# PALACE *of* PALMS

Also by Kate Teltscher

*India Inscribed:*
*European and British Writing on India, 1600–1800*

*The High Road to China:*
*George Bogle, the Panchen Lama and the*
*First British Expedition to Tibet*

KATE TELTSCHER

# PALACE *of* PALMS

*Tropical Dreams and the Making of Kew*

PICADOR

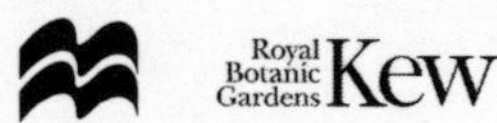


First published 2020 by Picador
an imprint of Pan Macmillan
The Smithson, 6 Briset Street, London EC1M 5NR
Associated companies throughout the world
www.panmacmillan.com

ISBN 978-1-5290-0485-4



1 3 5 7 9 8 6 4 2

A CIP catalogue record for this book is available from the British Library.

Map artwork by Hemesh Alles

Typeset by Palimpsest Book Production Ltd, Falkirk, Stirlingshire
Printed and bound by CPI Group (UK) Ltd, Croydon, CR0 4YY

*To the memory of my mother,*
*Maina Teltscher (1929–2020),*
*who always loved Kew Gardens*

# *Contents*


*Author's Note* ix

*List of Illustrations* xi

*Map* xviii

1. Opening the Door 1

2. The Inspectors 6

3. The Contenders 23

4. The Horticultural Tour 49

5. Father and Son 72

6. The Engineer and the Architect 94

7. The Landscape Designer 119

8. Deck Iron 137

9. The Great Experiment 159

10. The Princes of the Vegetable Kingdom 185

11. The Palm House Spectacle 215

12. The Museum 239

13. The Public 269

14. Closing the Door 296

*Notes* 311

*Bibliography* 347

*Acknowledgements* 365

*Index* 367

# *Author's Note*

The ornament used throughout as a chapter opener is based on the palmette design on the interior ironwork of the Palm House.

# *List of Illustrations*

## Integrated Illustrations

1. The Palm House door, detail from plan of 'The Royal Palm House' by Decimus Burton and Richard Turner, Kewensia, K92-79, Archives, RBGK (© The Board of Trustees of the Royal Botanic Gardens, Kew)
2. Kew Gardens, 1837–9, 1959 copy of plan by Thomas Chawner, Archives, RBGK (© The Board of Trustees of the Royal Botanic Gardens, Kew)
3. William Townsend Aiton, director-general of the Royal Gardens, Kew Images 18381645, RBGK (© The Board of Trustees of the Royal Botanic Gardens, Kew)
4. John Lindley, 1866 (Louis van Houtte, *Flore des Serres et des Jardins de l'Europe* (1865–7), vol. 16, pp. 92–3. Scan of original book from Botanicus, Public Domain, https://commons.wikimedia.org/w/index.php?curid=20837663)
5. Sir William Jackson Hooker, 1851 (Lithograph by T. H. Maguire, Wellcome Library 4329i. Credit: Wellcome Collection. Attribution 4.0 International [*CC BY 4.0*])
6. John Smith, 1876, *Gardeners' Chronicle*, 18 March 1876, RBGK (© The Board of Trustees of the Royal Botanic Gardens, Kew)
7. A sketch of Brick Farm in a letter from Sir William Hooker, W. J. Hooker to J. D. Hooker, 9 May 1841, JDH/2/10, f.114, Archives, RBGK (© The Board of Trustees of the Royal Botanic Gardens, Kew)
8. Loudon's ring-shaped glasshouse design, *Gardener's Magazine*, 8 (1832), p. 420 (© The Board of Trustees of the Royal Botanic Gardens, Kew)
9. Loudon's conical glasshouse design, *Gardener's Magazine*, 8 (1832), p. 422 (© The Board of Trustees of the Royal Botanic Gardens, Kew)

10. The Great Stove at Chatsworth (Chronicle / Alamy Stock Photo)
11. Joseph Hooker, chalk portrait by George Richmond, frontispiece of L. Huxley, *Life and Letters of Sir Joseph Dalton Hooker*, vol. 1 (London: John Murray, 1918) (© The Board of Trustees of the Royal Botanic Gardens, Kew)
12. Mount Erebus and Mount Terror, frontispiece of J. D. Hooker, *The Botany of the Antarctic Voyage*, vol. 1 (London: Reeve Brothers, 1844) (© The Board of Trustees of the Royal Botanic Gardens, Kew)
13. The conservatory at Killakee House, designed by Turner: C. McIntosh, *The Book of the Garden* (Edinburgh: Blackwood & Sons, 1853), vol. 1, plate 20 (© The Board of Trustees of the Royal Botanic Gardens, Kew)
14. Hammersmith Works, Dublin, letterhead engraved by John Kirkwood, EPH A852 (This image is reproduced courtesy of the National Library of Ireland)
15. Initial sketch of arboretum by William Nesfield, Archives, RBGK (© The Board of Trustees of the Royal Botanic Gardens, Kew)
16. The Palm House with radiating vistas and formal parterre, *The Garden* (17 August 1872), p. 151 (© The Board of Trustees of the Royal Botanic Gardens, Kew)
17. William Nesfield's plan for a national arboretum, Archives, RBGK (© The Board of Trustees of the Royal Botanic Gardens, Kew)
18. The Royal Botanic Society Winter Garden, J. C. Loudon, *Encyclopaedia of Gardening* (London: Longman, Green, Longmans and Roberts, 1860), p. 280 (© The Board of Trustees of the Royal Botanic Gardens, Kew)
19. Section and details of Palm House construction, *The Builder* (15 January 1848), p. 29 (© The Board of Trustees of the Royal Botanic Gardens, Kew)
20. The central section of the Palm House, detail from plan of 'The Royal Palm House' by Decimus Burton and Richard Turner, Kewensia, K92-79, Archives, RBGK (© The Board of Trustees of the Royal Botanic Gardens, Kew)
21. Chance Brothers Glass Works, Smethwick, 1857, PHS/1741 (Sandwell Community History and Archives Service)
22. The Campanile, chimney-cum-water tower, *Illustrated London News*

(2 September 1848), p. 132 (© The Board of Trustees of the Royal Botanic Gardens, Kew)

23. Burbidge and Healy's patent boiler, J. C. Loudon, *Encyclopaedia of Gardening* (London: Longman, Green, Longmans and Roberts, 1860), p. 614 (© The Board of Trustees of the Royal Botanic Gardens, Kew)
24. Sketch of the Palm House tunnel, sketch on reverse of Richard Turner's estimate for ironwork (WORK 16/29/8), f.23 (The National Archives)
25. Diagram of plant and animal life from Hitchcock's *Elementary Geology* (1840) (The History Collection / Alamy Stock Photo)
26. *Virginia in the Bath*, from W. S. Orr's edition of Bernardin's *Paul and Virginia* (1839). This illustration taken from the French edition of *Paul et Virginie* (Paris: Léon Curmer, 1838) (Public Domain, www.oldbook illustrations.com)
27. *Paul and Virginia* by William Calder Marshall (1843) (duncan1890 / iStock)
28. Holweck's monument to Bernardin de Saint-Pierre (1907) (Christophe. moustier – French Wikipedia, Attribution, https://commons.wikimedia.org/w/index.php?curid=1597401)
29. The plant collector deified: *Joseph Hooker in Sikkim*, engraving after Frank Stone (Wood engraving by Butterworth & Heath, Wellcome Library no. 4323i. Credit: Wellcome Collection. Attribution 4.0 International [CC BY 4.0])
30. The Palm House interior, *Illustrated London News*, 2 September 1848, p. 133 (© The Board of Trustees of the Royal Botanic Gardens, Kew)
31. An illustration from Gosse, *Wanderings through the Conservatories at Kew* (London: Society for Promoting Christian Knowledge, 1857), p. 96 (© The Board of Trustees of the Royal Botanic Gardens, Kew)
32. The Museum of Economic Botany (1855), frontispiece to W. J. Hooker, *The Museum of Economic Botany* (London: Longman, Green, Brown and Longmans, 1855) (© The Board of Trustees of the Royal Botanic Gardens, Kew)
33. A list of the multifarious uses of palms, from Sophy Moody, *The Palm Tree* (1864), p. 325 (© The Board of Trustees of the Royal Botanic Gardens, Kew)
34. *Oenocarpus bataua*, with blowpipe arrow and quiver, from Wallace's *Palm Trees of the Amazon* (1853), plate 11 (© The Board of Trustees of the Royal Botanic Gardens, Kew)

35. *Desmoncus polyacanthos*, the barbed climbing palm, from Wallace's *Palm Trees of the Amazon* (1853), plate 27 (© The Board of Trustees of the Royal Botanic Gardens, Kew)
36. The oil palm, *Elaeis guineensis*, John Jackson, *Commercial Botany of the Nineteenth Century* (London: Cassell & Co., 1890), p. 107 (© The Board of Trustees of the Royal Botanic Gardens, Kew)
37. Anti-slavery advertisement for Price's Distilled Palm Candles, SP2621/1 Archives, London Borough of Lambeth (This image was reproduced by kind permission of London Borough of Lambeth, Archives Department)
38. A sketch of germinating double coconut in cask in letter from Wenceslaus Bojer, W. Bojer to W. J. Hooker, 8 January 1852, DC/55/133, Archives, RBGK (© The Board of Trustees of the Royal Botanic Gardens, Kew)
39. Frontispiece of *Curtis's Botanical Magazine*, vol. 1 (3rd series) (1845) (© The Board of Trustees of the Royal Botanic Gardens, Kew)
40. The triumphal arch outside Hammersmith Works, *Illustrated London News*, 11 August 1849, p. 93 (© The Board of Trustees of the Royal Botanic Gardens, Kew)
41. Visitors at Kew (1851), Kewensia, DN-82-1724, Archives, RBGK (© The Board of Trustees of the Royal Botanic Gardens, Kew)
42. Visitors' map from William Hooker's *Kew Gardens, or, a Popular Guide* (1847) (© The Board of Trustees of the Royal Botanic Gardens, Kew)
43. The Palm House interior, *Illustrated London News*, 7 August 1852, p. 97 (© The Board of Trustees of the Royal Botanic Gardens, Kew)
44. Promenading around the Palm House gallery, *Illustrated London Almanack for 1853*, p. 13 (© The Board of Trustees of the Royal Botanic Gardens, Kew)
45. Richard and Thomas Turner's design for the Great Exhibition (Peter Berlyn and Charles Fowler Jnr. Engravings by George Measom [1818–1901]. The Crystal Palace: Its Architectural History and Constructive Marvels. Public Domain, https://commons.wikimedia.org/w/index.php?curid=29651105)
46. Joseph Hooker, flanked by palms, during his presidency of the Royal Society, 1873–8 (Wood engraving by W. G. Smith after himself. Credit: Wellcome Collection. Attribution 4.0 International [CC BY 4.0])
47. Queen Victoria's coffin lying in state in the Albert Memorial Chapel,

Windsor Castle, 1901, RCIN 2105792 (Royal Collection Trust / © Her Majesty Queen Elizabeth II 2020)

48. Design to rebuild the Palm House using arches from Elizabeth II's Coronation, Kewensia, Archives, RBGK (© The Board of Trustees of the Royal Botanic Gardens, Kew)

49. East entrance to the Palm House, P. H. Gosse, *Wanderings through the Conservatories at Kew* (London: Society for Promoting Christian Knowledge, 1857), p. 45 (© The Board of Trustees of the Royal Botanic Gardens, Kew)

## COLOUR PLATES

1. An imagined South American scene featuring two palms, K. F. P. von Martius, *Historia Naturalis Palmarum* (Leipzig: T. O, Weigel, 1823–53), vol. 2, Tab 52 (© The Board of Trustees of the Royal Botanic Gardens, Kew)

2 & 3. Maps showing the distribution of palms in the New and Old Worlds, K. F. P. von Martius, *Historia Naturalis Palmarum* (Leipzig: T. O, Weigel, 1823–53), vol. 1, Tabs. Geograph. 1 & 2 (© The Board of Trustees of the Royal Botanic Gardens, Kew)

4 & 5. The towering double coconut palm, *Lodoicea maldivica*, *Curtis's Botanical Magazine* (1827), vol. 54, Tabs. 2734, 2738 (© The Board of Trustees of the Royal Botanic Gardens, Kew)

6 & 7. The feathery plumes of the ivory-nut palm, *Phytelephas macrocarpa*. The fruit and the seeds, together with items fashioned from vegetable ivory: a box and a model of a llama, *Hooker's Journal of Botany and Kew Gardens Miscellany*, vol. 1 (1849), plates 6 & 7 (© The Board of Trustees of the Royal Botanic Gardens, Kew)

8. Examples of palms and their parts by the botanical artist and philanthropist Elizabeth Twining, *Illustrations of the Natural Orders of Plants* (London: Joseph Cundall, 1849–55), vol. 2, p. 145 (© The Board of Trustees of the Royal Botanic Gardens, Kew)

9. 'The Palm of the Plain' from Sophy Moody's *The Palm Tree* (London: T. Nelson, 1864) (© The Board of Trustees of the Royal Botanic Gardens, Kew)

10 & 11. The 'Palm of the Forest' and 'Palm of the Ocean' from Moody's *The Palm Tree* (London: T. Nelson, 1864) (© The Board of Trustees of the Royal Botanic Gardens, Kew)

12. A lithograph depicting the multiple uses of the date palm, Wellcome Library 28051i (Wellcome Collection. Attribution 4.0 International [CC BY 4.0])
13. Sir William Jackson Hooker, the first director of Kew, oil portrait by Spiridone Gambardella, 1843, Media ID 13252648 (© The Board of Trustees of the Royal Botanic Gardens, Kew)
14. Richard Turner, the iron founder and engineer. Courtesy of the National Botanic Gardens, Glasnevin
15. The architect Decimus Burton in the early 1830s, lithograph portrait by Maxim Gauci, after Eden Upton Eddis (Bridgeman Images)
16. The first curator of Kew, John Smith, Archives, RBGK (© The Board of Trustees of the Royal Botanic Gardens, Kew)
17. A plan of the Palm House produced by Decimus Burton and Richard Turner, Kewensia K92-79, RBGK (© The Board of Trustees of the Royal Botanic Gardens, Kew)
18. A plan of the area around the Palm House by the landscape architect William Nesfield, Archives, RBGK (© The Board of Trustees of the Royal Botanic Gardens, Kew)
19. Chemist and photographer Robert Hunt, Wellcome Library no. 9928i (Wellcome Collection. Attribution 4.0 International [CC BY 4.0])
20. A diagram recording Robert Hunt's experiments with samples of glass and juice extracted from palm leaves, Memorandum of the Principles upon which the Glass has been selected for the Palm House in the Royal Botanic Gardens at Kew, WORK 16/29/8, f.105 (The National Archives, ref. WORK16/29/8)
21. A daguerreotype of the Palm House nearing completion by Antoine Claudet, Media ID 1746343, RBGK (© The Board of Trustees of the Royal Botanic Gardens, Kew)
22. A daguerreotype showing the interior view of the Palm House under construction by Antoine Claudet, Media ID 1746341, RBGK (© The Board of Trustees of the Royal Botanic Gardens, Kew)
23. Visitors to Kew, coloured version of print from the *Illustrated London News*, 6 August 1859, Kewensia K92-49, Archives, RBGK (© The Board of Trustees of the Royal Botanic Gardens, Kew)
24. A nineteenth-century print presenting the gardens as an architectural spectacle, 'Great Palm House Kew Gardens', coloured print no. 42,

Archives, RBGK (© The Board of Trustees of the Royal Botanic Gardens, Kew)
25. An 1860s stereoview of the Palm House (Public Domain, www.flickr.com)
26. A sketch of Princess Mary, Sir William Hooker and Mr Craig, a Scottish gardener, by Ella Taylor, RCIN 918810 (Royal Collection Trust / © Her Majesty Queen Elizabeth II 2020)
27. Sir William Hooker in his later years, Media ID 10630916, RBGK (© The Board of Trustees of the Royal Botanic Gardens, Kew)
28. Joseph Hooker, who succeeded his father as director of Kew in 1865, Media ID 10630920, RBGK (© The Board of Trustees of the Royal Botanic Gardens, Kew)
29. The cover of the *Chemist & Druggist* magazine, July 1898, Kewensia pk92, Archives, RBGK (© The Board of Trustees of the Royal Botanic Gardens, Kew)
30. A 1950 linocut by Edward Bawden, 'The Palm House Kew Gardens' (© Estate of Edward Bawden, Bridgeman Images)

# ROYAL BOTANIC GARDENS
## KEW

*Plan showing the successive grants of land through which the Royal Gardens of Kew grew into the national botanic garden organized around the Palm House.*

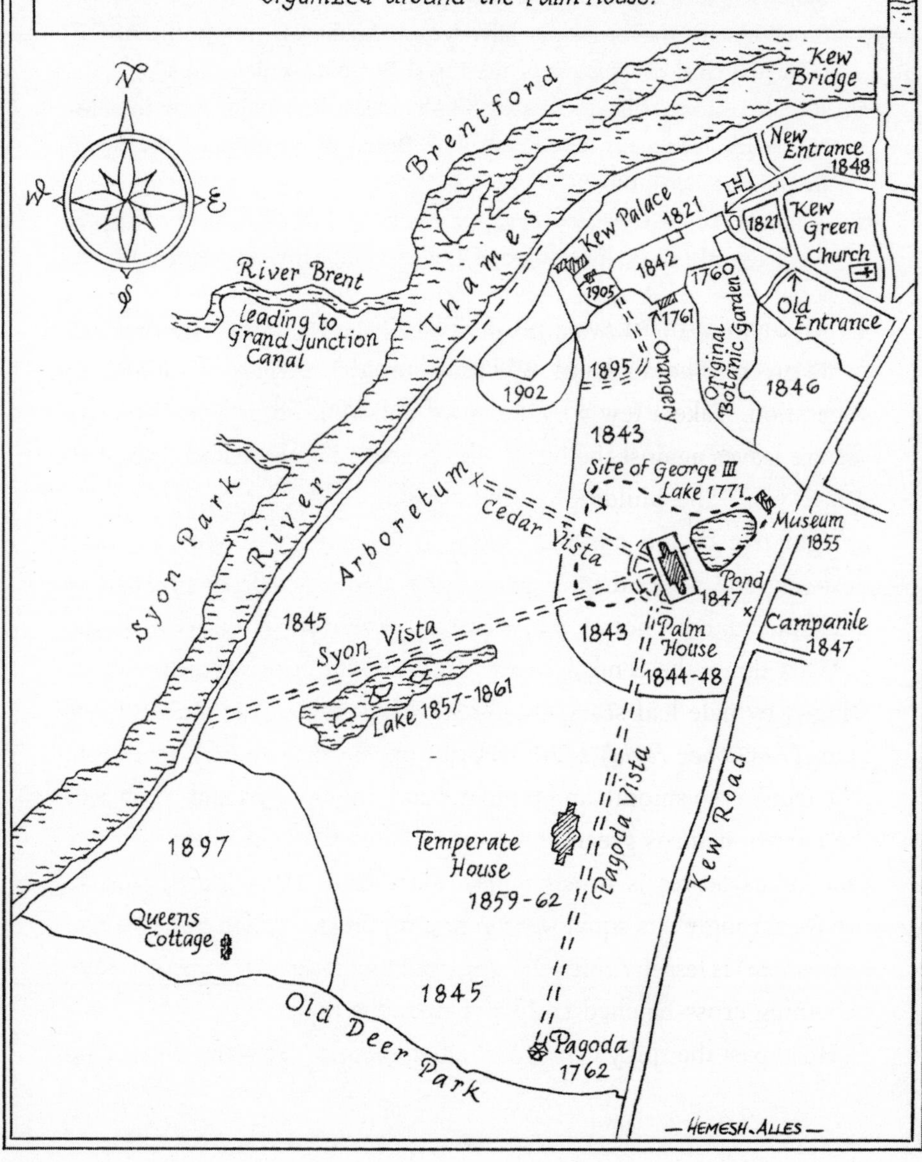

# 1

# Opening *the* Door

Push open the heavy Palm House door, and the world turns green. The air hangs hot and humid, smelling of unfamiliar vegetation. Take a few steps forward and look up. All that you can see are leaves against the light. The space is immense and the palms dwarf you. The building's slender columns and arches frame the upright trunks and curving stalks. On a quiet day, you can hear birdsong and water dripping from the plants. Inside, everything is intensified: larger, hotter, more vibrant. Even the sound is amplified.

Walk down the central path to find the tallest palm in the house. Ringed by pale leaf scars, the thick grey trunk of the Cuban royal palm (*Roystonea regia*) soars straight up, more than fifty feet high. The trunk is so smooth and regular that it invites the touch. Towards the crown, it turns green and then radiates out in feathery plumes. One of its leaves is brushing the glass roof. How long before it breaks through? Its squat neighbour, the Bermuda fan palm (*Sabal bermudana*) is less inviting. The ridged trunk is wrinkled and cracked, becoming cross-hatched and hairy near the top.

Head past the spiky cycad to the banana bed. Between the ragged banners of leaves dangle fat purple buds; higher up the stalks are clusters of unripe fruit, curving improbably upwards. The swoosh of a long frond, trailed by a gardener, momentarily distracts you. There, among the giant bamboo, is an ornate white staircase, spiralling through the stems. You begin to climb, but halfway up you hit a bank of yet more heat. Your reward is the gallery view: look down onto the patterned foliage, spread out in exquisite geometry, and up to the canopy of crowns, now so much closer. Turn to wipe the steam from the glass, and you can see the tree-lined avenues outside, stretching far into the distance.

For more than 170 years, the Palm House has provided the ultimate spectacle at Kew. Kept at a near constant heat, it defies the passage of the seasons. You can wander through the tropical regions of Africa, the Americas, Australasia, Asia and the Pacific in less than an afternoon. Embowered in vegetation, you can easily lose all sense of direction. The paths seem to loop endlessly, and the ever-changing views from the winding staircases disorientate you further. It is a manicured jungle: the leaves are swept up and the fruit is harvested, but the stone-flagged floor is puddled and branches reach out over the paths. Peering into the beds, you might spot robins or, more rarely, a Chinese water dragon that keeps the number of cockroaches down. Removed from the normal constraints of time and place, the Palm House is both inside and outside, real and staged, here and there.

I have been visiting Kew since my childhood, and have brought my own children to explore its grounds. Over the years in the Gardens, I've walked high among the treetops, marvelled at rhododendrons in bloom, and listened wonderstruck at dusk to music generated by a beehive, but nothing can compare to the thrill of the Palm House. It is memorable because the experience is so physical. The environment is overwhelmingly different, even as you encounter plants that furnish household staples at every turn: pepper, sugar, ginger, vanilla. Without doubt, the most magnificent of all the plants on display are the stately palms.

The Palm House is the principal attraction of any visit to Kew. Entering by what is now the main gate, you almost immediately encounter the building, fronted by the ornamental pond and colourful parterre. With its elongated form and elegant curves, the Palm House is at once light and imposing. The glass shell both contains and reveals its living collection. It changes appearance according to the weather and the time of day: silver grey when overcast, golden at sunset. As you walk the grounds, you view it repeatedly from different angles, framed at the end of long vistas: the focal point of the whole Gardens.

The Palm House has long been the emblem of Kew. Once seen, its bold outline is never forgotten. It is not whimsical like the Great Pagoda, or fussily extended like the Temperate House, but sleek and coherent: a masterpiece of design. In her short story 'Kew Gardens', first published in 1919, Virginia Woolf described the sudden illumination of the Palm House glass roofs 'as if a whole market full of shiny green umbrellas had opened in the sun'.[1] The graphic artist Edward Bawden repeatedly returned to the subject of the Palm House, celebrating its distinctive form in linocuts, illustrations and posters for the London Underground from 1930 to 1950 (see Plate 30). Steve Sekely's 1962 science-fiction horror, *The Day of the Triffids* (based on John Wyndham's novel), opened with an unsuspecting nightwatchman doing his rounds of the Palm House, stalked by a monstrous man-eating plant. Far-fetched though it may be, the film suggests the status of the Palm House as other-worldly: a place of outlandish plants and futuristic architecture. But although the building is much photographed and fêted, the history of the Palm House is oddly overlooked.

Why is the Palm House at the centre of Kew? To answer this

question, we need to go back to the opening years of Queen Victoria's reign, to the moment when the Gardens – a fraction of the size that they are today – were transferred from royal to public ownership. Over these initial years, additional grants of land greatly expanded the Gardens, and it became possible to imagine a project on the scale of the Palm House. The first director of Kew drove his grand scheme through with vision and determination, but it was long in the making. Six years would pass between an initial inspection of the Royal Gardens and breaking ground for the Palm House.

The breathtaking result came from creative collaboration between a number of remarkable individuals. The design was largely the work of a brilliant outsider who was prepared to risk everything to make his name, but received little public recognition in his lifetime. His exuberant invention was restrained by an urbane and experienced architect. Together, they employed the latest in glass and iron manufacturing techniques to construct a building of unprecedented lightness and grace. The interior display was managed by the curator, who tended his plants with fierce devotion. The surrounding grounds were laid out by an artist-turned-landscape architect who made the Palm House the centrepiece of Kew and, in effect, of the modern botanical world.

With its collection gathered from colonial gardens around the globe, the Palm House proclaimed the extent of Britain's imperial power. Its innovative design and advanced engineering made the building as much the object of public attention as its spectacular display. Without even boarding a ship, the public could experience the damp heat and lush vegetation of the colonies. In recreating the tropics on the banks of the Thames, the Palm House declared technology's victory over nature.

We have largely forgotten that palms occupied an unrivalled

position in nineteenth-century natural history, literature and art. Supplying every necessity of life, palms were thought to surpass all European vegetation in terms of beauty and abundance. They were associated with effortless bounty and dreams of exotic locations. This book recovers the nineteenth century's extraordinary fascination with palms. To explore the role played by palms in Victorian culture is to show how much of the world was conceived in terms of a palm zone: a broad region encircling the globe.

This is the story of the foundation of a public institution, a scientific discipline and a dynasty. It is an account of personal ambition and innovation, of science and plant hunting that connects Kew to the empire and the wider tropics. Just as the Palm House sits at the hub of Kew, so Kew once headed a network of colonial botanic gardens. These relations of plants and power are encapsulated in the Palm House. Now, as when it was built, the Palm House provides a glittering prism through which to view Britain's real and imagined place in the world.

1. *The door to the Palm House.*

# 2

# The Inspectors

It was quite the worst time for a government inspection of the Royal Gardens. A grey haze obscured the sky, and snow remained piled in heaps on the ground. The three inspectors rang for admission at the wooden door which served as the public entrance to the botanic garden on Kew Green. They had spent the previous week investigating frost-blasted gardens in and around London: Windsor Castle, Hampton Court, Buckingham Palace, Kensington Palace and the kitchen garden at Kew. They were authorized to examine the plants, survey the buildings, scrutinize the accounts and interrogate the staff. So far, they had not been impressed. 'We found all the gardens in excellent wretchedness, the most miserable places that were ever beheld', one member of the party confided to his wife.[1] The 'discipline of some of the Gardeners', they noted disapprovingly, 'is excessively lax, especially with respect to the sobriety of the men'.[2] Now it was the turn of the botanic garden at Kew.

The opening months of 1838 had been the coldest in London for a decade. On 20 January, the temperature had plummeted to well below freezing, and a deep frost had set in for a fortnight. The Thames had frozen over, and it had been possible to walk across the river by London Bridge. With the Port of London ice-bound, all river traffic had been suspended. Skittle grounds were set up on the ice, and midstream at Hammersmith, to the west of the city, a sheep was roasted whole. Among the few people to profit from the weather was Patrick Murphy, author of *The Weather Almanack (on Scientific Principles, showing the State of the Weather for every day of the year 1838)*, who had predicted the fall in temperature for 20 January. Despite the inaccuracy of his other forecasts, the *Almanack* became an immediate bestseller, Murphy earned a small fortune, and, for years after, the period was known as 'Murphy's Winter'.

By 19 February the thaw had started, and the Thames was once again navigable. Four miles upstream from Hammersmith, along an extravagant S-shaped bend, was a particularly busy stretch of the river. At this point, the Grand Junction Canal met the Thames, bringing barges down from the Midlands, laden with coal, pottery and glassware for sale in London. At the confluence on the northern bank sat 'one of the meanest looking towns . . . in all England'.[3] With its tenement blocks, cottages, inns and wharfs, Brentford was notorious for its squalor. The muddy High Street formed part of the main route connecting the capital to the West of England. Ten long-distance stagecoaches ran daily to Bath along the narrow road, with other services heading to and from London. There was a constant interchange of passengers and goods from carriages and carts to barges and boats. With its transport links and riverside position, Brentford attracted numerous industries – a soap factory, timber yard, breweries, distilleries, malt houses, tanneries and gas works – and a reputation for dirt, stench and drunkenness.

Happily for the residents on the opposite bank, a conveniently placed island had been planted with poplar trees to block Brentford's offensive chimneys from view. Here, across the toll bridge over the Thames, was a different world. On the Surrey side, set amid market gardens, pastures and the Royal Pleasure Grounds, lay the affluent village of Kew. Some ninety houses surrounded a triangular green, with a duck pond at one end, the neat brick church of St Anne's in the middle, and the entrance to the Royal Gardens at the far end. Clustered near the pond were the modest cottages of artisans and tradespeople. Bordering the north and south sides were the gracious homes of the wealthy: attractive, variegated terraces with bay windows and balconies, canopies and fanlights. Set back from the street were substantial houses belonging to two of the young Queen Victoria's elderly uncles: the Duke of Cambridge and the King of Hanover. Kew was a rural retreat, a 'courtly village' where the rich and influential could play at being country folk.[4]

But, this morning, Kew looked far from inviting. With the temperature just a few degrees above freezing, the snow was turning to dirty slush. Across the whole of the south-east, the severe weather had taken its toll on shrubs and trees. The frost had been so harsh as to split open the branches of evergreen oak. 'The winter of 1837–8 was in England more injurious to vegetation than any which has occurred in modern times', a paper read at the Horticultural Society of London declared. 'At no other time in the history of English gardening have there been so many rare exotics exposed to the naked influence of the climate'.[5]

Just eleven acres in extent, the botanic garden was wedged between the royal kitchen garden, the lawns of Kew Palace and the far more extensive Royal Pleasure Grounds. Kew's connections with the royal family dated back to the 1720s, when Queen Caroline, wife of George II, established the Richmond Lodge estate, which extended some 400 acres along the Thames, from Richmond (the site of a former Tudor palace) to Kew Green. The Prince of Wales and his wife Augusta occupied the White House, close to Kew Green, from the time of their marriage, in 1736. For Augusta, garden improvement was a passion. In 1759, she founded a small physic garden (which, by the time of the inspection, was known as the botanic garden) and commissioned the architect William Chambers to build fashionable follies throughout the Pleasure Grounds, including a one-roomed Alhambra, an ornate mosque and the famous ten-storey Pagoda, which, newly refurbished with brightly gilded dragons, remains to this day.

When Augusta died in 1772, her son George III inherited the White House and joined its garden to that of the neighbouring Richmond estate. From the time that the two gardens were combined, Kew Gardens was known by the plural form. During George III's reign, the royal family first made use of the gabled red-brick Dutch House – now known as Kew Palace – as a royal nursery and regular summer residence. For George III, Kew was a domestic haven away from court; a pastoral idyll where he could spend time with his family, adopt the life of a gentleman farmer and build his collection of exotic plants.

By the time of the inspection, the small botanic garden was open to members of the public. Under the watchful eye of an accompanying gardener, visitors could tour the walled garden. Located near the entrance was one of the greatest attractions: Napoleon's Willow, now weeping gently in the thaw. Originally a cutting from the willow that marked Bonaparte's tomb on St Helena, the tree had been nurtured from a slip under a bell jar by John Smith, the principal foreman who oversaw all practical work in the Gardens. On its first planting out, more than a decade after Napoleon's defeat at the Battle of Waterloo in 1815, the willow had drawn such crowds that the door to the Gardens had given way in the crush, 'the result being bruises and flattened hats and bonnets'.[6] The public flocked to see the fallen emperor transformed, as in some classical myth, into a graceful tree. A high trellis fence now defended it from those who might seek their own cuttings. French visitors had been known to kneel before the tree, heads uncovered, to pay their respects.

Sheltered by a shrubbery, the willow had survived the intense frost of 1838. In the small arboretum, packed with rarities, some of the less hardy trees, including Sir Joseph Banks' Pine (a prized monkey-puzzle tree from Chile), were bundled up in mats against the cold. The botanic garden's brick walls afforded a degree of protection to the acacias, myrtles and magnolias that were planted against them. But, at this time of year, neither the large circular bed of grasses nor the herbaceous borders were at their best. The three inspectors tramped the paths, stooping from time to time to examine specimens, surveying all corners of the Gardens.

In one area stood an irregular group of hothouses and greenhouses, ten in number, of varying size, age and condition, containing the spoils of voyages to the Cape of Good Hope, Western Australia and Botany Bay. Each 'stove', or hothouse, had its own furnace, and the soot from the chimneys blackened the greenhouse glass and plants around. 'The Botanical results of scientific Expeditions undertaken for many Years have been deposited at Kew', the inspection party learnt, 'and persons expressly engaged to collect Plants and Seeds in Foreign Countries have frequently sent the whole of their collections to this Garden'.[7] Picking their way through overstocked greenhouses, the inspectors fingered leaves and peered into propagating pits. The palms, in particular, were outgrowing their accommodation; the roof of the palm stove had been raised four feet, but fronds still regularly smashed through the glass.

The rich plant collection at Kew had been built up during the reign of George III, under the direction of Sir Joseph Banks, the great doyen of natural science in Britain. Cargoes of botanical curiosities had arrived from Australia, the Americas, Africa, India, China and the South Pacific. But, in the decades following the deaths of both Banks and George III in 1820, the botanic garden had fallen from royal favour. The two succeeding monarchs had little interest in rare plants: George IV had lavished more attention on the cast-iron palms of the extravagant Brighton Pavilion; his successor and brother, the less flamboyant former naval officer, William IV, had cut back on royal expenditure. By the time that Victoria inherited

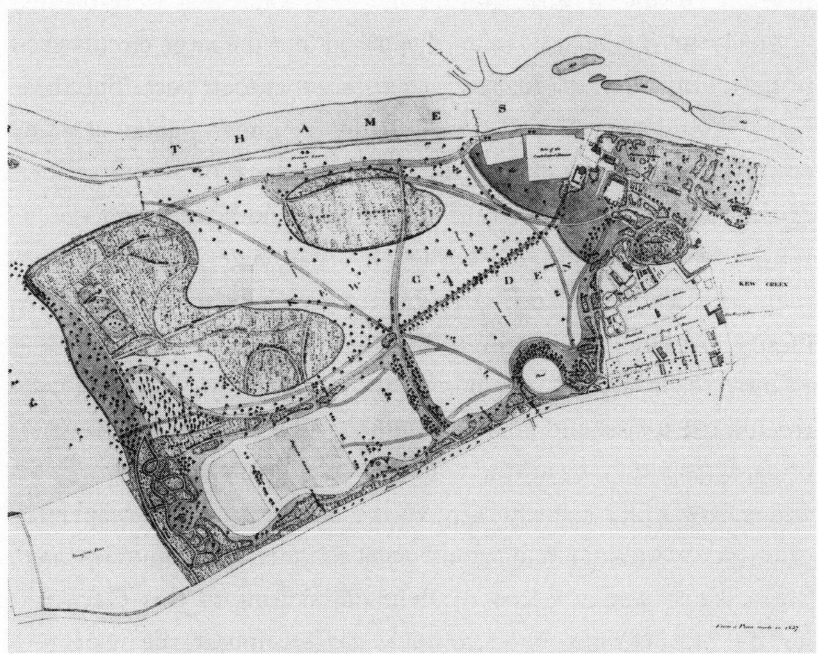


2. *Kew Gardens, 1837–9.*

the throne in 1837, spending on Kew had dwindled and standards had slipped.

An early priority for the young Victoria in the first months of her reign was to secure the Crown finances. Her limited private resources made it important that Parliament quickly approve the Civil List to set the royal income. This entailed a Treasury review of Royal Household expenditure that placed the Royal Gardens under particular scrutiny. For some years, the management of the Royal Gardens and, in particular, the botanic garden at Kew had been subject to sustained criticism in the horticultural press. In 1827, the pioneering Scottish landscape gardener and writer, John Claudius Loudon, had fired the first salvo. Loudon employed the language of political reform to suggest a complete overhaul of the Royal Gardens: 'The entire system of royal parks and gardens is rotten, and requires renewal, or radical reformation'.[8]

For Loudon, the botanic garden stood in the way of the progress of horticulture, which he saw as a potent means of social improvement. Loudon believed that gardening and public gardens contributed substantially to the happiness, education and refinement of taste of men and women of all classes. A passionate advocate of self-improvement, Loudon argued that gardeners should augment their practical knowledge through reading. Given their low rates of pay, professional gardeners could not afford to buy books, so employers should provide them with a library. In Loudon's view, the regime at Kew did little to foster the education or advancement of gardeners: the journeymen did not have access to botanical books and were paid the same meagre wages as those in commercial nurseries. As Loudon and various correspondents to his *Gardener's Magazine* pointed out, Kew received plants from all over the world, but did not distribute them to other gardens in Britain.

The campaign against Kew was reignited, ten years later, at the start of Victoria's reign, when the combative journalist George Glenny, notorious for his invective and heightened rhetoric, leapt into the fray. Denouncing Kew in the *Gardeners' Gazette* as 'slovenly and discreditable', the plants as 'disgracefully dirty' and so 'infested with insects' to 'justify their being called an Entomological Menagerie', Glenny announced that he would undertake 'the Herculean task of enforcing something like improvement'.[9] The main target of both Glenny's and Loudon's attacks was the seventy-two-year-old William Townsend Aiton, who had charge of the Gardens where he had spent all his working life (as his father before him). In his editorial, Glenny delivered a blunt message: 'we give Mr. Aiton notice to reform – or quit'.[10]

3. *William Townsend Aiton, director-general of the Royal Gardens.*

Aiton had long been one of the most powerful figures in the horticultural establishment. With Sir Joseph Banks and others, he had founded the Horticultural Society. He had crafted landscapes viewed daily by successive monarchs at Windsor and Buckingham Palace. From 1810 to 1813 he had issued the five-volume *Hortus Kewensis*, a monumental revised edition of his father's catalogue of the plants cultivated at Kew. For decades, he had exercised a virtual monopoly over the exotic plants contributed by government collectors, deciding whether – or, more likely, not – other gardeners would have the chance to cultivate new species. His reluctance to distribute plants generated considerable animosity in horticultural circles. According to the *Colonial Magazine*, the botanist Allan Cunningham used to say that 'more immortality could be earned by publishing a list of plants *dying* at Kew, than *living* in other gardens'.[11]

In the midst of the press campaign against Kew, the Parliamentary Committee on the Royal Gardens met to nominate members of the inspection party. To head the team, the Committee appointed Dr John Lindley, one of the leading figures of British botany and horticulture. In his late thirties, the hugely energetic Lindley held three jobs simultaneously: he was Professor of Botany at the newly founded University College London, assistant secretary to the Horticultural Society and director of the Chelsea Physic Garden. He was also the author and illustrator of numerous botanical and horticultural books and articles, often in collaboration with Loudon. The son of a failed Norfolk nurseryman, Lindley had never attended university himself, but published his first botanical work, a translation from the French, at the age of twenty, and thereafter worked his way into the highest botanical circles, gaining the patronage of Sir Joseph Banks. He lived in Turnham Green, just a few miles across the river from Kew, close to the Horticultural Society's garden at Chiswick. Rising at dawn, he habitually worked well into the night.

In term time, he would ride into central London to lecture (delivering up to nineteen different lectures a week), while also attending to matters at the Chiswick and Chelsea gardens. Lindley's immense productivity was driven both by intellectual curiosity and financial necessity; early in life, he had taken on responsibility for his father's debts, and had never managed to pay them off.[12]

The second member of the inspection team was the prodigiously talented Joseph Paxton, whose appetite for hard work equalled Lindley's, and whose own career trajectory would be even more remarkable. His formal education had ended at the age of fourteen, but Paxton excelled as a landscape designer, self-taught engineer and architect. Paxton had trained at the Horticultural Society under Lindley, and there attracted the attention of William Cavendish, the Sixth Duke of Devonshire, who was the Horticultural Society's landlord and one of the most important patrons of botany in Britain. Invited to work at the Duke's estate of Chatsworth in Derbyshire, Paxton seemed capable of realizing the Duke's most extravagant horticultural dreams. He had already established Europe's largest arboretum at Chatsworth, and was now in the process of building the Great Stove, a glasshouse of his own design which would be the most extensive in the world. Venturing into journalism, Paxton publicized his triumphs and dispensed gardening advice in the *Magazine of Botany*, the monthly journal that he edited. With Paxton's inventive genius, flair for publicity and grand ambition, Chatsworth would become the most famous private garden in mid-nineteenth-century Britain.

Paxton and Lindley were close allies and significant figures in horticultural circles, but the third member of the inspection team was a less obvious choice for public service. John Wilson was head gardener to the Earl of Surrey at Worksop Manor in Nottinghamshire. His only notable achievement had been to win a Horticultural Society medal in 1831 for grapes, peaches and nectarines. Wilson was doubtless recommended for the post by his employer, who had a seat on the Royal Gardens Committee as treasurer to the Royal Household. As the Earl of Surrey's man, Wilson may have acted as the voice of the Royal Household on the inspection team.

Together, the three men were instructed by the Committee to address two main issues: firstly, to advise on the most efficient way to run the kitchen gardens and forcing grounds that supplied vegetables, fruits and flowers to the Royal Household; and secondly, to direct their attention to the structure and purpose of the botanic garden at Kew. Should the Queen continue to finance the botanic garden, or should it become a publicly funded institution? What measures would be required to turn Kew into a leading centre of botanic science? What policy could be pursued to establish a fair distribution of Kew's duplicate plants? How could all parts of the British Empire both contribute to and benefit from the botanic garden?[13] In short, the inspection team was to devise a plan to determine the future of Kew.

Having surveyed the beds and hothouses, the inspection team repaired to one of the offices to interview the septuagenarian Aiton on his management of the botanic garden. The butt of mounting criticism in the press, Aiton was now obliged to justify his operations, answer detailed questions and open up his ledgers. He faced interrogation from a panel of men half his age, among them the rising stars of the gardening world.

The inspectors first asked Aiton to give an account of the botanic garden staff, their duties and rates of pay, starting with himself. Aiton enjoyed a handsome allowance of £1,000 a year (around four times the salary earned by Paxton at Chatsworth), a substantial house with rates and fuel paid, plus free forage for his horse. Next in line came John Smith, the principal foreman, in charge of the practical management of the Gardens. Smith received £100 a year, and was provided with a small house and weekly allowance for fuel and candles.[14] The team was told that Smith had embarked on the lengthy job of naming the plants. The correct identification of plants was of central importance to a botanic garden, a task which, according to Lindley, properly belonged to 'a man of high scientific attainments, aided by an extensive herbarium and considerable library', rather than 'a foreman, paid small weekly wages for cultivating plants', even one of Smith's outstanding 'zeal and assiduity'.[15] In a defensive move, Aiton said that he could not be held answerable for the plant names. Evidently much of the responsibility for the botanic garden had devolved upon Smith. Starting as a journeyman, Smith had worked at Kew for eighteen years, and had risen through the ranks by virtue of his skill, expertise and tremendous application. Now in his late thirties, Smith was in charge of ten gardeners (six trainees and four labourers), with additional staff in the summer, who each received a wage of twelve shillings a week.

Aiton was next required to lay the botanic garden records before the inspection party. The accounts showed that the annual funding for the botanic garden had decreased over the previous decade by around a third. Aiton also presented the books of incoming and outgoing plants: seven folio volumes to register plants received by the botanic garden, but only just over one full volume to record plants distributed – the disproportion apparently proving Aiton's reluctance to share the collection. Aiton had assumed that the botanic garden was a private garden, and so had only given plants to those likely to return the favour.[16]

In fact, the precise status of the botanic garden had always been unclear. How far could it be considered solely a private institution? While the Royal Household was responsible for the garden's foundation and maintenance, many of the exotic plants had been provided by government-funded collectors. This led Lindley to conclude that the botanic garden should not be regarded exclusively as the monarch's private property.[17] Members of the public were admitted every afternoon, save Sunday. The botanic garden suffered no damage from the public, Aiton reported, however the need to supervise visitors took labourers away from gardening duties. But, wondered Lindley, given the lack of any overall scheme of plant identification or attempt at classification, what possible advantage could a visitor derive from a trip to Kew, 'except that of a pleasant walk'?[18]

The day's interrogation left Aiton feeling shaken. Abrupt in manner, Lindley had been far from deferential in his questioning. Had he been wise, worried Aiton, to dissociate himself from the plant names supplied by Smith? He fired off a letter to Lindley to assert his belief in the importance of the correct scientific labelling of plants, 'for the advantage of the visitors generally, as well as for the instruction of the gardeners'.[19] Lindley, however, was unconvinced: 'It is difficult to reconcile this statement with the fact, that up to a recent period no means had been taken to carry such an object into effect'.[20] In a second letter, Aiton sought to explain the scant records of outgoing plants. 'Many plants, seeds and cuttings in small quantities have been given to amateurs, of which no account has been taken', he wrote.[21] But Lindley remained unpersuaded by Aiton's justification of his regime: 'it really does seem impossible to say that it has been conducted with . . . liberality or anxiety to promote the ends of science, and to render it useful to the country'.[22]

Aiton's concern was well founded. A week and a half later, Lindley's report was sent to the Committee. While commending Aiton's defence of the public's right of access to the Gardens and praising the good cultivation and state of the plants' health, even in overcrowded greenhouses, the report found that Kew lacked the most basic requirements of a botanic garden: there was no evidence of classification, no systematic arrangement, no comprehensive labelling, no regular communication with colonial botanic gardens. 'It is little better than a waste of money to maintain it in its present state', pronounced the forthright Lindley; 'it fulfils no intelligible purpose, except that of sheltering a large quantity of rare and valuable plants'.[23] As far as Lindley was concerned, there were only two options: 'it should either be at once taken for public purpose, gradually made worthy of the country, and converted into a powerful means of promoting national science, or it should be abandoned'.[24]

But, at this point, the whole tenor and tone of the report changed. What followed was an expansive vision of a transformed Kew, perfectly pitched to appeal to current ideas of scientific progress, national pride and imperial sentiment. The public botanic garden had long been accepted as a sign of civilization, Lindley asserted; how strange then that England, 'the most wealthy and most civilized kingdom in Europe', should lack one (particularly when Edinburgh and Dublin boasted such establishments).[25] Like Loudon, Lindley believed that public gardens improved the moral and educational condition of the nation. A public botanic garden would 'undoubtedly become an efficient instrument in refining the taste, increasing the knowledge, and augmenting the amount of rational pleasures' of the working classes, he declared.[26] Beyond this, the benefits of a public botanic garden at Kew would radiate even further. Widening his view to encompass the whole of the British Empire, Lindley asserted that Kew would act as the headquarters of a global network of colonial botanic gardens. With Kew at the centre, the botanic gardens in India, Australia, the Indian Ocean and the West Indies would be able to exchange information and supplies more effectively. Not only could plants and advice be provided to newly established colonies, such a system would also confer untold advantage to whole fields of British endeavour: medicine, commerce, manufacture, horticulture and agriculture. The colonies would offer up their natural resources to Britain, aiding 'the mother country in every thing that is useful in the vegetable kingdom'.[27]

This grand vision could be achieved with ease, Lindley claimed. All that was needed was to expand the present botanic garden by some thirty acres, build additional glasshouses, arrange and name the plants, develop nurseries and establish separate departments for medicinal, economic and agricultural plants. 'There is no sort of difficulty in effecting all this, and more, except the cost'. The initial sum Lindley estimated at £20,000, and then a £4,000 annual grant. It was 'inconceivable that Parliament would refuse the money for this purpose', he optimistically concluded.[28]

The force of Lindley's rhetoric and reasoning persuaded the members of the Royal Gardens Committee. They forwarded the report to the Treasury with the recommendation that financial responsibility for the botanic garden be immediately transferred from royal to government coffers. 'It appears worse than useless to keep it in its present state', they commented curtly. The Treasury should decide whether or not to maintain the botanic garden as a public institution, 'but we think the public would scarcely approve of its abandonment, and if it is to be kept up it should be maintained on a scale creditable to the Character of the nation, and to the present state of Botanical Science in this Country'.[29]

The Lords of the Treasury, however, thought otherwise. They had embarked on the review of royal expenditure with an eye to economy, and were in no rush to endorse a plan that entailed extensive spending. Equally unconvinced was Lord Melbourne, the Whig Prime Minister, who acted as Queen Victoria's trusted advisor. In her journal entry for 30 April 1838, Victoria recorded a conversation in which Melbourne signalled his disapproval of the Royal Gardens Committee. 'It does not seem a very prudent Committee', Melbourne had remarked. Although somewhat hazy on the details, Victoria recalled that 'a Dr. Somebody of the Horticultural Gardens, and the gardener of the Duke of Devonshire's at Chatsworth, who never thought of what was economy, were on the Committee'.[30] The Queen herself had no interest in the gardens and considered them a drain on the Royal Household finances. As she complained in her journal, 'there's that Botanical Garden at Kew, which I don't care at all about, and which it would be as well to give up'.[31] Lord Melbourne, however, restrained her from such precipitate action: 'the Public', he told the Queen, 'might possibly vote a sum for it'; in which case, the botanic garden 'became in fact, public property'.[32]

Far from acting immediately, the Treasury and the Commissioners of Woods and Forests sat on the report. There were more pressing matters occupying the government and Royal Household than the fate of the Royal Gardens. In May 1839, the so-called 'Bedchamber Crisis' erupted. After a government bill had been passed on the narrowest of margins, Melbourne tendered his resignation as Prime Minister. The Queen was compelled to invite the Tory Robert Peel to become Prime Minister, but then refused to comply with Peel's demand to dismiss a number of the Whig Ladies of the Bedchamber. Peel in turn declined to take up office, and Melbourne was swiftly reinstated. Following this governmental upheaval, there were two great state occasions to finance and orchestrate: the Queen's coronation in June 1838 and her wedding to Albert in February 1840.

For two years, the matter of Kew was shelved. Throughout this time, members of the government were aware that there remained the most economical course of action of all. They could always decide on the second of the two options outlined by Lindley, the outcome favoured by both the Queen and the Prime Minister: that the botanic garden could simply be abandoned.

# 3

# The Contenders

Whitehall may have chosen to ignore Kew, but for those directly affected, the botanic garden was a matter of consuming interest. Given the criticism contained in the report and his advancing years, it seemed likely that William Townsend Aiton would shortly resign or retire, but it was far from clear who might succeed him as director. Was this a post for a botanist or a horticulturist? A well-connected gentleman scientist or a practical gardener? How far would the government accept the terms of the report? And would the botanic garden even survive the policy of retrenchment? The uncertainty over the future of the garden would, in the words of the amateur botanist Frederick Scheer, shake the 'Botanical world' from 'the even tenor of its way'.[1]

At the time of the enquiry, Joseph Paxton boasted of his own chances of securing the £1,000-a-year post. 'I know I could get the place with the least exertion, if the Duke would part with me', Paxton wrote to his wife. 'I am sure Dr. Lindley is dying for me to get it – he thinks I should make something of Her Majesty's Gardens if I was at the head'.[2] But, Paxton added, he owed the Duke of Devonshire his loyalty and would not apply (although he would not omit 'to tell the Duke that all this has been within my mark').[3] He imagined that the job would be far from the sinecure that it had been, rather 'all anxiety and care', since the botanic garden would require a complete renovation. In any case, Paxton told his wife, the salary might be cut to £600, and then the post would not be worth having.[4]

It was perhaps just as well that Paxton did not put John Lindley's support to the test. From the very beginning, Lindley had set his own sights on the directorship of Kew. Lindley was always worried about his precarious personal finances, and he was beginning to grow weary of his extraordinary burden of work. A well-remunerated post at Kew would certainly ease his situation. In compiling the official report, Lindley had in some sense written his own job description. By emphasizing the scientific role of a reconfigured Kew, he

4. *John Lindley, 1866.*

implied the need for a future director with serious scientific credentials. Given Kew's projected significance in national and imperial affairs, the director should be capable of moving in the highest circles. Lindley's appointment by the Committee already proved the strength of his government connections. Over the years, he had carefully cultivated official, scientific and aristocratic contacts, including the Whig Duke of Devonshire. Lindley gave Devonshire a copy of his report and arranged for the institutions that employed him – the Horticultural Society and the University of London – to send petitions in support of the report's recommendations to the House of Commons. Aware that the directorship might soon become available, Lindley set about activating his acquaintances.

Among the first to be contacted was his long-standing friend Sir William Hooker, Professor of Botany at Glasgow University. Fourteen years Lindley's senior, Hooker also originated from Norfolk, and had preceded Lindley at Norwich Grammar School. A genial man, Hooker had helped Lindley from the start of the younger man's career. Hearing of Lindley's botanical aptitude, Hooker had encouraged the eighteen-year-old to consult his private library and herbarium. Then he had secured Lindley his first job by introducing him to Sir Joseph Banks. A decade later, when Hooker turned down the Chair of Botany at University College London, Lindley was appointed in his place. So it was with every assurance that, on the first day of the enquiry, Lindley dashed off a confidential note to Hooker: 'If anything worth having should originate out of this investigation I hope they will give it to me, for I want it much, and I hope I may calculate upon your interest . . . This however quite between ourselves'.[5]

Lindley's letter threw his friend into confusion. For years, Hooker had aimed at the directorship of Kew himself. He was a popular and charismatic figure at Glasgow University. Tall, handsome and energetic, Hooker had the gift of charming an audience. His lectures attracted members of the public as well as students. He was in charge of the Glasgow Botanic Gardens, which he had relocated and greatly expanded; he was the editor of the prestigious *Curtis's Botanical Magazine* and author of numerous botanical works; he had been knighted two years previously for his services to botany. To cap his career, Hooker longed for nothing more than to be appointed director of Kew. On an earlier rumour of Aiton's retirement, he had attempted to secure the post by lobbying politicians and aristocrats – in particular, John Russell, the Sixth Duke of Bedford, keen horticulturalist, botanist and head of the prominent Whig family. As a result of his campaign, the Duke of Argyll, then Lord Steward of the Royal Household, had assured Hooker that the directorship would be his, should a vacancy arise during his term

5. *Sir William Jackson Hooker, 1851.*

of office. On hearing the recent news about Kew, Hooker had immediately fired off letters to six of his most powerful advocates, setting the wheels of his own networking machine in motion.

Hooker was sharply aware that his former protégé might deprive him of his long-cherished goal. Up to this point, Hooker had been the senior figure in their relationship, but the balance of power seemed to be shifting. Lindley was situated close to the seat of government and was intimately involved in the process of restructuring at Kew. He had sent a copy of his report to Hooker's patron, the Duke of Bedford. It was unclear if his role in the enquiry would render him more or less likely to be appointed. Should Hooker reveal his interest to Lindley or bide his time? Would the rivalry affect their friendship? The day after receiving Lindley's letter, Hooker picked up his pen:

> *My dear Friend*
> . . . I write to you just now . . . because of what you state relative to Kew: & this I do not without some pain; – for I know how hard it is even for two very intimate friends to be Candidates for one & the same appointment, without some feelings of jealousy arising. Let me hope however that such will not be the case in the present instance. But it is impossible now that you have opened your mind to me in this matter that I can, as a man of honour, keep you in the dark respecting my views & feelings & wishes on the subject, even though such a communication may be prejudicial to my interests.[6]

With a disarming combination of frankness and rectitude, Hooker set about asserting his right to the post. First, he established a claim of priority: 'so long ago as the early part of the year 1834', he told Lindley, the directorship of Kew had been promised him by 'the Nobleman in whose gift it lay'. Not only this, but '(unknown to me) he had fixed upon me 6 years before'. It was 'a very sincere desire to return to England' that motivated him. Hooker concluded by comparing Lindley's financial situation and prospects with his own: 'I am truly sorry to hear you say that you want the situation much – for I really had an idea that your several appointments & occupations were very lucrative; – much more so than mine: & you have the high advantage arising from a residence near the Metropolis'.[7] Hooker clearly implied that he had an equal – if not greater – moral claim to the job than Lindley.

But Lindley was not prepared to concede the ground. In his reply, he justified his desire for the directorship in terms of relief from his heavy workload: 'I have as such a fairly good income, but no human being can imagine the labour with which it is acquired'. Appealing to his friend's sympathy – 'I am perfectly certain that I shall be able to bear such exertion but for a few years longer' – Lindley asserted that it was quite natural for him to seek a job that would produce the same income with less fatigue. While there might be no immediate prospects at Kew, he could match Hooker's assertions of long-standing interest and high-level backing (in his case, from the Tory former Foreign and Colonial Secretary, Lord Aberdeen). In a more conciliatory tone, Lindley expressed his faith in their enduring friendship: 'Pray believe me when I say that no one should feel more pleasure at your returning among us Southerners than myself, and if fate fixes you at Kew, so much the better as we shall be neighbours'.[8] Should the situation be reversed, he imagined that Hooker would be equally pleased for him. Reassured by these mutual protestations of good will, the two men set about the contest in earnest.

Hooker feverishly pressed his qualifications on everyone from the Prime Minister and the Chancellor of the Exchequer down. He approached Lindley's patron, the Duke of Devonshire, only to be told that the Duke had that very day written to recommend Lindley to Lord Melbourne.[9] His own advocate, the Duke of Bedford, lobbied his many political acquaintances, and asked his younger son, Lord John Russell, a member of Melbourne's cabinet, to explain to the Queen the importance of establishing Kew as a national botanic garden.[10] Hooker wrote to his friend, the mathematician, botanist and former Whig MP, William Henry Fox Talbot – then engaged in the optical researches that would lead to his invention of photography – to urge him to action: 'if the friends of Horticulture do not soon come forward, I fear Kew will be sacrificed'.[11] Fox Talbot took up the cause with the Linnean Society, the learned society devoted to the study of natural history (and named after the great Swedish naturalist Carl Linnaeus). Fox Talbot proposed a motion, unanimously adopted by the Linnean Society Council, to petition the House of Commons in support of Kew. 'Whether we shall do any good', Fox Talbot observed to Hooker, 'time will show'.[12]

Hooker related every move in his campaign to his confidant and father-in-law, Dawson Turner. Hooker seems to have learnt his networking skills and devotion to correspondence from Turner, a man of great energy and wide-ranging interests, who had made his fortune as a Norfolk banker, but spent his spare time in botanical and antiquarian pursuits (and would think nothing of writing twenty-two letters between dinner and bedtime).[13] Hooker first met Turner, who was just ten years his senior, in 1805, at the age of twenty-one. Hooker's calling card was a species of moss previously unknown in Britain. As his son later wrote, Hooker's subsequent visit to Turner 'led to the colouring of his future life'.[14] Turner swiftly set the young Hooker to work illustrating his magnum opus on seaweeds, proposed him for election to the Linnean Society and supplied the all-important introduction to Sir Joseph Banks. Turner found Hooker's assistance so invaluable and his company so congenial that he established him as the manager of a nearby brewery, encouraged his botanical pursuits and admitted him to the family circle.

The Turner household was run along unusual lines. Dawson Turner's wife, Mary, was an accomplished artist, and her six daughters were educated at home, tutored in Latin, Greek, French, German and Italian by their father, and trained as artists by the acclaimed watercolourist, John Sell Cotman. While Dawson Turner spent his day in the banking office situated on the ground floor, the female members of the family were occupied in scholarly and artistic activities overhead. As soon as they were old enough, the daughters joined the industrious family workshop, cataloguing and illustrating Dawson Turner's extensive botanical and antiquarian collections. Ten years after he had first made Turner's acquaintance, Hooker married the eldest of the Turner daughters, eighteen-year-old Maria. A reluctant and unsuccessful brewery manager, Hooker continued to pursue his botanical interests and, in 1820, through the recommendation of Banks, was appointed Professor of Botany at Glasgow University. As a parting gift, Turner donated his herbarium and – because Hooker's classical skills were somewhat lacking – composed Hooker's inaugural lecture in Latin.[15]

Ever-attentive to his son-in-law's career, Turner assisted Hooker in plotting his strategy for Kew. They agreed that Hooker's main advantage lay in his relative cheapness. Hooker imagined that Lindley would 'strain every nerve' to gain a handsome salary.[16] Lindley, as he confided to his father-in-law, would not be satisfied with anything less than £1,000 a year, whereas he himself would be happy with £600. In January 1839, Hooker made the journey from Glasgow to London to present his case in person to Thomas Spring-Rice, the

Chancellor of the Exchequer. 'I frankly told Mr. S. Rice what my present income was & what I would be satisfied with here', he reported to Turner. To Hooker and Turner's delight, Spring-Rice hinted that the appointment which Lindley 'had carved out for himself will come to nothing'.[17]

But as the months wore on, and the government's aversion to public spending became more marked, Hooker's optimism drained away. In April 1839 he had nothing satisfactory to report to Turner, and by July he was despondent: 'I almost despair of anything coming of Kew', he told Turner. 'The D. of Bedford & all my friends say that with the present state of finances Ministers will not consent to any additional outlay there'.[18] Then, in October 1839, Hooker's situation suddenly took an abrupt turn for the worse. During a trip to his Scottish estate for the annual grouse-shooting season, the seventy-three-year-old Duke of Bedford suffered a fatal stroke. All at once, Hooker's chances were significantly diminished. He had lost his most highly placed informant and staunchest supporter. Without Bedford's influential backing, Hooker feared that the path was left wide open for Lindley.

Locked in their rivalry and calculations, Hooker and Lindley only saw the other as a serious contender for the post. But the campaigning journalist John Claudius Loudon, who had initiated the call for the reform of Kew, fixed on a fellow Scotsman as a candidate: John Smith, the principal foreman at Kew. Writing in the *Gardener's Magazine* for April 1838, Loudon commented: 'we trust the merits of that modest and unassuming man, and thoroughly scientific botanist and gardener, Mr. Smith, will not be forgotten. If Mr. Aiton resigns . . . Mr. Smith is, we think, the fittest man in England for the Kew Botanic Garden'.[19] In backing Smith, Loudon was challenging the class assumptions that generally barred a working man from high office. His characterization of Smith as a 'thoroughly scientific botanist and gardener' also troubled the distinction between two socially differentiated occupations: the man of science on the one hand, and the practical horticulturalist on the other.

A self-taught botanist of humble origins, John Smith embodied the principle of self-improvement so greatly admired at the time – not least by Loudon himself. The son of a gardener in Fife, Smith had been educated at the parish school of Pittenweem. Like many rural children, he worked in the fields during the harvest-time holidays to help pay his school fees. His whole education, he claimed, cost no more than five pounds. He left school at thirteen, having just started to study Latin, to be apprenticed to his father, and, for a number of years thereafter, he worked as a

*6. John Smith, 1876.*

journeyman gardener in Fife. At nineteen, through his father's friendship with William McNab, the curator, he secured a place at the Royal Botanic Garden at Edinburgh, where he was permitted to attend the botanical lectures laid on for medical students. 'Here I met with minds congenial with my own', Smith recalled, 'and although four of us lived in a back shed one-roomed bothy, all personal discomforts were forgotten, our leisure time being entirely employed with books, and in drying specimens of plants'.[20] Out of his wages of nine shillings a week, Smith managed to purchase a Latin *Flora* of British plants, and he painstakingly worked his way through the descriptions, with the assistance of a glossary and Latin dictionary.

Two years later, armed with a letter of recommendation from William McNab, Smith journeyed south. Smith was part of the great exodus of nineteenth-century Scots who sought to improve their employment prospects by emigrating to England. With few opportunities at home, Scottish gardeners were much in demand in England, where they were generally considered better educated, more resourceful and steadier than their English counterparts. As an 1826 correspondent to the *Gardener's Magazine* recalled of his early days as a jobbing gardener in London: 'I had a good deal of employment at first, partly from the circumstance of being a Scotchman, being called by the people who employ jobbers, a professed gardener'.[21] The horticultural press advanced various theories to account for this preference for Scots. Trained to cope with challenging weather conditions, Scottish gardeners were thought to develop particular skills of attentiveness and persistence. The bothy system – where trainee gardeners lived together in basic lodgings – was credited with producing self-reliant individuals, whose bonds with fellow trainees gave them a firm sense of professional identity.[22] Smith himself ascribed the superior skills of

Scottish gardeners to the excellence of the education system: 'the parish school education being much more liberal and free than the national school class education in England', Scottish gardeners were 'acquainted with Geometry and mensuration, and had their scales and compasses with them, and the contrary with the English'.[23] Whatever the basis for their success, it is evident that Scots, working as gardeners, nurserymen and plant collectors, dominated nineteenth-century horticulture – as was also the case in the medical and engineering professions – not only in Britain, but throughout the empire.[24]

The Royal Gardens were no exception to this rule. Kew was, in fact, a central nexus in the Scottish horticultural network. The first supervisor of the Gardens at Kew had been William Aiton (father to William Townsend Aiton), who was said to have walked all the way from Lanarkshire to London to find work, first at Chelsea Physic Garden and then at Princess Augusta's garden at Kew. His son and successor had engaged the Ayrshire-born William McNab at Kew for the first decade of the nineteenth century, before McNab returned to Scotland to take up the curatorship of the Edinburgh Botanic Garden, where Smith encountered him. By the time that Smith arrived at Aiton's door, bearing a letter of recommendation from McNab, he was following a well-worn route and would have been assured of a friendly reception.

Aiton initially placed Smith in the kitchen gardens at Kensington Palace to learn the art of forcing pineapples, grapes and peaches for the royal table. Then, in 1822, Smith was transferred to Kew, where his early duties involved tending the hothouse furnaces. In weekly rotation, one of the junior gardeners would be designated 'fireman' and kitted out in uniform (which they all shared, whatever their size) to heave coals and cart ashes away. Once the working day was over, Smith devoted himself to study. With his personal library now amounting to four volumes, Smith was 'looked upon as the most learned in plants in the garden'.[25]

With his determination and attentiveness, Smith quickly rose through the ranks. Within a year, he was promoted to foreman of the hothouses and propagating department. To Smith's care were entrusted the new plants that arrived, in varying states of health, from collectors across the globe. He became accomplished at nursing plants back to vigour and coaxing seeds into life. In addition to his cultivating duties, Smith increasingly took charge of the management of the gardeners. A stern disciplinarian, Smith was a highly effective, if less than amiable, foreman. He kept a close eye on the gardeners. 'It was a rule at Kew, enforced by the penalty of dismissal, that no gardener should take tips from visitors', recalled J. W. Thomson, one of Smith's trainees, 'but I know this rule was often broken when a tempting *douceur* was offered'. Smith, however, never turned a blind eye, being 'an uncompromising stickler for the rules', which, according to Thomson, 'accounted, perhaps, for his unpopularity'.[26]

Smith's reputation for unwavering probity and the strict adherence to guidelines was forged early in his career. A year into his tenure as foreman, Smith's determination to pursue a miscreant gardener resulted in an extraordinary and widely reported trial at the Old Bailey. On the morning of 29 January 1824, Smith discovered that a number of rare plants had disappeared from the propagating house and noticed a trail of footprints outside. The missing exotics included *Banksia grandis* from Australia, *Jacquinia mexicana* from Central America, and two rare specimens of a climbing spiked palm, *Calamus niger*. Aiton and Smith went directly to the office of the Bow Street Runners to report the loss to the police. As a precautionary measure, Kew was placed on lockdown, with all the gardeners confined to a shed and provided with wooden benches and mats to sleep on.[27]

The investigating officer, George Ruthven, was famous for leading the dramatic arrest, four years earlier, of the radicals of the Cato Street Conspiracy, suspected of plotting to assassinate the Prime Minister and the entire cabinet. With his customary determination, Ruthven went with Smith the same day to track down the stolen plants at Colville's Nursery in Chelsea. Ruthven ordered Robert Sweet, the nursery manager and a respected botanical writer, to open up the glasshouses, and invited Smith to inspect the rows of plants. With typical assurance, Smith quickly located the specimens stolen from the propagating house, now repotted in Colville's glasshouse. On the basis of Smith's confident identification, Sweet was arrested and charged with 'feloniously receiving . . . seven plants, value 7*l.*, and seven garden pots, value 6*d.*, the goods of our Lord the King, which on the same day, at Kew, in the County of Surrey, had been feloniously stolen'.[28]

Sweet's trial was attended 'by many persons celebrated for their scientific and literary acquirements', reported the *Morning Chronicle*.[29] The prosecution case was that Michael Hogan, a gardener at Kew, had stolen the plants and sent them in a box to Sweet. A fellow gardener, Charles Noyes, testified that, on the evening of 28 January, Hogan had given him a box addressed to Sweet, which he had taken, at Hogan's request, across the river to the Waggon & Horses, one of the many pubs in Brentford that served as staging posts. On the morning of 29 January, according to Mary North, the pub landlady, and Thomas Oakshot, a tallow chandler-cum-deliveryman, the box had been loaded onto a coach and delivered by Oakshot to Sweet at Colville's Nursery on the King's Road. The following day, it was discovered that Hogan had absconded, without waiting to collect the six days' pay owed to him. Hogan had not been seen at Kew since.

In Sweet's defence, a number of prominent witnesses were summoned, including William Anderson, the curator of the Chelsea Physic Garden, and the bookseller and publisher John Ridgway, to testify to Sweet's unimpeachable character and reputation as 'the first practical botanist in Europe'.[30] One well-informed juror directly questioned John Smith on the witness stand (as was permitted in trials at the time). Had not a book by Mr Aiton recently been severely criticized in the horticultural press? Smith acknowledged that he had read an article in the *Botanical Register* in which Mr Aiton had been called a dunce. Might not Aiton, the juror asked, have set out deliberately to entrap Sweet in return for being pilloried in print? Smith vehemently refuted the suggestion, while John Ridgway asserted that Sweet was not the editor of the *Botanical Register*.

The *Morning Chronicle* reported that, in his summing up, Mr Justice Best greatly regretted 'that a gentleman to whom the public were so much indebted to for his works upon the most interesting science of Botany, should be placed in his unhappy situation'. But given the evidence, the judge 'expressed his fears that the Jury could come to no other conclusion than that the prisoner was guilty of the offence charged'.[31] Despite the judge's guidance, the members of the jury remained unconvinced. They might have been influenced by the entrapment theory, or been concerned by the absence of proof that the plants so confidently identified by Smith were in fact those that had been stolen. Whatever their doubts, after two hours' deliberation, they returned a verdict of Not Guilty.

The failure to secure a conviction would have infuriated Smith and Aiton. Smith admitted to having had strong suspicions about the culprit, and the trail of circumstantial evidence certainly seemed to implicate both Hogan and Sweet. The case might have strengthened Smith's habits of surveillance, but did not prompt any wider consideration of the factors that could have contributed to the theft. Rather than review the policy of non-distribution of plants or the low pay of gardeners, Aiton attempted to minimize the risk that valuable plants would be stolen by identifying the plants in the botanic garden only by number, and by keeping the lists of plant names securely in the garden office. If the nameless plants presented less of a target for thieves, they were also rendered useless for students of botany. Some four years after the trial, Smith suggested to Aiton that the benefits of naming the plants might outweigh the risk. Aiton reluctantly agreed to Smith's plan to identify the plants, on condition that Smith take full responsibility for the accuracy of the names.

The daunting task of identifying the plants in the botanic garden was one that Smith readily embraced. It raised him above the level of a practical gardener, contributed to his growing expertise and fuelled his drive for self-improvement. Smith's spare time was devoted to botany. He developed a specialist interest in ferns, building up his own collection of dried fern specimens, and was already developing a novel scheme of fern classification. So great was Smith's expertise that the Linnean Society elected him an associate in 1837, a rare distinction for a self-educated botanist.

Smith's fascination with ferns prompted him to strike up a correspondence with the renowned botanist Sir William Hooker. It was in the course of this correspondence that Smith informed Hooker of the impending government enquiry at Kew. By return of post, Hooker asked Smith for more information: 'I really should be glad to know more about the matter and whether a really good, and scientific Botanist is to be placed at the head of it'. Hooker acknowledged that the changes might have implications for Smith, but did not for a moment regard him as a potential rival. He reassured Smith of his prospects with gentlemanly condescension: 'For yourself, I should say from your long service in the Garden, and the excellent character I have always heard of you, that you have a claim to the Attention of the Committee, and that you deserve to be retained and promoted'.[32] Smith, for his part, deferred to Hooker as a man of influence. Fearful that his lack of official contacts might cause him to be overlooked or supplanted in any future reorganization, Smith requested that Hooker write on his behalf to the Commissioners; a recommendation from Sir William would surely weigh greatly in his favour.[33] Some months later, when Smith learnt that Hooker intended to apply for the directorship, he wrote to express his enthusiastic support.

It seems likely, then, that Smith would have been as surprised as Hooker to hear himself advanced by Loudon in the *Gardener's Magazine* as a candidate for the directorship of Kew. Picking up on the story, George Glenny, in the *Gardeners' Gazette*, leapt to the conclusion that Smith had proposed himself for the post, and roundly denounced his presumption. With characteristic extravagance, Glenny went on to blame Kew's problems on Smith, announcing that 'Gardeners know how much they are indebted to us for cleansing that *augean stable*, and Mr. SMITH ought to think himself well off that he was not kicked out with the dirt'.[34] What aroused Glenny's fury in particular was a report that Smith had banned the *Gardeners' Gazette* from Kew. According to Glenny, Smith had declared that any gardener caught reading the paper would be sacked on the spot. '[T]he silly fellow could not take a more effectual method of causing every man to seek it with the greater avidity', Glenny observed with some glee. He ended the article with the promise to his readers – and threat to Smith – of future disclosures: 'now Mr. SMITH thinks the GARDENERS' GAZETTE calculated to open the eyes of his men too much, we will take care he shall not be disappointed.'[35]

Such individual attacks were part of Glenny's signature style; Lindley and the Horticultural Society were also regularly harangued and Glenny liked nothing better than a good vendetta. In an article published the following autumn, Glenny railed at the lack of action on Kew. An immediate order should be put in place to name the plants, he declared. In Glenny's view, it was Smith who was responsible for obstructing the identification process: 'The man Smith, who takes a good deal on himself at Kew, objects to this measure; and as long as he has the power to defeat it, he will resist'.[36] Smith would no doubt have been incensed by the allegation, not to mention Glenny's patronizing reference to 'the man Smith'. But if Glenny's claims that Smith had banned the *Gardeners' Gazette* had any foundation, then Smith might not even have read the paper. It is more than likely that Smith would have considered Glenny and his paper as beneath contempt.

In any case, graver matters preoccupied Smith. The winter of 1837–8 had been a devastating one for the Smith family. The household had been struck by consumption, the disease that accounted for around a quarter of all deaths in the period. In the cramped conditions in which his family of eight lived, tuberculosis spread quickly. One after another, Smith's wife and two of his daughters were afflicted with the wasting disease; first they developed the enervating fever and digestive disorders, then they started to cough blood. Eleven-month-old Jane was the first to go, on 31 December 1837. Her mother, the thirty-five-year-old Ann Smith, succumbed just a few days later. Then, in February, the same week as the garden inspection, Smith lost Ann, his two-year-old daughter. Over two months, Smith and his ever-diminishing family followed each of the three coffins in grim succession to the small graveyard beside the church on Kew Green.

Consumption stalked the Hooker family too. In the autumn of 1839, one of the three Hooker daughters, Elizabeth, away at school in Kensington, contracted tuberculosis. The following summer, her younger sister, Mary Harriette, fell ill as well. Unlike the Smiths, the Hookers could afford to travel in search of health. First, the daughters were taken to Leamington Spa, then to Hastings, and finally to the milder climate of Jersey. Lady Hooker attended her ailing daughters, while Sir William divided his time between his lecturing duties at Glasgow and visits to Jersey. Elizabeth gradually recovered, but Mary Harriette did not. The doctors warned the family to expect the worst. After an agonizing six-month decline, Mary Harriette died in June 1841, at the age of just fifteen. For her family, Mary Harriette's unwavering Christian faith and uncomplaining demeanour made her death an exemplary one.

Lung troubles and a persistent cough also afflicted the elder of the two Hooker sons, William Dawson (known as Willy). But it was not just the state of Willy's health that concerned his family. He had qualified as a doctor and obtained a post as Professor of Materia Medica at Anderson's University in Glasgow, but frittered his time away in idle pursuits. In April 1839, he compounded the problem by eloping with one Isabella Smith, 'a person of no energy, no conversation, & almost as unwilling to exert herself as William himself is'.[37] The secret marriage caused a rift between Isabella and her parents. By the autumn of the same year, it became apparent that Willy needed to seek a warm climate for the sake of his lungs, ideally an environment suitable for botanizing, and to find a means to support his now pregnant wife. It was decided that he would set himself up in medical practice in Jamaica, and then send for Isabella, who would remain for the time being in the Hooker household in Glasgow. But, a mere month after his arrival in Jamaica, Willy was struck down by yellow fever. The progress of the disease was swift. He began to vomit black material and, within a few days, was dead. With tragic irony, an autopsy revealed no tubercles in his lungs.[38] His posthumous daughter was named after him, Willielma Dawson Hooker, 'a name that would be scarcely tolerable', her grandfather wrote, 'but for the recollections it brings'.[39]

The very week that Sir William received the devastating news of his son's death, the botanical world was alarmed by reports of government plans to close Kew. On 11 February 1840, John Lindley unexpectedly received a visit from Robert Gordon, Secretary to the Treasury. To Lindley's dismay, Gordon offered Kew's collection of plants to the Horticultural Society, 'as if', so one of the trainee gardeners later recalled, 'it were dead lumber'.[40] Lindley immediately issued a letter of refusal to the Treasury, called an emergency meeting of the Horticultural Society council, and wrote both to the Prime Minister and the Leader of the Opposition to notify them that he would have the issue raised in Parliament. Lindley's anger at the 'barbarous Treasury scheme of destroying the place' overrode all considerations of personal advancement. 'I of course was aware', he wrote subsequently to Hooker, 'that the stand I made and the opposition I created, would destroy all possibility of my securing any appointment'.[41]

But, if the Horticultural Society had refused to accept Kew's collections, there were other, more likely, takers. The recently established Royal Botanic Society of London was viewed by many as a rival to Kew. Founded in 1838 for 'the Promotion of Botany in all its branches, and its application to Medicine, Arts and Manufactures, and also for the formation of extensive Botanical and Ornamental Gardens within the immediate vicinity of the metropolis', the Society leased eighteen acres of the Inner Circle of Regent's Park.[42] The central London location was one of the Botanic Society's main selling points. Regent's Park was a 'highly aristocratic district' that already housed the Zoological Gardens, and it escaped the worst of the city smoke and odours because of the prevailing winds.[43] A membership subscription cost five guineas for a standard fellowship, ten guineas for a life fellowship, and one hundred guineas for life fellowship with the right to introduce friends and receive transferable tickets. The Society was founded as a select horticultural club, with the Queen as patron, whose members would enjoy the privilege of promenading around ornamental gardens in the heart of London.

As soon as William Hooker heard of the Botanic Society's foundation, he was concerned about its potential impact on Kew. Although the membership included few serious botanists and the list of patrons was 'of a most mixed character', the Society could well divert royal attention away from Kew.[44] Both he and John Smith were approached by the Society for appointments at Regent's Park. Indeed, Hooker's name was added, without his consent and to his considerable irritation, to the list of 'Vice-Patrons and Proposed Fellows' that featured in the Society's prospectus.[45] Although Hooker was tempted by the prospect of a well-paid post in London, he held out for the possibility of Kew. 'One thing is quite certain', he wrote to Dawson Turner, 'that a public national Botc. Garden is loudly called for at this time, & I feel sure that if Government does not bestir itself in the matter, the people will, & there will soon be as fine a Garden there as there is already a Zoological Institution'.[46] Hooker's misgivings about the Society's intentions were well placed. The Botanic Society approached the government in September 1838 with a proposal to take over Kew, and, in February 1839, accepted the Treasury's offer of Kew's priceless collections.[47]

At Kew, Smith was shocked to receive a letter from the botanist Aylmer Bourke Lambert, who informed him that 'Kew Gardens are to be broken up and the plants to be sent to the Horticultural [Society,] that is [if] they will accept of them – if not they are to be offered to persons belonging to the Regents Park'.[48] Even more disturbing was the report of the kitchen gardener that 'he had received instructions from Lord Surrey to take possession of the Botany Bay House, and convert it as soon as possible into a vinery, and that the Cape House was to follow, and to permit of him doing so he was to destroy the plants'.[49] The next day, Smith's old friend the fern enthusiast Robert

Heward visited the Gardens, and Smith raised the alarm. Heward, who was the former publisher of the radical journal the *Westminster Review*, sent an anonymous letter to *The Times*.[50] 'The miscalled Liberal Administration are at their shabby tricks again', the letter opened in thunderous vein, 'and if an exposure of their proceedings is not quickly made public, they will probably accomplish a most disreputable and detrimental affair'. To save a paltry sum, one of the finest collections of plants in Europe was threatened with demolition. 'How respectable will the country look in the eyes of foreigners', Heward asked, 'when it is told on the continent, that Great Britain cannot support the charge of the only national botanic garden in the country?' Ending with a vision of glasshouses repurposed 'to grow grapes and pineapples in', the letter invited the Editor of *The Times* 'to raise your voice against such a desecration'.[51]

Heward's rallying cry reverberated round the botanical community. 'Every one is up in arms about it', Aylmer Bourke Lambert told John Smith.[52] Within days, *The Times* published a letter from an unnamed government source denying that the government had ever intended to demolish the botanic garden. Gordon wrote to the Horticultural Society, hastily backtracking: he had only ever been exploring possibilities with Lindley and had not issued a formal proposal. Loudon devoted substantial articles to the necessity of preserving Kew as a national botanic garden in the March and April 1840 issues of the *Gardener's Magazine*. Like Lindley, Loudon activated his political acquaintances, approaching his fellow Scot, the radical MP Joseph Hume, who, despite his well-known commitment to government retrenchment, 'promised to speak of it in the house'.[53] On 3 March, Lord Aberdeen, Lindley's long-standing Tory patron, raised the matter in the House of Lords. 'The garden was maintained by the public as part of the state and dignity of the Crown', he declared, 'and ought not to be disposed of in the manner that had been proposed'. What is more, 'her Majesty could not have a more refined and elevated object than the protection of this delightful science'. Replying for the government, Viscount Duncannon issued a categorical denial, asserting that 'there was not, and never had been, the least intention of breaking up the garden'.[54]

Lord Aberdeen's call on the Queen to take an interest in Kew was reinforced, in a somewhat unlikely manner, by a letter written by John Smith to the botanist Aylmer Bourke Lambert. In a bid to appeal to Victoria's husband and cousin, Prince Albert of Saxe-Coburg and Gotha, Smith shrewdly described the garden's foundation by Princess Augusta of Saxe-Gotha. The well-connected Lambert showed the account to a lady visitor, who, as he informed Smith, 'is so delighted with the part of your letter relating to Saxe Gothas that she is copying it – she moves in the highest circles and . . . will take up the cause zealously'.[55] Smith's letter 'went to the throne', Lambert reported, and was 'read by her Majesty and Prince Albert, they were much interested with it'.[56] Kew would have attracted the recently married couple's attention not only because of the family connection, but also because of Albert's enthusiasm for science. Although previously dismissive of Kew, Victoria now dispatched a member of the Royal Household to visit the Gardens. Smith's well-timed missive transformed the botanic garden into an emblem of dynastic alliance and a token of the Queen's affection for her new husband.

The public campaign seemed to have paid off. There were behind-the-scenes negotiations about the terms of the transfer of Kew from royal to public ownership. In a Commons debate in May 1840, Joseph Hume demanded the publication of the Royal Gardens Committee Report.[57] More than two years after it was composed, Lindley's report on Kew was finally made public.

Surfacing from grief at the loss of his son William, the bereaved Hooker found that Kew was suddenly centre stage. Approaching his fifty-fifth birthday, Hooker was no longer young. Now was the time to make his move. But death had robbed him not only of his firstborn son, but also of his patron, the Sixth Duke of Bedford. Hooker could not afford to let the chance to secure the longed-for directorship pass him by. With his father-in-law, he devised an extraordinary plan to revive the Bedford family patronage. Together, they would prepare a volume to praise the deceased Duke's contribution to botany and horticulture: a eulogy that would not fail to mention Bedford's distrust of the Botanic Society and his favourite scheme to convert Kew into the national botanic garden, with Hooker at its head. Such a publication, they hoped, might persuade Francis Russell, the Seventh Duke of Bedford, and Lord John Russell, his politically influential younger brother, to honour their late father's memory by continuing to support Hooker. Much as Smith had invoked the royal lineage to promote Kew, so Hooker harnessed filial sentiment to further his campaign for the directorship.

The slim volume, printed for private distribution, purported to be a copy of a letter sent by Hooker to his father-in-law. It included judiciously edited excerpts from Bedford's correspondence about Kew. Initially, Hooker had thought that he would leave in Bedford's complimentary references to Lindley, to show that he had never sought to undermine Lindley with the Duke 'for any selfish purposes'. However, the instances where Bedford 'speaks most honourably of Lindley & as equally deserving with myself of an appointment at Kew' did not make the final cut.[58] 'A point always uppermost in the Duke's mind', wrote Hooker, 'was, that the management of the *reformed gardens* should be entrusted to my care'.[59] Rushed into print in April 1840, the volume was presented not only to members of the Bedford family, but also to the Queen – the copy remains in the

Royal Collection to this day – and, to cover all political bases, to the Tory Lord Aberdeen and the Radical Joseph Hume, advocates of Kew in the House of Lords and Commons respectively.[60] As John Smith later wryly observed, it was 'as fine a piece of sophistry and egotism as could well be written'.[61]

In Glasgow, Hooker waited impatiently to learn of developments at Kew, swinging wildly between optimism and pessimism. On 29 April he confided to Dawson Turner, 'I hear there is an opinion in London that I am to have Kew', but two days later wrote, 'As to Kew I have no hope'.[62] Lindley still appeared as his main rival, but he now started to view Smith as a possible cut-price contender. In the event of Aiton's retirement, Hooker feared that 'a common gardener would be preferred to fill up the place'; he had heard that 'Smith or some such man shd be Aiton's successor'.[63] He travelled down to London to lobby ministers in person, in a state of fretful anticipation. 'I am so anxious even to come & live near here and so certain that I can benefit Kew Gardens', he told his son Joseph, 'that I would almost come there for nothing & indeed have made such an offer that they cannot well refuse'.[64] But, by late June 1840, the years of manoeuvring were finally over. The Treasury at last gave its consent to the transfer of the botanic garden to the Office of Woods and Forests. Kew was no longer a royal garden, subject to the interest – or neglect – of individual monarchs, but a public institution. After a two-and-a-half-year-long campaign of persistent networking and assiduous lobbying, Hooker was finally approved as the director of the botanic garden.

The terms of the position were not finalized until the following winter, and it was only in March 1841 that the official letter was sent. Summoning Sir William from Jersey, Lord John Russell arranged a meeting between Hooker, the Commissioners of Woods and Forests and the Chancellor of the Exchequer. Taking Sir William at his word, the Treasury granted him a very modest salary indeed: £300 a year, plus £200 housing allowance (£100 less than Hooker had wanted). With the appointment still unannounced, the horticultural press continued to speculate about the directorship, with Loudon backing Smith in the *Gardener's Magazine*. When Hooker eventually travelled to Kew on 26 March 1841 for the formal handover of the botanic garden, he found Smith 'very gloomy and uncomfortable', and inferred that Loudon's support had needlessly raised his hopes. But Smith's resentment did little to cloud Hooker's sense of triumph. 'Aiton transferred the Gardens to me, & henceforth I am the Director', he gleefully reported to Turner.[65] At last he was in possession of the key to Kew, and could embark on a programme for the Gardens' transformation.

# 4

# The Horticultural Tour

Packing up in Glasgow, Sir William Hooker carefully prepared the dried plant specimens in his herbarium for removal. The finest private collection in the land, his herbarium was indispensable for his botanical work. Equally important was his botanical library. Plants, books, furniture and household items were all to be stowed in a smack, or sailing boat, for the sea voyage to London (the usual means of transporting goods from Scotland before the advent of long-distance railways). The final leg of the journey would be by barge – five vessels in all – from the London docks along the Thames. Hooker was exchanging life in a crescent town house in the West End of Glasgow for a spacious country residence. He had located a property large enough to accommodate both his herbarium and library: Brick Farm in Mortlake, some ten minutes' walk from the botanic garden, a handsome establishment with coach house and stables, set in seven acres of grounds, with fine trees and pastures stretching down to the river. From the study window, there was a view that took in lawn, meadows, the towpath, willows and the Thames. Across the river lay Chiswick, home to the Horticultural

Society garden run by John Lindley, and Chiswick House, the Duke of Devonshire's elegant Palladian villa with formal gardens and menagerie, used for grand-scale entertaining.

Carpenters and cabinetmakers were busy at Brick Farm building floor-to-ceiling bookcases in the drawing room, ante-drawing room and study, and fitting out a further five rooms with herbarium specimen cabinets. Surrounded by grazing land and market gardens, Brick Farm felt as if it was entirely in the country, yet it was within easy

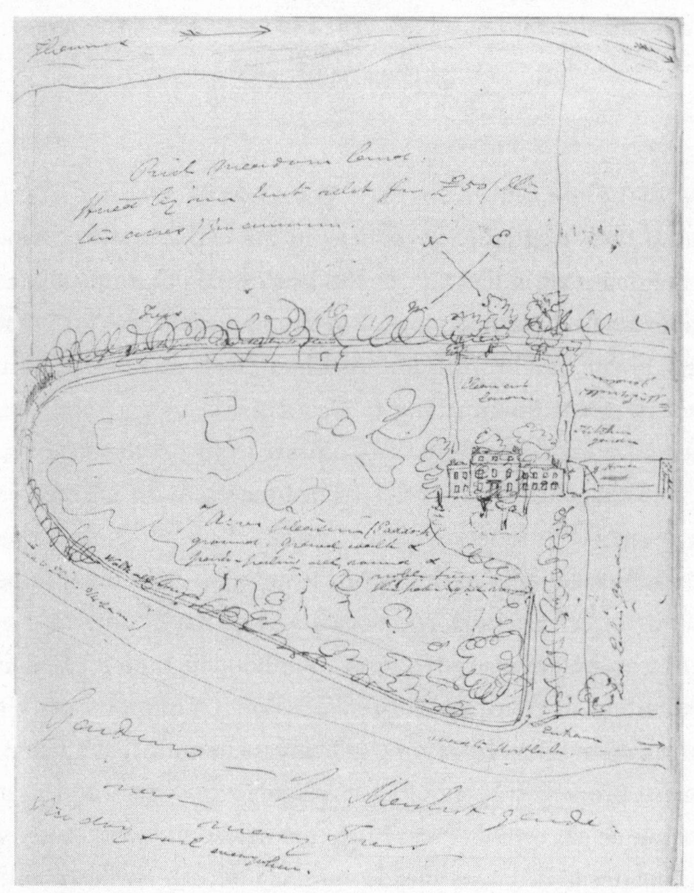

7. *A sketch of Brick Farm in a letter from Sir William Hooker.*

reach of town: 'from Kew Bridge', wrote Hooker, 'we have Coaches or Omnibuses every ¼ of an hour to London for a shilling'.[1] The establishment pleased Sir William in all respects save the name: 'Brick Farm' lacked sufficient dignity for a gentleman's residence. Although only renting the property, Hooker exchanged what his son Joseph termed 'a most plebeian name' for 'West Park', to match the neighbouring 'West Hall'.[2] Despite the grand-sounding address, Hooker was considerably impoverished by the move: the entire operation cost around £300 – the whole of his first year's salary.

What had this outlay – not to mention the years of anxiety, plotting and lobbying – won for Hooker? The botanic garden at Kew was just four acres larger than the grounds of his new house. It comprised an unrivalled collection of exotic plants, but these were crammed into ten run-down glasshouses. There were no records of any kind. In a parting shot that seemed to epitomize the meanness of his regime, Aiton had left with all the garden accounts, botanical drawings and books, claiming them as his private property. To add to the annoyance, Aiton had not completely departed: he still retained control of the adjoining Royal Pleasure Grounds, on an annual pension of £1,000 that dwarfed Hooker's salary.

Aiton's act of archival sabotage had effectively cleared the ground for Hooker to start anew at Kew. There was no model or precedent for a national botanic institution in Britain. Hooker was not issued with a set of official instructions, nor was he answerable to a board of trustees. In administrative terms, the botanic garden came under the government Office of Woods and Forests, and Hooker had to gain the Commissioners' approval for any new initiatives. The funding for major projects was subject to parliamentary vote and there was no guarantee of continued political support. To his friends, Hooker's situation appeared 'a very insecure foundation on which to build the object of his ambition, a Botanic Garden worthy of the nation'.[3]

But the lengthy campaign for the directorship had taught Hooker how to play the long game and think strategically. He was well aware that the discipline of botany rested on a system of international correspondence and plant exchange. During his time at Glasgow, Hooker had built up a worldwide botanical network, in part supplied by his former students who had studied botany in the course of their medical training and had since found employment as surgeons in the colonies. An inveterate correspondent, Hooker kept his contacts alive with regular requests and responses. At Kew, the volume of his correspondence greatly increased: he was usually at his desk by eight in the morning and only left it around midnight. His new position brought him close to London and made it possible to attend learned society meetings and keep up with the latest scientific developments. He was elected vice-president of the Linnean Society, and held fellowships of the Royal Society, Geographical Society and Society of Antiquaries. As the editor of a string of popular botanical journals, he was able to publicize Kew and influence public opinion. The prestige of his post granted Sir William access to the very highest social and political circles. A man of impressive bearing, courtesy and charm, Hooker was at ease in the company of visiting dignitaries. For the Swiss botanist Alphonse de Candolle, Hooker was '*un type de vrai* gentleman *anglais*'.[4]

Hooker put all those gentlemanly qualities to work on arrival at Kew. His first task was to conciliate his one-time rival, the principal foreman John Smith, who remained in charge of the practical management of the botanic garden. In the months that followed Hooker's appointment, Smith's family was once again visited by consumption. The disease that had carried off his wife, Ann, and two of their infant daughters, now struck his thirteen-year-old daughter, Mary. Over the summer of 1841, Mary's condition deteriorated significantly. By the end of July, she was emaciated and coughing blood, and, on 4 August, she died. 'It is my painfull duty to inform you that my dear child expired this morning at ½ past seven', Smith wrote with awful brevity to Sir William. 'It is needless for me to state my feelings on such an occasion especially to you and Lady Hooker, who know by a like bereavement the feelings of a parent for the loss of a beloved child'.[5] United by grief for daughters lost to consumption (the fifteen-year-old Mary Harriette had died less than seven weeks earlier), the two men both took refuge in their work. Smith seems to have buried himself in his after-hours studies of the intricacies of ferns and the problems of his new scheme for classifying the genus. He wrote a succession of articles that Hooker published in the *Journal of Botany* the same year. This new recognition of his expertise would no doubt have gratified Smith and demonstrated some of the advantages of working under Hooker. More concrete acknowledgement of Smith's skills and responsibilities came in the form of an increase in his salary – up a third, to £130 a year – and a new job title, curator, a designation then in use for those in charge of botanic establishments.

Hooker astutely turned Smith, one of the former gatekeepers of the royal collection, into an ambassador for Kew's new policy of openness. Little more than a fortnight after Mary's death, Smith was sent on a horticultural tour of England and Scotland. Smith's brief was to visit a range of gardens, large and small – the grand establishments of aristocrats and the specialized collections of enthusiasts, municipal botanic gardens and commercial nurseries – travelling by coach and steamer all the way to his former training ground, the Royal Botanic Garden in Edinburgh. Smith's task was to identify any plants that Kew lacked and put in requests for donations. These would be provided later, when the plants had reproduced or could be divided. In sharing their plants, donors could feel that they were contributing to the national garden without significantly diminishing their own collections.

By sending Smith on tour, Hooker at once demonstrated his respect for Smith's knowledge and broadened the curator's frame of horticultural reference. Smith's first stop was Woburn Abbey, where Hooker's particular ally, the Sixth Duke of Bedford, had lavished much of the family fortune on the estate. The twenty-eight-acre garden, landscaped by Humphry Repton, was studded with features testifying to the Duke's various botanical interests: the Grass Garden, Heathery, Willow Garden, British Rose Garden and Arboretum. Smith's guide was the head gardener, James Forbes, a fellow Scot, botanist and member of the Linnean Society. In 1837, Forbes had published an account of a European garden tour undertaken to build Woburn's collection of cacti, that 'curious tribe of plants' – the last of the Duke's great botanical passions.[6] Keen to record the glories of his garden, the Duke had financed Forbes' publications, including his earlier description of Woburn's grounds, *Hortus Woburnensis* (1833). Written by one 'more accustomed to the pruning knife than the pen', *Hortus Woburnensis* combined botany with gardening advice and was aimed at a market of both professional and amateur gardeners.[7] It started with a 'Descriptive Catalogue of upwards of Six Thousand Ornamental Plants' and continued with observations on the management of conservatories, hothouses and kitchen gardens. Forbes celebrated horticulture as a pursuit that could unify all ranks of society, from the peer in his greenhouse to the cottager in his vegetable patch. Always sceptical of grand claims, Smith is unlikely to have played on these high sentiments when requesting plants for Kew; more likely, he would have appealed to the gardener's self-interest by offering plants in exchange, from Kew's collection.

Travelling northwards, Smith broke his journey at Birmingham, where the Botanical Gardens, although less than a decade old, contained an impressive collection. Smith identified some 250 plants for Kew. Financed through subscription by the Birmingham Botanical and Horticultural Society, the Gardens in Edgbaston were a sign both of the increasing prosperity of the city's business and professional classes, and their aspirations for gentility. Mr Cameron, the gardener, was proud that so many of his plants should be thought worthy of being sent to Kew.[8] Here was acknowledgement of the quality of the collection and justification of the expense involved in obtaining rarities.

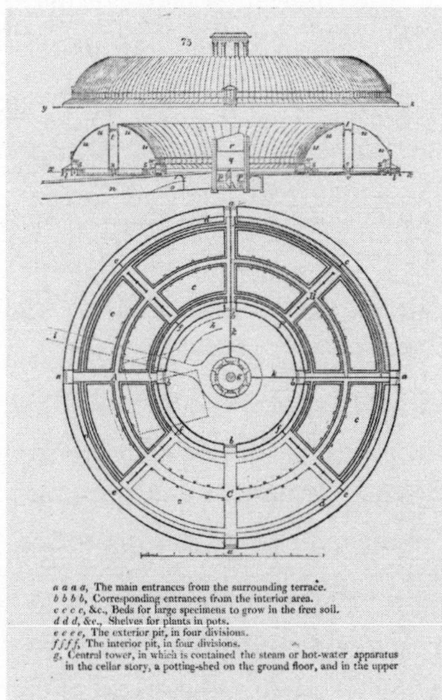


8. *Loudon's ring-shaped glasshouse design (see below).*

9. *Loudon's conical glasshouse design (see below).*

The members of the Society were wary of undue extravagance. They had employed the renowned John Claudius Loudon to lay out the grounds, but had drawn the line at Loudon's conservatory plans: one was in the form of a great ring, with a tower in the middle and glass-covered circular walks; the other, of even greater cost, was of conical shape, 200 feet wide at the base and 100 feet high, with a central spiral ramp leading to an upper gallery. Beguiled by the possibilities of the new iron and glass technology, Loudon had misjudged his clients' tastes and resources. In the end, the Society opted for a less flamboyant design submitted by a local company, Jones & Co. Glasshouses formed the greatest of all garden expenses: in addition to the initial expenditure for the building were the costs of supplying tropical plants and the continuing outlay for fuel and maintenance. Even the most modest stoves were a luxury, while the largest were the preserve of crowned heads and the wealthiest of aristocrats.

Few nobles came richer or more ostentatious than the Duke of Devonshire, whose estate at Chatsworth was Smith's next destination. Under Joseph Paxton, the gardens were being transformed into a magnificent showcase for the Duke's wealth and Paxton's talents. In recognition of Chatsworth's glories, John Lindley had invited the Duke to take on the role of president of the Horticultural Society. At the time of Smith's visit, Paxton's Great Stove had recently been completed and was in the process of being stocked with plants. Enclosing a near acre of ground under a barrel-vaulted roof, the Great Stove was 'the mammoth of its kind': the largest conservatory in existence.[9] With its soaring central nave and two side aisles, the building appeared to contemporaries like a vast cathedral. But the walls and roof were of glass rather than stone, and slender cast-iron columns rather than massy pillars supported the structure. The new glass and iron architecture created a wholly unfamiliar sense of space and light. 'The sensation, on entering the massive portal is not only one of surprise, but of pleasure', marvelled the garden designer Charles McIntosh: 'one feels as if entering a new world'.[10]

The Great Stove was the triumphant expression of Paxton's self-taught engineering skills. He perfected his designs through practical experiment, testing his ideas first in smaller buildings. Paxton was an enthusiastic advocate of curvilinear structures for hothouses: hemispherical forms which maximized the access of light both in winter and summer. To Paxton's mind, rounded roofs were not only superior in terms of performance, but also beauty: 'it is universally conceded', he wrote in the *Magazine of Botany*, 'that a curved line is more elegant than a straight and angular one'.[11] Designers had long debated the relative merits of iron or wood in the construction of hothouse roofs; Paxton favoured wood. At Chatsworth, he invented his own technique of layering wooden strips on a curved frame to increase the strength and curvature of the rafters. From Loudon, Paxton borrowed the idea of ridge-and-furrow glazing, a corrugated glass surface that caught the sun's rays both in the early morning and late evening. When viewed externally, the Great Stove's walls seemed to ripple.

Given the scale and expense of the project, the Duke of Devonshire sought reassurance from an established architect on the structural soundness of Paxton's design. He approached Decimus Burton, one of the leading city planners and architects of the day, responsible for laying out Regent's Park, designing Hyde Park Corner and planning the Zoological Society Gardens (his Giraffe House at London Zoo is still in use today). Burton was no stranger to monumental structures. In 1824, at the age of twenty-three, he had executed the

Colosseum in Regent's Park, one of the major attractions of nineteenth-century London. Based on the Pantheon in Rome, the Colosseum was a building full of wonders. It contained an 'ascending room' – London's first passenger lift – that transported visitors to a rotunda which displayed a 360-degree panorama of London, as seen from the cupola of St Paul's, and had a dome larger than that of the cathedral itself. The Colosseum also boasted an iron-framed conservatory, stretching some 300 feet, with tropical plants, exotic birds, fountains and a stalactite-encrusted grotto. According to the *Imperial Magazine* for 1829, the conservatories and water works exerted 'a talismanic effect on the mind, and manifest to the beholder the powerful restraints in which art is enabled to enchain nature'.[12] With such a pedigree in spectacular buildings, Burton willingly signed off on Paxton's designs.

Like the Colosseum, the Great Stove offered visitors the experience of an artificial world. To create a sense of surprise, it was located out of sight from the main house, and all workings were hidden from view. An underground railway delivered coal to the

10. *The Great Stove at Chatsworth.*

basement boilers, hollow cast-iron pillars doubled as drainpipes, and a flue channelled the smoke below ground to a distant chimney. The glasshouse contained both temperate and tropical zones. The ground rose and fell, and a mass of rockwork was fashioned into steps to lead to a gallery. The house was so large that a broad carriageway passed through the centre to allow grand visitors to view the botanical wonders from the comfort of their carriages. 'This stupendous structure is fast filling with choice plants', the *Derby Mercury* reported in May 1841. 'Here the grateful orange, the luxuriant musa, the oriental palms, the American agave, the Australian conifer, the Mexican cacti, and other rare plants, are blended in glorious confusion'.[13] With vegetation gathered from the world over, the Great Stove was a veritable heterotopia: a space outside the usual constraints of geography, at once all places and none. At the time of Smith's visit, the Great Stove's fame had already spread across the Atlantic. In 1841, the American *Magazine of Horticulture* hailed the Great Stove as 'the *ne plus ultra* of conservatories'.[14]

Stocking the Chatsworth glasshouse with the world's flora came at no small price. The previous year, *The Times* had reported the slow progress of a twelve-ton palm, transported from Buckinghamshire to Chatsworth, in a cart pulled by nine horses, at a rumoured cost of £1,000.[15] By far the most spectacular plants in the Chatsworth display were the palms. In the mid-nineteenth century, palms held an unassailable position in the British imagination. According to Charles Knight's *The Land We Live In*, palms demonstrated 'the very perfection of organisation', combining 'the highest imaginable beauty with the utmost imaginable utility'.[16]

More than any other family of plants, palms appeared to provide humans with every necessity of life: food, drink, oil, clothing, building material, weapons, tools, musical instruments and books. As an article in *Chambers's Edinburgh Journal* put it: the question is not 'What do they afford us? But what is there that they do not?'[17]

Then, as now, palms were associated with effortless bounty, heat and relaxation. George Lawson, demonstrator of botany at Edinburgh University, noted the ubiquity of the palm motif both in high art and wallpaper design: 'Whether in the finished painting of a Brazilian landscape, or on the paper hangings of a tap-room, the palm tree at once indicates in a manner which no other object could, the genial clime in which the scene is laid, and suggests a long train of thoughts on the luxury and ease which the inhabitants enjoy.'[18]

The wide band of the palm zone – then generally located between 35 degrees in the southern and 40 degrees in the northern hemisphere – encircled the globe. Dependence on palms united diverse regions and societies in a common palm culture. Identified with a range of locales – the Holy Land, the Orient and the Pacific, with desert islands and tropical jungles – palms were a kind of literary and visual shorthand for the non-European and the exotic. 'When the painter wishes to represent a tropical land', the *Illustrated Magazine of Art* observed, 'he depicts a landscape with palm trees'.[19]

The two most commonly known palms were the date palm (*Phoenix dactylifera*) and the coconut palm (*Cocos nucifera*). The date palm had a particularly venerable cultural lineage. The date palm was revered in the classical, Judeo-Christian and Islamic traditions; these parallels prompted nineteenth-century writers to draw analogies between the various cultures. 'No member of the vegetable kingdom', declared *Chambers's Journal*, 'has played as important a part in religion, history and poetry as the palm'.[20] In the classical world, palm fronds represented victory, and palm leaves retained this meaning in nineteenth-century figurative speech: 'we speak of awarding the palm', commented *Chambers's Edinburgh Journal*, 'without the privilege, in most cases, of a personal acquaintance with the exalted originals from which the expression sprung'.[21]

In the Bible, palms were identified with the female form, with triumph and upstanding virtue. The Song of Solomon likened the body of the beloved to that of a palm tree (7.8). Sermons, commentaries and works of popular botany glossed verses such as 'The righteous shall flourish like the palm tree' (Psalm 92.12) and elucidated the vision of the saved standing before God's throne 'clothed with white robes, and palms in their hands' (Revelations 7.9).[22] The supposed endogenous – or inward – growth of palms was taken as an apt metaphor for the inner spiritual growth of Christians, and their upright stature as an emblem of moral rectitude.[23]

For Muslims too, as Charles Knight noted, the palm was associated with upstanding virtue and abundance.[24] In the Islamic tradition, the date palm was thought to have been formed from the leftover clay that remained after the creation of Adam. As the sister of Adam, the date palm was to be cherished as a paternal aunt. *Chambers's Journal* outlined an elaborate parallel, attributed to a 'fanciful Arab author' (the thirteenth-century cosmographer and encyclopaedist, al-Qazwīnī), between humankind and date palms: as men are distinguished from the animals by their erect stature and beauty, so are palms; as humans are differentiated by their sex, so are palms; as men have a head, so palms have a crown – and, in both cases, decapitation results in death.[25] For reasons of decorum, *Chambers's Journal* omitted the original Arabic observation that the seeds of the palm smelt like human sperm.

With its associations with the ancient world, the date palm offered a direct link to the distant past. Nomadic cultures which depended on dates as their staple food appeared to have altered little since biblical times. According to Charles Knight, *Bheladal Dsherid*, the Country of the Dates in North Africa (covering parts of present-day Algeria, Tunisia and Libya), had 'remained for a longer period unchanged in its inhabitants and its productions than any other portion of the world'. Identifying the scriptural Ishmaelites with contemporary Bedouin, Knight argued that the date palm of Old Testament days was 'of the same use, and held in the same esteem, as it is now'.[26] To sit under a palm in the desert, mused *Chambers's Journal*, was to see in one's imagination 'all the incidents of the patriarchal life pass in procession'.[27] Indeed, the same article asserted, the date palm was linked to the very origins of humanity: 'At the foot of this tree, man first appears upon the earth, and for many ages his history and wanderings are confined to the country of the date-palm'.[28]

For many nineteenth-century writers, the date palm was one of the central elements that differentiated life in the Orient from that of Europe. In his fictionalized *Sketches of Persia*, published anonymously in 1827, the East India Company administrator and envoy to Persia, Sir John Malcolm, provided a paradigmatic tale which was much reproduced and elaborated.[29] Travelling in Persia, the British narrator is dismayed at the apparent contentment of 'ignorant, half-naked swarthy men and women broiling under a burning sun, with hardly any food but dates'.[30] How could people be happy in such a degraded state? Did they have no desire for improvement? An Armenian member of his party answers his questions with an anecdote. An Arab woman from the city of Bushehr (in present-day Iran) once worked for four years as a nursemaid to an English family. Returning home, she told everyone that England was 'like a garden; the people were rich, had fine clothes, fine houses, fine horses, fine carriages, and were said to be very wise and happy'. Her audience was filled with envy and gloom, until she happened to say, '"England certainly wants one thing . . . There is not a single date-tree in the whole country!" "Are you sure?" was the general exclamation. "Positive!" said the old nurse: "I looked for nothing else all the time I was there, but I looked in vain."' Immediately, the mood of her audience changed from jealousy to pity, and all who heard her 'went away wondering how men could live in a country where there were no date trees!' Reflecting on the story, the narrator starts to question his assumption that the spread of European knowledge would necessarily add to the sum of human contentment.[31] A kind of moral fable, the story at once makes fun of Persians for their cultural misapprehensions and criticizes the British for their notions of progress. The date palm emerges as an emblem of the Providential wisdom that supplies vegetation perfectly suited to the needs of humanity in every region.

Coconut palms, too, occupied a prominent position in British culture. They were associated in particular with the literature of childhood – with the island narratives in the tradition established by Daniel Defoe's *Robinson Crusoe* (1719). Although Defoe's novel never referred to palms and only once mentioned 'cocoe trees', nineteenth-century editions of the novel were full of illustrations of palms. The popularity of *Robinson Crusoe* generated a distinct genre of castaway narratives, known as the Robinsonade. Adventure tales, such as Frederick Marryat's *Masterman Ready* (1841–2) and R. M. Ballantyne's *The Coral Island* (1858), featured islands covered with palm groves. The lives of the South Pacific islanders in *The Coral Island* were so closely identified with coconut palms that palms were inscribed on their bodies in the form of tattoos: 'on the back of a man's leg, the roots rising, as it were, from under his heel, the stem ascending the tendon of the ankle, and the graceful head branching out upon the calf'.[32]

The global occurrence of the coconut palm prompted questions on the manner of its distribution. The shoreline habitat of coconut palms indicated a maritime route. In 1857, John Robertson published an article in *Household Words* called 'Coco-Eaters'; the title suggested a parallel between those who lived on the fruit of palms and the leisured *lotophagi* of Greek myth, and also alluded to Tennyson's 1832 poem, 'The Lotos-Eaters', which depicted the seductive oblivion of existence on a palm-bordered land. A comparable life of island ease, suggested Robertson, could be sustained by the coconut, spread around the world by both tidal and European means. 'The coco floats like a little boat', he observed.[33] Washed up on a new shore, the coconut would sink into the sand, germinate and take root. These seaborne methods of distribution were supplemented by the actions of Arabic traders and European colonizers. 'Civilisation', Robertson claimed, had been 'co-operating with Providence in disseminating the blessings of coco-palms, by planting the seeds where the currents could not carry them'.[34] Disregarding the possibility that coconuts might have been carried by other peoples, Robertson portrayed the worldwide transplantation of coconuts as one of the redeeming features of colonization. Europeans might have 'exterminated aboriginal races to gratify their ruthless rapacity', but such atrocities, Robertson claimed, were offset by their benevolent act of planting coconuts: 'Their intelligent and adventurous selfishness often made desert places fertile'.[35] Indeed, the imperial qualities of resourceful endeavour lauded by Robertson were also celebrated in the castaway narratives of the Robinsonade: the coconut made survival possible, even on the most remote of islands.

In his second novel, *Omoo* (1847), based on his experience as a sailor on a South Pacific whaling ship, Herman Melville devoted a whole chapter to 'The Cocoa-Palm': 'a tree by far the most important production of Nature in the Tropics'.[36] For the Polynesians, the narrator asserts, the coconut palm was 'emphatically the Tree of Life'.[37] In a lyrical paragraph, consisting of one endlessly lengthened sentence, he hymns the coconut's multifarious uses:

> Year after year, the islander reposes beneath its shade, both eating and drinking of its fruit; he thatches his hut with its boughs, and weaves them into baskets to carry his food; he cools himself with a fan platted from the young leaflets, and shields his head from the sun by a bonnet of the leaves; sometimes he clothes himself with the cloth-like substance which wraps round the base of the stalks, whose elastic rods, strung with filberts, are used as a taper; the larger nuts, thinned and polished, furnish him with a beautiful goblet: the smaller ones, with bowls for his pipes; the dry husks kindle his fires; their fibres are twisted into fishing-lines and cords for his canoes; he heals his wounds with a balsam compounded from the juice of the nut; and with the oil extracted from its meat embalms the bodies of the dead.[38]

The boundless utility of the coconut palm was one of the common themes of natural-history writing. 'It is a common saying', wrote James Wilson, 'that the cocoanut tree has ninety-nine uses, and the hundredth cannot be discovered'.[39] Melville's ever-extended sentence is one of the most elegant examples of a familiar enumeration of the all-encompassing bounty of palms. The coconut was often taken as 'the palm of palms', exemplifying all the useful properties of the whole family of palms.[40]

Melville also draws on a customary trope when he praises the beauty of palms. In *Omoo*, the coconut groves of Papeete Bay in Tahiti are surpassingly lovely: 'High overhead are ranges of green rustling arches; through which the sun's rays come down to you in sparkles. You seem to be wandering through illimitable halls of pillars; everywhere you catch glimpses of stately aisles, intersecting each other at all points.'[41]

The architectural qualities of palms were much celebrated by late eighteenth- and early nineteenth-century writers. Groves of palms often evoked Gothic cathedrals and provoked sensations of awe and wonder.[42] Some writers even claimed that the stems and proportions of palms provided the model for Greek columns.[43] The parallels with classical and ecclesiastical buildings endowed palms with a dignity that was ascribed to the Divine Architect himself.[44]

The widespread distribution of palms across the globe invited writers to draw parallels across cultures. In an article on the coconut, for instance, the military surgeon Henry Marshall compared his own observations on the coconut palm in Ceylon (present-day Sri Lanka) with biblical uses of the date, and contemporary accounts of palm practices in North Africa and Otaheite (Tahiti). In Ceylon, Marshall noted, palm fronds were employed as a sign of respect to people in power.[45] As an emblem of triumph and joy, palm fronds featured both in the Bible and current practice in Murzuq (present-day Libya). Eagerly tracing cross-cultural parallels, Marshall switched to the subject of headgear, comparing the bonnets of coconut leaves worn by women in Otaheite with the palm hats favoured by European soldiers in Ceylon.[46] Such a wide-ranging account, encompassing both past and present, suggested the endless proliferation of palms and their uses across the world. To the nineteenth-century imagination, the worldwide web of palm connections spanned times, regions and cultures.

However extravagant he might have found the Chatsworth display, Smith returned from his tour with an enhanced sense of the possibilities of horticultural spectacle. His garden visits helped to establish Kew as an institution with nationwide reach. By the time that he came back to Kew, Smith had forged links with a range of gardeners, both grand and modest, professional and amateur, and had established lines of communication and plant exchange across classes and regions. The tour also allowed him to gauge the level of horticultural activity throughout the country.

The provision of municipal gardens was high on the agenda of contemporary social reformers. 'Public walks' were seen as crucial for the health and welfare of the urban working classes. In cramped industrial cities, public gardens allowed access to much-needed fresh air and green space. The London air, according to the Irish writer John Fisher Murray, was 'a substantial vapour, gross and palpable. Sometimes you can smell it, oftener you taste it, and at intervals you may cut it with a knife'.[47] With the rise in lung diseases such as tuberculosis, the atmosphere of cities was of growing concern to doctors. As early as 1829, Loudon had published his 'Hints for Breathing Places for the Metropolis' in the *Gardener's Magazine*: a plan for concentric green belts in towns, so that 'there could never be an inhabitant who would be further than half a mile from an open airy situation, in which he was free to walk or ride, and in which he could find every mode of amusement, recreation, entertainment, and instruction'.[48] In addition to functioning as 'respirators', parks were also supposed to encourage orderly behaviour and social aspiration.[49] Rather than frequent the pub, artisans and factory workers were given the opportunity to accompany their families to the well-kept environment of the public park. 'A man walking out with his family among his neighbours of different ranks', noted the 1833 Report of the Select Committee on Public Walks, 'will naturally be desirous to be properly clothed, and that his Wife and Children should be so also'. Such decorous attire and respectable conduct would, according to the report, have 'the most powerful effect in promoting Civilization and exciting Industry'.[50]

It was commonly assumed by those who shared the liberal political views of the Whigs that the provision of public parks, botanic gardens and museums would educate and raise the taste of the people, thereby lessening discontent and the likelihood of unrest. Leisure time should be devoted to rational recreation – that is, to improving pursuits that strengthened both body and mind, rather than to low pastimes and the consumption of alcohol. An orderly, uplifting environment would encourage orderly, respectful behaviour. When questioned in 1841 by the Select Committee on National Monuments, Colonel Charles Rowan, one of the chief commissioners of the Metropolitan Police, observed that 'the more the people see that they are considered, the better their conduct becomes in consequence . . . they take an interest in preserving the things they are allowed to visit'.[51] To provide free amenities and to trust the working classes to behave appropriately became the mark of enlightened government.

The Queen, who was generally sympathetic to Whig principles, allowed increasing access to Crown lands over the course of the 1840s. In London, first Regent's Park and then the other Royal Parks opened their gates to members of the public – so long as they were respectably dressed. At Kew, Victoria recognized the need to expand the eleven-acre botanic garden to improve provision for the people. She acquiesced to Sir William's requests in 1841 and 1842 for successive grants of land from the adjoining Royal

Pleasure Grounds. Her uncle, the King of Hanover, however, proved harder to persuade. Writing to his father-in-law in July 1843, Hooker complained of being 'sadly annoyed by the K. of Hanover, who swore with horrid imprecations that I should not carry the contemplated alterations of the Garden into effect'.[52] Hooker had to use all his diplomatic skills to persuade the lesser members of the royal family to part with their shooting grounds, hayfields and fish ponds for the public good. He was obliged to be charmingly attentive to his royal neighbours, particularly the Duchess of Cambridge and her daughter, Princess Mary Adelaide (see Plate 26). When in residence, they took daily constitutionals in the botanic gardens and 'constantly invited him to accompany them in their walks, and were not backward in giving him their opinion of his operations'.[53] By comparison, Victoria's relative indifference was a blessing: 'I am sure it is a happy thing for the Garden', Hooker confided in Dawson Turner, 'that the Queen does not take an interest in Kew, like the Duchess of Cambridge; for as far as Her Majesty is concerned, I believe I might have every reasonable thing my own way'.[54] Hooker's confidence in his ability to persuade the monarch appears to have been well founded. By 1844, the botanic garden's territory had grown by sixty-five acres – nearly six times its original size.

Hooker was not only concerned with the extent of the Gardens, but also the aesthetics. In place of the boundary wall between the botanic garden and the Pleasure Grounds, he erected a wire fence that gave the illusion of greater space. He opened up views, laid out new walks and extended the lawns. 'I cannot tell you how much I have at heart the improvement of these fine Gardens', he told his son, Joseph. 'People say when they are in the Gardens they hardly know them again'.[55] His predecessor, however, did not appreciate the transformation. 'Mr Aiton is sadly annoyed at all these changes',

Lady Hooker wrote to Joseph; 'he says it half breaks his heart to see the paths altered which were planned by himself & George the III'. Not only did Aiton resent Hooker's innovations, he also regarded them as inauspicious. For a number of months after his arrival at Kew, Sir William had not been in the best of health. His wife attributed this to fatigue sustained from repeatedly travelling to and from Jersey, to the stress of moving house and to grief at the loss of their daughter, Mary Harriette. But, to Aiton's mind, Lady Hooker wryly observed, Sir William's ill health had been caused by 'the levelling of an unlucky wall & the substituting of a light wire fence, "which let in so much cold"'.[56]

Far from being cast down by his indisposition, Sir William would scarcely admit to being ill. He was absorbed by his new project and full of plans for Kew's future. Hooker now had more than enough space to pursue his ambitions for the botanic garden. 'When we take in our additional 40 acres', he boasted to his father-in-law in 1843, 'it will be the finest thing of its kind in Europe'.[57] Hooker's bold dream for Kew received admirable backing from John Lindley. Now that they were no longer competing for the same job, the two men resumed their friendship. Together, the director of Kew and the vice-secretary of the Horticultural Society constituted a formidable team. Hooker paid public tribute to Lindley by deferring to his report on the Royal Gardens. In the absence of any official instructions, Hooker took Lindley's vision of a future Kew as the starting point for his policy at the Gardens. He quoted extensively from Lindley's projection of Kew's national and imperial importance in his first annual report to the House of Commons.[58] Even John Smith grudgingly conceded that Hooker had the drive and commitment to realize Lindley's grand schemes: Sir William was 'the right man in the right place', to ensure 'that the principles embodied in Dr. Lindley's Report, would be carried into effect'.[59]

For his part, Lindley celebrated Hooker's early achievements in the editorial columns in the *Gardeners' Chronicle*, the weekly horticultural newspaper that he launched with Paxton in 1841. Now that visitors were able to walk freely through the Gardens without a supervising gardener in attendance, there had been 'a large increase of respectable company', Lindley reported.[60] Overturning Aiton's policy, Hooker had started to share duplicate plants in the collection, he noted approvingly. Lindley confidently predicted that travellers would willingly gather seeds, and gardeners donate plants to Kew, assured that their donations would not be neglected, and that their gifts would be reciprocated. The botanic garden would become a fount of horticultural and botanical information for the nation. 'We have ourselves seen the changes which are going on at Kew', Lindley observed, 'and we sincerely congratulate the country upon its renovation'. Under Hooker's directorship and given adequate government funding, predicted Lindley, Kew would swiftly assume its rightful place 'at the head of the Botanical Establishments of Europe'.[61] At the earliest opportunity, Lindley advised, Hooker should turn his attention to 'an entire renovation of the Palm-house', since many of the magnificent specimens were breaking the glass of their cramped quarters.[62]

# 5

# FATHER *and* SON

HOOKER'S OTHER GREAT PROJECT – IN ADDITION TO THE promotion of Kew – was the career of his surviving son, Joseph Dalton Hooker. Indeed, the two schemes were closely intertwined. Having plotted so long to obtain Kew, Sir William was reluctant to let it out of the family. But this would not be nepotism pure and simple: his son would have to attain a respected position within the field. Joseph had all the makings of an excellent botanist, but he was still young. To prepare Joseph as his successor would be a decades-long campaign involving all of Sir William's skills as strategist, negotiator and publicist.

Joseph's botanical career started early in life. Raised in a household with its own herbarium, a mother who was an accomplished botanical artist and a father who took him on regular plant-gathering trips, Joseph had honed his skills of observation, identification and drawing in childhood. Maria Hooker entered wholeheartedly into her husband's botanical pursuits and acted as his secretary and amanuensis. She loved music and art, was widely read and 'wrote with a facile pen steeped in all the copious rotundity of the Johnsonian school'.[1] Evangelical in belief, Maria Hooker brought up her five children – two sons and three daughters – to respect their elders and apply themselves to their lessons. At seven years old, Joseph and his brother Willy used to attend their father's early-morning botany lectures at Glasgow University (returning home in time for breakfast at half past nine). In the words of his biographer, Leonard Huxley – himself the son of Joseph's friend, the renowned zoologist Thomas Henry Huxley – Joseph Hooker 'did not so much learn botany as grow up in it'.[2]

Added to the advantages of his upbringing was Joseph's capacity for hard work. Fifteen months younger than Willy, Joseph strove to keep up with his elder brother. 'I think that Joseph would be the child to please you in his learning', Maria Hooker reported to her father, Dawson Turner. 'He is extremely industrious, though not very clever. Willy can learn the faster if he chooses, but while his elder brother sets his very heart against his lessons, Joseph bends all his soul and spirit to the task before him'.[3] His powers of application meant that Joseph excelled at school, but he was a nervous child who hated speaking in class. Following his father's example, Joseph loved to collect and classify; he built up his own herbarium and collection of insects (particularly beetles) and began corresponding with entomologists while still in his teens. So great was his pleasure in ordering the world that, on one occasion, 'earnestly and unprompted during his papa's absence', Maria Hooker told Dawson Turner, Joseph undertook 'the task of cataloguing every book in the house'.[4]

But, even for a botanist born and bred, the career path was not straightforward. Most naturalists were gentlemen of private means, who could pursue their scientific interests and travel to distant lands without being obliged to earn a living. This was not an option available to the Hookers. For an aspiring botanist, the best way to make one's name was to secure a berth on an overseas voyage; the more remote the destination, the better. In his own youth, Sir William had leapt at the opportunity to conduct a botanical survey of Iceland (all expenses paid by Sir Joseph Banks). Hooker did not confine his researches to botany, but also investigated Icelandic society, culture, geology and natural history. On his homeward voyage, however, the ship on which he was travelling caught fire. Laden with tallow and wool, the vessel was swiftly engulfed in flames. No lives were lost, but Hooker's botanical specimens, drawings and papers were all destroyed. From the sparse remains of his journal, augmented by manuscripts lent by Banks and his own recollections, Hooker worked up a two-volume *Journal of a Tour in Iceland in the summer of 1809* (1811). Initially, the *Journal* was privately printed, but a London bookseller deemed it sufficiently interesting to bring out an edition two years later.[5] It served to announce Hooker's arrival on the scientific and literary scene. From his own experience, Sir William knew the importance of publishing the findings of a voyage, however scanty or heterogeneous. On such foundations, a man could build his career.

For Hooker's son Joseph, a far greater – if far riskier – opportunity to travel presented itself. In 1838, the British Association for the Advancement of Science proposed an Antarctic voyage to locate the south magnetic pole. This would be a major government-funded expedition to take magnetic readings and establish magnetic observatories in various British colonies across the southern hemisphere – on St Helena in the South Atlantic Ocean, at the Cape of Good Hope in South Africa, and at Hobarton in Van Diemen's Land, off the south-east coast of Australia (modern-day Hobart, in Tasmania). By gathering sufficient data on magnetic variation, dip and intensity, scientists hoped to build an understanding of the laws that governed the earth's magnetic field and, in so doing, improve the accuracy of navigation. In their search for the south magnetic pole, the British faced competition from both French and American expeditions – all three nations eager to claim the prestige of discovery.

The Antarctic remained a void on the global map. The extreme climatic conditions had deterred earlier navigators from venturing beyond the Antarctic fringes. Fantastical tales of a great southern continent, *Terra Australis Incognita*, had circulated since classical times, but the existence and extent of Antarctica had yet to be confirmed. Although the expedition's primary object was to gather magnetic information, a secondary aim was geographical exploration. Venturing into the high southern latitudes, the expedition would have to brave pack ice and Antarctic storms in its attempt to advance as close as possible to the south magnetic pole. Two naval vessels, the *Erebus* and the *Terror*, originally designed to carry heavy mortars for bombardment, were to be specially reinforced to withstand the Antarctic seas. The success of the expedition would depend on the strength of the ships' hulls, on the weather and – for the faithful – on Providence.

Sir William and Joseph immediately saw the career-launching potential of a voyage that combined cutting-edge science with daring adventure. As it criss-crossed the southern oceans, the Antarctic voyage would provide an unrivalled opportunity for a botanist keen to survey unknown floras and study the geographical distribution of plants. Sir William, then still a professor at Glasgow University, lost no time in procuring an introduction for Joseph to the expedition commander, the seasoned Arctic explorer and expert on terrestrial magnetism, James Clark Ross. In 1831, the famously dashing Ross had planted the British flag on the north magnetic pole. Now, he wanted to do the same for the south. Already high on the list of heroic explorers, Ross aimed for the very top of the national pantheon. By contrast, the twenty-one-year-old Joseph was entirely untested. But Ross was prepared to take Joseph on in the role of assistant surgeon – provided that he qualify first as a doctor. With very little time available, Joseph applied himself to his medical and natural-history studies with fierce determination, managing to complete the medical curriculum within a year. Then it was discovered that, according to university regulations, Joseph would not be able to graduate in time. With typical dispatch, Sir William wrote several letters to highly placed contacts and his son's way was cleared. Although Joseph did not manage to secure his desired position of expedition naturalist, he settled for the lesser post of botanist. In September 1839, Joseph Hooker set sail on the *Erebus* as assistant surgeon and botanist, the youngest member of the expedition.

The Antarctic expedition, according to the president of the British

11. *George Richmond's chalk portrait of Joseph Hooker.*

Association for the Advancement of Science, was 'the most important and the best-appointed scientific expedition which ever sailed from the ports of England'.[6] The *Erebus* and the *Terror* each had strengthened ribs, a metal-sheeted hull, a heating system and double deck. They were provisioned for three years and carried massive ice-saws. To ensure the accuracy of the measurements, the Royal Society had supplied sets of the latest scientific instruments: magnetometers, chronometers, hygrometers, anemometers, electrometers. 'All expect much from you in such a voyage', Sir William wrote on parting from Joseph, 'and so do I dear fellow'.[7] Sir William's farewell sentiments were echoed in a patriotic poem addressed 'To the Officers of the Antarctic Expedition', published the same month in the *Literary Gazette*:

> Go forth, adventurers on the ocean.
> Go from your own, your fatherland,
> We hail you with a strong emotion –
> A brave – a noble-hearted band![8]

In an attempt to live up to the high public and private expectations excited by the voyage, Joseph devoted himself single-mindedly to his duties: collecting, classifying, drawing and recording. At each landfall, he went on botanizing trips, either on his own or with companions, in happy pursuit of specimens large and small, from tree ferns to lichens. He filled his vasculum, travelling portfolio and even his pockets with plants. At sea, he collected and drew marine creatures caught in the ship's towing net. His researches were encouraged by James Clark Ross, who himself had served as naturalist during his previous polar expeditions and had recently been elected to the Linnean Society. 'Captain Ross as soon as he heard that I was anxious to work, gave me a cabinet for my plants in his cabin', Joseph told his father; 'one of the tables under the stern windows is mine wholly, with a drawer for my microscopes & locker for my papers'.[9] Hooker and Ross would sit opposite each other in companionable silence, working away until the early hours – the captain busy at his log and calculations, Joseph intent on his drawings.

The first leg of the expedition, the voyage from Britain to Van Diemen's Land, lasted eleven months. The route took in Madeira, the Cape Verde Islands, St Helena, the Cape of Good Hope and the remote Kerguelen's Land (otherwise known by the ominous name of Desolation Island). On arrival at Hobarton, in Van Diemen's Land, the ship was greeted by the mail boat. 'None but a sailor knows what it is to see the first boat pull along side', Joseph told his sister Maria, '& oh how my heart pounded when Captain Crozier pulled along side & handed up the huge wash-beaten letter bag. A few minutes more & I should be happy'.[10] But among Joseph's haul of letters was one with black margins and a black seal. From the opening words of his father's address, 'My very dear & only son', Joseph knew that his elder brother was dead.[11]

Like his father, Joseph turned to botany in his grief: 'never before', he wrote to Sir William, 'could I have so deeply felt how much the study of our mutual pursuit tends to alleviate our distress'.[12] Even as he mourned the loss of his brother and childhood companion, Joseph was aware that he had now taken on a new role in the family. As the only son, the whole weight of parental love, expectation and anxiety would fall on him. 'Dear Joe', his father wrote, 'our minds naturally turn to you & we would cling to you with more affection than ever'.[13] Joseph's health amid the rigours of the Antarctic expedition became an object of even greater parental concern. 'Oh, may God ever have you in his holy keeping, give you a prosperous voyage & in due term, give you a safe return to your now afflicted Parents & Sisters!' his father prayed.[14] 'Nothing I can say', Joseph responded, 'can console you, but the oft repeated promise that you may prove me a faithful son & one that would make up your loss as well as he could'.[15] Throughout his childhood, Joseph had vied with William. Now, he was left in sad possession of the field.

In Van Diemen's Land, as throughout his voyage, Joseph encountered friends and associates of his father. Before Joseph's departure, Sir William had furnished him with introductions to his correspondents – colonial officials, doctors, traders and missionaries – spread throughout the world. On the Antarctic voyage, Joseph functioned as his father's global ambassador (much as John Smith, on his later tour of British gardens, acted as Hooker's domestic envoy). Sir William instructed his son to cultivate new contacts, to encourage botanic enthusiasts to send him specimens, seeds and plants. The Lieutenant-Governor of Van Diemen's Land was Sir John Franklin, former Arctic explorer and friend both of Captain Ross and Sir William. With his previous experience of polar exploration and magnetic science, Franklin was an enthusiastic supporter of the expedition. He set 200 convicts to work, building the magnetic observatory, and fêted the expedition officers with balls and receptions. Joseph visited Franklin at his residence, but disliked large gatherings and avoided the parties. He preferred to spend time with Ronald Campbell Gunn, the island's superintendent of convicts, a dedicated amateur botanist who supplied Sir William with a stream of specimens. The two men went on collecting expeditions together and Joseph relished his discussions at 'Mr Gunn's delightful fireside'.[16]

Departing from Hobarton in November 1840, the *Erebus* and *Terror* headed into 'an entirely unexplored region of discovery'.[17] In terms of exploration, the first tour was the most productive of all three of the expedition's Antarctic voyages. Breaking through the pack ice, the *Erebus* and *Terror* set their course due south. In January 1841, they sighted an immense land mass of ice-covered mountains, between 9,000 and 12,000 feet high. To mark the significance of the discovery – and to claim the land for Britain – Ross named the region Victoria Land. With considerable difficulty, a small party made its way to the shore, and the captain clambered onto a rocky promontory, staying just long enough to plant 'a little silk Union Jack, the present of some lady . . . and all the hands gave three cheers'.[18] The flag had been intended for the south magnetic pole, but since Victoria Land now frustratingly blocked the ships' passage, this might be the nearest the expedition would approach to that elusive goal. The makeshift performance was perhaps not quite the ceremony envisaged by the writer of a poem, 'On a Flag Presented to Captain Ross by a Lady, to be planted on the South Magnetic Pole', printed in the *Literary Gazette* in 1839. The final lines celebrated the moment when the 'beauteous banner' would 'start into new life' and:

> the shout triumphant tell the tale,
> That Man's proud foot o'er Nature doth prevail[19]

Although man's victory over nature was far from complete, Ross had not entirely given up the pursuit of the magnetic pole. Victoria Land might, after all, prove to be an island, around which they could sail. Accordingly, the expedition proceeded along the coast. The next day, they were stunned by the magnificent sight of a snow-covered volcano, emitting a plume of black smoke. Enraptured by the spectacle of fire and ice, Joseph wrote home:

> I can give you no idea of the glorious views we have here, they are stupendous & imposing, especially when there was any fine weather, with the sun never setting among huge bergs, the water sky both as blue or rather, more intensely blue than I have ever seen it in the tropics, & all the coast one mass of beautiful peaks of snow & when the sun gets low they reflect the most brilliant hints of golden yellow & scarlet & then to see the dark cloud of smoke tinged with flame rising from the volcano rising in one column, one side jet black & the other reflecting the colours of the sun.[20]

With a sentence as long and breathless as the view was breathtaking and grand, Joseph attempted to convey the overwhelming impact of the scene. Like many travellers to polar regions, Joseph saw the landscape in terms of the sublime: at once terrifying and ravishing, inspiring both wonder and awe. With his artist's eye, Joseph carefully recorded the luminous colours and made several sketches of the scene.

In the rugged terrain, Captain Ross found a way of guaranteeing the lasting fame of the expedition. He named the active volcano Mount Erebus, after his own ship, and its dormant fellow Mount Terror, after the companion vessel. Later the same day, a further wonder loomed into view: an immense wall of ice, rising some 150 feet above the sea, barring all but the highest mountains from sight. For 300 nautical miles, the expedition followed the line of the great ice barrier – later known as the Ross Ice Shelf – before the captain made the decision to turn back to Hobarton.

The following two Antarctic summers, the expedition again ventured to the far south. Beset by foul weather and hazardous conditions, neither voyage contributed greatly to the existing stock

12. *Mount Erebus and Mount Terror.*

of knowledge. In late November 1841, storms prevented the ships from landing on Chatham Island, to the east of New Zealand. From mid-December 1841 to early February 1842, the ships were stuck fast in the pack ice. The stranded crew saw in the New Year with an elaborate ball on the ice, opened by Captain Crozier of the *Terror* and 'Miss Ross' of the *Erebus*. But the desperate revelry did little to mask the severity of the situation. It was sheer good fortune – or, as most believed, the guiding hand of Providence – that freed the ships from the ice. Worse was to follow. In an attempt to avoid an iceberg in stormy waters, the two ships collided and inflicted serious damage on each other. 'I suppose no naval annals in the world could record such a narrow escape', a letter from an officer, printed in the *Athenæum*, declared; 'however, we did escape, and, what was more fortunate, without the loss of a single life'.[21]

In his correspondence home, Joseph shielded his family from the horrors of the Antarctic. It was only after the final, particularly taxing and unrewarding Antarctic trip that he admitted to his father how much he detested the voyages to the far south. 'I cannot tell you how rejoiced we are now to be leaving it for good & all!!' he exclaimed, with palpable relief.[22] Nothing could compare to the tedium and terror of life on board the *Erebus*. In stormy weather, with hatches battened down and the continuous pitching, the only possible escape was in the pages of books. The hours of darkness were haunted by the constant fear of unseen icebergs. 'How can one sleep at night under such circumstances?' Nothing would tempt him to return to the region: 'I am sure I would not for a Baronetcy'.[23]

Delighted as he was that an end was in sight, Joseph knew that he had profited greatly from the expedition. The periods spent ashore had afforded him an unparalleled opportunity to botanize in Van Diemen's Land, New Zealand and the Falkland Islands. The collections that he amassed during this period would form the basis of his future botanical career. Although the specimens were officially the property of the Admiralty, Joseph privately dispatched duplicates to his father for safekeeping. And when, halfway through the expedition, he learnt of Sir William's appointment at Kew, he had added incentive to contribute to the national store. His father's letters excitedly reported developments at Kew. His call for plants had been met with an overwhelming response: 'botanical treasures are pouring in upon me from all quarters: & I no sooner skim through one new arrival than another comes in'.[24] The Queen had consented to his expansion plans and his superiors had readily agreed to send a collector to the West Indies. 'Natural History in all its branches is more flourishing than ever', he announced optimistically, '& I hope our Kew Gardens will be instrumental in giving an impulse to Botany'.[25]

With Sir William's encouragement, Joseph focused his efforts on plants that might attract scientific or public attention, such as the Kerguelen Land's cabbage. Confined to one remote island, the distinctive Kerguelen Land's cabbage was valued by sailors as protection against scurvy. Joseph wrote the first botanical description of the plant and dispatched seed to his father, who longed to have such a rarity at Kew. But Sir William could not get the seed to germinate, much to his frustration and Joseph's incredulity. 'I have had fifty plants of it from seed', Joseph boasted; 'I had it growing in a bottle! (hanging to the after rigging) . . . during all our second cruise in the Ice'.[26]

The diverse environmental and climatic conditions encountered at every landfall on the expedition presented Hooker with the opportunity to address issues of plant geography. Comparing the vegetation of different locales, Hooker started to ask larger philosophical questions of how and why species were distributed across the globe. Remote islands in particular engaged his attention. Why was it, for instance, that the vegetation of the southern Indian Ocean island of Kerguelen's Land bore little resemblance to that of the nearest continent, Africa, but had more affinity with the plants of South America? Why did the Kerguelen's Land cabbage grow only on that island and nowhere else in the world?[27] This willingness to grapple with fundamental issues of plant distribution would later bring Joseph into correspondence and friendship with the greatest natural historian and scientific theorist of his day: Charles Darwin.

From the very outset of the voyage, Darwin had been Joseph's model and personal hero. Some eight years older than Hooker, Darwin had set sail as naturalist on HMS *Beagle* in 1831, also at the age of twenty-two. Hooker had aimed for the post of expedition naturalist, rather than botanist, because he aspired to the same position as Darwin. In 1838, Darwin published the findings of the expedition as the *Journal of Researches* (now known as the *Voyage of the Beagle*). While still a medical student, Joseph had been lent the proofs of Darwin's text, which he kept under his pillow, so eager was he to read them last thing at night, first thing in the morning. The Antarctic voyage followed part of the *Beagle*'s route and Joseph found Darwin's remarks 'so true and graphic wherever we go' that his account was 'not only indispensable but a delightful companion & guider'.[28] Joseph framed his ambitions in terms of Darwin's achievements. He, too, wanted to travel, observe, collect and write his way into scientific fame.

Joseph documented his four years of travels in journals, drawings and letters home. He never published an account of the voyage to rival Darwin's, but his father ensured that his most remarkable discoveries came to public attention during the course of the expedition. Strictly speaking, this contravened naval regulations which stated that all accounts, drawings, records and collections were to be kept confidential and surrendered to the Admiralty at the end of the voyage. Captain Ross rigorously enforced this code, limiting even the amount of information that he communicated in his official dispatches, much to the annoyance of the Admiralty in London. But, with characteristic expediency, Sir William found ways around the rules. Private correspondence, to his mind, was exempt from the official ban. Copies of Joseph's letters circulated widely among the Hookers' friends and acquaintances. 'Your letters of which we constantly read the non-confidential portions call forth exclamations of wonder & delight', Elizabeth Hooker told her brother. 'The compliments which are paid to the style & expression in your writing, I cannot attempt to repeat, indeed I fear that if you were likely to be conceited, such flattery would turn your head'.[29]

Particularly appreciated by the Hookers' social circle were two drawings sent by Joseph to be copied by his father's resident botanical artist, Walter Hood Fitch. The first depicted Mount Erebus, venting a column of black smoke, 'its margins tinged white by the sun, with a distinct red tinge from the fire below'.[30] The second sketch was a moody night-time seascape, featuring an iceberg pierced by a hole. Joseph supplied atmospheric hints for the colouring: 'it was blowing hard and there were some black scudding clouds near the moon, which was reflected on the tips of the waves, close to the edge of the berg. The water should be of intense cobalt blue, and it should reflect a white glare on the sea'.[31] As Elizabeth fondly told her brother, Fitch's copies of his drawings, 'one of the Burning mountain & the other of the floating berg', were 'subjects of great admiration to our friends here'.[32]

But, far from being gratified by the praise, Joseph was offended. Had he not repeatedly told his parents to keep his correspondence within the immediate family circle? Was he not old enough to know his own mind? On shore in the Falkland Islands, he happened to encounter a young midshipman, from another ship, who informed him that he had heard extracts from Joseph's letters read aloud by his aunt in Dublin. Joseph was outraged. The midshipman's aunt? In Dublin? What business did friends of friends have in sharing his letters? 'I was always very averse to any society but that of persons whose pursuits were similar to mine', he reminded his father. By nature both shy and arrogant, Joseph cared only to be known by foremost 'Botanists & men of Science, with them my own industry must introduce me'. Storming with youthful indignation, Joseph told his father, 'my repugnance to any such notoriety is so strong that if these wishes cannot be complied with I must give up writing any thing but simple statements'.[33]

But Joseph's outburst did not reach Britain in time to check his father's instinct for publicity. The many months' delay in communication gave Sir William a chance to promote his son's career. Joseph's drawings of Mount Erebus and the iceberg, 'neatly copied by Fitch, in his best manner', were shown at the Geographical Society. 'And now', Lady Hooker exclaimed to her son, 'Prince Albert wishes to see them & has commanded your father to bring them to him . . . they are now gone to be mounted in a superior style!'[34] On 29 March 1842, Sir William went to Buckingham Palace, bearing his son's letters and the copies of his Antarctic drawings. Prince Albert interrogated Sir William for around an hour. 'He has been asking me 50 questions about you & the Voyage, & the wonders you have seen', Sir William excitedly reported to Joseph the same day. 'He listened with the greatest attention to the extracts I read him from your letters relating to the extreme southern regions'. Admiring the pictures, the Prince 'begged to show them to the Queen, which he did & brought them back with the thanks & expressions of Her Majesty's pleasure'.[35] Rarely had paternal pride been so thoroughly gratified: 'the first person in the realm', Sir William beamingly observed, 'is warmly concerned in your success'.[36]

News of his social triumph somewhat mollified Joseph. 'Of course the honor is far too flattering to allow me to be angry, even had I cause', he conceded, semi-apologetically.[37] If Prince Albert continued to show an interest in the Antarctic venture, then, by all means, his father should satisfy royal curiosity with passages from his letters. In any case, Joseph was beginning to chafe at the restrictions imposed on him by the Admiralty. He began to suspect Ross's motives for restricting the flow of information. 'He seems to wish all the news to come home with him, to astonish the world like a Thunder-clap', he grumbled, with a new note of cynicism. But Ross's scheme might backfire: 'if the knowledge of our proceedings be stifled, it will beget indifference, instead of pent-up curiosity, ready to burst out on our firing one gun at Spithead'.[38] If Joseph could not risk openly defying the captain's rules, his father was under no such obligation.

To Sir William's mind, the most notable of Joseph's botanical discoveries should be broadcast widely. He consulted with the Admiralty hydrographer, Francis Beaufort (famous for creating the wind scale that bears his name), who had been an enthusiastic promoter of the Antarctic voyage from the start. Whenever Beaufort saw Sir William, he pumped him for news of the expedition, saying that Hooker knew far more from his son's letters than the Admiralty ever learnt from Ross's dispatches. With Beaufort's backing, Hooker decided to draw up an account of the expedition, with excerpts from Joseph's letters and descriptions of the most significant botanical discoveries. He would submit the account to the Admiralty for approval, and then publish it both as a stand-alone volume and as an article in his own *London Journal of Botany*, a magazine aimed at the growing market for popular botanical books. With typical dexterity, Sir William would at once gain official sanction to bend the rules, promote his son's career and fill the pages of his own publication. The account, he promised his son, would be 'just enough to whet the public appetite for more'.[39]

When it was published as a single volume, William Hooker's *Notes on the Botany of the Antarctic Voyage* (1843) was dedicated 'with permission' to Prince Albert because 'His Royal Highness has felt and expressed a most lively interest' in the success of the Antarctic expedition.[40] If the dedication trumpeted Hooker's royal connections, the opening sentence amplified the fanfare: 'Since the days of the illustrious Cook . . . perhaps no voyage, undertaken for the purpose of scientific research, has ever excited so deep an interest in the public mind'.[41] The passages that Sir William selected – and sometimes heavily worked up – from Joseph's correspondence constructed an image of the young naturalist-adventurer as a successor to Darwin and the great Prussian geographer, Alexander von Humboldt, who reconfigured the European view of the natural world with his travel accounts that combined scientific rigour with a sense of the sublime. Joseph was rendered an heroic figure, battling to collect plants amid the freezing gales of Kerguelen's Land. Like Humboldt, he was presented as a man of Romantic sensibility, open to the awe-inspiring spectacle of nature: '"Often as I have sate", says the botanist, "on the summit of the cliffs which hem in this iron-bound bay, it was impossible to grow tired of watching the fearful surf, continually roaring and lashing against a mile of precipices, surmounted by high, snow-capped mountains"'.[42]

Hooker included his son's painterly description of Mount Erebus, but added his own gloss referring to Captain Ross's wise leadership and reflecting on man's place in creation:

> This was a sight, so surpassing every thing that can be imagined, and so heightened by the consciousness that we have penetrated under the guidance of our commander, into regions far beyond what was ever deemed practicable, that it really caused a feeling of awe to steal over us, at the consideration of our own comparative insignificance and helplessness, and at the same time an indescribable feeling of the greatness of the Creator in the works of his hand.[43]

As the editor of his son's letters, Sir William was careful to craft his son's reputation as a bold and dedicated naturalist, a man of science and art, a loyal and pious officer: a young man of prodigious talent and promise.

Sir William judged that the public would be most interested in plants with commercial potential. It was while Joseph was overwintering in the Falkland Islands that he had first been struck by the economic possibilities of the peat-loving tussock grass. Growing in coastal locations, in lofty clumps up to six feet high, tussock grass was much grazed by cattle and horses. Joseph thought that it might be transplanted to otherwise unproductive areas of the British Isles for use as fodder. This scheme was entirely consistent with Kew's role, as envisaged by John Lindley, to supply and transplant valuable plants across the colonial world. To promote Joseph's plan, Hooker included extensive observations on tussock grass in *Notes on the Botany of the Antarctic Voyage*. Joseph managed to communicate his enthusiasm to the young Governor of the Falklands, Lieutenant Richard Clement Moody, who established an experimental tussock-grass garden. Moody asked Joseph to write a botanical description of tussock grass, which he sent with his official dispatches to the Colonial Office.[44] In a letter that was reprinted extensively in the London and provincial press, Moody excitedly claimed that the 'splendid Tussack Grass is the gold and glory of the Falklands', which might 'make the fortune of Orkney and the owners of Irish peat-bogs'.[45]

In London, Sir William joined forces with Moody's equally redoubtable father to deliver a paper on tussock grass to the Royal Geographical Society. Sir William predicted that tussock grass might 'ere long form an important pasture on some otherwise barren coasts of England, and especially on those of Scotland and Ireland'.[46] As a result, Kew was inundated with requests for tussock grass. 'You have no idea the quantity of letters I have from strangers in all quarters, from the south coast of Kent to John o'Groats, & from the East of Fife to the west coast of Connaught', Sir William gleefully reported to Joseph, 'humbly begging me, the happy Father of so renowned a son, to give them but the tithe of a fibre of the root, or one seed; or in default of them a piece of a leaf'. Sir William proceeded to mock those who imagined that 'the most wonderful

Grass . . . is to make the fortune of all Highland & Irish Lairds who have bogs for bogs – "pates" they will have it, are the proper soil for the plant'.[47] But, in this case, Sir William's publicity drive did not pay off. In the first place, he could not supply the demand because he had yet to receive any seeds at Kew. In the longer term, the dreams of tussock grass waving over the coasts of the British Isles proved unrealizable; despite extensive trials, transplanted tussock grass failed to thrive.

Ever active on his son's behalf, Sir William started to lay plans for Joseph's next career move. 'I have a scheme, when, please God, you return to us, for you to publish a *Flora of N. Zealand* and of the *Antarctic Regions*, including Van Diemen's Land', Sir William plotted. 'This would be an honourable thing to do & nobody can have such materials as you will, & you can have access to the collections of the British Museum, Darwin &c. for things you do not possess'.[48] As far as financial support was concerned, Sir William assured his son that he would be able to receive government funding, and, for the rest, Sir William would be happy to provide what he could. 'The scientific world will expect it from you', he urged.[49] What is remarkable is that Sir William's plan came to fruition in almost every respect – even if it took fifteen years for Joseph to complete publication of the *Floras*.

As Sir William had anticipated, some ten months later, Charles Darwin wrote to offer Joseph access to the *Beagle* plant collection: 'I am very glad to hear you talk of inducing your son to publish an Antarctic Flora . . . all my collection . . . will be joyfully laid at his disposal'.[50] This letter opened the way for a scientific correspondence and friendship between Joseph and Darwin that would prove the most sustaining of both men's lives. Joseph's fascination with plant geography and the distribution of species struck an immediate chord with Darwin. The younger man quickly became an important sounding board for Darwin's theories. Such was Darwin's confidence in Hooker that, a matter of months after they had started to correspond, Darwin chose to confide in Joseph his heretical and long close-guarded idea 'that species are not (it is like confessing a murder) immutable'.[51] So it was that Joseph Hooker became the first of Darwin's peers to learn of his theory of natural selection – although it would take years of discussion before he was convinced of its validity.

As the expedition drew to a close, Sir William set out his view of Joseph's longer-term career options. To support himself, Joseph could either practise as a doctor or work as a university professor, but his father did not suppose that he would like either medical practice or the 'drudgery of lecturing'.[52] In which case, Sir William continued, 'perhaps you might not object to follow me in my Horticultural occupations . . . I would not say that I have been here, at present, long enough to ask anything in this establishment for you: – but by and by it is possible I might be allowed to resign in your favour, and really & truly I do not think you could have an appointment more congenial to your tastes'.[53] Knowing his son's temperament, Sir William depicted his role – not entirely accurately – as one wholly devoted to intellectual pursuits, reassuring him that the director had charge of the 'correspondence and scientific department, not the cultivation and mechanical department' and that he was 'in contact with men of Science and education & cultivated minds'.[54] For the time being, his father was more than happy to support him. Joseph should devote himself to his botanical studies and appear 'before the public in the character of a Botanist', and then, as had been the case with Sir William himself, 'industry will in time meet with its reward'.[55] In his final expedition letter, sent on the last leg of the voyage, Joseph wrote that he did not wish to be a financial burden to his father, so hoped to be of use as an assistant. His thoughts were now fixed on his return and their forthcoming reunion: 'I never looked forward to the fulfillment of any Day or Night dream with so much pleasure as I do to meeting you again, & the more so because we shall shake hands in the home you have so long looked forward to, & I have so often wished you to obtain, – I mean as at Kew'.[56]

# 6

# The Engineer *and* *the* Architect

A month after Joseph's return in the autumn of 1843, Sir William made his way excitedly along the road from West Park to Kew Green. Although the early-October sky was overcast, Sir William was in buoyant mood. The previous day, he had received a message from Windsor to expect a royal visit. The Queen and the Prince Consort wanted to inspect the newly renovated Kew Palace to see if it would be suitable for use as an occasional base for their growing family – three infants so far, ranging in age from five months to nearly three years – and Sir William was instructed to conduct them on a tour of the recently extended botanic garden. To give the royal party complete freedom of movement, Hooker had ordered the public entrance to be closed. He would do his best to interest the monarch in the Gardens and build on his friendly relations with Prince Albert. Today was an opportunity to show off his improvements and set out his future plans.

Sir William greeted the royal couple as they alighted from their carriage at the King of Hanover's house, not far from the mahogany door to the Gardens on Kew Green. With his long experience of university lecturing, Sir William was the consummate tour guide. Courteous and engaging, he pointed out recent acquisitions and unusual specimens, and diverted his guests with information on the plants' properties and uses. Prince Albert took a lively interest in botany and horticulture. The German court culture in which he had been raised emphasized the importance of gardens. 'Among the German sovereigns', observed John Lindley, 'a taste for gardening has grown up in a degree unknown in any other country except among the English'.[1] The various duchies, principalities and kingdoms that made up the German Confederation boasted numerous castles with splendid gardens. Among the most magnificent were those at the imperial summer palace of Schönbrunn in Vienna, where the hothouses contained 'the most rare palms . . . and birds of Africa and America there fly from branch to branch'.[2] The kingdoms of Prussia and Bavaria possessed rich botanic gardens: Berlin's royal botanic garden was 'justly considered the first in Germany', and Munich's botanic garden, under the direction of famous palm expert Carl Friedrich Philipp von Martius, had an unsurpassed collection of Brazilian plants.[3] Given the Hanoverian royal connection, there had been over a century's exchange of horticultural and botanical expertise between Britain and Hanover. In addition, Hooker could again remind the Prince Consort of the specific association between Kew and the Saxe-Gotha dynasty, with the garden's foundation by Albert's ancestor, Princess Augusta.

Sir William's route took in the whole of the grounds and all the hothouses, which, as Victoria noted in her journal, were 'full of the rarest & most curious plants, all in excellent order'.[4] In the company of her garden-loving husband, Victoria evinced greater energy and enthusiasm for Kew than Hooker had anticipated: 'I had no conception', he wrote to Dawson Turner, that 'the Queen could have borne the fatigue of going through all the Houses'.[5] Both the Queen and Prince Albert professed themselves delighted with Hooker's alterations and the fact that the Gardens had not suffered damage from the increased access of the public – over 20,000 visitors in the previous twelve months.[6] Hooker was thrilled when Albert 'enquired particularly for Joseph & expressed a wish to see him'.[7] Summoned post-haste, Joseph was introduced to the Queen and Prince Consort, and was invited by Albert to show his drawings from the Antarctic voyage at Windsor or Buckingham Palace. Watching with pride – and perhaps a touch of relief – Sir William reflected that 'Joseph behaved very nicely, & without being at all elated is evidently pleased with the compliment'.[8]

Next to his son's advancement, Hooker's most cherished wish was to enhance the reputation of Kew. One project, more than any other, appeared to him essential to assert Kew's status as a public botanic garden: a new palm house. The Queen and Prince's tour of Kew provided the occasion for Hooker to present his grand vision.

A palm house was a matter of national prestige. In 1838, Charles McIntosh had bemoaned Britain's lack of a public glasshouse: 'the government in this respect is much behind that of France, Austria, or Prussia'.[9] A great palm house functioned for McIntosh as a symbol of an affluent, advanced nation, and Britain was in danger of losing out to its European rivals: 'No one can view the houses in the Jardin des Plantes at Paris', McIntosh wrote, 'without regretting that we should be in this respect so much behind our less wealthy neighbours'.[10] The Paris hothouses, erected between1834 and 1836, were hailed as 'a magnificent series of conservatories built of iron, with an extraordinary extent of glass, arranged in the most scientific manner'.[11] According to John Claudius Loudon, the Jardin des Plantes was 'unquestionably the first establishment of the kind in Europe'.[12]

Britain had so far failed to establish a comparable institution, despite its vast colonial possessions. As the *Colonial Magazine* pointed out with a grand rhetorical flourish in 1840, Kew had yet to profit from the rich botanic possibilities offered by Britain's imperial network:

> Colonies in every quarter and in every clime; governors, secretaries, and agents unnumbered; a fleet of vessels in the constant service of the government, of all sizes and capacities, sailing in every sea, crossing every ocean, floating before every wind, and encountering every season; opportunities for sending out collectors at the smallest expense, and of bringing home their collections in the shortest time and at the cheapest charge – what might not have been expected?[13]

Like McIntosh, the *Colonial Magazine* considered Britain's lack of botanical achievement a source of national shame: 'Let us compare what has been here effected, with what we behold at Berlin, at Vienna, at Munich, and we must blush!' Unlike Germany, Britain could draw on its worldwide imperial resources: 'Truly heaven gave us chances, such as no people possesses, but we have yet to learn how to use them'.[14] A splendid palm house at Kew would provide a showcase for the botanic spoils of empire – a magnificent display of colonial vegetation and natural products.

Hooker was acutely aware that the present palm stove was far from impressive. At sixty feet long, the existing house was becoming dangerously overcrowded. 'Some of the palms are getting too high for their spacious prison-house', warned Frederick Scheer in 1840, 'and will break through it unless it be speedily enlarged'.[15] At the start of his tenure, Sir William had contemplated several palm-house schemes. He initially imagined that he might be able to erect a new palm house over the old one, dismantling the original structure only when the new one was complete, to avoid exposing the tropical plants to the air.[16] He first favoured an 1834 design for a wooden stove, drawn up (but never built) by Sir Jeffry Wyatville, the architect responsible for remodelling Windsor Castle.[17] But, by 1843, with the expansion of the botanic garden, Hooker was convinced that a far grander scheme was required. To view the latest in glasshouse engineering, Hooker visited two palm houses designed by the renowned Joseph Paxton. The first was at Loddiges' Nursery in Hackney, just outside London. Loddiges was famous for its rich plant collection and pioneering hothouse heating and sprinkler systems. Paxton's curvilinear palm house provided a spectacular frame for Loddiges' tropical display. 'Passing into the centre of this building, the mind is struck with a feeling almost of awe as we stand in the midst of the noble palm-trees which tower above', marvelled *Chambers's Edinburgh Journal*. 'He must be apathetic, indeed, whose thoughts are not elevated by such a scene'.[18]

More impressive still was Hooker's second destination: Paxton's Great Stove at Chatsworth, previously visited by Kew's curator, John Smith. Chatsworth House, with its magnificent architecture and extensive art collection, had long enjoyed pride of place on Derbyshire tourist itineraries. Among the new highlights of the garden tour was the Great Conservatory, 'like a sea of glass when the waves are settling and smoothing down after a storm, which is the result of its *undulating* structure'.[19] The Stove had cost the Duke of Devonshire a staggering £33,000. How could Hooker, on government funds, ever hope to compete? An invitation from the Duke or Paxton was required to actually enter the Conservatory, so it was only the select few, like the King of Saxony, who could be transported to the 'tropical scene with a glass sky'.[20] Surely a public institution should not be outclassed by a nobleman? To Sir William's mind, 'it was neither fitting nor desirable that a national establishment for the reception of tropical plants, and for the promotion of science in this country, should be so greatly inferior to many establishments of the same kind in the possession of private individuals'.[21]

Set out in the conservatory at Kew at the time of the royal visit was a model of a palm house, designed by Mr Robinson, the local clerk of works who had accompanied Hooker on his recent glasshouse tour. Inspired by Chatsworth, Robinson's design was a slightly scaled-down version of Paxton's showpiece. 'It is intended that this building shall be 200 ft. long (exclusive of the approach or vestibule), 100 feet wide, and 55 high', the *Gardeners' Chronicle* reported. 'Like the great Conservatory at Chatsworth, it will have a lofty centre surrounded by aisles (forming one interior), with a carriage drive through the middle'.[22] To Sir William's delight, the model so pleased the Queen and Prince 'that they asked if so handsome a structure would be seen from the Palace'.[23]

The royal enthusiasm for the scheme allowed the Palm House to assume a new prominence within the Gardens. The Commissioners of Woods and Forests had previously instructed Hooker that the building should be hidden among a grove of trees. A secluded situation, feared Hooker, would limit the amount of light available to the tropical plants. On aristocratic estates, such as Chatsworth, the glasshouse was typically concealed from the main residence to avoid the dissonance of clashing architectural styles. However, the botanic garden at Kew was no longer part of the Crown estate, and large portions of the Royal Pleasure Grounds were being transferred to public use. The royal couple's question about the visibility of the Palm House from the Palace recognized the autonomy of the botanic garden and at the same time suggested a certain reluctance to relinquish Crown control. It was clear that the Palm House could now function as a bold landscape feature, occupying a central position in the Gardens. 'This was the very thing I wished for', Sir William reported to his father-in-law that evening, basking in the glow of his and Joseph's social and botanic success. 'Indeed', he concluded in satisfied vein, 'the visit has been a very agreeable one in every point of view'.[24]

To promote Kew, Hooker knew that he had to cultivate allies in government circles. Now that the royal couple had approved the Palm House scheme, Hooker convinced the Earl of Lincoln, the First Commissioner of Woods and Forests, that they should go beyond the clerk of works' cut-price version of Chatsworth. A grand Palm House would function as a national status symbol, a popular attraction and an emblem of the new prominence accorded to botanical science. Enthused by Hooker's vision, Lincoln took an active interest in the development of the Palm House. As *Chambers's Edinburgh Journal* declared, 'a national conservatory . . . would form a noble and eloquent trophy to science, and one as useful and instructive as noble'.[25]

Glasshouses were at the forefront of nineteenth-century building technology. With their innovative forms and materials, they occupied a position at the intersection of architecture and engineering. The use of iron in construction rendered conventional ideas based on stone architecture obsolete. It became necessary for designers to rethink the relationships between mass, volume and structure. This revolution in architectural thinking required the expertise of engineers – a profession previously devoted to military works and the construction of roads and canals. No formal qualifications existed for structural engineers at the time. The Institution of Civil Engineers had been established in 1818, but it functioned more as a club for the exchange of ideas than as a professional training body. The creators of innovative iron-framed buildings came from a variety of backgrounds in garden design and glasshouse manufacturing. They picked up the skills and knowledge that they required on the job. In his *Encyclopædia of Gardening*, Loudon claimed that the 'grand cause of the improvements which have been made in hot-houses may be traced to their being no longer, as formerly, under the control of mansion architects'.[26]

Well might Loudon pronounce on the matter: in 1817, he had revolutionized glasshouse design by inventing the flexible wrought-iron glazing bar, which made it possible to construct curvilinear glass walls and roofs. For Loudon, functionality was key to hothouse design. 'Fitness for the end in view', he asserted, 'is the basis of all beauty in works of use, and therefore, the taste of architects . . . may safely be pronounced as radically wrong'.[27] But those who commissioned large-scale glasshouses wanted the reassurance and prestige provided by a professional architect. Much as he valued the ingenuity and skill of Joseph Paxton, the Duke of Devonshire had called in the prominent architect Decimus Burton to approve the structure of the Chatsworth Great Stove. Likewise, to create the Palm House at Kew, the Earl of Lincoln thought it necessary to engage the services of both an architect and an engineer.

While he was on the lookout, Lincoln encountered Richard Turner, a Dublin iron-founder recently arrived in London. Turner was reputed to be the leading glasshouse manufacturer in Ireland. He had travelled to London in the hope of building up an English clientele. Overflowing with ideas, Turner was irrepressible: 'a man of singular inventive genius', according to the Dublin architect Thomas

Drew, 'with a stock of daring and original projects always on hand'.[28] Eager to land a major commission, Turner aimed high and tendered low. Might he, Lincoln wondered, be the man for the job?

Turner came from a relatively modest family of Protestant ironmongers, but had profited handsomely from Dublin property speculation in the 1820s and 1830s, and could afford the lease on a six-acre site in Ballsbridge, a village on the River Dodder, to the south-east of Dublin. There, he built the aptly named Hammersmith Works, a substantial iron foundry with an imposing gateway and grand facade that extended for some 200 feet along Hammersmith Place, and included a lane of modest workers' cottages to the rear. Adjoining the works was Hammersmith House, a handsome villa for Turner's family of eight children, which showcased the foundry's own ironwork: an ornate veranda, high-level iron balustrade, decorative railings and conservatories. From 1834 on, the Hammersmith Works produced all manner of ironware suitable for domestic purposes: gates, railings, balconies, and baths with boilers for hot running water – the latest in luxury plumbing. With his business partner, William Walker, Turner introduced a recently patented hot-water system to Ireland. But Turner's speciality was iron glasshouses. He built hothouse ranges at Colebrooke in County Fermanagh and Killakee in County Dublin, a sweeping curvilinear glasshouse for Belfast Botanic Garden, and a peach house for the Viceregal Lodge in Phoenix Park, the most extensive iron glasshouse range in Ireland at the time. He came equipped with the highest testimonials from members of the Irish gentry and nobility.

Ireland lacked sufficient reserves of iron ore or coal to develop its own mining industry, so the Hammersmith Works, like all Dublin foundries, relied on coal and iron imported from England. By the mid-nineteenth century, Britain was the world's largest iron producer, and iron was regarded as the 'all-conquering metal'.[29] Advances in

13. *The conservatory at Killakee House, designed by Turner.*

military technology, industry, engineering and transport were all founded on iron; indeed, some historians have suggested that the dependence on iron was such that the Industrial Revolution might as well be termed the Iron Revolution.[30] Iron appeared infinitely adaptable and endlessly useful: 'capable of being cast in moulds of any form', wrote the chemist Andrew Ure, 'of being drawn out into wires of any desired strength or fineness; of being extended into plates or sheets; of being bent in every direction; of being sharpened, hardened, and softened at pleasure'.[31]

Nineteenth-century construction revelled in the myriad possibilities of cast and wrought iron. Cast iron lent itself to decorative features. With its high levels of silicone, it flowed smoothly when molten, and could be cast into elaborate shapes. More importantly, cast iron possessed great compressive strength, which made it suitable for the supporting elements of buildings, such as columns. But the high carbon content of cast iron also made it brittle and liable to fracture without warning. Among the notorious failures of cast-iron structures was the collapse, in 1833, of the Anthaeum, a vast domed glasshouse under construction at Hove, on the south coast. According to *The Times*, the Anthaeum would have been larger than St Peter's in Rome, and 'would have formed one of the most splendid ornaments in the world'.[32] But the cast-iron ribs that made up the dome lacked the necessary support from diagonal cross-braces. Shortly after the scaffolding was removed, the great iron ribs started to swerve and crack, then fell with a thunderous roar and 'such a galaxy of immense sparks, as to produce the effect of a powerful flash of lightning'.[33] The tangled wreckage of the pleasure dome remained for decades on the seafront: a melancholy monument to the hazards of cast-iron construction.

Such disasters, coupled with new mechanized production techniques, prompted a move towards the increased use of structural wrought iron. The greater availability, cheapness and pliancy of wrought iron transformed engineering and architecture in the 1840s and 1850s. Wrought iron was so called because it had been worked – repeatedly heated, stirred, beaten and rolled – to remove the carbon content. This process of 'puddling' resulted in a purer form of iron that was more flexible and less brittle than cast iron, and, crucially, as strong in tension as in compression. Unlike cast iron, wrought iron was appropriate for the elements of a building that were exposed to lateral forces. The increased malleability of wrought iron encouraged innovation in all forms of construction, and the material was particularly attractive to glasshouse engineers. Eminently suited to roof beams and sash bars, wrought iron allowed for the creation of structures that had slim supporting frames which did not block the light.

Turner was convinced that wrought iron was the wonder material of the future. He was greatly influenced by Loudon's ideas and designs, and followed all developments in applications of wrought iron closely. By the early 1840s, he was experimenting with wrought-iron ribs and glazing bars in combination with cast-iron pillars. Turner made a compelling advocate for the advantages of wrought iron in the construction of glasshouse roofs. In May 1843, despite having missed the tender deadline, Turner managed to convince the Royal Dublin Society to abandon their plans for a wood and iron glasshouse, and adopt one composed entirely of iron.[34]

But the febrile political climate of 1840s Dublin made an uneasy environment for Turner's ambitious business plans. The city was at the heart of the campaign to repeal the 1801 Act of Union that bound Ireland to Great Britain. The leader of the Repeal Association was Daniel O'Connell, the first Catholic Lord Mayor of Dublin, who argued that Ireland would never prosper under Westminster's control. In 1843, the Dublin Corporation joined the Catholic bishops to declare support for repeal and the establishment of an Irish parliament. In April that year, Dubliners organized protest meetings against a government decision to transfer the mail-coach contract from a Dublin company to a Scottish one, involving the loss of 2,000 jobs in the city. On 8 October 1843 (just a few days after Victoria and Albert had visited Kew), a mass rally in favour of repeal had been planned to the north of the city. Although previous 'monster meetings' had been peaceful, Sir Robert Peel's Tory government feared armed insurrection. Two warships steamed into Dublin harbour, the rally was banned and the city bristled with troops. Alarmed at the possibility of bloodshed, O'Connell cancelled the protest. In the event, the day passed off without incident, but O'Connell was arrested, charged with conspiracy and sentenced to a year's imprisonment.

In this atmosphere of political tension, Turner made a public show of his political allegiances. Dominating the main gate of the

Hammersmith Works was an enormous cast-iron royal crest, adorned with crown, lion and unicorn. This declaration of loyalty would have reassured Turner's customers, neighbours and landlord. His clientele was drawn from the wealthy ranks of the Protestant landowning classes, and Ballsbridge was a staunchly Unionist area. The foundry and Turner's earlier property developments were situated on the Pembroke Estate, which comprised much of County Dublin and was owned by Sidney Herbert, a Tory politician and Secretary to the Admiralty in Peel's administration. Turner seems to have cultivated good relations with his landlord, for it was Herbert who supplied Turner with one of his most useful introductions in London: to the Earl of Lincoln, Hooker's government ally, the First Commissioner in charge of expenditure at the Office of Woods and Forests.

Turner met Lincoln when he travelled to London in the summer of 1843 to submit his most ambitious scheme yet: a design for an immense winter garden to be erected in Regent's Park by the Royal Botanic Society – the rival institution to Kew. A model of Turner's proposed glasshouse, measuring seven by five feet, was placed on display for a week at Exeter Hall, on the Strand. A large domed structure, connected to four smaller circular houses, would cover 'an *acre and a half*, or upwards!' the exhibition handbill breathlessly exclaimed.[35] Turner was also in the market for more modest

14. *Hammersmith Works, Dublin.*

conservatories. The advertisement boasted that Turner's glasshouses were stable, light and well ventilated, and 'for Beauty, Elegance and Utility' were 'beyond parallel'.[36]

Turner was the master of the sales pitch, as charismatic as he was articulate, and keen to acquire new clients in London. According to Drew, Turner was as 'remarkable for his rough-and-ready powers of illustration' of his schemes, as for his 'eloquent, plausible, and humorous advocacy of them'.[37] The Earl of Lincoln was readily won over. The next target of Turner's charm was the director of Kew himself. On 30 January 1844, Turner brought the model of his Royal Botanic Society glasshouse to show Sir William Hooker and his long-term ally, John Lindley. He expanded on the virtues of wrought-iron construction, demonstrated the benefits of curved glass, and explained the relative merits of steam and hot-water heating. Turner's command of the technicalities was second to none. After three mornings in his company, Hooker declared to Lord Lincoln that Turner knew 'more about Hothouses & greenhouses & the best principles of heating them than any man I ever met with'.[38]

However, as an Irish innovator and entrepreneur, Turner was at a distinct disadvantage. He was unfamiliar with the workings of Westminster and had to contend with the dominant British prejudice against Irish workers, who were considered backward-looking and unproductive. But, ever alert to opportunity, Turner tried to make the most of his Dublin connections. A few days after the meetings with Hooker, he followed up with a letter pointing out the political advantage of employing a Dublin-based ironworks at a time of growing support for repeal in the city. Although the numbers employed by his Hammersmith Works were relatively small, such a high-profile government contract might, Turner argued, help to assuage public anger at the recent loss of jobs in the mail-coach industry.[39] But, as the Repeal Association might have anticipated, the

Commissioners showed little interest in matters of Irish public opinion and levels of employment. The Office of Woods and Forests focused its attention entirely on the tender process and the need to monitor public finances.

To oversee the Palm House project, approve the design, liaise with the engineer and contractor, and keep an eye on the finances, Lord Lincoln required the services of an experienced and well-regarded architect. The Commissioners needed someone who would provide trustworthy advice, was familiar with the workings of government and had a particular knowledge of glasshouses. The obvious choice was Decimus Burton, the architect who had signed off Paxton's Great Conservatory at Chatsworth. Then in his mid-forties, Burton had long experience of working on all scales, from grand commissions for parks to schemes for domestic architecture. He was well known to the Office of Woods and Forests and had shaped many of the public spaces in London. With an extensive network of clients, he enjoyed a reputation for unimpeachable good taste. As Hooker boasted to his father-in-law, Burton was considered 'one of the best & most expensive Architects'.[40]

Decimus Burton had shot to prominence early in his career. His youthful ascent was fuelled in equal measure by his ambition, appetite for work and family influence. His father, James Burton, had been London's major property-developer, erecting some 3,000 houses in the capital. Working with John Nash, James Burton had developed the fashionable areas of Regent's Park and Regent's Street, and was responsible for building much of Bloomsbury. With his immense wealth, James Burton moved in the highest social circles. He developed the seaside resort of St Leonard's, near Hastings, on the south coast, where guests included the Duchess of Kent and her daughter, Princess Victoria.

Like many self-made men of the period, James Burton aimed to secure his family's social position. He encouraged his first son, also named James, to train under the eminent architect John Soane. But James only lasted a few weeks in Soane's office, before attempting and failing at successive careers. If James was the black sheep of the family, Decimus was its golden boy. The very model of industry and respectability, he seems to have inherited his father's business acumen and drive. Decimus completed his architectural studies under John Soane at the Royal Academy, and worked for his father from an early age. Before he was eighteen, Decimus designed The Holme, a splendid villa for his family, overlooking the lake in Regent's Park (which remains among the grandest private residences in London today).[41] Decimus planned other magnificent houses in Regent's Park, including Grove Lodge for the geologist George Greenough, who had a side interest in botany and horticulture. Attached to the house was a conservatory which the architect Charles Cockerell praised for its elegant form, adding, with a touch of concern, that it looked 'as fragile as a blubber [jellyfish]'.[42]

In his early twenties, Decimus started to land major commissions, refashioning London's ceremonial cityscape with grand entrances for Hyde Park and Green Park, most notably the monumental arch and screen at Hyde Park Corner. He was appointed architect to the Zoological Society and the Royal Botanic Society of London. He won acclaim for his Greek-revival designs, but could equally turn his hand to rustic cottages or Italianate villas, and devoted much of his time latterly to the development of the Calverley Park estate in Tunbridge Wells, the original garden suburb.[43] As a leading neoclassical architect, Burton had in recent years seen his own designs fall from favour in the wake of the Gothic revival. However, he still exercised considerable influence in architectural circles and, in 1839, the Royal Institute of British Architects appointed him vice-president, in acknowledgement of his position as a 'ruling power and light in the profession'.[44]

By the 1840s, Burton was considered an authority on glasshouses. He had long experience in designing architectural conservatories for private residences, but his reputation rested on his association with the Great Stove at Chatsworth.[45] Burton's actual involvement with the project appears to have been minimal; the Duke of Devonshire only called in Burton to approve Paxton's design at a late stage in the construction process.[46] But such was the renown of the building that Burton was keen to be known as the conservatory's architect (and he even wrote a letter of complaint to the author of a guidebook which omitted to mention him).[47] Just a couple of months previously, the Queen and Prince Consort had visited Chatsworth, and reports of the splendid Stove filled the press. On the back of Paxton's triumph, Burton became *the* glasshouse architect.

With his professional activities ranging across the British Isles, Burton's earlier career had intersected with that of Richard Turner in Ireland and Sir William Hooker in Scotland. During the 1830s, Burton had been responsible for laying out the Viceregal estate of Phoenix Park, in Dublin, where Turner had erected a peach house in 1836–7. In Glasgow, in 1840, Burton was employed to draw up a plan for the development of the Kelvinside estate. He assigned the first plot as the new location for the Botanic Garden, which was then still under Hooker's care. As architect to the Royal Botanic Society, Burton would have known of Turner's ambitions to erect the glasshouse at Regent's Park. But it was only when Burton was called in to advise on Turner's design for the Palm House, in February 1844, that the three men were placed in direct contact.

1. One of the many magnificent illustrations from the most important book on palms, the *Historia Naturalis Palmarum* (1823–53), by Carl von Martius. This imagined South American scene features two palms: *Leopoldinia pulchra* by the cascade and *Astrocaryum jauari* rising high above the forest canopy.

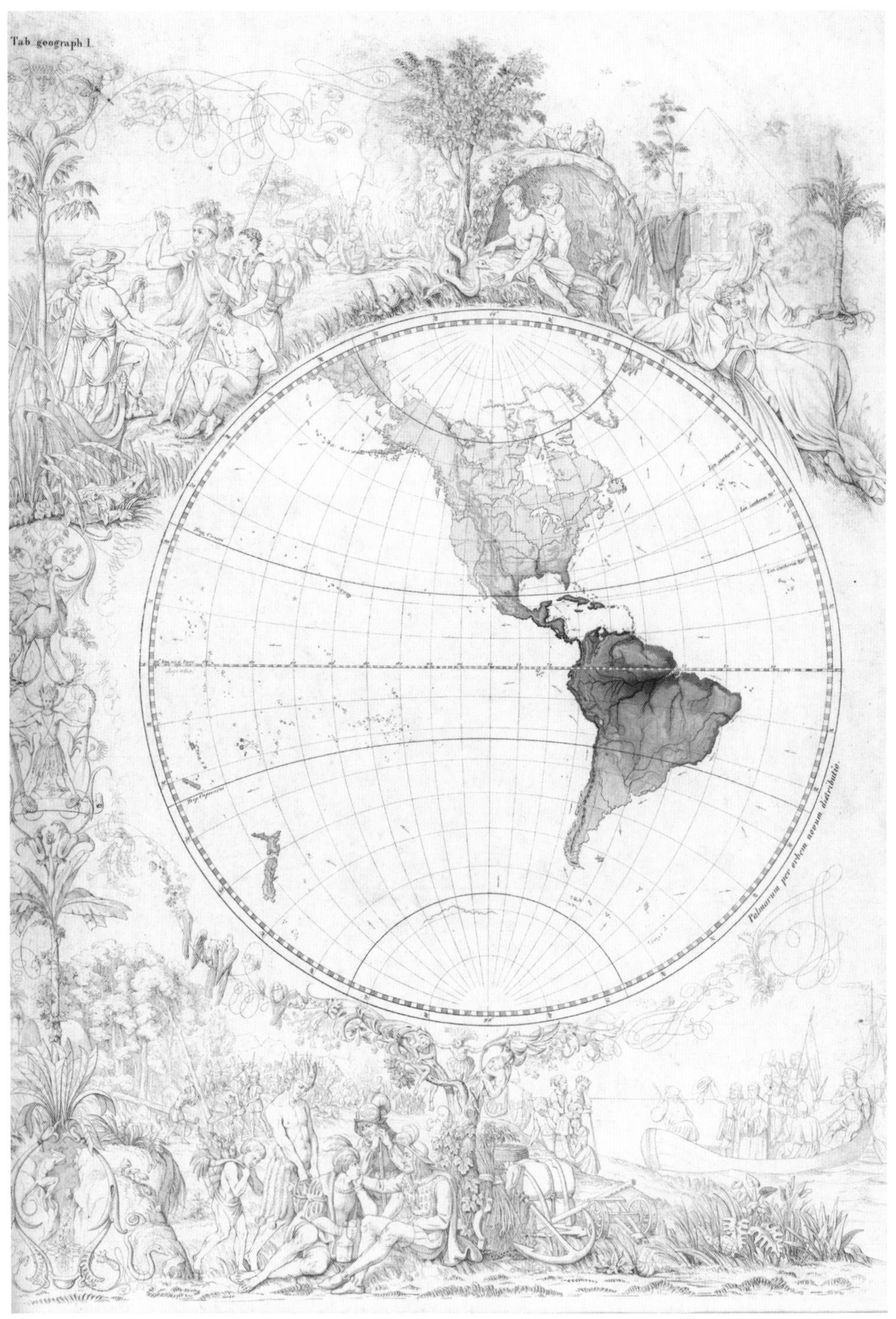


2. The *Historia Naturalis Palmarum* included maps which, for the first time, showed the distribution of palms in the New and Old Worlds. The exuberant engravings that surround the hemispheres depict palms, fantastical creatures and the encounter between Europeans and indigenous peoples.

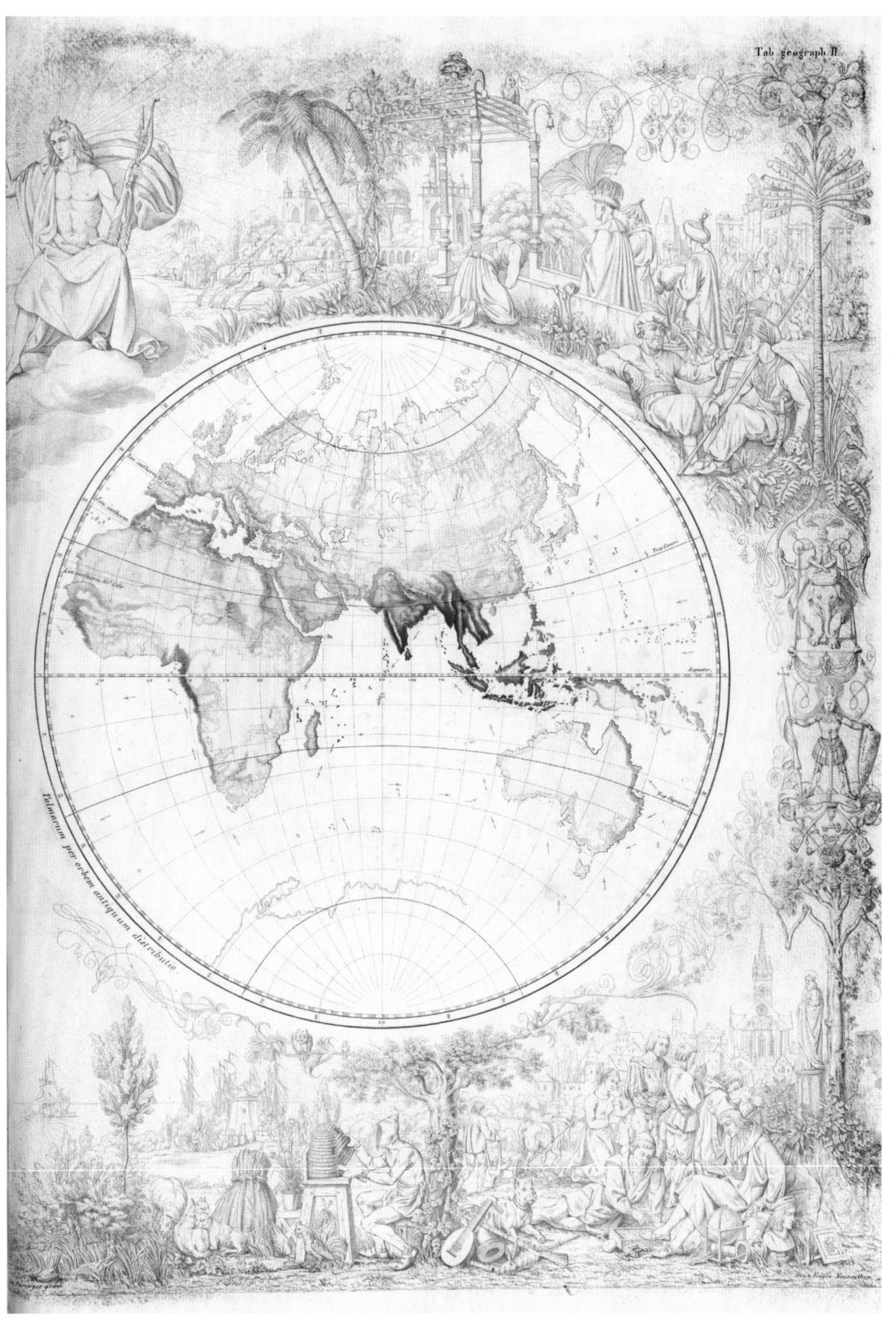


3. Martius imagined that palms were the offspring of Mother Earth (Terra) and the sun god (Phoebus). This new-minted myth is represented above the maps: Phoebus presides over the western corner of the Old World (plate 3), while Terra is seated on the eastern slope of the New World (plate 2), holding a palm in her hand.

4 & 5. The towering double coconut palm (*Lodoicea maldivica*) bears the heaviest fruit and largest seed in the world (below). The seed was a prized curiosity in Europe and regarded as a universal panacea in China. Its distinctive rounded form earned the plant its early botanic name, *Lodoicea callipyge*: 'beautiful buttocks'. Many attempts were made to cultivate the palm at Kew.

6 & 7. The feathery plumes of the ivory-nut palm (*Phytelephas macrocarpa*) grow from a short or underground stem, with the fruit resting on the ground. William Purdie, a Scottish plant hunter, was sent to New Granada (Colombia) to collect specimens for Kew. Pictured in the lower plate are the fruit and the seeds, which were used as a cheap ivory substitute, together with items fashioned from vegetable ivory: a box and a model of a lama.

8. The botanical artist and philanthropist Elizabeth Twining published the lavish two-volume *Illustrations of the Natural Orders of Plants* (1849–55). A member of the famous tea-merchant family, Twining lived in nearby Twickenham and drew plants at Kew. This plate shows examples of palms and their parts, including the dwarf fan, date and climbing rattan.

9. Combining botany and piety, Sophy Moody's *The Palm Tree* (1864) celebrated palms as the only biblical tree to encircle the globe. The illustrations chart the variety of geographical locations associated with palms. This image, entitled the 'Palm of the Plain', conjures up an oriental – probably Indian – setting.

10 & 11. Illustrations from Moody's *The Palm Tree* locate palms in contrasting environments. With its crouching jaguar, the 'Palm of the Forest' suggests the hazards of the Amazon rainforest. The tranquil seas and advancing sailing ship of 'Palm of the Ocean' (above) associate palms with desert islands and sea-faring adventure: one of the most enduring of European stereotypes of palms.

12. Victorians celebrated palms as the most useful of all plants. This lithograph from *Plants of Other Lands, which are Useful to Man* (1843) depicts the multiple uses of the date palm: the fruit for food, the fronds for ritual, the leaves for basketry, the stone for fodder, the sap for alcohol and the stem for timber.

With Burton's approval, Turner was instructed by the Commissioners to draw up more detailed plans for the Palm House. He returned to his workshop in Dublin to prepare the scheme. In just over a week, he produced a Gothic-style design consisting of a central nave and two flanking wings. The nave's distinctive feature was a double row of columns: the inner row bore the weight of the central roof, and the outer carried a horizontal bar, or purlin, that helped to support the roof of the aisle. This was an elegant engineering solution, which Turner had used in his earlier glasshouses, that avoided the need for bulky columns with trusses. The outer columns were just two inches wide, and doubled as stakes for climbing plants.[48]

Eager to clinch the Kew deal, Turner returned swiftly to London. He made his way to his lodgings, a modest hotel in the city, near the General Post Office. He instructed his staff to send the plans after him, but had not factored in the vagaries of the postal system. He spent several days dashing from post office to coaching inn to railway station in frantic pursuit of them. He wasted hours meeting every incoming train at Euston Square station. When he finally took receipt of the plans, he delivered them directly to Burton's office.

Far from sharing Turner's sense of urgency, Burton took a more measured approach. Accustomed to the ways of the Office of Woods and Forests, Burton knew that the tender process would be a lengthy procedure, dependent on the weekly meetings of the Board of Commissioners. Turner seems to have had little sense of the pace of government decision-making, and somehow imagined that Hooker could exert pressure to speed up the process. Impatient to secure the contract, Turner urged Hooker 'to take Time (as we call it) by the forelock in getting on soon, as every way now is of importance, with a view to the Glazing being done before the next Winter storms'.[49]

But Burton wanted time for his own deliberations. He generally approved the layout and practicality of Turner's design, but took exception to the double row of columns and the neo-Gothic elements. He considered Turner's Gothic flourishes both unnecessarily expensive and fussily ornamental: all 'fret work, crockets, perforated parapets'.[50] His reservations were related to his lack of sympathy for the current vogue for the Gothic style. Like Loudon, Burton held that glasshouses should not be influenced by any particular architectural style. 'I do not think that it would be judicious', Burton wrote in measured tones to the Commissioners, 'to adopt in a building constructed of Glass and Iron where light is the great object, any decided style of architecture such as exists in buildings erected of masonry'.[51] In advocating such an approach, Burton set glasshouses apart as a distinct class of building, and prioritized functional design. He advised the Commissioners on the desirability of a pared-down style 'suitable for horticultural purposes' for the Palm House, and persuaded Sir William of its merits.[52] In a letter to Lord Lincoln, Hooker declared himself 'quite delighted with his [Burton's] views of the simple form that ought to be adopted in our stove'.[53]

But Turner was far from delighted when he discovered that Burton was not just criticizing elements of his design, but actually engaged on his own plans for the Palm House. From conversations with Burton's draftsman, Turner learnt that Burton's design involved a semicircular roof, as at Chatsworth. This 'fatal semi-arch' would, in Turner's estimation, cut the available light in winter by as much as a quarter.[54] Equally damaging was Burton's omission of any roof ventilation to dispose of 'the exhalations of the plants'.[55] When he finally sweet-talked the draftsman into giving him a private view of Burton's plans, he was horrified. In place of his row of slender columns and supporting purlin, Burton proposed bulky pillars with thick trusses. This would ruin the interior space. Turner dashed off a note summoning to London his much-valued Dublin foreman, 'a Practical as well as a scientific man'.[56] Then he wrote in strict confidence to Hooker, to warn him of Burton's scheme. 'It seems to be wildly extravagant', he declared, 'its interior will be much in cumbered, no doubt, with a series of these immense massive trussed arched supporters'. Enjoining Hooker to secrecy, Turner confessed that he himself would have to adopt a pose of complete ignorance: 'I am not to appear to Mr Burton to know any thing of this at all . . . Please to keep me harmless & Blameless, and as you kindly know my Motives, I am confident of your favor in forgiving'.[57]

Turner trusted that Hooker would play along. Just a few days earlier, Turner had written, 'quite Entre nous', to alert Hooker to his misgivings. In going behind the architect's back, Turner attempted to strengthen his relationship with the director of Kew. He earnestly avowed his dedication to the project: 'my Ambition and most anxious solicitude is to have a Botanical or Horticultural Structure, that has not yet had its Equal, nor never shall be surpassed, such a one as will be Creditable to me, and most satisfactory to all interested, But most particularly to You, who feels so deeply interested in it'.[58] Turner's fervent declaration reflects both the scale of his ambition and his understanding of the extent of Hooker's personal investment in the project. Allying himself closely with Hooker's aspirations, Turner pledged to create a Palm House of unparalleled splendour that would at once elevate Kew, make his own name and secure Hooker's legacy.

Turner's audacious intervention appears to have paid off. Hooker consulted with his curator, John Smith, who also objected to Burton's thick, trussed pillars because they would obstruct the arrangement and growth of the palms. Hooker wrote to Burton to emphasize the importance of the interior space. 'Your letter has set me thinking', Burton replied with a touch of irritation, 'and as that which you propose knocks on the head all previous plans, it is fortunate that I did not finish my report for yesterday's board. I have sketched out another design to meet your new ideas'.[59] The same day, Turner's foreman arrived in London. With scant regard for social niceties, Turner procured an invitation for the foreman to Burton's imposing offices in Spring Gardens, just off Trafalgar Square.

Cooperation was to win out. For the first week in March, Turner and his foreman remained closeted at Burton's offices in Spring Gardens, revising the plans. They made an unlikely team: the grand establishment architect, the ebullient Irish iron founder and his level-headed foreman. Various proposals were advanced and rejected. Should they go for the grandest possible design? Or would it be wiser to curtail their ambitions in the hope that the Commissioners would commit funds for the entire project at the start? Updating Hooker regularly, sometimes twice daily, Turner dashed off notes detailing the changes. At different times on 7 March, the central portion of the house was to be 145 feet long, then 137 feet 6 inches long. In the end, prudence prevailed. One great advantage of the more modest dimensions was that they allowed for the use of parts of standardized length which could be manufactured off-site.[60] The Palm House would be among the earliest prefabricated buildings.

The most difficult challenge was the problem of how to achieve an unobstructed central span to accommodate the largest palms. When Turner and his foreman finally arrived at a solution, Turner wrote in triumph to tell Hooker. They had devised a way to span an unprecedented width of fifty feet with just a single row of columns on either side. This opened up the interior space to wonderful effect. The aisles would be twenty-five feet long by twenty-five feet high. The curves of the roofs would echo each other. With such strong geometry, the building would be very beautiful. Turner promised Hooker 'a very noble Structure . . . commensurate with the object of a National Garden like what the Royal Botanic of Kew is now becoming under your able Guidance & Direction of it'.[61] Such flattery could not but appeal to Sir William. The design was finalized just in time for the meeting of the Board of Commissioners, the following day. 'I do believe', declared Turner, 'it will be as near what might be termed perfection, as we can expect to almost ever arrive at'.[62]

Despite the central role of Turner and the foreman, Burton presented the revised Palm House scheme as entirely his own. Edward Diestelkamp has suggested that Burton omitted to mention Turner and the foreman in his official report to preserve the appearance of impartiality: since Burton was to advise the Commissioners on the award of the contract, he might have thought it necessary to dissociate himself publicly from Turner.[63] Equally, Burton might simply have regarded the scheme, drawn up in his offices, as his own. Judging from his conduct at Chatsworth, it appears that Burton was never averse to claiming more credit for his involvement than was strictly his due. In Burton's own estimation, and probably that of the Commissioners, his professional and class status as architect completely eclipsed those of an Irish iron founder and his foreman.

For his part, Turner does not seem to have been aware that Burton assumed entire responsibility for the scheme. He was more concerned by the news that he had a competitor. Presented to the Board the same day was a rival bid from Jones and Clark, a hothouse manufacturer based in Birmingham. John Jones had been responsible for the glasshouse range at Birmingham Botanical Gardens in Edgbaston. Unusually for glasshouse designers, the company employed copper rather than wrought-iron glazing bars. In a confidential letter to Hooker, Turner comprehensively condemned copper as 'too ductile a metal . . . so heavy and dead in itself, no elasticity, it wd. not regain its own position again & as such would be fatal to the glass'. The idea of a sixty-five-foot-high copper glasshouse 'was so truly silly and ridiculous in the extreme that it wd. amount to a kind of insanity'.[64] In more temperate language, Hooker expressed his own reservations about the scheme and, importantly, Burton also dismissed it.

Despite his disapproval of Jones and Clark's design, Burton invited the company to tender for the revised plan. Unconvinced by Burton's assurances that this was simply a matter of procedure, Turner feared losing out to the Birmingham company. It was grossly unfair. So much effort and ingenuity had gone into the Palm House design. He and his foreman had come up with a truly innovative plan. Turner wrote to Hooker in considerable agitation: 'it is too Bad to have all my schemes & with all my considerations & my Foreman's all to be handed over to Jones'.[65] Turner returned despondently to Dublin to attend to his business, leaving Burton to employ a civil engineer to produce detailed drawings of the scheme. Over the next few weeks, Turner worried that his rival might not only snatch the contract, but also steal his engineering secrets from him.

Towards the end of April, Turner returned to London to view the civil engineer's drawings and submit his estimate for the central section of the glasshouse. 'I went 1200 miles since I left this house in great haste to get back in time here!' he exclaimed to Hooker.[66] But all his eager expectation turned to despair when he saw the drawings. The civil engineer had completely misinterpreted his scheme. Although following the design in broad outline, the drawings departed greatly in detail of construction – 'a most absurd set of plans', as he later called them.[67] But there was no time to amend them now, and, once again, Turner had to trust to his powers of persuasion. 'I had nothing for it', he said, 'but to tender for it, hoping that if my tender was accepted, I could prevail in convincing the parties how discreditable and unwise it would be to carry it out'.[68]

But the issue of the tender was itself fraught with difficulty. At what level should he pitch the estimate? This was a far larger and more prestigious project than any of Turner's previous undertakings. He had invested considerable time and money to get thus far: neglecting his business in Dublin while cultivating his contacts in London. He had boasted of the project to his acquaintances, and had – perhaps unwisely – let it be known that the contract was as good as his. He could not bear to lose out at this stage. It would be best, he decided, to cut down on his profits and keep the estimate as low as possible. For the central section, he calculated a price of £18,500.

Never strictly businesslike in his proceedings, Turner submitted his estimate with a disarmingly personal covering letter addressed to the Board. The Office of Woods and Forests followed a firm policy of awarding contracts only to the lowest bidder. Should his estimate turn out to be higher than his rival, Turner begged that he still be awarded the contract:

> I have been most anxiously solicitous, and ambitious, to obtain this order & particularly now after my absence from home being so long prolonged, the numerous Inquiries for me at home, was informed of my object here, so that, in fact, I also now feel quite ashamed, not to take home with me the order, which I so confidently expected, and almost fully calculated upon, that I have spoken with great certainty, almost, upon my success, and which I shall always feel most grateful for your Kindness in Causing me to be successful in.[69]

But, in the event, Jones and Clark's estimate came in much higher, at over £25,000. When he learnt this informally from Burton, Turner wrote a second thoroughly unprofessional letter. He claimed to the Board that he had been so apprehensive of losing the order, that he had reduced the sum that he had originally calculated. He begged the Commissioners' leave to raise the estimate to his original figure of £20,900. Unsurprisingly, he was turned down.

Turner continued to wait for official confirmation that he had been selected as the Palm House contractor. Ever impatient, he was exasperated by the delay. 'I don't yet know the result', he complained to Hooker, '& all this & former proves to me, that Patience is a Virtue'.[70] After more than a week, the Commission's letter of appointment finally arrived. Turner's relief at securing the contract was tempered by anxiety about the terms. 'I am glad altho its at the very low regime of £18,500 that they have decided upon me', he wrote to Hooker.[71] Worse still, Turner learnt that he would have to make do with £5,000 until April of the following year. 'This circumstance', he admitted, 'is rather a damper'.[72]

Financial considerations aside, Turner signed off with customary enthusiasm and confidence: 'I have no doubt whatever, we shall have the Best & choicest House yet in Europe . . . I am determined to make Character & Fame & Building a Structure which I antisipate [*sic*] you will pronounce to be perfection'.[73] Of course, there remained the issue of the civil engineer's ridiculous plans. But, with typical optimism, Turner assumed that 'Mr Burton is that kind & Gentlemanly Man that will allow these modifications which will be essential improvements important to be done'.[74] Eager to be home, Turner set out for Dublin the same evening. On the boat, he was already thinking of ways to enhance the design.

# 7

# The Landscape Designer

John Smith, the curator, was beside himself. Could they not see that this was the worst possible place for the Palm House? The architect had barely been half an hour in the Gardens before he selected a site to the north of the pond. He wanted to erect the glasshouse at the end point of a grand walk leading from the Kew Green entrance. But he had chosen the lowest-lying spot in Kew; an area which, as Smith well knew, was a bog for much of the year. Back in the reign of George III, it had even been the location of a lake. Earlier still, the whole area had been marshlands, fed by the Thames. Now, all that remained was a pond bordered by weeping willows, but the surrounding ground was not to be trusted. Dig a few feet down and you would be sure to hit water, Smith told Burton. Yet the architect persisted in thinking the site suitable for a glasshouse with boilers in the basement. He brushed aside all of Smith's concerns with an offhand, 'Oh, we will make that alright'.[1]

But the curator knew his Kew and he knew his duty. He warned the director of the dangers of flooding. He told him more than once. But it seemed that his twenty years of experience counted for nothing.

Sir William paid him no heed. Smith's final opportunity arrived when the architect's assistant came to stake out the site. He could not bear to watch the man make his measurements. So, he told him – in no uncertain terms. The assistant must have made a complaint. The director wrote the same day to censure Smith for interfering in a matter in which he had no business. The curator had used disrespectful language not only to Sir William, but to all persons involved. All further communications with Smith on the subject of the new Palm House were now closed.

Unaccustomed to reprimand, Smith reached for his pen. He had not intended to insult the director or any other person, he wrote. 'I may have used strong words condemnatory of the situation', he admitted, 'but the moment had now come to give my last word against the chosen site of the palm house as I considered it the worst that could have been chosen in the garden'. Not one to back down, Smith restated his case, 'being quite certain that much evil would arise consequent on the furnace rooms being below the level of the ground and therefore liable to be flooded'.[2] The following day, Hooker attempted a reconciliation. 'On his coming to the garden the next morning', recalled Smith, 'the first thing he did was to shake hands, and he said, he now knew that I did not mean any disrespect and he admitted I was only doing my duty'. But Hooker also reasserted his authority. Reminding the curator of his place, Sir William told Smith that he 'had no right to speak, as the Commissioners had left the choice of a situation to the Architect, and that he (Sir W. Hooker) approved the site'.[3]

But the decision was neither so simple nor so final as Hooker suggested. The director had omitted to mention that the planning process also involved a landscape gardener: William Andrews

Nesfield. In January 1844, around the same time that Lord Lincoln had first introduced Richard Turner to Hooker, he had also recommended the services of William Nesfield. Lord Lincoln knew of the landscape gardener through his work at Clumber Park, the Nottinghamshire seat of his father, the Fourth Duke of Newcastle. Well connected and self-assured, Nesfield had built up a clientele among the aristocratic and landowning classes. Like Turner, he was ambitious and keen to take on a high-profile public project. But, unlike the iron founder, he possessed little personal charm and tended to be inflexible.

Nesfield had taken an unusual route into landscape gardening. He was the son of a clergyman in County Durham, and had already pursued two seemingly unrelated careers. After training as a cadet at the Royal Military Academy, Woolwich, he had served in the army, first in the Peninsular Wars in Spain and then, during the War of 1812 with the United States, in Upper Canada. His family connections had gained him the post of aide-de-camp to Lieutenant-General Gordon Drummond, commander of the troops and later Governor of Canada. After six years in the army, Nesfield was weary of military life. He resigned his commission and embarked on a second career as a watercolourist. He set himself up as a painter in London and toured Europe and Britain seeking out picturesque sites. According to the great art critic John Ruskin, he was the master of 'the radiant cataract', capable of capturing what Ruskin called 'the colour and the spirituality of a great waterfall'.[4] For over a decade, Nesfield led the life of an artist, but by the mid-1830s, he had a wife to support, and cascades could no longer cover the household bills. To make ends meet, he turned his hand to garden design.

Landscape gardening was perhaps not so remote from Nesfield's previous occupations as might at first appear; his military training at Woolwich had endowed him with practical drawing, surveying and engineering skills, and his years as a watercolourist had taught him to view landscape in picturesque terms. Major theorists of the picturesque, such as Uvedale Price, held that there was little to distinguish the artist from the garden designer; both were engaged in the pictorial fashioning of landscape. Nesfield conceived of garden design in terms of three planes derived from landscape painting: the foreground, middle ground and background. For Nesfield, the hand and eye of the artist were everywhere at work in garden design.

With his extensive network of contacts and reputation as a painter, Nesfield was in considerable demand. 'Mr. Nesfield', Hooker told his father-in-law, 'has the character of the best Landscape Gardener'.[5] In his schemes for private estates, Nesfield combined a highly formal approach to the areas of the garden close to the house with the naturalistic treatment of the more distant parkland. In the mansion's vicinity, he created terraces, balustrades and intricate box-lined parterres – *parterres de broderie* – based on seventeenth-century French patterns, often incorporating heraldic devices or initials to flatter his patrons. Nesfield's particular skill lay in managing the transition from the formal gardens to the informal park. To unify the whole, he created grand vistas which, when viewed from the main doors or windows of the house, emphasized the extent of the estate, stretching all the way to the horizon.[6]

On their first meeting, at the end of January 1844, Hooker was struck by Nesfield's intelligence and his appreciation of the beauties of Kew. It was evident, Hooker reported to Lord Lincoln, that Nesfield had grasped the Gardens' potential and had clear ideas for their improvement. From their brief acquaintance, Hooker judged him well qualified for the task. At the same time, Sir William had some misgivings about Nesfield's enthusiasm for the French style. 'He perhaps favours too much the formal or what he called the "geometrical" arrangements', Hooker told Lord Lincoln. While he appreciated that 'so noble a piece of ground' might merit a degree of formality, Hooker trusted that Nesfield would have 'too much good sense to carry it too far'.[7]

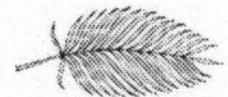

Nesfield's brief at Kew was to lay out an arboretum – that is, a collection of trees, planted according to botanical order. An arboretum fitting Kew's status as the national botanic garden should aspire to provide a systematic display of all the trees and shrubs suited to a temperate climate. The existing arboretum at Kew occupied just five acres. In his official report on the Royal Gardens, John Lindley had criticized it as 'not very extensive', and the plants as 'too much crowded'.[8] Small as it was, the arboretum contained 'many very fine specimens of hardy exotic trees and shrubs'.[9] A number of these had originally been cultivated in the mid-eighteenth century by the Duke of Argyll, at his estate in nearby Whitton. Others had travelled greater distances and by more surprising routes. In his *Records of the Royal Botanic Gardens*, John Smith told the story of the Chile pine or monkey-puzzle tree, the first to be cultivated in Britain. Archibald Menzies, the surgeon on Vancouver's four-year naval survey of the coast of north-west America (1791–5), had attended a dinner in Santiago where 'part of the dessert consisted of nuts which Menzies (who was a good botanist) had not before seen. Instead of eating all his share, he took some with him on board, and having obtained a box of earth, planted them, where they sprouted, and he succeeded in bringing five plants to England, which were safely received at Kew'.[10] Much as he relished the biographies of individual trees, Smith was even more attached to the arboretum itself. With a surprisingly modern-sounding appreciation of its wilderness aspects, he considered it a woodland idyll: 'a remarkable spot', like 'the interior of a large forest crowded with underwood . . . the resort of hundreds of birds'.[11] Much to Smith's regret, Hooker ordered the arboretum to be thinned and had the undergrowth cleared away. As a result, Smith claimed, the lichens and mosses died, as did many of the shrubs and trees.[12]

In opening up the arboretum, Hooker had been aiming to display the specimen trees to their best advantage. To fulfil its botanic function, an arboretum was supposed to give a clear view of the characteristic shapes of trees. To Hooker's mind, overcrowding was just one of the old arboretum's shortcomings. In addition, it failed to conform to current schemes of botanic classification. The arboretum was arranged according to the system devised by Carl Linnaeus in the eighteenth century. The Linnaean system was simple to master, but, by the 1840s, was considered inadequate for serious botanic study. Linnaeus had classified all living organisms within a ranked hierarchy which ranged from the broad to the specific. All plants were identified with a binomial (a two-part name) which designated both their genus and species – a system which is still in use today. For instance, the common English oak was named *Quercus robur* and the closely related Turkey oak, *Quercus cerris*. The class and order of plants were determined by their reproductive organs: the number of stamens (the flower's male parts) and carpels (female parts). As these features were easy to identify, the system was straightforward and widely used. However, because the system focused only on the plants' reproductive organs, the resulting groupings showed little obvious affinity; plants of entirely different form would be grouped together simply because they shared the same number of reproductive parts. For these reasons, botanists such as Lindley and Hooker regarded the Linnaean system as 'artificial', and appropriate only for children, beginners and, inevitably, ladies.

Even before the appointment of Nesfield, it was clear to Hooker that Kew needed a new arboretum that was both more extensive and organized according to the 'natural' system then in favour. Developed by two French botanists by the name of de Jussieu (uncle and nephew) and two Swiss botanists called de Candolle (father and son), the natural system took into account features such as the plants' leaves, stem, roots, the form and relative position and numbers of organs. The greater complexity of the classifying process, which involved detailed observation and comparison using dissection tools and microscopes, meant that the natural system was more challenging to master. However, this approach resulted in groupings which displayed far greater affinity than those in the Linnaean system, and lent themselves more effectively to planting schemes. An arboretum arranged along natural lines produced a much more coherent display than a Linnaean one.[13]

The great champion and popularizer of both the natural system and arboreta – as of so many matters botanical and horticultural – was John Claudius Loudon. In 1830, Loudon announced his intention to publish a comprehensive record of all the trees and shrubs growing in Britain. This was not a project that he could undertake alone. In an early example of what we now call citizen science, Loudon invited readers of the *Gardener's Magazine* to participate by providing descriptions, drawings and seeds of the trees in their region. He distributed some 3,000 questionnaires for completion and received responses from over 800 contributors. Eight years in the making, the mammoth *Arboretum et Fruticetum Britannicum* (1838) consumed much of Loudon's legendary energy and always precarious finances. Comprising eight volumes, the *Arboretum Britannicum* was arranged according to the natural system. It was illustrated by 400 specially commissioned portraits of individual trees from within a ten-mile radius of London. It was intended to spread arboricultural knowledge and to encourage the taste for establishing plantations and arboreta throughout Britain. Nothing like it had ever been published before.

For Loudon, trees were not only 'the most striking and grand objects of the vegetable creation', but also 'those which contribute the most to human comfort and improvement'.[14] Trees provided much of humanity's food and drink. Wood was essential for the construction of houses and ships, and the practice of agriculture. Without trees, Loudon asserted, there would be no settled communities and no trade. The transfer of trees across the world, Loudon argued, was a benign form of imperialism: 'it is the beautiful work of civilisation, of patriotism, and of adventure, first to collect these all into our country, and next to distribute them into others . . . thus contributing almost imperceptibly, but yet most powerfully to the progress and equalisation of civilisation and happiness'.[15]

Loudon's view of the universal benefits of global tree transplantation was shared by Hooker. Reviewing the *Arboretum Britannicum* in 1839, while still a professor at Glasgow University, Sir William had warmly recommended the work to botanists, cultivators and 'to every nobleman and gentleman of landed estate, who is desirous of improving his property and enlarging the resources of his country'.[16] Reiterating Loudon's grand assertions of the value of trees, Hooker had concluded that Loudon's work was of 'vast importance . . . to this country, to every part of Europe and the temperate parts of North America; and we may even say, to all temperate parts of the civilized world'.[17] Now, as director of Kew, Hooker had the chance to put these bold claims for the global significance of arboriculture into practice.

What Sir William needed was space. When the Queen gave the botanic garden an additional forty-five acres from the Pleasure Grounds in 1843, the area was swiftly designated for an arboretum. Preparations and purchases were made: 'a considerable collection of trees and shrubs was obtained from the various nurseries in this country, as well as from the Continent', recalled Smith; 'plans of arrangement and calculations were made for space to be allowed for each genus'.[18] But before this scheme had time to progress far, Lord Lincoln proposed that Nesfield should draw up a design for an arboretum.

To plan an arboretum was to think large-scale and long-term. It was necessary first to consider the whole of the ground available and then project decades ahead, to imagine the scheme when the trees were full grown and their crowns had reached their greatest extent. Nesfield wanted to create a national arboretum, but even with the additional acres he had to limit his ambitions to fit the confines of the botanic garden – the area delimited from the neighbouring Pleasure Grounds by a light wire fence. It was not only the growth of trees as they advanced towards maturity that Nesfield had to consider. Space would have to be left for additional future planting; with each new plant-hunting expedition, trees would be added to the various groupings of genera. An arboretum was a living, ever-changing collection. There would be no quick returns on such an endeavour; to plant an arboretum was to provide for the future.

But an arboretum was not simply a utilitarian or scientific resource. It was also a striking landscape feature. Well-established trees conferred a sense of permanence and dignity to the grounds. They were a central element in both landscape design and picturesque theory. According to Uvedale Price, 'the great art of improvement' consisted in 'the arrangement and management of trees'.[19] Presenting endless diversity of shape, form and colour, trees could be used to catch the eye, create avenues and frame views. In a picturesque landscape, wrote Price, trees surpassed all other natural objects in the 'infinite *variety* of their forms, tints and light and shade', and their 'quality of *intricacy*'.[20] In addition to their aesthetic value, trees carried a wealth of cultural and geographic associations. 'They remind us of the climes whence they come, of the scenes with which they were associated', wrote George Sinclair, head gardener at Woburn Abbey.[21] To walk an arboretum was to travel the world. 'In exploring a well-selected arboretum', Sinclair continued, 'the eternal snows of the Himalaya, the savannahs of the Missouri, the untrodden forests of Patagonia, the vallies of Lebanon, pass in review before us: we seem to wander other climes, to converse with other nations'.[22]

The art of laying out an arboretum was to strike a balance between the aesthetic and cultural qualities of trees on the one hand, and taxonomy on the other. Hooker instructed Nesfield that it was important both to maintain the park-like grandeur of Kew and to follow the rules of the natural system. But, as the landscape gardener pointed out, these two principles might come into conflict. 'I am anxious to know whether it is absolutely necessary that the Orders sh'd be planted according to rotation', Nesfield wrote to Hooker.[23] To adopt a strictly systematic method was likely to cause problems with the overall design: 'if we are to be thus fettered, there will be immense difficulty in managing the artistical department because high growth may happen to come where we want low or open glade & vice versa', he warned.[24] With his artistic background, Nesfield inevitably privileged aesthetic considerations and advocated a flexible approach which responded to the needs of a particular location.

At the beginning of March 1844, Nesfield drew up a rough plan of the arboretum, using the limited space available. He decided to approach the commission as if he were laying out an estate, but, in an exceptional and innovative move, to treat the Palm House as if it were a country house. Unaware of its precise shape and dimensions, Nesfield blocked out the conservatory as a simple rectangle. But, even at this early stage, he knew that it should function as the grand focus of Kew. The Palm House was thus accorded prime position at the centre of the design. The scheme would change and expand over the years, but the germ of the idea was in place from the start: the glasshouse would attract visitors' attention and command views over the whole grounds. As Nesfield explained to Hooker, the Palm House would be 'the one great point of sight'.[25]

As with his designs for country estates, Nesfield's layout ranged from the artificial to the naturalistic. In the immediate vicinity of the Palm House, Nesfield planned a terrace, ornamental parterres and gravel walks. Radiating out from the centre of the Palm House, Nesfield sketched three great vistas, a *patte d'oie* or goose-foot arrangement, reaching beyond the confines of the botanic garden into the Pleasure Grounds. One headed in the direction of Syon

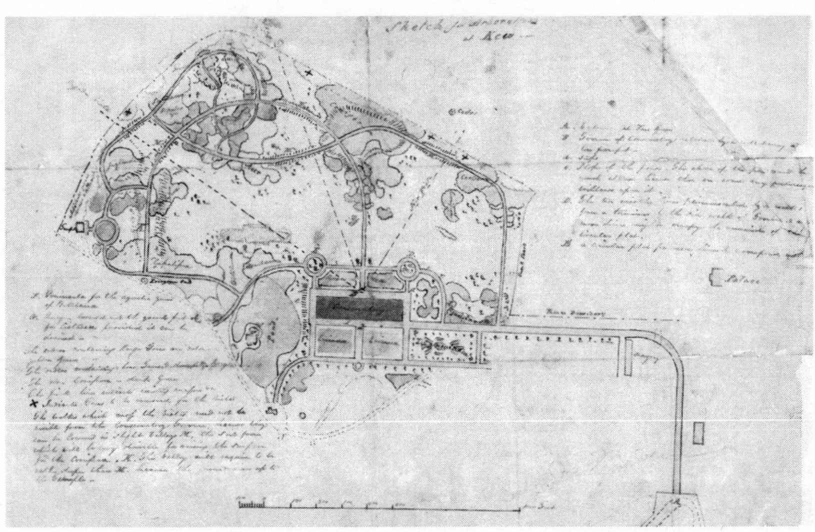


15. *An initial sketch of an arboretum by William Nesfield.*

House on the opposite bank of the Thames, home to the Duke of Northumberland, himself an enthusiastic patron of botany and plant hunting. One stretched towards Richmond, terminating in the splendid prospect of William Chambers' Chinese-style pagoda, over half a mile distant. The third had yet to find its object of sight. Conferring a grandeur and spaciousness on the scheme, these vistas served to link the Palm House to aristocratic power in one direction and the exotic East in the other: two potent influences on British garden design.

Nesfield's main concern was to respect Hooker's instruction to preserve Kew's 'Park-like character'.[26] Guided by aesthetic considerations, Nesfield left the middle ground clear. He mapped out irregular, picturesque groupings of orders of trees in the background, arranged according to height, graduating from low to high. Despite

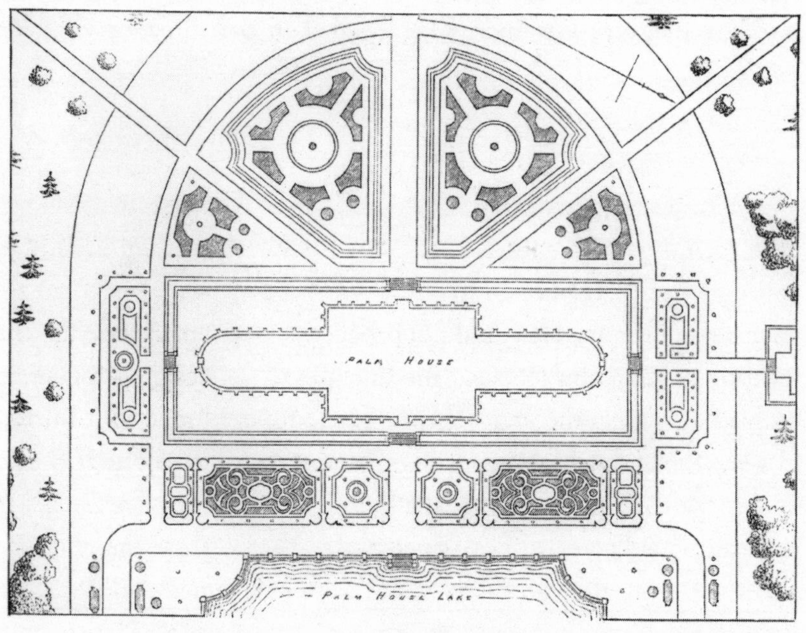


16. *The Palm House with radiating vistas and formal parterre.*

some reservations about formal arrangement close to the Palm House, Hooker appears to have been impressed. Writing to his father-in-law just a few days after viewing Nesfield's plan, Hooker could not resist boasting: 'If our views are carried into effect, the Garden will be finer than I ever could have anticipated'.[27]

The first practical step to take on the ground, Nesfield informed Hooker, was to conduct a thorough inspection of all the trees at Kew. A list should be drawn up to determine which trees should be saved, which moved and which felled. Every tree would be ranked according to its botanic importance, general shape and state of health. If the director would be so good as to supply a team of ten or twelve axemen, Nesfield would 'run over to Kew soon to do the needful'. But 'as signing death warrants is a serious responsibility', Sir William should 'be present as judge advocate'. Adopting a blackly humorous tone, Nesfield acknowledged the finality of the decisions (and the expense of his rates): 'my rule is never to strike a blow without convincing reason, consequently I ought to have someone to reason with – a good force of executioners will save my time & consequently the cash of the Commis[sioners]'.[28]

But the executions were stayed. Much to Nesfield's frustration, the project progressed extremely slowly. Every decision had to be approved by the Office of Woods, and funding was dependent on government grants. He could not proceed with the plans because the location of the Palm House – the linchpin of his design – remained unfixed. Towards the end of April 1844, Nesfield met with Burton to view the architectural drawings. The architect told Nesfield that he was contemplating moving the Palm House twenty-five feet from its position at the end of the main walk that led from the entrance on Kew Green. But, for months, the matter remained undecided. In June, Nesfield wrote to inform Hooker that he had 'a Plan upon a large scale begun for the Arboretum', but added with evident annoyance, 'the question is, when will it be required? – at all events it cannot be finally accomplished till the site for The House is fixed'.[29] At length, in August 1844, Hooker and Burton concluded that the Palm House should be relocated from the north to the west side of the pond. This was not in any way a response to John Smith's concerns about flooding, but rather to allow for a reflection of the Palm House in the water to mirror and enhance the translucence of the structure.

The various elements of the design were now falling into place, but Hooker was losing faith in Nesfield. With his head full of picturesque prospects, was he really the man to lay out an arboretum? He seemed more interested in creating an attractive park than a place for botanic study. While Sir William desired beauty and spectacle, he also wanted scientific precision. Kew had both to attract the public and demonstrate its botanical pre-eminence. Perhaps a practical gardener would be better suited to the job. In December 1844, Hooker was approached by Robert Glendinning, the Scottish proprietor of Chiswick Nursery, just across the river. Glendinning had previously been head gardener at Bicton, in Devon, where, following advice from Loudon, he had laid out an arboretum. Loudon had praised the arrangement and planting of the Bicton arboretum in the pages of the *Gardener's Magazine*, noting Glendinning's 'excellent taste in landscape-gardening, as well as enthusiastic love of trees and shrubs'.[30] With his horticultural experience, the nurseryman would, no doubt, be better informed than Nesfield. Would it be possible, wondered Hooker, to engage Glendinning as assistant to – or replacement for – the landscape designer?

But the architect, Burton, continued to back Nesfield, despite the landscape designer's increasing exasperation with the project. Angered by the lack of progress and lack of available space for the arboretum, Nesfield wrote privately to Burton, vowing that 'if only a National Paddock is to be created', he had 'come to the fixed determination to have nothing to do with Kew, directly or indirectly'.[31] Burton was dismayed. He had come to rely on Nesfield's judgement and good taste. While he and Hooker both shared Nesfield's desire that a greater extent of land be made available from the Pleasure Grounds, they knew – unlike the impatient landscape gardener – that any decision involving the Office of Woods would have to be handled delicately, and would inevitably involve bureaucratic delay. Burton was used to managing complex schemes and smoothing over problems, but even he allowed his irritation to show. In a confidential letter to Hooker, he noted curtly, 'Mr N. declines to act professionally in laying out Kew Garden & Arboretum'.[32] Nevertheless, Burton attempted to mediate between Hooker, Nesfield and the Office of Woods. He managed to devise a letter that did not close down any of the options. This masterly piece of diplomatic communication left 'the door open for Mr. Nesfield should the Board desire his services & should he be disposed to afford them'; it also allowed Hooker, should he so wish, 'to bring in the experienced nurseryman'.[33]

Burton's letter bought enough time for the crisis to blow over. By early summer 1845, the situation had altered significantly. After more than fifty years and approaching the age of eighty, William Townsend Aiton, the former superintendent of the Royal Gardens at Kew, was finally contemplating retirement from the Pleasure Grounds. The old royal estate was likely to come under Hooker's care (although, as he admitted to his father-in-law, Hooker largely saw it as a means to augment his salary). Adjoining the botanic garden, the Pleasure Grounds comprised of woods, open land and walks, nearly 200 acres in extent, which had changed little since they had been originally laid out in the eighteenth century. Aiton's retirement was the perfect opportunity to request additional space for the arboretum – the very chance for which Nesfield, Burton and Hooker had been waiting.

All the interested parties realized that now was the time to patch up their differences. Hooker sent conciliatory letters to Nesfield and Burton, who both responded positively. 'I augur well for the public service', the architect wrote optimistically to Hooker, 'that so good an understanding happily exists between us'.[34] Hooker and Burton had long lobbied Lord Lincoln about the need to enlarge the arboretum. Now it was Nesfield's turn to add his voice. He would submit a report outlining his expanded scheme and follow up with plans. It was to be hoped that Nesfield's previous behaviour would not count against him, although, as Hooker confided to his father-in-law, 'Mr. Nesfield does not stand well in Ld. L's opinion'.[35]

In his report, Nesfield made the case for establishing an arboretum worthy of the nation: 'It is reasonable to infer', he wrote, 'that a national Arboretum ought to be the Head Quarters of every variety of Tree & shrub which will stand this Climate'.[36] Given the arboretum's public function, it was 'not only to be a place for instruction and botanical reference but of ornament and should be designed after the manner of park scenery'.[37] With the Palm House at its centre, the surrounding arboretum had to be correspondingly large. The arboretum's extent was dictated 'by reason of the magnitude of the proposed palm house which naturally prescribes a given scale for its accompaniments . . . as it inevitably must form the focus of chief artificial attraction of the place'.[38]

Nesfield's ambitious scheme claimed 150 acres for the arboretum. With this additional ground, Nesfield had the scope to create a 'National Arboretum', as he called it on the plan. The decision to

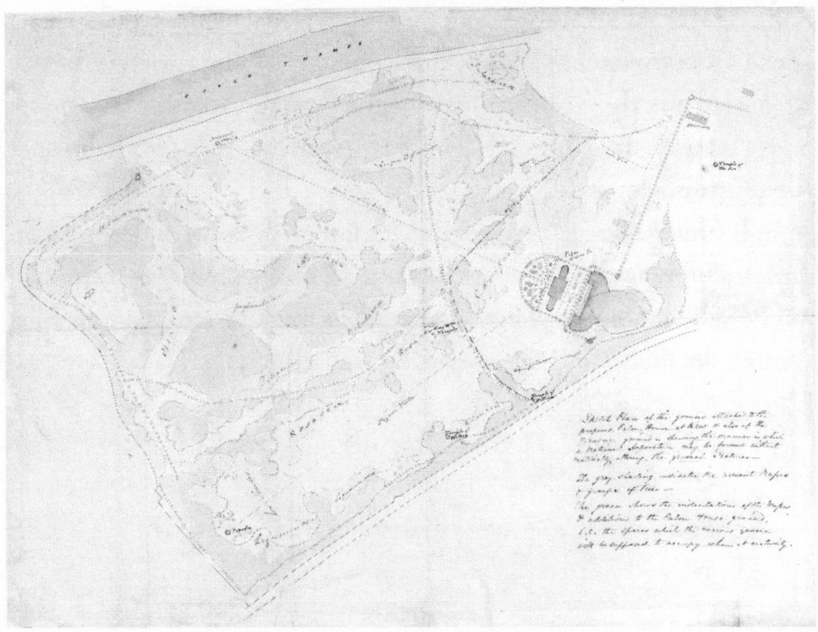

17. *William Nesfield's plan for a national arboretum.*

relocate the glasshouse to the west of the pond allowed Nesfield to devise a much cleaner, more coherent layout of the grounds, with the Palm House dominating the design. After eighteen months of planning, disagreement and tension, a truly beautiful scheme had emerged. From the entrance, the main walk headed towards the pond, bordered by conifers which shielded the Palm House from view. At the pond, the path turned a sharp right to reveal, all at once, the Palm House facade (see illustration 17 above, and Plate 18). Raised on a terrace, the Palm House was fronted by flower beds, with steps leading up to its doorway. Nesfield envisaged that visitors would follow a route that ran from the entrance gate, along the main walk, around the pond and into the Palm House. Once they had viewed its tropical wonders, visitors would emerge at the back of the Palm House into the temperate zone of the arboretum. The rear door of the Palm House was directly aligned with Syon Vista, a broad avenue stretching nearly three quarters of a mile to the Thames. To the left and right, at forty-five-degree angles, extended the Pagoda and Cedar Vistas. The scheme was grand in scale, yet simple in design. It made perfect sense of the space.

In July 1845, Hooker reported to his father-in-law that 'Poor Aiton, with tears in his eyes, gave me possession of the pleasure-grounds'.[39] With this symbolic transfer of power, Hooker's vision of a new Kew, centred on the Palm House, came a step closer.

# 8

# Deck Iron

Back in Dublin, Richard Turner was worrying about money. Turner delighted in winning clients and in solving their technical problems, but rarely paid much attention to the accounting side of his business. His initial excitement at securing the deal for the central portion of the Palm House quickly dissipated on learning, near the end of June 1844, that he was now obliged to supply the names of two bondsmen: respectable individuals who would be prepared to stand surety, should he fail to meet the contract. The appointment of bondsmen would necessarily entail enquiry into his own financial standing, a scrutiny which Turner would prefer to avoid. Only three years previously, bankruptcy proceedings had been commenced against him in Dublin. Although he had come to an agreement with his creditors, he had been required to appear at the Court of Bankruptcy on two occasions, and this fact had been announced in the Dublin press.[1] Would it be possible, Turner enquired of Burton, to waive the sureties in favour of withholding a quarter of the payment until the work had been signed off?

But there was no way around the regulations. The Treasury kept a strict eye on spending at Kew. The Chancellor of the Exchequer in Robert Peel's Tory government was Henry Goulburn, a staunch advocate of economy, and particularly wary of expensive schemes for public 'improvement'. Kew received its funding from two sources: parliamentary grants were allocated for major building works, such as the Palm House, while the Land Revenues of the Crown, administered by the Commissioners of Woods and Forests, covered salaries and running costs. Expenditure on the Palm House was listed as a separate item in the accounts published by the government.[2] The Treasury was aware that the cost of building the Palm House would be the subject of public interrogation, particularly by Radical critics of government spending. For Burton and the Office of Woods, therefore, it was important to be seen to be exercising due caution when appointing a contractor.

By August 1844, it became apparent that Turner would not be able to provide the necessary sureties. Without bondsmen, he could not be named as the contractor for the Palm House. Faced with the prospect of losing the job, Turner accepted demotion to the position of subcontractor for the ironwork. One of the leading building companies of the day, Grissell and Peto, was appointed as the primary contractor in his stead. Grissell and Peto were at the forefront of many of the building projects that defined mid-nineteenth-century Britain. They had laid large sections of major railway lines, recently erected Nelson's Column, and were involved in the ongoing construction of Charles Barry's neo-Gothic Palace of Westminster. Unlike the Hammersmith Works, Grissell and Peto had the capital, experience and reputation to obtain sureties with ease. At Kew, they were engaged to lay the Palm House foundations, form the basement boiler rooms and dig a service tunnel. As at Chatsworth, the extensive heating apparatus required by the immense glasshouse would be housed underground. A tunnel –

containing a track for trucks to transport coke and ashes, and a flue for the discharge of smoke – would link the glasshouse to a coal yard. Although their actual contribution to the project would be limited to the initial stages, Grissell and Peto, as the main contractor, would be responsible for the entire works. Finally, on 17 August 1844, the contract for the central portion of the Palm House was signed. Much to Turner's dismay, appended to the contract were the civil engineer's contemptible plans.

As a self-taught engineer, Turner kept abreast of technical developments by reading the various magazines devoted to engineering and construction that had proliferated in recent years. By mid-century, these publications contributed to the prevailing idea of Britain as a nation which claimed superiority over others through its technological expertise. Two innovations in particular – the railways and the steamship – were key to this national image; they promised to revolutionize communication, boost commerce and strengthen imperial power. Railway construction was at its height in the 1840s, with new lines linking the major cities and manufacturing areas throughout Britain. In 1842, the Peninsular and Oriental Steam Navigation Company (later known as P&O) launched a steam service between Britain and India, and the British Navy commissioned its first iron steam vessels the following year. The engineering press followed these developments with avidity. In its opening volume, the *Civil Engineer & Architects Journal* proclaimed that the 'great development of steam navigation and railways . . . contribute extensively to the character of an age which may justly be marked among the eras of human civilization'.[3]

One of the functions of the technological press was to publicize new patents. In October 1844, the *Civil Engineer* hailed a patent granted to Kennedy and Vernon, an engineering and shipbuilding duo based in Liverpool, as 'an improvement in shipbuilding of the greatest importance'.[4] At the time, it was common practice in shipbuilding to use rivets to join the various wrought-iron elements in a ship's frame. This made each joint a potentially weak spot and added to the ship's overall weight. To address this problem, Kennedy and Vernon devised a method to produce wrought-iron beams, rolled all in one piece, with projecting ribs or flanges. Strong and light, this 'deck beam' was a timely invention, as the *Civil Engineer* pointed out: 'Iron ship building is daily an object of the greatest importance, it having been recently adopted by government, it is therefore necessary that shipbuilders and engineers should turn their immediate attention to the construction of vessels in the strongest manner with as small a weight as possible'.[5]

Vernon and Kennedy's patent caught Turner's eye. Could this deck beam, he wondered, have applications beyond shipbuilding? Strength and lightness were the very qualities that he sought in his glasshouses. Turner was particularly arrested by the design of one of Kennedy and Vernon's beams: the 'bulb-tee' section, a length of wrought iron rolled into a near 'I' shape. It was with mounting excitement that he realized this section might be suitable for the frame of the Palm House. With the instinct of an intuitive engineer, Turner was able to make the imaginative leap between ships and buildings. In this he showed remarkable prescience; the 'bulb-tee' was a predecessor of the I-beam, which was to become one of the most commonly used building elements. Turner was the first person to grasp its structural potential.[6]

For Turner, the new patent offered an elegant solution to the civil engineer's inept drawings. Vernon and Kennedy's rolled wrought-iron ribs were of the appropriate dimension for the Palm

House roof. Although deck beam was more expensive than cast iron, less of the metal would be required. Turner calculated that the reduced quantity would offset the higher cost. All that was required was to persuade Burton, Hooker and the Commissioners of its benefits. Commencing his campaign, Turner wrote to Hooker of his determination to substitute rolled wrought iron 'in lieu of the tremendously prodigious, & Gigantic affairs proposed – of which we shall have a most happy Riddance'. Not a man to use one word where five would do, Turner invited Sir William to join him in denouncing the cast-iron ribs, 'not only as a Blemish but a dreadful Nuisance, Unsightly, Unsuitable & Unnecessary'.[7] He declared that a wrought-iron frame would be 'exceedingly more satisfactory to you, and ten Thousand times more Creditable to me'.[8] He promised Hooker beauty, stability and strength. So great was his confidence that he even invoked the spectre of failure: 'I would not for a vast deal do a thing that would be wrong in such a structure, committing an Error on such important occasion how could I ever recover myself and what an inexcusable injury I might do save me from it!?'[9]

Such an outpouring of conviction was not merely a sales pitch. Turner was perfectly genuine in his desire to create a glasshouse of unprecedented grace. His reputation, livelihood and future were all at stake. His emphatic tone was just one aspect of his effusive manner and energetic approach. Whether he was attempting to persuade a client or provide a solution, Turner was equally relentless. Luckily, many people also found him charming. Sir William, for one, was won over. Turner even managed to persuade Hooker to help him extend his business in England by recommending his services to his aristocratic friends and acquaintances.

When Hooker learnt that Lord Derby was considering building a conservatory, he suggested Turner for the job. Not only was he extremely pleased with Turner, wrote Sir William, 'even Decimus Burton, our Architect, owned himself under many obligations to Mr. Turner in the planning of our great stove'.[10] That an architect should acknowledge his indebtedness to an iron founder was offered as testimony to Turner's exceptional qualities. 'His character too stands very high not only as a most efficient workman but as a strictly honest man', continued Hooker. 'Indeed the only fault ever heard of him is that he does work a great deal too cheaply'.[11] This final observation served both as a recommendation and caveat, for, if a tradesman's estimates were too low, he might not manage to execute a contract. At times, a touch of colonial condescension entered Hooker's view: 'He has a little Irish exuberancy, but with a little management he is a most useful man'.[12] In the event, Lord Derby and his estate manager were not convinced. Derby complained of the 'undeniably unworkmanlike paper' that Turner had submitted 'as a sort of Contract and Estimate', and explained that they had decided against employing him because he 'was too vague & I may say it, flighty for us'.[13] Evidently, Turner's business methods and Irish exuberancy were not to everybody's taste.

On the Palm House contract, however, Turner did his utmost to avoid giving the impression of flightiness. He assured Hooker that he was 'putting all the requisites for satisfying all the Scientific Gentlemen, Mr D. Burton & all of the vast improvement & Utility & numberless advantages' of deck iron.[14] In December 1844, he was back in London to attend a meeting with Decimus Burton, Thomas Grissell (representing the primary contractor) and William Malins of the iron masters Malins and Rawlinson, the company appointed by Kennedy and Vernon to manufacture their patent deck iron. At the meeting, Turner undertook, at his own risk and expense, to produce a pair of trial Palm House 'ribs', which would be tested for strength by Grissell and Peto. To prepare the trial framework, Turner thought, might take around two weeks.

But, as with any new technology, the process was far from straightforward. The deck iron was manufactured by Malins and Rawlinson in twelve-foot lengths. When the rolled wrought-iron bars arrived at the Hammersmith Works, Turner's first challenge was to find a way to weld the sections together to form a single rib, forty-two feet long. He discovered that it was extremely hard to fuse the I-shaped beams, end to end. His existing machinery and furnaces were inadequate to the task. Advancing through trial and error, Turner made slow progress; the predicted two weeks stretched into months. He had to work out an entirely new process, build the necessary equipment and instruct his staff. He purchased a new blast furnace, capable of achieving high temperatures through concentrated hot-air blasts. No accounts of Turner's method survive, but it is likely that he heated the ends of the beams in the blast furnace and united them together using either a screw device or hydraulic press. The rib thus formed was bent to the required arc, while still hot, around a template.[15] In all, the experimental process took nearly six months.

The trial ribs finally made their way from the Hammersmith Works in Dublin to Grissell and Peto's yard in Lambeth in June 1845. Erected in the builders' yard, the ribs were subjected to two days of stress testing. Burton reported to Hooker that Lord Lincoln himself had 'assisted . . . the 2d. trial of the iron' and was 'much pleased'.[16] More importantly, Grissell and Peto announced themselves satisfied by the strength of the ribs. On the basis of Turner's calculations, Grissell and Peto were prepared, at no additional expense, to exchange Burton's bulky cast-iron ribs for the slender wrought-iron ones proposed by Turner.

The memory of his triumph remained with Turner for the rest of his life. A year before his death, he told the Dublin architect Thomas Drew that the decision 'gave Sir William Hooker, and Mr. Decimus Burton as well, the utmost pleasure and satisfaction, being then convinced of the sad error they were saved from, for anything more foreign from Mr. Burton's design it would be difficult to imagine'.[17] It is possible that the passage of thirty-five years sweetened the memory, or that Turner's propensity for self-promotion remained undiminished in old age. But, without doubt, this was a moment of vindication for Turner.

For all Turner's engineering brilliance, he was often a frustrating working partner. Over the coming years, Burton was to gain extensive experience of managing relations with Turner. At the same time that the two men were engaged on the Palm House, they were working together on another project: the Winter Garden for the Royal Botanic Society at Regent's Park. It had been the chance to win this contract that had originally attracted Turner to London, but the extravagant model that he had displayed at Exeter Hall had not been the design adopted by the Society.

Despite its glittering membership, the Botanic Society did not have limitless resources. Members were invited to contribute to a Conservatory Building Fund, with the subscription list headed by HRH Prince Albert (donation: twenty-one pounds).[18] In June 1844, the Society selected a glasshouse design submitted by Decimus Burton. But, with the sums raised, the Winter Garden Committee could only contemplate erecting the central portion of the scheme. Burton had drawn up two versions of the conservatory – one in iron, the other wood. On the architect's advice, the Committee opted for the more economical wooden version. But, the following year,

Turner submitted a tender for an iron structure of 'the most lightsome and handsome appearance' that came in at £150 cheaper than the rival bid for a wooden conservatory.[19] Not only was Turner's price appealingly low, but he also undertook to erect the conservatory in less than six months. This proved a winning combination; the Winter Garden contract was signed on 20 June 1845 – just a week after the successful test of the Palm House ribs.

But, as Burton had already experienced in his dealings with Turner, the iron founder tended to take much longer to execute work than he had anticipated. Whether this originated in an eagerness to win the contract or an overly optimistic disposition, Turner habitually underestimated the length of time required for a job. In the case of the Winter Garden contract, there was a penalty clause that obliged Turner to finish by 29 November 1845, or pay a sum of twenty pounds for every subsequent week that the work remained incomplete. On the deadline date, with the conservatory half-built, Burton was summoned to a special Committee meeting to 'take such steps as will be deemed necessary in the present unfinished state of the Building'.[20] Turner was not in attendance, but wrote a letter requesting an extension until the following February, 'within which Month', he claimed, he would 'have it quite perfect & complete'. In a long postscript, partly defiant, partly explanatory, Turner accounted for the delay:

> P. S. Permit me to mention it was too short a time say only 5 months for erecting a work of such immence magnitude the tediousness of manufacturing is very great indeed owing to such a very great deal of jointing halvings and fitting requiring so much accuracy and perfect truth for exactness &c. all in the wrought Iron, and the Castings too are longer in hand owing to the extensive Railway Contracts interfering

> with all sorts of workmen &c. But our Tradesmen have been attentively getting on but the period was too short to do it in and the shortness of the days renders the erection more tedious. But I shall accomplish all heating and Glazing and everything within February and wait in you of your goodness in compliance by giving me till then.[21]

The rush of Turner's various explanations gives a sense of the complexity of the manufacturing and building operation, both at the Hammersmith Works and on the ground in Regent's Park. This was precision work, requiring highly skilled labour. It was evidently difficult to recruit sufficient numbers of iron smiths and labourers at the height of the railway-building boom; Irish 'navvies' made up a third of an estimated 250,000-strong workforce employed in laying the railways. At the same time, the list of endlessly proliferating problems suggests Turner's tendency to exonerate himself. Nowhere does he acknowledge that he had freely agreed to meet the November deadline.

The Society council was not disposed to leniency. A letter was dispatched to Turner, refusing his request for an extension and reminding him of the penalty clause in the contract. The curator of the gardens was instructed to take stock of the plants destined for the Winter Garden, to make arrangements to preserve them and keep track of the expenses incurred (limited to fifty pounds). Burton was directed to write a report on the current state of the building and to account for the materials on site. But it was not only the delay that created difficulties for the architect; Turner's conduct was also a matter of concern. On his own initiative and without consultation, Turner had made alterations to the building that would impede its possible extension at a future date (the central portion that Turner was commissioned to erect only made up a quarter of the proposed glass complex). Burton reported that he had been obliged to deliver a formal reprimand to Turner: he was told 'not to deviate in any point from the Contract'.[22] Turner was required to send a letter to the Society's secretary undertaking, somewhat improbably, to follow all the architect's future directions: 'I shall be perfectly satisfied to be guided in all respects – relative to the whole by Mr. Burton', a chastened Turner wrote. 'I hereby commit every thing to his views from beginning to end and guarantee his decisions shall be always final & binding upon me'.[23]

When February arrived – the month promised for completion – Turner was absent in Dublin and the Winter Garden still unfinished. The Committee, 'having expressed great dissatisfaction upon the progress of works', summoned Burton and Turner's foreman, Mr Morris.[24] The delay, Morris reported, arose from the difficulty in recruiting workmen; he anticipated that the building would be finished by April. 'I feel it is my duty to inform you', Burton wrote sternly that day to Turner, 'that . . . the Chairman stated to your foreman Mr. Morris, the certainty that the Society will levy the penalties accruing under your contract for non fulfilment of the works within the stipulated period'. Given how far Turner was behind, it was clearly in his interest to expedite proceedings: 'I strongly therefore advise you to increase the number of workmen so as to complete the works with the utmost dispatch'.[25]

At the end of March, the Botanic Society received word that the Queen and Prince Consort wished to inspect the new Winter Garden. Unfortunately for the Society, Victoria and Albert were shown around while the workmen were still putting their finishing touches to the building. The Winter Garden had taken twice as long to erect as initially agreed. But the building itself was a triumph. The filigree

18. *The Royal Botanic Society Winter Garden.*

glass structure was elegant and exceptionally light. 'Not an inch is there of unnecessary rafter to interrupt the light', admired Charles Knight.[26] The doors were formed of simple glass panels and the internal pilasters were faced with green and red ground glass. The delicate wrought-iron frame and absence of obvious means of support created a place of wonder: 'a veritable fairy land, transplanted into the heart of London', marvelled Knight; 'an actual garden of delight, realizing all our ideal'.[27]

Frustrating as it was to deal with Turner, the quality of his craftsmanship was undeniable. Although he paid scant regard to architect plans and contract deadlines, Turner's workmanship could not be faulted. The ambivalence that Turner aroused in his clients is evident in a passage initially drafted for the Royal Botanic Society's annual report for 1846:

> Although much dissatisfaction has been felt by the Council and considerable loss has been sustained by the Society in consequence of the delay in the completion of the conservatory beyond the time specified in the contract and announced to the Fellows in the Report of last year, it is due to the Contract to state that, as far as their present limited experience and the expressed opinions of persons familiar with buildings of a similar description enable the Council to form a judgment, they have every reason to believe that the work has been skilfully and efficiently executed.[28]

In fact, the drafted passage was struck through; an annual report was evidently not the place to express the conflicting sentiments generated by the wayward genius of Turner.

The Winter Garden proved a fashionable success. Fitted out with 'pretty little iron tables', it was ideal as a venue for genteel socializing, particularly for ladies.[29] It provided the centrepiece for Royal Botanic Society garden parties and flower shows, and in the evenings was used as a venue for concerts. It never reached the size originally planned. In the 1870s, however, sufficient funds were raised to allow Turner's son, William (who took over the business), to add two apses and a covered way to link the building to the road. But the Royal Botanic Society was never a serious botanic or horticultural institution and did not pose a challenge to Kew. It fell from favour in the early twentieth century, and the Winter Garden was demolished in 1932.

In October 1845, Turner started the process of erecting the ribs of the central portion of the Palm House. Forged at the Hammersmith Works in Dublin, the massive ribs were conveyed by ship and barge to Kew. Like an enormous, elaborate kit, the Palm House was made up of thousands of prefabricated individual components. Each element had a dual function both to bear the structure and support the exterior shell. Every part of the frame was linked to another. At the lower level, the central portion consisted of a series of half arches of deck iron. These half arches met twenty hollow cast-iron columns (which doubled as drainpipes) that supported the gallery and the arched upper level. The columns were fixed to the gallery with cast-iron brackets that evoked branching palm-leaf stalks. The ribs were braced together using a purlin of Turner's own design. Running horizontally throughout the entire building, the purlin consisted of a wrought-iron rod enclosed within an iron tube. Once the ribs and the purlin were in place, the wrought-iron rod was pulled taut, placing the whole framework under tension to knit the structure together. This innovative form of post-tensioning created a framework that was at once rigid and flexible, allowing for a degree of expansion and contraction. Turner's tubular purlin was much slimmer and lighter than the one specified in the civil engineer's drawings – yet another amendment to the architect's plans.

Over the course of 1846, the framework of the central portion was gradually erected. At the upper level, a viewing gallery was constructed. Burton had originally planned two small spiral staircases at opposite corners to the gallery, but Turner was concerned that this might weaken the structure. It was agreed to substitute a single, larger winding staircase to the midpoint of the gallery. If this were to prove inadequate, a second stairway could be added later. On ascending, visitors would be afforded a striking central view of the Palm House interior. With

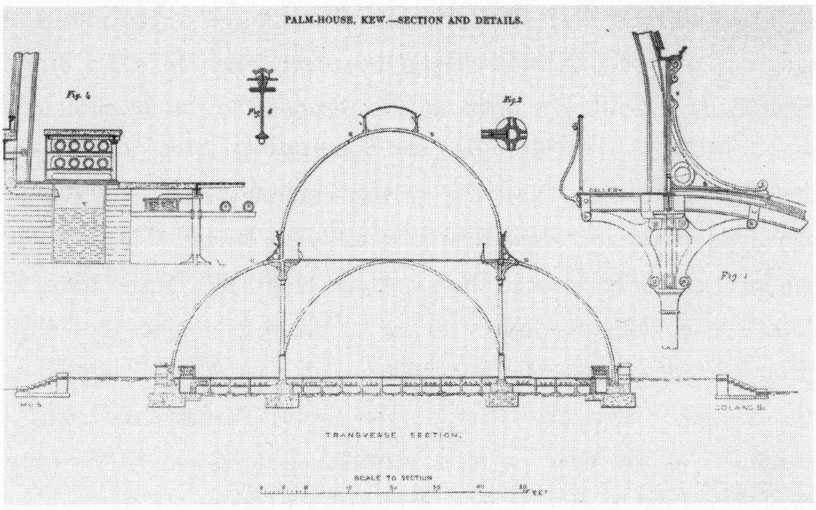


19. *A section and details of Palm House construction.*

his customary exuberance, Turner introduced little decorative flourishes throughout the ironwork: rosettes to cover bolted joints; palmettes, flowers and scrolls to adorn the staircase railings.

Following Kennedy and Vernon's example, Turner registered a patent for his innovative use of iron. But, unlike the shipbuilding patentees, Turner anticipated new structural applications for his inventions. From his experience with the Palm House, Turner recognized that deck beam could be used to span great widths. Nowhere was this quality more required than in the construction of railway-station roofs. In an environment where accidents were common, supporting columns posed a hazard: if an engine were to collide with a pillar, the roof would collapse. In deck iron, Turner saw a solution to this problem. Turner's 1846 patent for 'Certain Improvements in the Construction of Roofs of Railway Stations and Roofs and Floors of Other Buildings' included the structural use of deck iron and the new purlin. As an entrepreneur, he of course realized the extent of the market for wide-span railway buildings.

The following year, Turner submitted a design for an immense single-span roof – an unprecedented 153 feet wide – for Lime Street Station, Liverpool. His proposal, he recalled, 'in the first instance was considered perfectly visionary and chimerical'.[30] In the face of steadfast opposition from the railway-company engineer, Turner managed to convince the directors to adopt his design. The company engineer not only doubted the plans, but distrusted Turner himself: 'Mr. Turner does not inspire in me so much confidence as I wish proper in the person who undertakes such a work', he confided to the company secretary.[31] But, in the event, Turner's roof was a triumph: 'at the time of its execution', judged the engineering publisher John Weale, it was 'unquestionably one of the boldest pieces of construction in existence'.[32]

At Kew, Turner relied on an exclusively Irish workforce. For the American landscape architect Robert Leuchars, this demonstrated the benefits of engaging experienced workers: 'the material and workmen were all brought across the channel, costing nearly as much as if brought to America; yet the workmanship was superior, and the cost said to be less, — proving that practice and knowledge of the details lessen the original cost of construction'.[33] In adopting a purely economic view, Leuchars grouped Irish workers together with the material: both were equally transportable. But, in reducing Irish workers to the status of iron components, Leuchars ignored the most significant contemporary cause of the mobility of Irish labour: the Great Famine. From 1845, when the potato blight first struck, Ireland suffered a crisis that was exacerbated by government inaction. Rural communities were the most gravely afflicted, but

Dubliners also experienced severe hardship. The city was overwhelmed with streams of people fleeing starvation, seeking a means of survival or passage to England or America. While the Hammersmith Works might not have directly employed famine refugees, Turner's preference for Irish workmen was explained by his English contemporaries 'as a motive of kindness to those suffering around him'.[34] But Turner was not a particularly generous employer. Dublin wages were lower than London ones, and the Irish smiths at Kew considered themselves ill paid. In March 1846, the Irish Palm House workers went on strike for higher wages. Already concerned that he had underestimated the cost of construction, Turner reluctantly agreed to increase their pay.

In November the same year, Turner also had to deal with labour problems at the Hammersmith Works. The *Freeman's Journal* reported that Turner summoned fifteen of his workers to appear at the Dublin police office. The men had objected to working with an engineer by the name of Patrick Dunn; if Dunn remained in post, they declared, they would quit.[35] The smiths, Turner stated, had previously been exemplary workers: 'they were a capital set of men, and always acted in the mildest manner, and he was very sorry that they had acted so erroneously at present'. The presiding police magistrate thought that Turner might have a case, and advised the men to reconsider. Turner said that he would be happy to accept the workers back; 'he had no ill feeling to the men', he declared, 'even if he could he would not punish them, but he would retain Pat Dunn, or any other man he pleased in his employment, without being dictated to'. Turner's mixture of benign paternalism and fierce resolution, backed by the threat of legal action, appears to have had the desired effect. Even the solicitor representing the smiths urged the men to return to work, 'as there was not a better employer in Ireland than Mr. Turner'.[36]

The fact that the Palm House was fabricated and built by Irish workers was rarely publicly acknowledged. The famine years saw a great increase in the number of Irish immigrants in Britain; during the 1840s, London's Irish community swelled by some 46,000, to around 130,000. This steep rise was accompanied by the growth of anti-Irish sentiment. Denigrated as violent and lazy, Irish labourers were generally seen as unreliable and prone to disorder. In an attempt to rehabilitate the reputation of Irish workers, a correspondent to the *Builder* in 1848 praised the Irish workmanship on the Palm House. 'As nearly all the work of this building has been executed by Irishmen, who are grateful for the employment it has afforded them', the writer observed, 'I hope you will consider it a proof that the mechanics of that country are disposed to earn their bread in honesty and peace, and are capable of executing works of that kind to the satisfaction of the professional gentlemen of this country'.[37] Tellingly, the correspondent's views were relegated to a footnote.

The crisis in Ireland also had an indirect impact on the management of Kew. In view of the worsening Irish situation, in February 1846, Robert Peel removed Lord Lincoln from his post as First Commissioner of Woods and Forests to appoint him Chief Secretary of Ireland. With the departure of Lincoln for Dublin, Hooker lost his most powerful government advocate: the man who had introduced him to Turner, and who enthusiastically backed the Palm House. The position of First Commissioner was taken by Lord Canning. But no sooner had Hooker begun to establish relations with Canning than Peel's ministry fell. By June 1846, there was a new Whig First Commissioner: Lord Morpeth. Hooker regarded his appointment with concern. 'Ld. Morpeth considers that there has been too much expended on the Garden', he confided to his father-in-law. 'This frequent change of Chief Commissioners is a very bad thing for me as well as the Gardens'.[38]

Given Kew's dependence on government finances, any political change was a cause of anxiety for Hooker, but he had long-established and close associations with the family of the new Prime Minister. Lord John Russell was the son of the Duke of Bedford, Hooker's staunch ally in the campaign to establish Kew as a public garden. Less than a month after he had expressed his fear over the appointment of Lord Morpeth, Sir William wrote in much happier vein to his father-in-law: 'I have had a pleasant interview today with the Commissioners at Whitehall & many gratifying expressions of regard & what is still better a hope held out to me that my salary would ere long be increased by £300 a year'.[39] Under the Whigs, Hooker's salary rose to £800 per annum. In addition, he would no longer personally have to bear the cost of purchasing botanical books for his library. So congenial was the meeting that Hooker felt emboldened to propose an extraordinary deal to the Commissioners: 'I told them I would be willing to give the Herbarium if they would make my Son my Assistant & Successor'.[40] Sir William was prepared to bargain the herbarium – his invaluable tool, greatest asset and prized bequest – in the attempt to guarantee a botanical career for Joseph. This was Hooker's first explicit move in the long game to secure Kew for his botanical dynasty.

From the very start of the Palm House project, Hooker had tried to guard against the possibility that only the central portion of the glasshouse would be built. With such an expensive undertaking, it was always possible that government finances would not stretch to the whole scheme, or that it would only be completed in very gradual stages. In his first annual report to the House of Commons, Hooker had stressed that the 'noble structure . . . if carried into complete execution' would be 'second to none in Europe'. He emphasized that it made economic sense to approve funding for the wings before the centre was completed: 'thus a great saving of expense will be effected in the scaffolding and temporary ends that will otherwise have to put up in the grand centre'.[41] Government funding was dispensed in tranches of varying amounts, every financial year. In his annual reports, Hooker tried to convey a sense of momentum with the building works, even if, as in 1845, the actual progress was slow. So, it was much to Hooker's relief that, the same year, Parliament sanctioned a further grant for the Palm House. In June 1846, the Commissioners instructed Burton to commence work on the wings.

Ever optimistic, Turner had already started to make preparations. 'I felt so well satisfied and persuaded in my own mind, that the Wings of the New Palm House at Kew, would be ordered', Turner told Burton in July 1846, 'that at all Peril, I proceeded with the works for them'. Echoing Hooker's suggestion for a seamless continuation, Turner proposed 'to Erect them simultaneously with the Centre, using the same Scaffolding, machinery & workshop as I have now at Kew'. Furthermore, he offered to build the wings 'for the same very moderate Sum' originally proposed: £8,500.[42] There would be

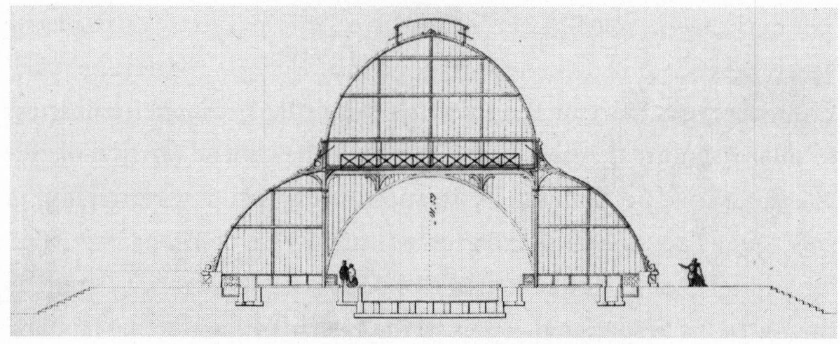

20. *The central section of the Palm House.*

no repeat of the previous delay, he promised. The workmen were now 'familiar with so novel a Structure, as was never before attempted'. The wings would be executed 'with singular dispatch' and the work completed within the year.[43]

The Commissioners did not share Turner's confidence. Nor did they heed Burton's advice that Turner's price was very moderate, that he had 'a large number of men habituated to the peculiar description of wrought iron work', and that in the 'machinery now made expressly for the purpose of bending the wrought iron ribs', Turner had 'a facility which no other Contractor possesses'.[44] Rather than regard Turner as a uniquely skilled engineer, the Commissioners considered him a tardy contractor. The wings, they decided, should be put out to tender. They instructed Burton to prepare detailed drawings and invite estimates from Turner and his English rival, John Jones of Birmingham.

Fortunately for Turner, Jones declared himself too busy to tender. Thus unopposed, Turner saw an opportunity to increase his original estimate. In his new plans, Burton had extended the length of each wing by an additional bay. But the expansion alone did not account for Turner's new price. The increase of £2,400 Turner justified in terms of the actual costs of construction – nearly double the amount that he had anticipated. The earlier figure he attributed to his inexperience and careless business practice. The previous estimate, he freely admitted, had been made 'in an offhand way, & not the result of figures, or Calculations, but in a wholesale manner supposed it would do, and was eager to secure the whole Job together'.[45] Surprisingly, his candour did not spoil his case. Burton stated that he thought the amount fair and moderate. Turner's original estimate, he told the Commissioners, had been wholly unrealistic. On Burton's advice, the Commissioners accepted Turner's increased price.

At the start of September 1846, the Commissioners appointed

Turner the contractor for the wings, and Grissell – who had recently parted company with Peto – the subcontractor for the masonry work. With his design skills and bespoke machinery, Turner had engineered himself into the position of primary contractor. But the very ingenuity that had won him Burton's regard came at considerable personal cost. Turner's ceaseless desire to innovate would soon bring him to the brink of financial ruin.

# 9
# The Great Experiment

The Palm House was more than a building; it was an elaborate scientific experiment. To engineer an artificial climate required the careful regulation of multiple elements: heat, light, air and water. Whatever the weather outside, the Palm House had to be maintained at a constant temperature of 80 degrees Fahrenheit (26 degrees Celsius). Any miscalculation or fluctuation could prove fatal for the plants within. According to John Claudius Loudon, the unnatural environment of a glasshouse threatened its inmates: 'the plants inclosed are in the most artificial situation in which they can be placed', he observed in 1824; 'constant and unremitting attention' was needed 'to counteract the tendency of that artificial situation to destroy them'.[1]

How, then, could glasshouses be designed to keep plants alive? There were many competing theories in the horticultural press. For some, the most important issue was the quality of the glass; others stressed the significance of ventilation. The advocates of hot-water-pipe heating systems opposed the devotees of steam. Some suggested planting in pits, others pots. To address such questions, Hooker drew on practical expertise both at Kew and elsewhere. He sought to combine the most advanced technology with the latest scientific research. As the recipient of government funding, the Palm House could not afford to fail. But it was no easy matter to recreate the tropics on the outskirts of London.

To gather information, Sir William dispatched envoys – in the shape of the architect and his own son – to visit the Jardin des Plantes in Paris, Kew's main European model and rival. Hooker was particularly interested in the performance of the pair of iron conservatories erected between 1834 and 1836 by Charles Rohault de Fleury. In December 1844, in the course of a trip to Paris, Decimus Burton reported that the two glasshouses were heated by a steam system with 'only 2 boilers' and reached a mere 60 degrees Fahrenheit at the time of his visit.[2] He noted ventilation points 'at the bottom of the sides of the houses at the top & also in the wall at the back – & at the summits of the roofs', but added that the garden staff did not 'think it advisable to use all the modes of ventilation even in summer'.[3] The palms and bamboos were grown in tubs in a sunken area, and were moved outside for the summer months. 'As regards the appearance & beauty of the house', Burton was 'decidedly of opinion that these are more satisfactorily produced by avoiding sunk pits – & having the mold at the level of the paths'.[4]

A month later, Sir William sent his son to Paris. This was Joseph's first destination on a tour of France and the Low Countries to establish his reputation among European naturalists: to make contact with leading botanists, compare botanic collections and arrange for plant exchanges.[5] He bore a letter of introduction to the illustrious scientific traveller Alexander von Humboldt, an old friend of his father. On first meeting with the seventy-five-year-old Humboldt, Joseph was taken aback, as he related to his mother: 'I went in and saw to my horror a paunchy little German instead of a Humboldt'.[6] Although lacking in physical presence, Humboldt's mind was as alert as ever, Joseph told his father: 'Humboldt I saw very often, sometimes three times a day, for he was never tired of coming to ask me questions about my voyage, he certainly is quite a most wonderful man; with a sagacity & memory & capability for generalizing that are quite marvellous: I gave him my book, which delighted him much'.[7] Joseph well knew how pleased his father would be to hear that his son had won over the grand old man of European science.

Joseph was delighted by the museum at the Jardin des Plantes, but far from enchanted by the gardens themselves. Lacking the green expanse of Kew, the Jardin des Plantes appeared poorly laid out: 'there is no grass & the walks have too public an appearance. The great avenues quite hide either the Galleries or Hot-houses', he complained.[8] Joseph visited the conservatories twice, and judged the collection to be much larger than that of Kew – perhaps double the number of species – but considered the plants themselves in 'a very inferior condition'. As for Rohault de Fleury's 'great square houses', the glass roofs were blackened with soot: '3 chimneys in the back wall pour out volumes of smoke on the roof itself – this latter is not sloped enough for the water to wash it in rain time'. The roofs were further disfigured by 'a wire protection from hail'. In contrast to Burton, who had noted multiple points of ventilation, Joseph observed, with condescending incredulity, that they had 'no ventilation whatever', and that the gardener and botanist who showed him around seemed 'surprised that their things burn in the summer'.[9]

Despite their conflicting reports, Burton and Joseph concurred on the necessity of ventilation. This was an issue much debated in the horticultural press. According to John Lindley, 'the vice of hothouse architects' lay in their neglect of adequate ventilation.[10] Lindley argued that hothouses should not only be ventilated, but that plants would be strengthened if the air were kept in active circulation, mimicking the action of a breeze. The Palm House was designed to allow air to enter through boxes low in the wall and exit through sashes high in the gallery and upper lantern. At an early stage in the planning process, Turner proposed 'Roof Sliding Sashes for Ventilating and Getting rid of the impure air from the Summit of the House'.[11] He designed a lever mechanism that connected the rolling sashes in the roof and vertical sashes in the lantern, so that, with one easy winding motion, they could all be opened and closed simultaneously.

As the future custodian of the Palm House, John Smith was invited to contribute his views on the practical arrangements. According to Smith, it was in the course of a discussion with Turner on ventilation that he first raised the matter of the glass. What kind did Turner plan to use? Holding up his hands in an expansive gesture, Turner exclaimed, 'Glass, you won't see there is Glass it will be so clear'.[12] Turner's flamboyant response surprised the down-to-earth Smith. Turner derived his vision of dazzling translucence from Loudon's notion of the 'almost perfect transparence' of curvilinear glass-houses.[13] According to Loudon, there was no limit to the architectural potential of glass, 'this elegant material produced from seemingly the most useless debris of our globe'.[14] Loudon projected '*houses of magnificent forms, and almost as light within as the open day*', with roofs 'raised to the height of a hundred or a hundred and fifty feet from the ground, to admit of the tallest oriental trees'. He imagined hothouses-cum-menageries with monkeys and 'the undisturbed flight of appropriate birds' among the tropical trees.[15] For Loudon, as for Turner, the near invisibility of glass allowed for a marvellous, transformative flood of light.

But such visions of transparency did not impress Smith. 'This will be very pretty', he replied to Turner, 'but how are the plants to be shaded in summer?'[16] There was a real danger, he warned, of scorching. On bright summer days, the plant houses at Kew were covered with canvas shades, fixed on roller blinds of Smith's own devising. But, for a structure the immense size and complex shape of the Palm House, such a system was both impractical and prohibitively expensive. The only way to overcome the problem, suggested Smith, would be to use green glass. '"Green glass", repeated Mr Turner, with some degree of astonishment'. Yes, confirmed Smith, the type of glass formerly used in the plant houses at Kew, which Mr Aiton called 'Stourbridge green'.[17]

In proposing 'Stourbridge green', Smith was suggesting a cheap form of crown glass, tinged green by traces of iron oxide. By the 1840s, it would have been considered old-fashioned and poor quality. In his *Encyclopædia of Gardening*, first published in 1822, Loudon recommended using the best crown glass in hothouses, condemning green glass as insufficiently transparent. 'Economy, as to the quality of the glass', wrote Loudon, 'is defeating the intention of building hot-houses, which is to imitate a natural climate . . . as perfectly as possible'. He warned that green glass blocked 'a free influx of light', and that the plants took on a 'sickly pale etiolated appearance'.[18] But Loudon recognized that the price of glass posed a problem for gardeners. Until 1845, a hefty excise duty was imposed on glass manufactured in Britain: twice the actual value of the product. One way to avoid the tax, the horticultural writer Charles McIntosh suggested, was to reduce the size of the greenhouse panes. 'If economy be an object of consideration', advised McIntosh, the crown glass could be 'cut under the size subject to duty', which would 'make a considerable difference in the expense'.[19]

The last thing that Turner wanted was to give the Palm House a cut-price look. The plans specified the use of large, curved panes of sheet glass. Considerably more expensive than crown glass, sheet glass was manufactured according to a new process that had originated in France. The size of the panes allowed for the admission of more light, but the price placed it beyond the reach of most gardeners; McIntosh considered the use of sheet glass in hothouses the 'utmost extravagance'.[20] But the deep pockets of the Duke of Devonshire had stretched to sheet glass at Chatsworth, and Burton had followed suit in specifying its use at both Regent's Park and Kew.

One of the reasons that sheet glass was so expensive was the level of duty that it attracted. Luckily for Turner, six months after he had signed the initial contract for the Palm House, Robert Peel announced the repeal of the glass tax. This was a move designed to stimulate the glass industry, to 'give full and unrestricted play to capital and enterprise in this country', as Peel announced in his budget speech. 'It is difficult to foresee', the Prime Minister declared, 'to what perfection this beautiful fabric may not be brought . . . to what new purposes glass, manufactured by our own skill and capital, may not be applied'.[21] The repeal of the duty was welcomed across the political spectrum. The *Mechanics' Magazine*, a low-priced, scientific weekly aimed at working men, hailed the 'emancipation' of glass manufacture 'from the fiscal restrictions by which it has been so long enthralled'.[22]

But the expansion of the glass industry and the technical advances anticipated by Peel were not immediate. There was a serious shortage of skilled glass-blowers in Britain, and major glass companies competed to recruit workers from France and Belgium. The British glass industry currently lagged far behind its European competitors. Over the course of a few months in 1845, the *Mechanics' Magazine* serialized a 'Memoir on the Manufacture of Glass in Bohemia' to diffuse 'knowledge of the processes by which the unfettered manufactures of other countries have attained to such superior excellence'.[23]

In November 1845, Turner looked to Europe to source glass of the highest quality for his prestigious hothouse projects. In a letter which acknowledged the problem of scorching – but ignored Smith's recommendation of green glass – Turner informed the Office of Woods that he was planning a continental trip:

> going to Antwerp, and possibly to Bohemia, in pursuit of a very superior coloured glass, the violet tinge; or azure hue, which I understand will be a wonderful improvement for the Royal Palm House and Inner Circle Winter Garden, and indeed, all horticultural structures, as it beautifully softens the light, and hinders the rays of bright sunshine destroying as much as it does when transmitted through the clear glass, which is found to scorch and wither the tender foliage, as they first appear, and subsequently the blossoms, except they are most carefully blinded by some artificial means.[24]

There is no record of the Office of Woods' response, but it is unlikely that the Commissioners welcomed Turner's proposal, either for patriotic or, more likely, for economic reasons. In any case, the following week, Hooker came up with a far more attractive proposition – one that had the advantage of being both domestic and scientific.

Given the technical problems involved in engineering an artificial climate, Hooker suggested that the issue of tinted glass should be referred to Robert Hunt, 'the only person in the Kingdom' capable of giving an informed view of the matter. Hunt had conducted a series of 'ingenious experiments' on the effect of coloured glass on the growth of plants.[25] What was more, Hooker told the Commissioners, Hunt was employed within their very own government department.

Robert Hunt had just started work at the Museum of Economic Geology, in Whitehall, collecting mining statistics, organizing geological maps and arranging specimens. The museum was part of the Geological Survey of Britain – effectively, the first government-funded scientific research institution. The Survey was the creation of Sir Henry De la Beche, a man driven by a deep conviction in the power of science. Of radical persuasion, De la Beche aimed to foster science at all levels of society. He promoted a collegial atmosphere among the young men employed by the Survey, and encouraged the autodidact Hunt, newly arrived in London, to pursue his own scientific research.

For Hunt, the position at the Survey marked his arrival at the heart of metropolitan science. He was in his late thirties, and had forged a scientific career for himself through a combination of aptitude, hard work and self-promotion. Unlike most men of science, Hunt had no private means. He came from a modest West Country background, and began his working life as a chemist and druggist. Initially, he had literary ambitions, but his early ventures into poetry and playwriting met with little success, so he turned his hand to scientific experimentation. Hunt was particularly excited by photography, a technology then very much in its infancy. The daguerreotype had been invented in France in 1838, and the calotype was patented in Britain in 1841 by William Fox Talbot (who had been one of Hooker's supporters in the campaign to secure Kew). Hunt was confident enough to begin a correspondence on photochemistry with the renowned mathematician and astronomer Sir John Herschel, the most eminent figure in British science. Herschel was keenly interested in photography, and had discovered, in 1839, how to fix images by using a sodium hyposulfite bath (which, to this day, forms the main constituent of photographic fixing solutions). Herschel recognized Hunt's talent and aspirations, and adopted him as a protégé.

With Herschel's support, Hunt embarked on his own photochemical experiments, and started to make his way in scientific circles. In 1840, he was appointed secretary to the Royal Cornwall Polytechnic Society, a foundation devoted to public education and technical innovation. Through contact with the Cornish tin-mining industry, he developed an interest in mining and geology. From 1841 on, Hunt presented papers at the British Association for the Advancement of Science (where Herschel was president of the mathematics section). It was through such activities that Hunt came to the attention of De la Beche, who invited him, in 1845, to take up the post of keeper of mining records at the Museum of Economic Geology, in London.[26]

To supplement his income and boost his reputation, Hunt developed a parallel career as a popular science writer. He submitted articles to a range of scientific and art journals, and published two books: *A Popular Treatise on the Art of Photography* (1841), which offered the first history of the new technology, and *Researches on Light* (1844), which combined an account of the photographic process with investigations into the properties of sunlight, including the sun's influence on plant growth. While much of Hunt's work summarized the findings of others, he also included accounts of his own experiments.

Hunt reported his initial findings to the 1842 meeting of the British Association for the Advancement of Science. He had prepared six boxes, with different coloured glass lids, in which he had sown a variety of seeds – mignonette, parsley and cress – and planted bulbs and tubers. He noted the different rates at which the plants grew and any changes in their patterns of development and health. His results were encouraging enough to convince him 'of the existence of some secret principle in light' that he hoped 'to render evident to the senses by its operations, although it may not be sensible to the human eye'.[27] Extrapolating from the photographic process, Hunt proposed that the sun generated not only heat and light, but also the invisible force of *energia*, which he later renamed *actinism*: the power to effect chemical change. Hunt identified actinism – 'ray power' – as the secret principle of sunlight that governed not only photography but, more significantly, plant life on earth.

Over the course of several years of experimentation with plants and coloured glass, Hunt discovered that blue glass prompted germination. From this, he concluded that blue glass admitted the least light and the greatest quantity of chemical or actinic rays. Red glass, he found, stimulated flowering and transmitted the most heat. Yellow glass admitted a high level of light but a low level of actinic rays, and promoted the formation of woody tissue. Of all the types of glass tested, green glass interfered the least with the plants' natural patterns of growth. It blocked the scorching rays of the sun, but allowed for the transmission of near normal levels of light and actinic radiation.[28]

It was a measure of Hunt's growing scientific reputation that Hooker requested his view on the matter of the Palm House glass. In his report, Hunt dismissed Turner's suggestion of blue or violet glass: 'these colours would, by obstructing light, give an increased action to the chemical principle of the sun-beam, and consequently excite an unnatural growth in the palms'.[29] Hunt had no hesitation in recommending glass 'coloured with oxide of copper to a tint which may be called pea-green'. Green glass would 'admit light and chemical power in the same proportions as white glass', but would obstruct the rays 'which produce the "*scorching*" desired to be avoided'.[30]

To be consulted on such a high-profile building raised Hunt's status both in official circles and the scientific community. For the first time, he could put his theories into practice by advising on an actual horticultural structure. For Hunt, the Palm House functioned as a kind of grand laboratory. 'The Royal Palm House', he proudly told an audience at the Society of Arts, 'is an experiment on a great scale'.[31] Hunt's ideas on glazing were indeed innovative. In attempting to identify a glass which would prevent the sun's scorching effect but allow for the healthy development of plants, Hunt was breaking new ground. As Henrik Schoenefeldt has pointed out, Hunt's attempts to develop a spectrally selective glass anticipated the solar control glass commonly used in modern structures.[32]

Hunt's work on the Palm House glass prompted increased interaction between the Geological Survey and Kew. At the start of 1846, De la Beche approached Hooker for advice on appointing a botanist to work on fossil flora for the Survey. Never one to miss an opportunity, Sir William suggested his own son. While Joseph was no expert on paleobotany, he had collected fossil wood during the course of the Antarctic voyage. Since returning from his tour of France and Belgium, Joseph had not yet managed to land a permanent job. He had held a temporary post lecturing in botany at Edinburgh University, but, despite letters of recommendation from figures as august as Alexander von Humboldt, he had failed to secure the professorship at Edinburgh for local political reasons. Now, he was back at West Park, living on an annual naval allowance of £200, working on the *Flora Antarctica*. The position at the Geological Survey offered Joseph a salary of £150 a year, the opportunity to deploy his botanical expertise, and the chance to join the lively group of young scientists assembled by De la Beche. Given the scarcity of botanical openings, he gratefully took up the post procured by his father.

Joseph found his work at the Survey both fascinating and frustrating. It required all his ingenuity to extrapolate the structure of plants from their fragmentary fossil remains. His focus was the vegetation of the Carboniferous period, when large swamp forests covered much of what was to become northern Europe, and, greatly as Joseph relished the challenge of seeking 'to reclothe the globe with the vegetation to whose decomposition we are indebted for coal', he recognized that it was an impossible task: 'the number of species, genera, and even orders, of which scarce a trace remains, must far outnumber those which are recognizable'.[33] Over the summer of 1846, he visited the coalfields of South Wales, Somerset and Bristol, to search for fossil remains. His research into coal would have brought him into close contact with Robert Hunt, in his capacity as keeper of mining records.

While Joseph was poring over the peculiarities of the structure of *Stigmaria* (fossil roots), Hunt was setting up experiments to determine the precise shade of glass required for the Palm House. In July 1846, the Commissioners of Woods informed Hunt of their decision to adopt glass of 'the tint commonly called pea-green'; but, 'as the adjustment of the tint may be of great importance, and involve some nicety' in matters which Hunt alone could judge, he should be responsible for selecting the specimen glass.[34] Hunt requested that Turner procure 'from all parts of the Kingdom, green glasses of every degree of intensity and variety of shades; in the manufacture of which the chemical colouring ingredients were necessarily very different' – thirty-seven samples in all.[35] Many of the glass samples were specially prepared for the purpose by Charles Cowper, the chemist employed by the largest and most innovative glass company of the day, Chance Brothers – the same manufacturer that had supplied the glass for the Great Conservatory at Chatsworth.

Hunt wanted to compare the samples of new glass with the traditional 'Stourbridge green', the crown glass previously used at Kew. He applied to John Smith for some panes, which were prised from the roof of one of the old plant houses. Hunt had a second, more unusual request for Smith. He planned to measure the effect of the various types of glass on actual plant material. Could the curator kindly supply him with the 'leaves of palms to experiment upon'?[36]

Smith duly dispatched a variety of palm leaves, including foliage from the dwarf-fan, cabbage-tree and date palms. But Smith was deeply sceptical of Hunt's experiments:

> it is a puzzle to one, how he, sitting in a room in London, in the month of November, with palm leaves before him which he had perhaps never seen before and [k]new nothing of this nature, could determine by any scientific process the degree of opacity to be imparted to glass of whatever color it may be, that would prevent the sun in summer from scorching the palm-leaves, and at the same time not injure their health.[37]

Smith was always suspicious of scientists who claimed to understand horticultural matters, but it is likely that he was not alone in his scepticism. To guard against such a response, Hunt detailed his methods in his report of December 1846 to the Office of Woods; to publicize his experiments and raise his scientific profile, he explained them at greater length in lectures delivered to both the British Association for the Advancement of Science and to the Society of Arts.[38]

Hunt subjected every piece of glass to various sets of experiments to determine the level of light, heat and actinic radiation that it admitted. First of all, he extracted the colouring matter from the palm leaves, and used it to form a solution and to stain paper. Then, to measure the degree of chemical change, he followed methods devised by Herschel, using light-sensitive silver-chloride paper and the palm-leaf-stained paper. To determine the amount of scorching, he exposed vessels filled with the palm-leaf solution to the action of sunlight, transmitted through the different kinds of glass. The length of time that the palm-leaf solution retained its green colouring was used to gauge the level of scorching (see Plate 20). While Hunt admitted that 'a very considerable difference may exist between the effects produced upon a living plant, and its dead juices', he was nevertheless confident that he had identified the glass sample best suited to the Palm House.[39]

It was a glass of the palest yellow-green; its shade more a hint than a colour. According to Hunt's experiments, the glass admitted all the light and actinic radiation, but obstructed the scorching rays. The specimen glass had been prepared by Cowper, and was free of manganese oxide, which was generally used in the manufacture of sheet glass. Hunt had insisted on excluding manganese oxide because it imparted a pinkish hue to the glass that would allow for the entrance of scorching rays. The glass selected, Burton calculated, would add an extra £350 to the cost of the glazing. Hunt himself received a fee of twenty-five pounds for 'experimentally examining and reporting upon the samples of Glass'.[40]

The specimen glass was sent for approval to Hooker. Before passing judgement, Hooker sought a second opinion from Charles Daubeny, the Oxford Professor of Chemistry and Botany. A decade previously, Daubeny had conducted his own research on the effect of light on plants, and was concerned that the glass might be insufficiently transparent. He asked the opinion of a colleague, Professor Baden Powell, a mathematician and physicist, who had also conducted investigations into the operation of light. Powell did not raise any significant objections, but Daubeny still urged caution. He advised

Hooker to test the glass on a smaller scale before applying it to his 'magnificent Palm House'. 'Light', he reminded Sir William, 'is the only element which art cannot supply for growing Plants'. Hooker should think carefully before taking a decision that might diminish 'the quantity of light which the Sun in this murky climate of ours doles out to us'.[41]

Hunt's methods were so new that the eminent professors felt unqualified to judge his findings. The functioning of the glass could only be ascertained through a trial, but there was no time to erect and monitor a test structure. Instead, the matter was decided over dinner. One evening in January 1847, Hunt and Hooker were invited to dine at Burton's town house to discuss the Oxford professors' letters.[42] Hunt must have acquitted himself to Sir William's satisfaction. The fact that he had selected a pale green hue much like that of the widely used crown glass was in his favour. The tint had effectively already been tried and tested, as Sir William wrote to the Commissioners:

> Even before Mr Hunt had instituted his important experiments with glass . . . I had expressed a wish that we might be provided with a kind which should more resemble that of the 'ordinary' kind of glass . . . which in practice has been long found better suited to the vigorous state of plants than pure sheet glass. Mr Hunt's admirable Report has proved, upon scientific principles, the superiority of this kind, and I am of the opinion that the glass selected by that gentleman is well suited to our purpose.[43]

Echoing Hooker, Hunt also used the parallel with horticultural practice to validate his findings. 'The tint of colour is not very different from that of the old crown glass, and many practical men state that they find their plants flourish much better under this kind of glass than under the white sheet glass which is now so commonly employed', he told the members of the British Association for the Advancement of Science. 'It is satisfactory thus to find practice confirming the conclusions of science'.[44] Others were less charitable. Charles McIntosh observed that 'the experiments of Mr Hunt do little more than lead us back to the days when good crown glass of a greenish hue was in high repute for hothouse roofs'.[45] John Smith was even more dismissive: Hunt 'furnished an elaborate report, full of scientific terms, which it is not necessary to comment upon, which ended with recommending the specimen of glass sent him, as the best. Thus Mr Aiton's "Stourbridge Green" in its old age received the stamp of science'.[46]

It is evident that horticulturalists received Hunt's findings with a degree of scepticism. His experiments were considered worthy of satire by *Punch*. 'Mr Hunt', the magazine reported in 1844, 'held a buttercup over a lighted candle, and, though the buttercup was not melted, the flower was considerably damaged'.[47] But his theories gained widespread acceptance and circulation (due, in part, to Hunt's own prolific publishing activities). Charles Darwin found Hunt's ideas convincing, and entered into a correspondence with him, requesting his help in locating coloured glass so that he could carry out similar experiments himself.[48] Without hesitation, Hunt recommended that Darwin approach the company that had supplied the glass for the Palm House: Chance Brothers – the most skilled and technically advanced glass manufacturers in the country.

Spread over many acres, the vast establishment of Chance Brothers in Smethwick, near Birmingham, appeared more like a town than a factory. Bisected by a canal, connected by roads and alleyways, the glassworks contained rows of sheds, furnaces, kilns, warehouses and cottages for workers. 'If seen from a certain distance by moonlight, when quiet and smokeless', the American consul Elihu Burritt wrote in 1868 (by which time the company had expanded even further), the works might look 'to an imaginative eye like a great nest of cathedrals and Turkish mosques . . . lofty brick spires tapering all the way but not to a point; towers and turrets of all dimensions; conical domes elongated at the top into a chimney.' But when, as often occurred, the factory worked all through the night, the romantic vision turned into a hellish spectacle: 'all aglow with its fiery industries', the scene became one 'which Virgil and Dante would have described'.[49]

Chance Brothers dominated the rapidly expanding British glass industry. By 1847, just two years after the glass tax had been repealed,

21. *Chance Brothers Glass Works, Smethwick, 1857.*

the number of British glass firms had risen from fourteen to twenty-four. 'The demand for glass was so great, that the manufacturers were in despair', recalled Henry Chance, the proprietor. 'Glass-houses sprang up like mushrooms. Joint-stock companies were established to satisfy the universal craving for window panes'.[50] As an established sheet-glass works, Chance Brothers enjoyed a distinct advantage. It had been the first company to introduce the sheet-glass process from France to Britain, in 1832. In addition, the company had secured its own supply of sulphate of soda (required in sheet-glass production) by constructing a chemical works in neighbouring Oldbury.

Barges bearing sand, coal and clay delivered directly to the factory wharves. The clay was required to fashion immense pots to contain the molten glass. With a life expectancy of some seven weeks, each pot could hold about two tons of 'metal', as the vitreous liquid was called. Sometimes pots would shatter, flooding the furnace with their white-hot contents. There was usually no explanation for these 'catastrophes of pots', Henry Chance sadly observed.[51] The entire glass-making process was hazardous and unpredictable. Exposed to the terrible heat of the furnace, the workers wore no protective clothing, and were often bare-legged and shoeless. The length of time required to bring the 'metal' to working temperature was so variable that labourers might be roused to start their shifts in the middle of the night.

The whole enterprise effectively depended on the skills of individual glass-blowers, in particular on the French and Belgian workmen whom the company had recruited for their sheet-glass expertise. The vocabulary of the Smethwick glassworks was peppered with French words: boys in the workforce were known as *gamins*, the instrument for flattening sheet glass was a *polissoir*, and shifts were called 'journeys', from the French *journée*.[52] Not altogether fancifully, Elihu Burritt imagined the company as a great vessel powered by the glass-blowers' lungs. 'The human breath forced through all those iron pipes', marvelled Burritt, 'if put in one volume, ought to be enough to propel a ship of the line across the Atlantic'.[53]

To perform their key role, the glass-blowers stood on platforms located in front of holes in the furnace wall, wielding their iron pipes dipped in molten glass. The platforms were erected over a pit to allow the glass-blowers to swing their pipes from side to side, while simultaneously blowing the glass into long cylinders. To maintain the consistency of the cylinders, the glass-blowers would, from time to time, raise the pipes vertically above their heads, blowing all the while. Whirling their pipes in great arcs, the blowers steadily inflated the liquid glass into cylinders six feet long. Burritt struggled to express their extraordinary movements: 'Nothing in the working of other metals is like these strange manipulations. That is not the word for them either, for the mouth seems to have more to do in the matter than the hand'.[54]

When the glass-blower judged that the cylinder had reached the required length, he removed its ends. The cylinder was then split open along its inner surface with a diamond-tipped cutting rod. The opened cylinder was next conveyed to the flattening furnace, where it was placed on a stone and a flattener applied the 'polissoir' – a wooden block attached to a handle – to iron the wavy surface of the glass smooth. Finally, the sheet was taken to a kiln, where it was annealed: reheated and slowly cooled, to toughen the glass. Then the panes would be taken to the warehouse for sorting into grades of varying quality: best, seconds, thirds, fourths, and lastly 'H', which designated poor-quality glass, assigned to horticultural purposes.

But, of course, the 'H' category did not apply to the glass for the Palm House. The immense order for Kew specified robust 21-ounce glass (the thickness of sheet glass was measured by weight, in ounces per superficial foot). Charles Cowper personally oversaw the constituents of the Palm House glass. Following Hunt's instructions, he made sure that the pale yellow-green tint was achieved through the addition of copper oxide. To avoid any hint of pink, all manganese oxide was excluded. Towards the end of the manufacturing process, a further step was required. Of the 16,000 panes of sheet glass produced, almost all were bent into the gentle curve required to match Turner's wrought-iron sash bars. Finally, the panes were packed for dispatch by barge. The canal system offered a far safer route for the transport of glass than the potholed roads. What was more, the Grand Junction Canal extended all the way from Birmingham to London, joining the Thames at Brentford, just across the river from Kew.

The most important mechanisms in the Palm House were the heating and watering systems. Between 1845 and 1846, Grissell and Peto formed the furnace rooms and dug the tunnel at Kew. The underground passageway linked the Palm House to the coal yard at the garden boundary, by the road from Richmond to Kew Green. It carried a railway track for the transport of coke and ashes, and flues for the discharge of smoke from the boilers. The 'subterranean chimney', as Hooker termed it, led to an 'ornamental shaft, at a considerable distance from the building itself', designed by Burton to resemble an Italian bell tower.[55] The campanile, as it is known, ingeniously functioned both as a chimney and water tower. On its upper level, a water tank and steam pump powered a pressurized sprinkling system to produce artificial rain in the Palm House. Positioned near the garden wall, the chimney did not interfere with the view of the glasshouse, and provided a striking termination to

22. *The Campanile (chimney-cum-water tower).*

Nesfield's main avenue, the Broad Walk, leading from the entrance to the pond.

As with all elements of the Palm House, the heating arrangements went through a number of modifications during the design process. The contract specified that Turner was required to fit a heating apparatus capable of maintaining the glasshouse at a temperature of 80 degrees Fahrenheit (26 degrees Celsius) when the external temperature was 20 degrees Fahrenheit (the equivalent of −6 degrees Celsius). This might appear an exacting requirement, but winters in nineteenth-century London were harsher than those of today, and the mercury could easily drop to well below freezing. Although precise in the matter of temperature, the contract did not specify the type of heating system to be supplied. This left Turner free to determine the best mode of heating the immense structure. But, inevitably, on a matter as critical as heating, both Hooker and Smith had their own opinions. Advancing through consultation, trial and error, the decision-making process was driven, as always, by Turner's restless ingenuity.

Turner immediately rejected the heating plans drawn up by the civil engineer employed by Burton. The architect had envisaged a steam heating system powered by six large marine boilers, with steam pipes running beneath the base of a sunken planting area. Turner preferred a more recently invented system combining hot-water pipes and tanks. He devised a plan whereby hot water would circulate in cast-iron pipes running along the sides of the building and in open ironwork cases beside the paths. Large hot-water tanks would extend beneath the sunken plant pits and under the stone flags of the paths. The combination of tanks and pipes was intended to deliver heat to plant roots and raise the temperature and humidity of the atmosphere.

Hooker and Smith, with a focus on day-to-day practicalities, were concerned that the heating system should be able to respond swiftly to changes in external temperature. They thought that greater flexibility and speed would be achieved with twelve average-sized boilers, rather than six large ones. Accordingly, the plans were changed to include a dozen Burbidge and Healy patent boilers, located in two basement boiler rooms. These were round boilers with a ribbed surface and sliding fire doors, generally considered to be both efficient and resilient. The number of boilers in use could be increased or decreased, according to the weather. This would allow for greater precision in regulating the Palm House climate.

The underground heating arrangements also impacted on the Palm House planting scheme. Both the director and curator were concerned about the pits. Hooker had initially thought that sunken areas would be useful to accommodate the tallest palms, but, after discussion with Smith and other gardeners, he changed his mind. Pits were unsightly

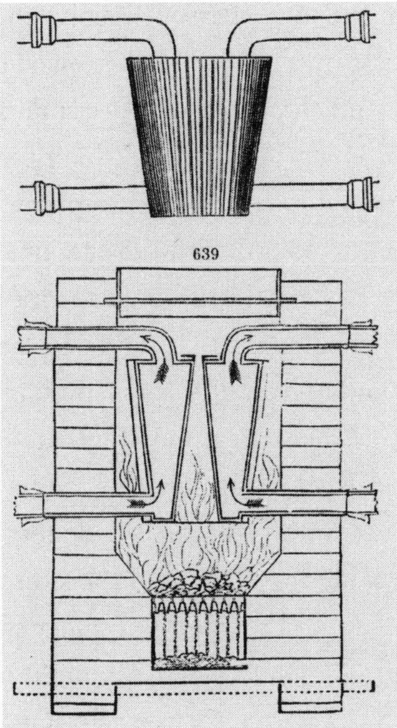


23. *Burbidge and Healy's patent boiler.*

and gloomy, he told Burton in December 1846. Labourers would find it difficult to manoeuvre the immense pots in and out of the pits. Worse still, stagnant air would gather in the hollows, which would have an unwholesome effect on the vegetation. 'We shall do better', he declared, 'to have the whole area of the House of one uniform level'.[56]

Then, in May 1847, three years into the project, Turner abruptly insisted on a change. The heating scheme which he had installed at the Winter Garden in Regent's Park was not working properly. The underground pipe system was incapable of generating even the more moderate heat required for the Winter Garden. The terms of the Kew contract made Turner directly responsible for the success (or otherwise) of the heating system, so it was imperative that he ensure its proper functioning. He quickly revised the plans. There would be only one tank now, he determined. Rainwater falling on the roof would drain through the hollow cast-iron pillars into the tank. The hot-water piping would be greatly extended: an intricate network would loop its way throughout the Palm House for an astonishing four and a half miles. The stone flooring would have to go. In its place, Turner substituted an iron grating, much to John Smith's dismay: 'it was with a degree of horror', wrote the curator, 'that I learned that the floor on which the plants were to be grown, was to be of perforated cast iron squares with hotwater pipes underneath it'.[57] Not only was this an unwelcome alteration, it was also expensive: a four-foot square of cast iron cost three pounds, a scandalized Smith noted.

But, in the end, even Smith had to concede that the heating system seemed to work. 'I may here say', he noted in his account of the Gardens, 'that I was satisfied that the 12 ribbed boilers of Messrs Burbidge and Healy were more than amply sufficient to maintain a temperature suitable to the cultivation of palms and other tropical plants'.[58] The problem, as far as the curator was concerned, was the underground conditions. The garden labourers had to push great trucks of coke in the sweltering

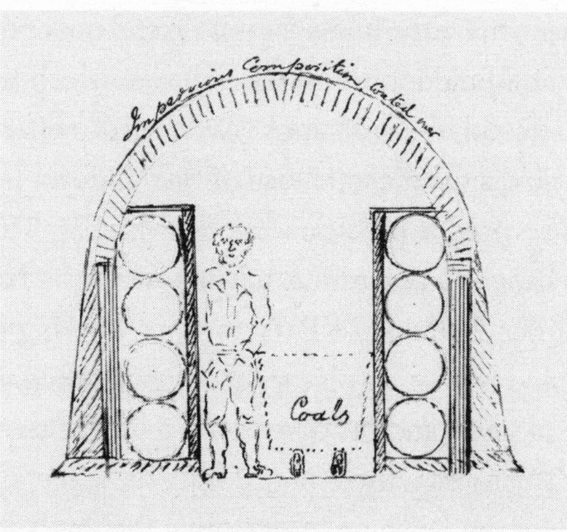


24. *A sketch of the Palm House tunnel by Richard Turner.*

confines of the 550-foot tunnel: 'the flues become so excessive hot for a considerable distance from the boilers', Smith complained to Hooker, 'that the heat is almost unbearable by the men conveying the fuel'.[59]

And then there was the flooding. As Smith had said from the very start, the Palm House had been built in the wrong place. Water had started to seep from the boggy ground into the furnace rooms and tunnel as soon as they had been built. 'Oh, we will make that alright', Mr Burton had reassured him. 'And heedless of the water, the furnaces were erected and the boilers fitted'.[60] The architect had not given a thought to the practical implications. Furnaces did not work well on damp coke. Smith had been obliged to install a pump, and keep men working it constantly, to make sure that the boiler rooms remained reasonably dry. These problems would not disappear.

On 24 July 1847, the French daguerreotypist Antoine Claudet packed up his equipment at his premises at the Regent's Park Colosseum. He had only recently moved his photographic studio to the Colosseum, in the hope of expanding his clientele. After a period of decline, the building designed by the young Decimus Burton had recently reopened and was once again attracting the spectacle-hungry crowds. Claudet was the most prominent of a handful of commercial photographers licensed to practise Daguerre's technique in London.[61] He was best known as a portraitist, having photographed the French King, Louis Philippe, and Queen Victoria's mother, the Duchess of Kent. But he was also a man of science, a correspondent and friend of William Fox Talbot, and the inventor of various improvements in the photographic process, which he had patented and communicated to the Académie des Sciences, the Royal Society, and the British Association for the Advancement of Science. Robert Hunt was well

aware of his activities, and had discussed Claudet's findings in his 1844 book, *Researches on Light*.

But Claudet's commission today was unusual. He had been invited to take the portrait not of an eminent individual, but of a building – and an unfinished one at that. Sir William wanted to record the Palm House as it neared completion. Only the new art of photography could catch the great work in progress: one technological innovation to commemorate another. The wrought-iron framework of the Palm House had been completed, but only the central portion of the building was glazed. To take an external view, Claudet set his apparatus up at a distance, beyond the Broad Walk. It was only possible to capture the full extent of the structure at an angle. The delicate green sheen of the glazed centre contrasted with the long skeletal wings. The interior bore all the signs of recent building work: scaffolding, ladders, planks and a rigged tarpaulin. But these did not obscure the grace of the wide arches and spiralling stairs.

The daguerreotypes remain in Kew's archives today (see Plates 21 and 22). Posed at the centre of the interior view are two gentlemen in top hats and black tailcoats: one, with crossed arms, drapes himself casually on a high box; the other, stouter, squats on a low stool. Who are these seated figures? They have variously been identified as Decimus Burton and Richard Turner, and as Sir William and Joseph Hooker. Further back, in the middle ground, stands a bare-headed man in a light-coloured coat. His clothing suggests that he is less of a gentleman. A working man, keeping his distance. Might he be John Smith? Most obscure of all is the possible form of a top-hatted figure, erect on the stairs. For a biographer of the Palm House, the anonymity of the figures is at once frustrating and strangely fitting. The Palm House was not the product of any one individual. It was created through collaborative effort. And, as in the daguerreotype, the human figures are ultimately dwarfed by their achievement: the grand structure itself.

# 10

# The Princes *of the* Vegetable Kingdom

By July 1848, the workmen were putting the finishing touches to the Palm House. The last panes of glass were being fixed, the boilers fired up and the ironwork painted a shade of deep blue-green. Inside the Palm House, John Smith and his foreman surveyed the empty space. The new glasshouse was immense. It covered more than half an acre: four times the combined area of the former hothouses. For the time being, Smith could only hope to fill the central section. The wings would have to wait until sufficient numbers of fast-growing species had been raised in the nursery stoves.

In the vacant glasshouse, every surface seemed to throb with refracted heat. Smith cast his eyes around the structure with growing dismay: 'looking up, nothing but iron was to be seen in every direction in the form of massive iron rafters, girders, galleries, pillars, and staircase, and the hot iron floor on which we stood and the smooth stone shelves and paths round the house'. To Smith, the building appeared unrelentingly industrial, more like 'some dock-yard, smithy or iron railway station than a hothouse to grow tropical plants in'. However, he had little choice in the matter: 'but there it was, I was to make the best of it, and to be responsible for the good cultivation of the plants which were commenced to be put in'.[1]

Smith's sense that the iron structure was ill-suited to exotic vegetation arose partly from practical concerns – that the heat was too dry – and partly from cultural considerations. The idea that European industrial modernity was at odds with the luxuriance of tropical nature was well established. The speaker in Tennyson's poem 'Locksley Hall' (1842), for instance, fleetingly imagines escaping to an oriental island with 'Breadths of tropic shade and palms in cluster', where 'Droops the heavy-blossom'd bower, hangs the heavy-fruited tree'. In such an island paradise, the young man supposes that he might find

> enjoyment more than in this march of mind,
> In the steamship, in the railway, in the thoughts that
> shake mankind.

But the dream of tropical island life is banished almost as soon as it is entertained. The speaker ends by exhorting the reader to join him in the march of industrial and imperial progress, closing with a stirring – if somewhat confusing – image of the globe spinning into the future on railway tracks:

> Forward, forward let us range,
> Let the great world spin for ever down the ringing
> grooves of change.[2]

The challenge for Smith at Kew would be to unite the disparate spheres of iron modernity and tropical vegetation in a convincing spectacle. With its novel design, the Palm House – like Tennyson's poem – announced the triumph of technology. Smith's task was to mount a display that would evoke landscapes which most members of the public had only ever encountered through texts and images: in botanical works, novels, poetry, collections of voyages, illustration and landscape drawings. For, although they might never have experienced the tropics themselves, most visitors to Kew would have travelled there in their imaginations. The accounts of early nineteenth-century scientific travellers, Alexander von Humboldt foremost among them, created a popular appetite for natural history and botany. To draw the crowds, the Palm House would have to provide a convincing version of that fantasy realm. And the undisputed stars of the tropical show were the plants that lent their name to the building: the great palms of Kew.

Distinguished by their distinctive form from native trees, palms exceeded all European norms in terms of their height and the size of their leaves, their generative organs and fruit. Most palms produce a single stem which grows to its full diameter before it emerges from the ground. Unlike the trunk of a conventional tree, which expands in girth throughout its life, the stem of a palm maintains its fixed diameter and only gains in height. In the mid-nineteenth century, palms were generally classified as *endogens* – that is, as plants with inward growth (as opposed to *exogens*: plants with outward growth, which expand in diameter). These categories – long since rejected by modern biologists – arose from early observations of palm stem anatomy. It was mistakenly believed that the scattered vascular bundles which conduct water and carbohydrate throughout the plant originated in the palm stem's centre. The theory provided an explanation for the regularity of the column-like stems which bear the familiar leafy crowns. Palm leaves can be broadly divided between the pinnate (feather-shaped) and the palmate (fan-shaped) – like an outspread human palm. On the basis of this resemblance to the hand, the Latin word *palma* was applied to the whole family of plants.

The botanist P. Barry Tomlinson likens palms to 'an engineering structure, built by continually adding appendages of fixed dimensions to a central axis'.[3] This regular pattern of growth made palms the ideal plants to exhibit in the grand engineering structure of the Palm House. The shape of the palms was echoed in the Palm House design. Whether intentionally or not, Richard Turner evoked the junction of palm-leaf stalks to the trunk in his design of the cast-iron brackets atop the Palm House pillars. With the building's ironwork painted green, the slender columns would double the stems, and the curved ribs mirror the fronds. Such a perfect match between the man-made and the natural had the potential to overcome the cultural clash of iron modernity and lush vegetation.

But of more immediate concern to Smith was the need to agree a plan with his foreman on the best positions for the palms – not only those from the old hothouses, but also new specimens promised by donors, now that Kew was able to accommodate large palms in a suitably spacious glasshouse.

The grand scale of the Palm House was entirely fitting because of the particular cultural status of palms. Botanists and popular writers unfailingly began their descriptions of the palm family with the observation that Linnaeus regarded palms as the *principes*, or princes, of the vegetable kingdom. Linnaeus's massive work of taxonomy, the *Systema Naturæ*, was first published in 1735, and went through twelve editions during the author's lifetime. It provided eighteenth-century naturalists with a framework for viewing and naming the world; indeed, scientists still use the binomial nomenclature popularized by Linnaeus today. The second volume of Linnaeus's great work, the *Regnum Vegetabile*, was devoted to plants. An English translation, *A System of Vegetables*, prepared largely by the philosopher-botanist-poet, Erasmus Darwin (grandfather of Charles), appeared in 1783. At the start of the volume, the various orders of plants were classified according to the ranks of human society. Heading the list were the princely palms; beneath them came the trees (nobles) and the grasses (plebeians), followed by, among others, the ferns (colonists), the mosses (servants), the algae (slaves) and the fungi (vagabonds). Linnaeus asserted that palms were 'eminent for their prodigious height, beautiful for their unvaried simple perennial stem, crowned with an evergreen tuft of leaves, and rich with the choicest treasures of fruit'.[4] Not only did the size, beauty and productivity of palms justify the regal analogy, the foliage provided the crown and the fruit suggested jewelled adornment. With such an accolade from the founding father of the discipline, palms were assured of their place both within botany and the popular imagination. While botanists working on other plant families may have ignored the human rank assigned by Linnaeus, palm specialists have long celebrated the princely status of palms. It is notable that, until relatively recently, the journal of the International Palm Society was called *Principes*, only changing its name to *Palms* in 1999.

According to Linnaeus's hierarchical model of nature, the princes of the vegetable kingdom were closely associated with the princes of the animal kingdom: mankind. Palms were '*tributary to the Primates, or the first order of animals; in particular to the Prince their cohabitant*'.[5] For Linnaeus, this pairing of palms and humanity went back to the earliest times. In the *Systema Naturæ*, Linnaeus divided *Homo sapiens* into five races – wild man, American, European, Asiatic and African – and suggested that palms provided humanity with its original food source: 'Man dwells naturally within the tropics, and lives on the fruits of the palm tree; he *exists* in other parts of the world, and there makes shifts to feed on corn and flesh'.[6] To describe those who subsisted on palm fruits, Linnaeus used the Latin phrase

'*Palmis Lotophagus*', which evoked the *lotophagi*, the languorous lotus eaters of Greek mythology, encountered by Ulysses on his voyage. Unlike the favoured palm-zone dwellers, those in temperate climes were compelled to work to produce sufficient food through farming and hunting. For Linnaeus, as for many Europeans, the palm was an emblem of nature at its most benevolent, associated with abundance and a life of seductive ease.

The parallel established by Linnaeus between man and palm extended across the natural sciences. A standard nineteenth-century textbook on geology, for instance, Edward Hitchcock's *Elementary Geology* (1840), was illustrated with a chart that showed the occurrence of fossil plants and animals in various geological eras.[7] This

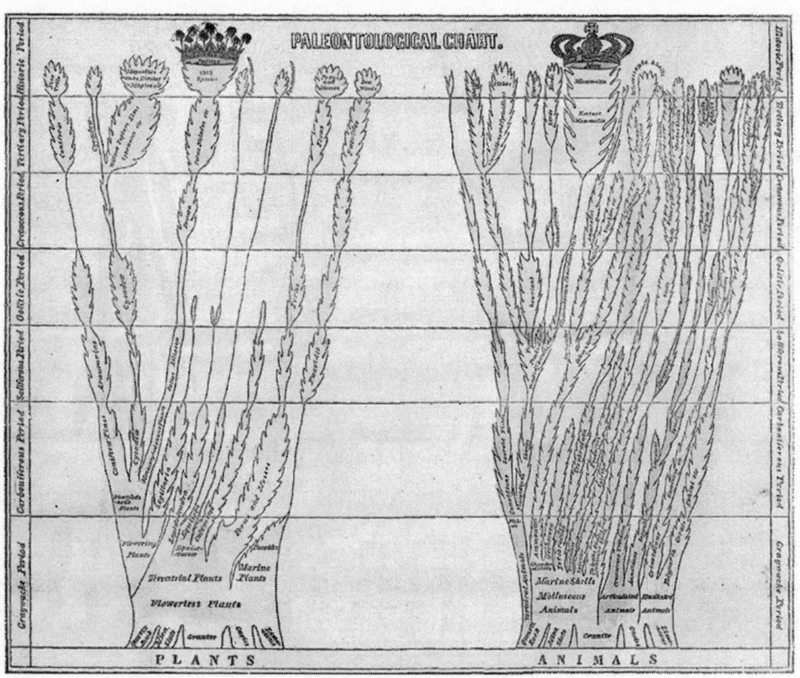


25. *A diagram of plant and animal life from Hitchcock's* Elementary Geology *(1840).*

was an early example of the diagram of the tree of life, subsequently made famous by Darwin.[8] On the chart, plant and animal life were represented as separate tree diagrams. Linnaeus's observation that palms were the princes of the vegetable kingdom was figured here in graphic form. The tree of plants was topped with a coronet of palms, and the tree of animals crowned by Man. In this vision of the biological past, palms and humanity were twinned as the ultimate expressions of life on earth.

Linnaeus's method of plant classification was sometimes known as the 'sexual' system because the reproductive parts of plants determined their particular class and order. In his 1760 *Dissertation on the Sexes of Plants*, Linnaeus cited an experiment carried out in Berlin, in 1749, on a Mediterranean fan palm, *Chamaerops humilis*. The Berlin Botanic Garden possessed a long-established female fan palm which had not fruited for over sixty years. To demonstrate that the female palm required fertilization from the male, an inflorescence, or complete flower head, from a male specimen in Leipzig, more than a hundred miles away, was conveyed by mail coach and suspended over the flowering Berlin palm. The 'experiment succeeded so well', a Berlin correspondent to London's Royal Society reported in 1753, 'that our palm-tree produced more than an hundred perfectly ripe fruit; from which we have already eleven young palm trees'.[9]

Such was the fame of this demonstration that later literature simply referred to it as the *Experimentum Berolinense* (the Berlin Experiment). So compelling did Linnaeus find it that he obtained some of the Berlin fruit for himself: 'some dates, the offspring of this impregnation, being planted in my garden, sprung up, and to this day continue to grow vigorously'.[10] The Berlin Experiment provided Linnaeus with neat proof of the existence of the sexes of plants. Although it was just one piece of evidence offered by Linnaeus, the Berlin

Experiment was sometimes presented by later writers as foundational for the whole of the sexual system. 'It was this circumstance chiefly that led Linnæus to the important discovery of the sexes of plants, upon which he based his system of classification', the author of *The Palm Tribes and their Varieties* claimed.[11] Thus palms appeared to be responsible for the whole system of Linnaean classification. Having furnished evidence for one of the key experiments in botanical science, the Berlin *Chamaerops humilis* survived, remarkably, until 1934; after its death, the trunk was placed on display in the entrance hall of the Berlin Botanical Museum, where it remains to this day.[12]

Unlike Linnaeus, the natural philosopher and novelist Jacques-Henri Bernardin de Saint-Pierre (1737–1814) advocated an aesthetic approach to nature. In his novel *Paul et Virginie* (1788), Bernardin created one of the most beguiling of tropical fictions. Generations of Europeans grew up on his tale of innocent love played out under palms and plantains. In contrast with the pastoral lovers depicted in the European literary tradition 'on banks of rivulets, in flowery meads, and beneath the shade of beech trees', Paul and Virginie reposed 'under cocoa, banana, and citron-trees, in blossom'. His intention, Bernardin announced in the novel's preface, was 'to blend with the beauty of nature between the tropics, the moral beauty of little society'.[13] Set on the Île de France (present-day Mauritius), *Paul et Virginie* appealed directly to Romantic sensibilities. It depicted a life at one with nature, far from European corruption and materialism, where the French protagonists lived in happy harmony with slaves. The characters 'knew the time of day by the shadows of the trees; the seasons, by the times when those trees bore flowers or fruit; and the years, by the number of their harvests'.[14]

The novel recounted the lives of two French women – one, a well-born widow; the other, a peasant abandoned by her seducer – who give birth and raise their children, Paul and Virginie, in a secluded spot on the Île de France. Dwelling in simple huts, the families have all their needs supplied by tropical abundance – and a pair of devoted slaves. Paul and Virginie grow up as brother and sister, generous of spirit and pure in morality, ranging freely through the island groves, enjoying the kind of natural upbringing advocated by Rousseau. At twelve years old, Paul is an accomplished landscape gardener, embellishing the enclosure with date palms, tamarind, mango, guava and breadfruit trees. Inseparable from an early age, Paul and Virginie appear destined for each other. But material considerations intervene: Virginie's mother dispatches her daughter back to France to gain an inheritance. After years of absence, Virginie makes the return voyage to the island, but her ship founders near port. Inhibited by European-taught modesty, Virginie refuses to strip to save herself by swimming. Paul witnesses Virginie's death by drowning, and succumbs to despair; within two months, he too is dead.

The pathos of the young lovers' fates and their early carefree existence proved irresistible to readers. The novel was swiftly translated into numerous European languages. In the first decade alone, *Paul et Virginie* went through fifty-six editions, including twenty translations. Of the several English translations, the most successful was Helen Maria Williams' *Paul and Virginia* (1795). The novel continued to sell well into the nineteenth century. So popular was it that, in 1834, the *New Monthly Magazine* published a sonnet, 'On Reading Paul and Virginia in Childhood', by Felicia Hemans, in which she declared:

> Midst thy palms
> And strange bright birds, my fancy joy'd to dwell.[15]

Two years later, on the voyage of the *Beagle*, Charles Darwin anticipated visiting the Île de France. 'Oh, that I had a sweet Virginia to send an inspired epistle to', he jokingly exclaimed to his second cousin. 'A person not in love will have no right to wander amongst the glowing bewitching scenes'.[16] The novel's many descriptions of tropical verdure provided endless opportunities for illustration. There were Paul and Virginie paintings, prints, picture books, figurines, sculptures, wallpaper designs and furnishing fabrics, all densely patterned with tropical foliage.

In the novel, Bernardin established a pair of intertwined coconut palms as the central emblem for his two protagonists. To mark the birth of her child, each mother plants a coconut. In the absence of church or state, the two palms 'formed all the records of the two families'. Their growth and inclination mirror the development of the children and their affections: 'one was called the tree of Paul, the other the tree of Virginia. They grew in the same proportion as the two young persons of an unequal height; but they rose at the end of twelve years above the cottages. Already their tender stalks were interwoven, and their young branches of cocoas hung over the bason of the fountain.'[17]

By embodying his two young lovers in palms, Bernardin reinforced the connection established by Linnaeus between humans and palms. The palms' gendered identities ('the tree of Paul', 'the tree of Virginia') reminded readers of the association between palms and plant sex, demonstrated both by Linnaeus and the Berlin Experiment (although the coconut, *Cocos nucifera*, is in fact monoecious, each plant bearing both male and female flowers). The palms' entwined stems inevitably suggested an analogy between plant and human sexuality.

These associations were reinforced by a scene later in the novel which represents the moment of Virginie's sexual awakening. One hot, moonlit night when she cannot sleep, the adolescent Virginie makes her way to the bathing spot beneath the coconut palms. She immerses herself in the cooling pool: 'She saw in the water, upon her naked arms and bosom, the reflection of the two cocoa trees which were planted at her own and her brother's birth, and which interwove above her head their green branches and young fruit. She thought of Paul's friendship, sweeter than the odour of the blossoms, purer than the waters of the fountain, stronger than the inter-twining palm-trees, and she sighed.'[18]

With the reflection of the branches and young fruit of the palms rippling over her naked body, Virginie intuits the possible outcome of her friendship with Paul. Suddenly her imagination grows 'disordered', the water feels hot, and, alarmed by her arousal, Virginie flees back to the safety of her mother, 'in order to find a refuge from herself'.[19]

In the figure of the two palms, Bernardin found a suggestive metaphor for human sexuality, unconstrained by convention. While the young lovers remain virtuous and their desire unconsummated, the two palms are entwined and fruitful. The many artists who illustrated the novel certainly revelled in the abundance of tropical nature. In 1839, the publishing company W. S. Orr brought out an English version of a French edition which boasted a staggering 330 illustrations. Virtually every page carried an image of palms, fruits or flowers: a tropical cornucopia. The sheer number of illustrations suggested the lush sensuality of the tropical environment.

Wreathed with exotic foliage and playful monkeys, the frontispiece featured two palms inclined towards each other over a pool. Somewhat daringly, the volume included an illustration of 'Virginia in the Bath'. The heroine was poised, nymph-like, in decorous profile on the pool's bank, embowered by vegetation and palm leaves.

26. Virginia in the Bath, *from W. S. Orr's edition of Bernardin's* Paul and Virginia (*1839*).

But it was perhaps the sculptor William Calder Marshall who went furthest in imagining the human figures merged with the palm. In *Paul and Virginia*, exhibited in 1843 at the Royal Academy, the characters are represented as young children, but still in a somewhat erotic manner. The young pair are supported by – and seem to grow out of – a palm stem.

The visual representations emphasize the whiteness of the European protagonists. Paul and Virginie are at once at home and radically out of place in the tropical environment. The seclusion in which the characters dwell allows the novel and illustrations largely

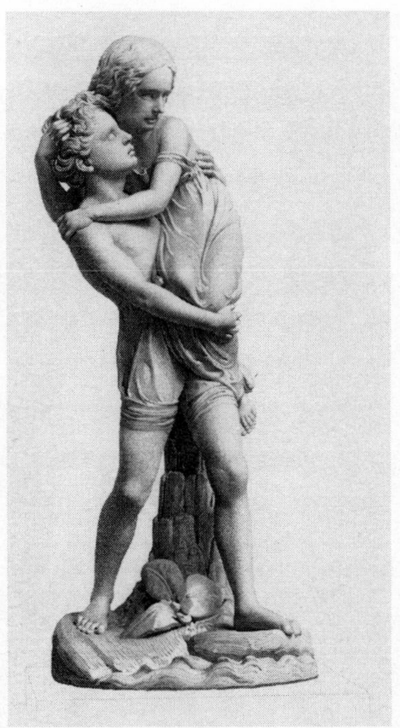

27. Paul and Virginia *by William Calder Marshall (1843).*

to ignore issues of colonial exploitation and oppression.[20] For the most part, the only black figures to make an occasional appearance in the text and illustrations are the kindly treated household slaves, who are usually relegated to the background or frame of the scene. Conveniently emptied of its inhabitants, the Île de France is reimagined as a tropical garden. In the novel, the island is a fertile and apparently uncontested space for Europeans to entertain the fantasy of a return to nature.

Given his role in fashioning a tropical garden for the European imagination, it seems peculiarly appropriate that Bernardin should have been appointed superintendent of the Jardin des Plantes in Paris, four years after the publication of *Paul et Virginie*. To this day, Bernardin is commemorated with a sizeable monument in the

28. *Holweck's monument to Bernardin de Saint-Pierre (1907).*

Jardin des Plantes. Louis Holweck's 1907 bronze sculpture depicts a pensive figure, atop a plinth. Unusually for a monumental sculpture, the pedestal is highly ornamented.

The base houses an equally large bronze sculpture: a verdigris Paul and Virginie, seated within a tropical bower so abundant that the foliage extends beyond the monumental frame. Truly, this is a monument not just to Bernardin, but also to the enduring appeal of his tropical idyll.

Among the most influential devotees of *Paul et Virginie* was the eminent natural historian and geographer Alexander von Humboldt (who, late in life, would meet Joseph Hooker). A famous polymath with an extraordinary memory, Humboldt made connections between previously distinct areas of study and laid the foundations for new disciplines such as environmental science. Overflowing with ideas, Humboldt was an electrifying conversationalist and moved in the highest intellectual circles. He counted among his friends the renowned poet and scientist Johann Wolfgang von Goethe. With Goethe, Humboldt could debate botanical theories, including Goethe's notion of the *Urpflanze*, or primal plant, an archetype that was at once ideal and real, embodying all existing plant forms and patterns of development. The idea of the *Urpflanze* first occurred to Goethe on a visit to Padua Botanical Garden, as he contemplated the fronds of a Mediterranean fan palm, *Chamaerops humilis* (the same species as the palm of the Berlin Experiment).

Humboldt united a Romantic appreciation of nature with empirical rigour. The connections that Humboldt saw between plants, climate and geology across the world were based on precise measurement and experiment. Humboldt made his name with an epic five-year South American journey, from 1799 to 1804 – travelling along the Orinoco by canoe, ascending the high peaks of the Andes and mapping Mexico by mule – accompanied by the botanist Aimé Bonpland. For Humboldt, travelling in the tropics was transformative. His account of the dangers and wonders of his journey, the multi-volume *Relation historique du voyage* (1814–25), was swiftly translated into English as the *Personal Narrative of Travels to the Equinoctial Regions of the New Continent* (1814–29) by Helen Maria Williams, who had previously translated *Paul et Virginie*. It became the model for subsequent scientific travel accounts (including Darwin's *Voyage of the Beagle*), and made Humboldt the ultimate hero-naturalist, equally bold in feats of physical and intellectual daring.

Although he travelled comparatively lightly – at least by the standards of most nineteenth-century expeditions – Humboldt found room in his baggage for a copy of Bernardin's *Paul et Virginie*. Over the years, both he and Bonpland read and reread the novel, 'in the calm brilliancy of a southern sky, or when, in the rainy season, the thunder re-echoed, and the lightning gleamed through the forests that skirt the shores of the Orinoco, we felt ourselves penetrated by the marvelous truth with which tropical nature is described'.[21] In particular, Humboldt recalled how, three weeks into his boat journey down the Orinoco, he was transfixed by a view of clusters of palms rising a hundred feet above the forest canopy – a sight that immediately recalled the description of 'a forest planted upon another forest', from *Paul et Virginie*.[22] Bernardin 'knew how to paint nature', Humboldt asserted, 'not because he had studied it scientifically, but because he felt it in all its harmonious analogies of forms, colours, and interior powers'.[23] For Humboldt, Bernardin's novel testified to the power of the artist to evoke the immense scale and intense verdure which distinguished tropical from European vegetation. 'In describing a small spot of land in an island of the Indian Ocean', Humboldt observed, 'the inimitable author of Paul and Virginia has sketched the vast picture of the landscape of the tropics'.[24]

The wonders of tropical nature, Humboldt argued, could best be conveyed to those in colder regions through literature and art. In *Ansichten der Natur* (*Aspects of Nature*), first published in 1808, Humboldt encouraged landscape painters to view plants 'not merely in hot-houses or in the descriptions of botanists, but in their native grandeur in the tropical zone'.[25] At this stage in his career, relatively recently returned from his travels, Humboldt considered glasshouses a poor substitute for the experience of tropical nature. This lack could only be supplied by the works of writers, poets and artists, 'from whence our imagination can derive the living image of the more vigorous nature which other climes can display'.[26] Still to publish his own narrative account, Humboldt promised to transport readers into a vibrant tropics of the imagination.

In the *Personal Narrative*, Humboldt attempted to convey the unparalleled beauty of the tropics. Continuing down the Orinoco, the members of the expedition first heard, and then saw, the churning waters of the cataracts of Maipures. The view of the cascades from the neighbouring mountain of Manimi was otherworldly: 'far as the eye can reach, a thick vapour is suspended over the river, and through this whitish fog the tops of the lofty palm-trees shoot up'.[27] Returning at different times of day, Humboldt never wearied of the spectacle. 'Sometimes the hilly islands and the palm-trees project their broad shadows, sometimes the rays of the setting sun are refracted in the humid cloud . . . coloured arcs are formed, and vanish and appear again'.[28] The memory of the 'sea of foam and palm-trees' was long lasting, as vivid as any impression created by a great work of art or literature.[29] For the Romantic Humboldt, the spectacle evoked 'all our feelings of what is grand and beautiful'.[30] Reproduced in nineteenth-century magazines and school readers, Humboldt's description of palms emerging from rainbowed clouds became a potent emblem of the tropical sublime.[31]

Like many nineteenth-century European travellers in remote areas, Humboldt imagined that the voyage down the Orinoco was like a journey back to the earliest times. 'In those wild regions', he observed, 'are we involuntarily reminded of the assertion of Linnæus, that the country of palm-trees was the first abode of our species'.[32] The people who lived on the banks of the Orinoco, he learnt, depended for months of the year on the *pijiguaio* palm (*Bactris gasipaes*), which produced bunches of hundreds of yellowy red fruits, much, to Humboldt's eye, like peaches. Humboldt named it the peach palm (the name by which it is still known today). In the nutritious starchy fruits, Humboldt believed that he had found proof of Linnaeus's claim that 'man is essentially palmivorous' – that is, first subsisted entirely on palms.[33] According to the *Oxford English Dictionary*, this description offers the earliest recorded use of the word 'palmivorous': a wonderful coinage introduced by Humboldt and his translator, Helen Maria Williams.

Further evidence for the palmivorous nature of mankind was provided by the Mauritia palm (*Mauritia flexuosa*), which grew in vast stands in wetlands throughout the Orinoco and Amazon basins. Mile upon mile was solely occupied by ranks of its tall grey trunks and massive fan-shaped fronds. Humboldt was struck both by the dominance of the palm in marshland areas and its centrality to the lives of the indigenous peoples. Termed the 'tree of life' by the Spanish missionaries, the Mauritia palm provided food, drink, building material and thread for the Guarani people.[34] Local mythologies even considered the Mauritia palm as the source of human existence itself. Humboldt reported that the Tamanaks of the Orinoco believed that, following the great flood, the world had been repopulated by people sprung from the fruit of the Mauritia palm.[35] The Guaranis built their huts on stilts made from the cut trunks of Mauritia palms, with floors woven from its fibre, coated with mud. At times of flood, they could live entirely in the trees. Humboldt reproduced the reports of earlier travellers, including Sir Walter Raleigh, who maintained that the Guaranis built their household fires directly on the mud-caked flooring of their huts, high up in the palms. 'The navigator', wrote Humboldt, 'in proceeding along the channels of the *delta* of the Oronooko at night, sees with surprise the summit of the palm-trees illumined by large fires'.[36] Like the earlier images of forests layered upon forests or palms piercing the clouds, the elevated fires of the Guaranis defied all European expectations.

Humboldt regarded this palm land paradoxically as both the site of freedom and of human degradation. Never conquered, the Guaranis 'owed their liberty and their political independence, for ages, to the quaking and swampy soil . . . on which they alone know how to walk in security, to their solitude in the *delta* of the Oroonoko, to their abode on the trees'.[37] But the very circumstances which guaranteed the Guaranis' freedom also placed them, in Humboldt's opinion, on 'the lowest degree of human civilization'.[38] He compared the lives of the Guaranis in the palms to those of apes, and likened their dependence on the Mauritia palm to that of specialist insects: 'the existence of a whole tribe, depending on one single species of palm-tree' was, for Humboldt, 'similar to those insects which feed on one and the same flower'.[39] The very abundance of the palm might, in some cases, be less a natural blessing than a barrier to human progress.

As a philosophical and scientific traveller, Humboldt's interests ranged across many disciplines, but he was particularly fascinated by botany and the geographical distribution of plants. In an extensive note to the *Aspects of Nature*, Humboldt suggested that much botanical work remained to be done in South America on the palm family. Many species had yet to be described systematically, but there were immense practical obstacles to collecting the necessary specimens. With only three or four palm species occurring in an area of, say, 3,000 square miles, collectors had to cover huge distances. Flowering seasons might only last a few days, so that 'one almost always arrives too late, and finds the fertilization completed and the male blossoms gone'.[40] Even when the botanist had the flower in his sights, there was the difficulty of actually reaching it. In the midst of swamps or dense forests, flowers might hang tantalizingly out of reach, atop fiercely spiked sixty-foot stems, defeating even the best-equipped naturalist:

> A traveller, when preparing to leave Europe on an expedition in which natural history is one of his leading objects, flatters himself with the thoughts of shears or curved blades fastened to long poles, with which he imagines he will be able to reach and cut down whatever he desires; he dreams, too, of native boys, who, with a cord fastened to their two feet, are to climb up the highest trees at his bidding. But, alas! very few of these fancies are ever realised; the great height of the blossoms renders the poles useless; and in the missions established on the banks of the rivers of Guiana, the traveller finds himself among Indians whose poverty, stoicism, and uncultivated state, renders them so rich, and so free from wants of every kind, that neither money nor other presents that can be made to them will induce them to turn three steps out of their path.[41]

In this account, the naturalist cuts a far from commanding figure, finding himself frustrated both by nature and the local people. But while he made fun of the unseasoned traveller, deriding his expectations, tools and useless money, Humboldt established an enduring image of the botanist battling against adversity. The physical trials of hunting large palms, which the American botanist L. H. Bailey called 'the big game of the plant world', feature even today in accounts of fieldwork by palm specialists.[42]

But the rewards of bringing home such a trophy were equally great. When, after five years of travel, Humboldt and Bonpland returned to Paris, they needed a suitably spectacular discovery to announce their arrival at the heart of metropolitan science. As Michael Dettelbach has noted, they publicized their expedition by presenting an account of a strikingly unusual palm to the Institut National de France.[43] Like Linnaeus, Humboldt considered palms 'the loftiest and noblest of all vegetable forms, that to which the prize of beauty has been assigned by the concurrent voices of all nations in all ages'.[44] Besides being tall and elegant, the palm presented by Humboldt and Bonpland was remarkable in being covered in a waxy substance. Even more extraordinarily, the palm had been encountered as Humboldt and Bonpland hiked over the Quindío Pass in the western Andes (in present-day Colombia), one of a group of mountain palms growing at higher altitudes and in lower temperatures than any other known species of palm. They named it *Ceroxylon alpinum* (although later botanists would rename the species *Ceroxylon quinduense*). With his enthusiasm for precise measurement, physical exertion and plant distribution, Humboldt had discovered 'in the tropics a peculiar group of mountain palms' that were 'entirely unknown', he boasted, before his South American journey.[45] To emphasize the exceptional nature of the discovery, Humboldt termed them 'Alpine Palms', uniting in a seeming oxymoron the landscape of Europe with the quintessential tropical plant.[46]

Answering Humboldt's call for further botanical work on South American palms was a twenty-two-year-old Bavarian botanist, Carl Friedrich Philipp von Martius. He joined a party of naturalists travelling to Brazil in 1817, in the suite of the Archduchess Leopoldine, the daughter of the Emperor of Austria, on the occasion of her marriage to Dom Pedro, the eldest son of the King of Portugal, Brazil and Algarve. The dynastic match offered an opportunity to conduct an ambitious scientific survey of Brazil. Martius and his travelling companion, the zoologist Johann Baptist von Spix, were appointed by Maximilian I Joseph, the King of Bavaria, to join the Austrian scientific team to gather information not only on the flora and fauna, but also the geography, geology, resources, climate and indigenous peoples of Brazil. Following the royal wedding celebrations in Rio de Janeiro, Martius and Spix set out for the Brazilian interior. 'One may easily imagine the feelings of the two travellers, especially of the youthful and enthusiastic Martius, when they stood upon the soil of the wonderful country that lay before them with all its treasures of nature – the very El Dorado of a naturalist', exclaimed the archaeologist Charles Rau in 1871.[47]

Martius and Spix embarked on an arduous 1,400-mile journey, lasting some two and a half years, through arid lands and dense rainforest, along the Amazon and, in the case of Martius, up the hazardous Japurá River. They mapped and surveyed; they investigated customs and languages; they braved rapids and life-threatening illness. But mostly they collected: minerals, rocks, birds, amphibians, fish, insects, spiders, crustaceans and plants. In the course of his travels, Martius amassed a staggering 6,500 species of plants, largely dried, but also a number of living specimens. Even more remarkably, the entire natural-history collection made it back, intact, to Munich. The plants and seeds found a home in the Royal Botanical Garden, and the natural-history items were displayed in a specially constructed Brazilian Museum.

Following the long, ignoble tradition of European explorers, Martius even collected people. On the final leg of his journey, he instructed a slave dealer to capture children for him. He purchased two girls and three boys, and later acquired another boy. Two of these children he left in Brazil, but four embarked on the ship for Europe with the naturalists in 1820. Of these, only two – a girl and boy – survived the voyage. Initially known as Miranha and Juri – not their actual names, but those of the tribes to which they belonged

– they were renamed Isabella and Johannes. Aged around twelve or thirteen, they did not share a common language, and so could not communicate with each other. The children's arrival in Munich was reported in the newspapers, they were shown at court, inspected by visiting intellectuals and displayed to the public at an inn. Sadly, they did not survive this treatment long. Juri succumbed to pneumonia in less than a year. Miranha lived a year longer, making progress in her education and language learning, before dying of an intestinal complaint in 1822. A wax copy of Juri's head remained on display in Munich University's Institute of Anatomy until the mid-twentieth century.[48]

While the expedition cut short the lives of Miranha and Juri, it made Martius's career. Immediately on his return, the twenty-six-year-old was knighted by the King and rewarded with membership of the Royal Bavarian Academy of Sciences and the post of assistant curator at the Botanical Garden at Munich. He was later appointed Professor of Botany at Munich University and subsequently promoted to curator of the Botanic Garden. The Brazilian collection was so extensive that he worked on little else for the rest of his life. Following the model of Humboldt, Martius and Spix published a narrative account of their travels, *Reise in Brasilien* (1823–31), the first two volumes of which were translated into English as *Travels in Brazil* (1824). In addition, Martius published a three-volume folio botanical work, *Nova genera et species plantarum Brasiliensium* (1823–30), to describe the new plants discovered in Brazil. But the palms he reserved for separate treatment.

The *Historia Naturalis Palmarum* (1823–53) was a uniquely lavish work devoted to all the known species of palm across the world (including those newly discovered by Martius). Thirty years in the making, it was issued in instalments, on unfolded broadsheets, building up to three volumes of very large format (known in the antiquarian book trade as 'Atlas' size, twenty-five inches tall – one up from 'Elephant'). The botanical descriptions were written in Latin, still the pan-European language of botany. Somewhat confusingly, Martius started by publishing the second and third volumes, depicting palms of the New and Old Worlds. The first volume, a collaborative work with two fellow botanists, Hugo Mohl and Franz Unger, was the last to be published. It offered a general introduction to the structure, form, geographical distribution and fossilized remains of palms.

Remarkably, Martius published the work at his own expense. But he did have access to a network of royal patronage that made his subscription list read like a roll-call of the crowned heads of Europe: the Emperor of Austria; the Tsar of Russia; the Kings of Bavaria, the Netherlands, Prussia and Saxony; the Grand Dukes of Tuscany and Saxe-Weimar-Eisenach – to name but a few. Forbiddingly expensive, this was a work aimed at members of the social and scientific elite. The decades-long process of preparing the *Historia Naturalis Palmarum* for publication placed Martius under severe financial constraint. In 1849, the naturalist Philip Henry Gosse reported that he was 'grieved to have seen it recently announced that Von Martius has ruined himself by the publication of his magnificent work on the Palms, and now offers some copies of it at a greatly reduced price'.[49]

The splendour and expense of the magnum opus lay in its 245 illustrative plates. These full-page lithographs were individually hand-tinted, the rich colours evoking the intensity of tropical verdure. A somewhat cheaper uncoloured version was also available. The first volume was illustrated with precise scientific drawings, including cross sections, diagrams and detailed copies of microscopic slides. The second and third volumes contained hundreds of botanical plates depicting the parts of palms: the leaves, spathes, flowers, fruits and seeds. Images of curving inflorescences, spiralling stems and outspread leaves were artfully arranged to fit the page. The accuracy of the botanical illustrations was such that, according to the Danish palm specialist Henrik Balslev, they can still be used for identifying specimens today.[50] For Balslev, the plates 'provide the special pleasure of seeing and disentangling the details of nature', and give 'one the same feeling as when pressing palm specimens in the field'.[51]

Unusually for a botanical work, the *Historia Naturalis Palmarum* also contained landscape scenes. Interspersed between the botanic plates were views of palms on seashores and rocky outcrops, by waterfalls and wooded mountains, in clearings and the depths of the forest. In contrast to the botanic plates, with their dissected parts placed in careful patterns across the page, the landscape scenes were full of atmospheric detail, enclosed within a frame of coloured wash (see Plate 1). Many of the plates featured figures: hunters poised with bow and arrow, fishermen with spears and nets, European botanists collecting and sketching. There were animals too: rearing snakes, slain leopards, fleeing ostriches. Although their ostensible subject was palms, the landscapes, with their arresting details, drew the viewer deep into imagined tropical scenes.

The dual scientific and aesthetic appeal of the *Historia Naturalis Palmarum* was first recognized by Goethe. In 1823, Martius introduced himself to Goethe by sending the initial two instalments of the book with a letter boldly asking the grand man to review his work. The following year, Goethe complied with his request, praising Martius's skills as an artist, both in the scientific drawings and the landscape plates. The work would appeal, Goethe predicted, not only to the 'erudite connoisseur', but also to 'every nature lover', the varied landscape scenes 'stimulating and at the same time satisfying our minds, imagination and emotions', giving viewers the sense 'of being entirely present and at home in a faraway part of the world'.[52] In his review, Goethe identified the wider appeal of palms to the nineteenth-century public. They were at once objects of scientific fascination and creative fancy, allowing Europeans both to think and to dream.

Building on Humboldt's ideas of plant distribution, the *Historia Naturalis Palmarum* identified a global palm zone. At the end of the first volume, Martius included two splendid maps: the first of the New World, the second of the Old (see Plates 2 and 3). In reorientating the world around palms, Martius prioritized the New World over the Old (as he also did in the numbering of his volumes). The two maps indicated, in different shades of red, the distribution and density of palms across the world. The African interior remained blank – it had yet to be charted by Europeans – but, in other respects, the maps broadly correspond to current ideas of palm distribution today.

At the same time as the *Historia Naturalis Palmarum* offered a pioneering phytogeographic map, it delineated a cultural mythology of palms. Martius endowed palms with a quasi-classical pedigree by terming them 'the noble offspring of Terra and Phoebus'.[53] This new-minted myth was illustrated in the frames of the maps. On the New World map, Terra (Mother Earth) is depicted as a majestic robed goddess, resting on the eastern curve of the northern hemisphere. With one hand she presents a palm, rather than her traditional symbol of flowers; the other hand she rests on the shoulder of a child holding the flowing vessel of a river deity, perhaps representing the Amazon. Acknowledging Terra with upraised hand is Phoebus Apollo, the sun god, seated in clouds above the western corner of the Old World. Radiating light, Phoebus Apollo bears his emblem of a bow and arrow. The classical deities ennoble both Martius's work and the whole palm family. Indeed, Martius's invented palm mythology was often repeated in popular nineteenth-century works on palms.[54]

The maps are surrounded by decorative foliage and historical-allegorical vignettes of New- and Old-World cultures, and the encounter between the two. The Old World is bounded at the bottom by scenes of European agriculture and apiculture, by emblems of learning and Christian faith. At the top, an oriental potentate progresses in state, shaded by a palm-leaf parasol. Beneath the New World, a boat bearing European soldiers and a cleric heads towards a shore, enacting the moment of arrival. At the base of the New World, Europeans are cherished by Native Americans bearing baskets of tropical fruit. In the distance, however, battle scenes rage, and a European soldier oversees the felling of a tree. At the top, a European appears to be buying an enslaved captive. The scenes of cross-cultural encounter, hostility and trade are linked by decorative palms and exquisite curlicues, sporting exotic birds and half-human, half-monkey hybrids (one wearing native dress, another wielding a pick in a mine). The history of the world is reinterpreted through vegetation, mythical creatures and an invented cosmology of palms. The *Historia Naturalis Palmarum* offers a new way of looking at the world: one that unites the usually separate tropics and Orient in a wide palm zone, girdling the earth.

From his institutional position at the Munich Botanical Garden, Martius corresponded with botanists throughout Europe. When Hooker was Professor of Botany at Glasgow, Martius sent him collections of plants and letters in Latin. In July 1837, for instance, Martius wrote to inform Hooker that he had dispatched some Brazilian plants for him, and complained about the slow progress he was making with the palm book.[55] When it was finally complete, Hooker purchased a hand-tinted edition of *Historia Naturalis Palmarum* for one hundred guineas.[56] The edition still remains in the library at the Royal Botanic Gardens, Kew, today. Each volume is so heavy that it is difficult to lift; so large, that you have to stand to read it. The initial pages are foxed, but the botanical plates remain startlingly lifelike and the landscapes glow with colour. To handle the volumes is to be left in no doubt about the prestige, beauty and ambition of the work.

The magnificence and sheer size of the *Historia Naturalis Palmarum* reinforced the notion that palms were the largest and most noble of plants. The book remained, for the most part, carefully guarded on the shelves of private libraries and scientific institutions, inaccessible to the general public. But, as the garden historian Brent Elliott has discovered, versions of its lithographs did reach a wider public.[57] Plates from the *Historia Naturalis Palmarum* were used as the basis for the cheap woodcuts illustrating articles on palms in the *Penny Cyclopaedia*. Issued between 1833 and 1844, in weekly instalments, by the Society for the Diffusion of Useful Knowledge, the *Penny Cyclopaedia* was central to the Society's campaign for public education. The project was part of the explosion of cheap scientific and instructive publishing following the invention of the steam-powered printing press. The botanical articles were written by Hooker's friend and ally, John Lindley, at the Horticultural Society. It was evidently on Lindley's instruction, and presumably from his own copy of *Historia Naturalis Palmarum*, that the woodblock maker copied the portraits of palms to accompany Lindley's descriptions. For the price of a penny, the working classes could buy crude but still accurate versions of the plates from one of the most exclusive of all botanical publications.

The impulse towards public education was shared by Hooker, at Kew. No greater emblem of the democratization of knowledge existed than the Palm House. Once the glasshouse was finally stocked, members of the public would be able to brush shoulders with the princes of the vegetable kingdom. This act of enlightened government was also conceived as a national triumph. 'To put the public in possession of this noble family, has been for the last twenty years the ambition of many governments and of many powers', the *Illustrated London News* asserted.[58] The paper then outlined a brief history of European palm-hunting and palm cultivation: 'The great Maximilian of Bavaria, aided by his scientific travellers, Spix and Martius, led the way; the French, in the conservatories of the Jardin des Plantes; the Spanish, in the gardens of the Escurial; and in our own country, Messrs. Loddiges, at Hackney, and his Grace the Duke of Devonshire, at Chatsworth, followed with much – but necessarily limited success'.[59]

Outshining all these attempts – be they public, royal, commercial or aristocratic – was the Palm House at Kew. 'The great attempt to rear the entire family in one vast establishment has been reserved for the English Government', declared the *Illustrated London News* with patriotic fervour. Anticipating the moment when the Palm House would be arranged, the article concluded that 'we can imagine no more striking exhibition of the great Creator's works than the offspring of Terra and Phoebus, as they have been termed, will present, or one more directly calculated to raise the public taste'.[60] The task to create a display that would meet these grand educational, religious and political aims fell to the curator, John Smith.

Four years in the making, the Palm House was finally ready to receive its plants. All the available garden workforce was involved in the operation to transfer the tropical specimens from the old hothouses. Carpenters were constructing seventy oak plant boxes, and repairing and repainting seventy more. A contractor was building a platform with moving rollers to transport the largest palms. The most prized of Kew's hothouse specimens risked damage from accident or exposure. The tallest palms would have to be uprooted with considerable force – but also with tremendous care. Of all the operations that Smith had overseen in the Gardens, this would be the most complex yet.

# 11

# The Palm House Spectacle

The greatest challenge in the moving process was posed by two immense fan palms (*Sabal bermudana*). Although short of stem, they possessed enormous root balls and a dense mass of broad, blue-green leaves. The two palms had been under Smith's care for twenty-five years, but in Kew's collection for much longer. Smith conjectured that it had been Captain William Bligh who had brought them to Kew in 1793. The palms, Smith supposed, were part of a substantial consignment of West Indian plants gathered on the return voyage of Bligh's second attempt to transfer the breadfruit from Tahiti to the Caribbean (the first having been famously thwarted by the mutiny on the *Bounty*). Standing at either end of the old glasshouse, the two palms had struck the young Smith with wonder. Their leaves – up to fifteen feet high by ten feet broad – regularly broke through the glass in the hothouse roof. To accommodate them, in 1828, Smith had expanded the palms' brickwork beds and raised the glasshouse roof by some four feet. Now, they more than filled the space. With prime plots allocated in the Palm House, the two fan palms would at last have room to grow. But, first, they needed to get there.

To extract the palms, the hothouse had to be partially dismantled and the brickwork beds excavated. With neither the staff nor the equipment to manage an operation on this scale, John Smith engaged the services of two engineers from Deptford Dockyard. Under Smith's fierce supervision, a team of dockers and gardeners repotted the palms in vast eight-foot-square wooden plant boxes. Then, using a cradle truck and moving tackle, the engineers carefully hoisted one of the palms, weighing seventeen tons, onto the specially constructed rolling platform. Secured in place, the palm was painstakingly conveyed the slow half-mile to the Palm House. The central entrance of the Palm House was opened to its full extent, three times the normal doorway height. Winched up the steps by a windlass, its crown barely clearing the doorway, the *Sabal bermudana* finally arrived in its new home, where it was installed in the nave. The procedure was then repeated for its fellow. The whole operation cost over one hundred pounds.

Following the two *Sabal bermudana*, other occupants of the old palm stove were trundled along the path to the Palm House. Among the tallest were two stately date palms (*Phoenix dactylifera*), a pair of handsome Himalayan fan palms (*Trachycarpus martianus*) and two Indian wine palms (*Caryota urens*), with leaflets resembling fishtails. More impressive still was a licuri palm (*Syagrus coronata*) donated the previous year by Sir George Staunton. While still a boy, Staunton had accompanied his father on Lord Macartney's diplomatic mission to China (1792–4). A gifted linguist, the twelve-year-old Staunton had learnt Chinese, and was the only member of the British embassy to converse directly with the Qianlong Emperor (who had rewarded him with a silken purse). As an adult, Staunton served with the East India Company at Canton, and retired at the age of thirty-six, his fortune made. He became a Tory MP and purchased Leigh Park in Hampshire, where he constructed a landscape garden with views as far as the Isle of Wight. The grounds were dotted with exotic follies, including a Chinese boathouse, fort and bridge, a Turkish kiosk, and a shell house for curiosities acquired on his travels: a stuffed crocodile, a sea hedgehog, a toucan's bill. In the hothouse, he grew bananas and mangoes which won gold medals at Horticultural Society shows. Among his prized stove plants was the Brazilian licuri palm, purchased from Loddiges' Nursery in Hackney. Over the years, the palm grew to a height of thirty-seven feet, endangering the Leigh Park hothouse roof. In 1847, Staunton offered the licuri palm to Sir William Hooker for the new Palm House at Kew. The enormous palm, its feathery fronds carefully arranged, was packed into a specially constructed wooden case, forty-two feet long. The boxed plant was then loaded onto a London-bound train for the seventy-mile rail journey to Kew, where it awaited transfer to its suitably magnificent setting.

After successive journeys with the rolling platform, the various palms were manoeuvred into position in the nave, to form the grand centrepiece of the display. There were four pits for the largest palms, but otherwise the plants were to be accommodated in pots. Smith was relieved to see that 'although some distance apart they made a goodly appearance'. But the curator remained unconvinced that the building would allow the palms to flourish. In an uncharacteristic moment of whimsy, Smith imagined 'that if they could speak, they would say that they were not happy in this dry air, and iron domicile erected for us, the principes of the vegetable kingdom'.[1]

It fell to Smith and the Palm House foreman to create the most congenial atmosphere possible for the palms. They oversaw the ventilation, cleaning and care of the hothouse plants. The palms were watered regularly with rainwater collected on the roof and channelled down the internal columns that doubled as drainage pipes. In addition to the overhead sprinkling system (which was never very satisfactory), the palms were hand-syringed from the gallery with Thames water, leaving the foliage coated with a fine dusting of chalky residue. It was far from easy to simulate the conditions of the tropics. For the gardeners assigned to the Palm House, working conditions were extremely difficult. Even in shirtsleeves, the Palm House temperatures were near unbearable, and the sheer size of the plants made every operation cumbersome. To avoid slipping and to keep out the damp, gardeners were supplied annually with a pair of 'clogs' – boots with leather uppers and wooden, iron-tipped soles, which rang loudly as they walked on the grated flooring of the Palm House. 'No one who has not experienced it can have any idea of the nature of the gardener's work in such houses as the Palm House', a later gardener complained.[2] The schedule was punishing: 'Ten hours a day for six days in the week, seven days in every fourth week, in a tropical temperature, often doing heavy work, trying to keep the plants healthy under the most artificial, often unfavourable conditions is an experience without parallel in horticulture'.[3]

To stock the vast expanse of the Palm House, Sir William called on his extensive network of contacts, both at home and overseas: landed aristocrats and nursery owners, horticulturalists and plant collectors, the directors of botanic gardens across Europe and the empire, colonial officials, naval officers, diplomats and missionaries. Palms were the undisputed stars of the show, but the house also contained a wide variety of tropical plants from around the world. With its global collection, the Palm House embodied the wide reach of Britain's imperial power. Combining tree ferns with bananas, coffee shrubs with bamboo, the Palm House created a tropical fantasy that defied the laws of plant distribution.

By far the largest donor of plants to the Palm House was the

Calcutta Botanic Garden; over the course of ten years, Nathaniel Wallich, the superintendent, sent to Kew some 500 'plants of the rarest and most valuable description'.[4] But Hooker also extended a wider public invitation. He contributed a chapter to the *Manual of Scientific Enquiry*, published in 1849 by the Admiralty for 'the use of Her Majesty's Navy and adapted for travellers in general'. Hooker advised that seeds should be gathered when ripe, wrapped in brown paper, and kept on board ship in an airy part of the cabin. Young plants could be transported in the 'now generally known and most deservedly esteemed' Wardian case: a portable glass box which functioned as a miniature greenhouse, keeping plants moist and – with any luck – alive.[5] With the increase in steam shipping lines and the reduction in the duration of voyages, far fewer specimens died en route. Packages addressed to 'Sir Wm. J. Hooker, Royal Gardens, Kew' were given free passage on naval vessels, Royal Mail steamers and the fleet of the Oriental Steam Navigation Company.

Situated at the centre of a network of colonial gardens, Kew collected botanic products from all over the empire, directing plant exchange between different tropical locations. The Scottish journalist James Hannay, in an article for Charles Dickens' magazine, *Household Words*, imagined the Gardens as 'a sort of bank to which botanical currency flows for transmission. Is something curious or valuable discovered anywhere? Seeds and specimens reach Kew – from thence other great European collections – and so a product of one side of the globe may, through this organization, be cultivated by us, in the corresponding climate of any of our colonial possessions'.[6] Transplanting medical plants, economic and food crops across continents, Kew engineered environmental and social change worldwide. The *Quarterly Review* (1851) named Kew the 'metropolis of plants' and declared that 'the reign of Victoria will be chronicled as the era of a mutual distribution of the vegetable productions of the world'.[7]

To acquire specific rarities, Hooker also directly commissioned plant collectors. In 1844, around the time that the Palm House plans were first being drawn up, Hooker instructed William Purdie, a Scottish plant hunter, jointly financed by Kew and the Duke of Northumberland, to extend his collecting activities from the West Indies to New Granada (present-day Colombia). Purdie was tasked with finding and dispatching live specimens of the ivory-nut palm. The ivory nut was in fact a seed. When dry, its endosperm (or nutritional tissue) formed a hard yellow-white substance which resembled ivory. As a cheap ivory substitute, it was exported to Europe and America to manufacture umbrella and cane handles, buttons, billiard balls and toys. (Today, with the international ban on the ivory trade, vegetable ivory from Ecuador is marketed as a way to save the African elephant.) Despite its widespread use, the actual palm, *Phytelephas macrocarpa* (literally, 'plant elephant large fruit'), had yet to be botanically described. No specimen existed in European glasshouses. Hooker noted that not even Martius, in 'his "Opus magnificum" on the Palms', had included a full description of *Phytelephas macrocarpa*.[8]

For two years, in New Granada, Purdie pursued the ivory-nut palm. At points, he was reduced to near destitution: 'I arrived here with only a *real* and a half (nine-pence English) in my possession', he informed Hooker from Bogotá, 'in debt with my servants and my clothes almost reduced to rags'.[9] With his usual eye for publicity, Hooker published extracts from Purdie's letters and journals, and illustrations of the ivory-nut palm, in his botanical magazines (see Plates 6 and 7). Readers followed Purdie's progress as he headed across the Sierra Nevada de Santa Marta, in the wet season, with four mules: one to ride, one to carry specimens and plant pressing paper, and two for the baggage and further specimens. The paths generally followed the course of the rivers, and often, Purdie despairingly wrote, 'the mules capsize and hurl rider and load into the water'.[10] Frequently drenched, he was laid up for weeks in mountain villages with recurrent bouts of fever. But, at last, in July 1845, Purdie reported sighting the *Phytelephas*: a graceful palm, known locally as the *tagua*, with pale green feathery leaves, its heavy fruits, the shape and size of a human head, resting on the ground.

To give a full botanic description, Purdie had to record all the plant's parts, which, as Humboldt noted, was particularly challenging in the case of dioecious palms (with separate male and female plants). It was many months before Purdie managed to catch a male *Phytelephas* in flower. In April 1846, he joyfully wrote to Hooker, 'I am happy to inform you that I have had, at last, the good fortune to detect the male flowers of the Ivory-Nut Palm, for which I long sought in vain'.[11] In the dense forest, his attention was first attracted by the sound of humming insects and the overwhelming scent. 'The fragrance is most powerful and delicious, beyond that of any other plant, and so diffusive, that the air, for many yards around, was alive with myriads of annoying insects', he informed Hooker.[12] Claiming his prize, Purdie carried the three-foot-long male flower head for twelve miles through the forest, his sense of triumph somewhat marred by the attendant cloud of flies: 'though I killed a number of insects that followed me', he complained, 'the next day, a great many still hovered about it, which had come from the wood where it grew'.[13]

Purdie harvested a quantity of the *Phytelephas* nuts, which he packed snugly in a box lined with moss. He selected some young specimens and planted them in a Wardian case, sprinkling additional fresh seeds in the soil. Having watered the plants, he sealed the lid tight with putty and screws. But, however much care Purdie exercised in preparing the boxes for Kew, he could not guarantee their safe arrival. 'If these should unfortunately suffer by the voyage', he wrote to Hooker in July 1845, 'I can procure more on my way down the river and am therefore peculiarly desirous to know their fate, without delay'.[14] In this instance, luck was on Purdie's side. In October 1845, Hooker reported that germinating seeds and living plants had reached Kew safely. The young plants were nurtured in the hothouse nurseries before making their public entrance in the Palm House.

In the course of his travels in the Sierra Nevada de Santa Marta, Purdie also encountered a species of mountain wax palm similar to that which Humboldt and Bonpland had presented with such a flourish at Paris, on their return from South America. In 1827, the French chemist and agronomist Jean-Baptiste Boussingault had followed Humboldt and Bonpland to the Quindío Pass to study the wax palm and analyse its wax, with a view to possible commercial applications. Boussingault had collected young plants, but failed to keep them alive. With the advantage conferred by the Wardian case, Purdie managed to dispatch living specimens of the wax palm, *Ceroxylon alpinum*, to Kew. Each palm, Purdie told Hooker, produced around fifty pounds of wax, which was used to make candles; but, he added regretfully, the palms were felled before the wax was scraped from their trunks.[15] Sir William was delighted to receive the consignment. Here was another trophy, as notable for its remarkable properties as for its association with the famed Humboldt, to add to the Palm House display.

Even though Kew had shared the cost of Purdie's expedition with the botanically minded Duke of Northumberland (whose London residence was just over the river from Kew, at Syon House), the Office of Woods and Forests raised concerns about Purdie's expenses and put pressure on Hooker to recall him. Operating with his customary diplomacy, Hooker resolved the situation by recommending Purdie for the post of curator at the Trinidad Botanic Garden. More generally, at a time of financial constraint, plant-collecting expeditions were not high on the government's list of spending priorities. In September 1847, Hooker had to deploy all his authority, charm and high-ranking connections to negotiate a botanic expedition to India. He managed to broker a deal whereby the Treasury and Admiralty would pay half the cost and he himself would make up the remaining £1,000. Sir William was prepared to countenance this enormous sum because the designated plant collector was none other than his own son, Joseph Hooker.

With his work on the *Flora Antarctica* at an end, and tiring of paleobotany at the Geological Survey, Joseph was keen to return to the field and wanted to develop his knowledge of tropical botany. A voyage to India would not only make him the complete botanist, but also equip him with indisputable credentials to succeed his father at Kew. Sir William contacted Lord Auckland, the First Lord of the Admiralty and former Governor General of India, who agreed that Joseph could remain on naval half-pay while on a two-year expedition to India. Joseph travelled out to India, free of charge, on the same ship as the newly appointed Governor General, Lord Dalhousie. It so happened that Dalhousie's late mother had been a keen botanist, who had not only corresponded with Sir William, but had bequeathed her herbarium to him. Before Joseph's departure, Sir William did not fail to write to remind Lord Dalhousie of the personal connection and to secure his interest for his son. By the time the ship had reached Egypt, Joseph was in such favour with Lord Dalhousie that he was invited to join the Governor General's suite.

Not content with securing influential introductions, arranging and part-financing the venture, Sir William celebrated his son's expedition in the various magazines that he edited. The *London*

*Journal of Botany* (1847) announced the appointment of Dr Hooker, 'one of the most enthusiastic votaries of Botany . . . by H. M. Government to investigate the vegetable productions of India, and especially of the Himalaya Mountains'.[16] Hooker also printed a long personal letter, in French, written by 'the distinguished Humboldt' to Joseph. Warmly addressing Joseph as his excellent friend, Humboldt praised his character, knowledge, ardour and disinterested devotion. He enthusiastically anticipated that Joseph would render eminent services to the disciplines of plant geography, meteorology and geology. In travelling to the Himalayan regions, Joseph would be carrying out his own lifelong dream, Humboldt declared. He appended a long list of questions and instructions for Joseph, requesting that he pay attention to matters such as the measurement of altitude for various plant families and species of fish in mountain lakes. In printing Humboldt's letter, Hooker positioned his son as an intellectual heir of the great naturalist.

To meet the growing demand for popular botany, Hooker decided in 1849 to launch his cheapest monthly magazine yet: *Hooker's Journal of Botany and Kew Garden Miscellany*, priced at a shilling. With a title that both enhanced his own reputation and the fame of Kew, *Hooker's Journal* aimed, in the words of the *Literary Gazette*, to 'afford a popular means of recording the discovery of remarkable plants, to communicate intelligence and observations of travellers abroad on botanical expeditions, and to illustrate the nature of vegetable substances in familiar use'.[17] To fill its pages, Hooker drew on his extensive network of correspondents. Letters from 'travellers abroad on botanical expeditions' made up a large proportion of its contents. In an unashamed exhibition of paternal pride (not to say nepotism), Hooker used the *Journal* to publicize the Indian travels of his son. In 1849, for instance, 'Extracts from the Private Letters of Dr J. D.

Hooker written during a Botanical Mission to India' made up almost a third of the volume. Far from being solely focused on matters botanical, Joseph's letters ranged in content from an account of an alligator attack and a visit to inspect a thug, a dacoit and a poisoner in the Mirzapur prison, to a description of Benares and a report of the operation of the opium trade in Patna. The letters would form the basis for the *Himalayan Journals* (1854), the book of travels which would bring Joseph Hooker to full public notice, much as the *Journal of Researches* (*Voyage of the Beagle*) had established the reputation of Joseph's close friend and mentor, Charles Darwin. The children's author 'Captain' Thomas Mayne Reid would even base a novel on Joseph Hooker's travels: *The Plant Hunters, or, Adventures among the Himalaya Mountains* (1859).

At times, Joseph's travels did indeed resemble an adventure story. In pursuit of orchids and rhododendrons, he headed to Darjeeling, a hill station on the edge of the Eastern Himalaya, acquired by the British for use as a sanatorium in return for an annual payment to the neighbouring kingdom of Sikkim. Relations between the British superintendent of Darjeeling, Dr Alistair Campbell, and the dewan (chief minister) of Sikkim were considerably strained. It was the dewan, rather than the *Chogyal* (ruler), who held political power in Sikkim. The dewan was a Tibetan, and favoured the Tibetan policy of excluding foreign influence from the region.[18] However, after protracted negotiations conducted by Campbell, Joseph was admitted into Sikkim, an area hitherto unmapped by the British. Travelling with an entourage of over fifty porters, servants and plant collectors, Hooker lived in relative comfort. Every night, his staff set up camp; a blanket slung over tree branches formed his tent. 'I entered my snug little house, and flung myself on the elastic couch to ruminate on the proceedings of the day', he recollected, 'waiting for my meal, which usually consisted of stewed meat and rice, with biscuits and tea'.[19] Hooker divided his time between botanizing and surveying, producing maps which would later prove invaluable to the British military.

Campbell used Hooker's expedition as an occasion to ally himself with a rival of the dewan, and to attempt – unsuccessfully – to seek an audience with the *Chogyal* of Sikkim. Prevented from meeting

29. *The plant collector deified:* Joseph Hooker in Sikkim, *engraving after Frank Stone.*

the ruler, Campbell responded by provocatively flouting border regulations. In November 1849, he and Hooker crossed into the forbidden territory of Tibet. 'I put spurs to my pony and gallopped ahead on the sandy plains of Thibet', Joseph wrote exultingly to his father, 'determined to stay away all day and see what I could'.[20] The Tibetan trespass lasted four days, before Campbell and Hooker were arrested and imprisoned by the dewan.

Campbell, as the main political prisoner, was placed under stricter confinement than Joseph. The two were kept separate, but were allowed to send notes to each other. 'I hope that you may not have had causeless alarm from evil reports of my safety having gone to England', Joseph wrote home, attempting to reassure his father. 'I am a prisoner under the Sikkim Rajah, along with Campbell, but my bonds are not very heavy & I am under no apprehensions whatever on my own or Campbell's account'.[21] Joseph was free to use his instruments, plants and books, and was keeping himself busy. 'I have now to beg & implore you not to make a stir about this', Joseph entreated his father. 'Pray . . . do not allow my Mother to harbour dismal thoughts of any description'.[22]

In the event, the British press denounced the pair's treatment and the colonial authorities threatened to invade. After two months, Hooker and Campbell were released, and were back in Darjeeling by Christmas Eve. But, the following year, the British responded in true imperial fashion: they refused to make the annual payment for Darjeeling, and retaliated by annexing some 640 square miles of Sikkim.

Following the incident, Hooker returned to less audacious pursuits. He met up with an old friend, the surgeon and botanist Thomas Thomson, then stationed in India, who, like Joseph, had grown up in Glasgow, the son of a university professor. They had undertaken medical training together, and Thomson had studied botany under

William Hooker. The two friends had long planned a joint botanical venture, and they now travelled together in the Khasi Hills in eastern Bengal, accumulating a vast collection of specimens which would form the basis of their later *Flora Indica* (1855). This was intended as the first in an ambitious series that would cover the entire flora of British India. But the project failed to attract official funding, and never progressed beyond the initial volume.

In Britain, Sir William indefatigably promoted his son's activities. He featured Joseph's discoveries – a staggering twenty-five new species of rhododendron – in his popular botanic magazines. The rhododendron seeds and plants which Joseph sent to Kew were to be planted in a sheltered vale near the Thames to create the vibrant display that became known as the Rhododendron Dell (which still attracts crowds of visitors when it explodes with colour in the late spring).

For his influential aristocratic, political and botanic friends, Sir William edited a de-luxe three-volume edition of plates, *The Rhododendrons of Sikkim Himalaya* (1849–51). The volume was fulsomely dedicated to the sixteen-year-old Princess Mary, the daughter of the Duke and Duchess of Cambridge, who lived on Kew Green and took a lively interest in the Gardens. To add an exotic touch, Sir William included descriptions of the Himalayan setting, with the frontispiece bearing a vignette of Kangchenjunga, 'the loftiest mountain yet known in the world'.[23] The preface related Joseph's awe at the 'stupendous scenery', which was tinged gold and red at sunrise, then suddenly, 'like the work of magic', shrouded in mist. 'Such is the region of the Indian Rhododendrons', exclaimed Sir William.[24]

The first species to be featured in the volume was the most beautiful of Joseph's discoveries: a large white bloom resembling the Bourbon lily, with rose tints and a lemon-scented fragrance, named

*Rhododendron dalhousiae*. Joseph provided an elegant explanation: 'to the Lady of the present Governor-General of India, I have, as a mark of grateful esteem and respect, dedicated the noblest species of the whole race'.[25] Even as Joseph and Thomson were still out botanizing in the Khasi Hills, a copy of the finished volume arrived at Government House, Calcutta. The younger Hooker was fast learning the necessary art of botanical flattery.

There was no formal opening ceremony for the Palm House. The first visitors were admitted in late summer 1848. At the start of September, the *Illustrated London News* published prints of external and internal views of the Palm House. The interior view depicted couples and families as onlookers to the scene of labour: piles of

30. *The Palm House interior,* Illustrated London News, *2 September 1848.*

planks and a trolley occupied the foreground, while a group of gardeners manoeuvred a palm into place in the middle ground.

On 21 August, William Hooker proudly reported to his father-in-law that Queen Victoria had visited Kew '3 times in less than 6 weeks', adding that 'The Palm House, now it is filled, is the admiration of every body & the view of the Palms from the Gallery is most striking. The Queen was enchanted with it'.[26]

The Queen's delight with the gallery view was echoed by contemporary writers and journalists. It was the highlight of a tour of the Palm House, even if it was several degrees hotter than the ground floor. To open the Palm House door was to be assaulted by heat, humidity and the smell of damp vegetation. 'It is the heat of India', the *London Journal* exclaimed, 'and there are you, within the distance of an hour's walk from London, without trouble or expense, amid the vegetable glories of the tropics!'[27] In an instant, visitors were transported to the realm of princely palms. 'Such regal forms bathing their green crowns in that atmosphere of warmth and light! – such coronets of plumes upborne to an astonishing altitude! – leaves, long and pointed, cast over a vast area! – leaves, broad and shadowy, as if inviting to coolness, shelter and repose!'[28] Overdressed and gasping, ladies gazed upwards, awed by the sheer size of the palms. 'And all the fanning in the world isn't any use', declared *Punch*, 'for the more you fan, the hotter you get'.[29]

Once the eye had adjusted to the tangled mass of foliage (and the elderly had wiped the mist from their glasses), visitors began to make out unfamiliar fruit hanging from the trees. There were clusters of bananas, as yet unknown in Britain: 'the fruit is esteemed a delicacy, and although somewhat "soapy" to some tastes, is highly agreeable', the *Ladies' Cabinet* informed its readers.[30] There were mangoes, secured from the light-fingered in muslin bags. Some mango varieties were 'no better than tow and turpentine', judged the *Quarterly Review*, but 'first-rate numbers' left 'a delicious taste in the mouth, which is remembered for years and years'.[31] Entwining the pillars were flowering creepers, reaching up to the gallery. A tour of the Palm House was an overwhelmingly sensory experience: the body responded to the heat, humidity, smells and imagined tastes of the tropics. The physical reaction not only made the visit more memorable, but entirely immersed the visitor in the tropical scene.

With its spectacular plants from all over the world, the Palm House provided a kind of exotic stage set for the free play of the imagination. It was a scene emptied of inhabitants, allowing it to be peopled by the visitors themselves. In an 1850 article for *Punch*, the novelist William Makepeace Thackeray, writing in the guise of a penniless

31. *An illustration from Gosse,* Wanderings through the Conservatories at Kew *(1857).*

Mr Punch, invited the reader to join him to enjoy the free diversions afforded by Kew: 'I will sit with him under a spreading palm-tree as if he were an Arab Sheik, or under a banyan tree as if he were a Bramin'.[32] The *Quarterly Review* imagined Palm House encounters of a more threatening kind: 'a tiger might start out from among those tree-ferns, a boa-constrictor might be climbing the trunk of that cocoa-nut palm'.[33] The Palm House allowed visitors to experience a tropical setting with none of the actual hazards of distant travel: inconvenient locals and alarming animals.

The two tall date palms (*Phoenix dactylifera*) evoked the enchanted realm of *The Thousand and One Nights*, and the orientalist romances of Robert Southey and Thomas Moore. The Orient depicted in Southey's *Thalaba the Destroyer* (1801) and Moore's *Lalla Rookh* (1817) was at once fantastic and full of authenticating detail: the focus in *Thalaba*, for instance, could shift within the space of a few verses from a dialogue with a demon to a scene of weaving baskets from palm leaves.[34] In both poems, the beautiful forms of date palms were likened to that of women. A quatrain from *Lalla Rookh* that described a *peri*'s (fairy's) view of a palm grove was particularly widely cited in guides to Kew:

> Those groups of lovely date-trees bending
> Languidly their leaf-crowned heads,
> Like youthful maids, when sleep descending
> Warns them to their silken beds[35]

Despite – or perhaps because of – its fanciful context and hint of sensuality, these lines were much quoted in botanical works. Nineteenth-century popular scientific writing did not observe strict disciplinary boundaries; plant descriptions were often supplemented with verses of poetry, demonstrating both the author's poetic taste and aesthetic appreciation. There was a fluid exchange between botany and poetry, rather as the Palm House functioned both as a scientific showpiece and a space for fantasy.

The gallery was by far the favourite location for tropical dreaming. Ascending the spiral staircase to the thirty-foot-high walkway allowed an uninterrupted view of the canopy: an illusion of endless foliage that transported excursionists into a tropical forest. It was Humboldt who established the glasshouse gallery as *the* site of tropical reverie. Humboldt attributed his youthful wanderlust to visits to the Berlin Botanic Garden and his fascination with an old dragon tree and the fan palm made famous by the experiment to establish the sexes of plants. As a student in Cambridge, Charles Darwin too was prompted to travel by the heady combination of glasshouses and Humboldt's *Personal Narrative*: 'my head is running about the Tropics: in the morning I go and gaze at Palm trees in the hot-house and come home and read Humboldt', he wrote to his sister, Caroline; 'my enthusiasm is so great that I cannot hardly sit still on my chair'. Merely to describe his state was to re-enflame it: 'I have written myself into a Tropical glow', he declared, before signing off.[36]

When Humboldt initially returned from his South American travels, he disparaged glasshouse displays as pale imitations of the tropics; but, as an elderly man, he came to value hothouses for their ability to ignite the imagination.[37] In his final work, *Cosmos*, Humboldt numbered 'the cultivation and arrangement of exotic plants' among 'the most precious fruits of European civilisation'.[38] A great palm house, such as that at Loddiges' Nursery, Humboldt proposed, provided the most convincing spectacle of the tropics:

> When . . . we look down from the high gallery . . . on the luxuriant reed and tree-like palms below, we feel, for a moment, in a state of complete delusion as to the locality to which we are transported, and we may even believe

> ourselves to be actually in a tropical climate, looking from the summit of a hill on a small grove of palms . . . the illusion is more perfect, and exercises a stronger effect on the imagination than is excited by the most perfect painting. Fancy associates with every plant the wonders of some distant region, as we listen to the rustling of the fan-like leaves, and see the changing and flitting effect of the light, when the tops of the palms, gently moved by currents of air, come in contact as they wave to and fro.[39]

The gallery view offered Humboldt an aesthetic experience that surpassed even the effect produced by visual art. Humboldt's state of transport seems analogous to a reader's total immersion in a world of fiction – the condition famously described by Coleridge as a 'willing suspension of disbelief'.[40] But, while the poetic world of Coleridge's reader was entirely fabricated, the palm-house spectacle was at once a work of art and a living display. 'So great is the charm produced by reality', wrote Humboldt, that 'the recollection of the artificial care bestowed on the plants certainly exercises a disturbing influence'.[41] The tropical dream was only broken by the recognition of the effort – both horticultural and technological – involved in staging the hothouse show.

Repeatedly, in accounts of the Palm House at Kew, a visit to the gallery provided the occasion for a moment of Humboldtian rapture. The writer was carried away into a fantasy realm, before being summoned back by the intrusion of the everyday. 'I climbed, with a sensation like swimming in herbage', wrote James Hannay in *Household Words*.[42] At the top of the spiral staircase, the visitor was 'perched above the forest . . . The palms were slowly swaying, and the feathery tops of the tall bamboos fluttered . . . The heat and the coloured light still the fancy into a dreamy mist – but an attendant passes you. You awake to fact; this gallery is the place whence the plants are watered'.[43] Like Humboldt, the narrator drifts into a tropical reverie, only to be roused by a gardener doing his rounds. The Palm House occupied a space between illusion and reality – part theatre, part working environment.

While Hannay modelled his description of the Palm House on Humboldt's account, the German botanist Berthold Seemann went a step further. He dedicated his *Popular History of the Palms* (1856) to Humboldt, and printed the great naturalist's gratified response as part of the prefatory material. Raised in Hanover, Seemann was one of a number of German gardeners and botanists who profited from the Hanoverian royal connection with Kew. University educated and linguistically gifted, with interests ranging across the natural sciences, literature, anthropology and music, Seemann had determined on a career as a plant collector. From 1845 to 1846 he trained at Kew, where his talent and ambition brought him to the attention of Hooker. Sir William recommended Seemann for the position of naturalist on the *Herald*, then undertaking a survey of the Pacific, but which was later diverted to polar regions to search for Sir John Franklin's lost Arctic expedition. The *Herald*'s voyage became a circumnavigation of the globe, and Seemann's travels in Panama, Peru, Ecuador and Mexico, western Canada and Hong Kong furnished the material for two major publications: *The Botany of the Voyage of H.M.S. Herald* (1852–7) and the *Narrative of the Voyage of H.M.S. Herald* (1853). Seemann evidently took the journey and publications of Humboldt and Bonpland as his model (he even adopted 'Bonpland' as his scientific name when elected to membership of the prestigious German imperial academy, the *Academia Naturae Curiosorum*).

Thanking Seemann for the dedication of the *Popular History of the Palms*, Humboldt singled out for praise Seemann's account of Kew's Palm House, and in particular his lengthy description of the gallery view. In the introduction to the *Popular History*, Seemann somewhat disingenuously refused to rank the great European glasshouses, before celebrating that erected by his patron, Sir William Hooker. To 'see the Palms to their greatest advantage, in an æsthetic point of view', Seemann advised, it was best to visit the Palm House on a dull or rainy day, to evoke 'the gloom of the virgin forest'.[44] The prospect from the gallery, Seemann asserted with a grand rhetorical flourish, recalled the exploits of those naturalists – including Humboldt, Bonpland and Joseph Hooker – 'who disregarding dangers and mental and bodily exertions, explored trackless forest, climbed steep mountains, traversed pestilential swamps – the abode of myriads of mosquitos, – and crossed dreary deserts and monotonous steppes' to gather the specimens.[45] Continuing his sentence – now grown to epic length – Seemann lauded the heroism and endurance of naturalists, and concluded that the visitor could not but feel grateful to those naturalists who had laboured so hard in the pursuit of knowledge 'to inspire us all with love and reverence for the infinite!'[46] Such musings would transport the visitor, so that 'gradually . . . the verdant masses will assume before his [the visitor's] mind's eye more extensive dimensions than they actually possess, become endless forests, where strange animals and barbarous peoples have taken up their abode'.[47] In providing a space to recall and re-enact the adventures of plant collectors, the glasshouse offered a monument to muscular botany. For Seemann, the Palm House attested to the advance of European science over the rest of the world.

But Seemann had not finished yet. The longer the visitor surveyed the gallery view, the more he would become convinced of 'the grandeur of the subject before him'. Why was it that northern climes were deprived of such beautiful and useful plants as palms? 'Why have we to go to Africa for our dates, to America for our cocoa-nuts, and to Asia for our sago?' The answer could only lie in the wisdom of

Nature, who, 'by distributing her gifts in such a manner, wished to point out the mutual dependency of one country or one man upon another, thus practically teaching us peace, humility, love! – the three great watchwords, without which human society cannot prosper, and human happiness becomes an impossibility'.[48] Bringing his introduction to a resounding close, Seemann suggested that Nature (rather than God) had distributed palms throughout the world so as to link humanity through the bonds of trade. In reaching this conclusion, Seemann knew that he would appeal to Humboldt, who advocated transcontinental commerce as a means to overcome the isolation of nations and contribute to humanity's development.[49] According to Seemann, the Palm House gallery offered nothing less than a view of the progress of civilization itself.

In contrast with the grand prospect from the gallery, the view below ground was far from promising. As John Smith had predicted, it was impossible to keep the boiler rooms dry. Although two pumps worked day and night, the stokers were knee-deep in water. It was fearsomely hot and the air stank. Going 'coking' was the worst job in the gardens, frequently assigned as punishment duty. The furnace rooms and boilers were a perennial source of anxiety for the curator. 'I can bear testimony', recalled Smith, 'to the consequences of the alarming words – "Please, sir, the boiler has burst"'.[50] By November 1848, the water was almost as high as the furnace doors. Two additional fire engines were set pumping. On 1 March 1849, Smith noted in his diary: 'Tunnel full of water, more men required'. The following day: 'Water in tunnel like a swimming stream'. On 5 May 1849: 'Water rising faster. Men quite exhausted with pumping'.[51] For the next four years, the workforce would struggle to keep the flooding at bay.

Contemporary accounts of the Palm House scarcely mentioned the labour involved in its functioning. The *Quarterly Review* imagined the underground railway tunnel as 'convenient to walk in, and lighted and ventilated by shafts from above'. Information on 'these subterranean wonders' could be gleaned from 'the well-behaved gnomes' who gave 'the first impulse to the machinery which elaborates the beautiful vegetation overhead'.[52] With a hyperbolic flourish, Smith and the garden staff were transformed into a magical workforce to tend the 'gigantic bubble' of tropical illusion, situated at the heart of Kew.[53]

But, for the British public, the tropics were not only the site of fantasy but also the source of commercial gain. While the curator and his team laboured hard to maintain the Palm House spectacle, Smith's son was busy cataloguing the plant products that drove the British economy.

# 12

# The Museum

The fourteen-year-old Alexander Smith, one of the two surviving children of Kew's curator, had been sent home from boarding school. A shy child, he had been afflicted by a nervous speech disorder which put an end to his formal schooling. If there was one thing that John Smith could not abide, it was idleness. To occupy the boy, Smith told him to sort the vegetable products in the old fruit store of the former royal kitchen gardens. The retiring Alexander – so unlike his forthright father – was at his happiest attempting to impose order on the haphazard collection. There were samples of seeds, oils, baskets, blowpipes, bonnets and walking sticks. Given that the boy seemed to take to the work, his father added him to Kew's payroll in June 1847. Alexander received a wage of a few shillings a week. It was a great comfort to John Smith to know that he had secured his only son a position at Kew.

The collection of plant products that occupied Alexander had originated in the specimens amassed over the years by Smith and Hooker. These were now to form the basis of the Museum of Vegetable Products, which opened to the public on 20 September

1847.[1] The museum was housed in the old fruit store, converted by Decimus Burton through the addition of a long skylight, gallery, glazed table cases and cabinets along the walls. The first of its kind, the museum aimed to demonstrate the uses of plants, both in their local and global context. The idea had been born out of Hooker's desire to prove the utility of botany and justify the public spending on the Gardens. By demonstrating the multifarious uses of plants, Kew could play its part in stimulating trade and industrial innovation.

The nineteenth-century British economy was heavily reliant on

32. *The Museum of Economic Botany (1855).*

plant products, either grown in the colonies or acquired through global trade. In 1853, Thomas Croxen Archer, who worked in the Import Department of Liverpool Customs, estimated that at least three quarters of the total value of British imports was made up from articles of vegetable origin.[2] To signal the commercial significance of plants and to confer a sense of scientific rigour to the collection, Hooker renamed the display the Museum of Economic Botany (most likely following the lead of De la Beche's Museum of Economic Geology).[3] In so doing, Hooker helped to establish 'economic botany' as the disciplinary term to denote the study of useful plants.[4] 'The ship-builder, the carpenter, the cabinet-maker, the general merchant, the manufacturer, the weaver, the physician, the druggist, the dyer, the oil and colourman &c. &c.', Hooker proudly listed, 'will here find, systematically arranged, the several objects in which they are interested, accompanied by their correct appellation, the countries whence they come, and the names of the Plants from which they are procured'.[5] With the long – and infinitely expandable – list of tradesmen, Hooker suggested the endless application of vegetable products.

To build the collection as inexpensively as possible, Hooker issued an open invitation to travellers to contribute plant items. In the chapter on botany which Hooker contributed to the *Manual of Scientific Enquiry* (1849), for the use of the Navy and travellers in general, he included suggestions for vegetable products and advice on sending dried and preserved plant material. Almost immediately, the packages flooded in: sections of tree trunks, flowers in alcohol, garments, fishing nets, musical instruments. Merchants and manufacturers in Britain donated samples of trade goods and finished products. Important donors received the gratification of public acknowledgement in the director's annual reports. In February 1848 Hooker reported that, since the museum's opening in September the previous year, the collection had more than quadrupled. Four years later, Hooker was boasting of its world-leading significance. 'This museum has been formed at a trifling expense; and, even in its present infant state', Hooker asserted, 'nothing of the same nature so practically useful to the scientific and commercial world exists in the capital of any country, or in any other Botanic Garden'.[6]

With such a large influx of material – much of it, inevitably, duplicating existing holdings or of questionable quality – it was important to fix an overall organizing principle. Initially, items were grouped according to end product, in categories such as food, fibres, oils and drugs. But, since individual plants could be used in multiple ways, this proved impractical, and the display was soon reordered around plant families, based on the natural system. Hooker's approach was partly modelled on Sir Henry De la Beche's Museum of Economic Geology, which, like Kew, came under the governance of the Office of Woods and Forests (and which employed Robert Hunt, who had advised on the Palm House glass). De la Beche placed rock samples beside associated metals and manufactures; following suit, Hooker exhibited plant materials next to locally produced items and European finished goods.[7] The resulting displays suggested the multiple ways that British industry could profit from local knowledge. The museum cabinets brought cultures together in unlikely conjunction. 'In striking proximity are articles of everyday use amongst ourselves', noted the writer, Sophy Moody, 'and strange and almost inexplicable things brought from the dwellings of savages'.[8]

Just as palms were the main attraction of the Palm House, so too were they the highlight of the museum. Hooker envisaged the display in the museum as a complement to the living collection in the Palm House. Visitors would derive 'twofold gratification and twofold instruction' from first being able to view tropical specimens in the

SUMMARY. 325

a strangely varied list of articles which are subjoined.

FOOD.

Fruits, various kinds
Bread (sago)
Honey.
Sugar.
Oil.
Cabbage.
Gruel.
Sweetmeats.
Puddings.
Palm-nut soup.
Preserves.
Pickles.
Salt.
Yeast.
Fruit beverages of various kinds.
Wine.
Milk.
Toddy.
Arrack.
Vinegar.
Food for cattle, camels, pigs, poultry, and all animals.

CLOTHING.

Ready-made cloak.
Do. apron.
Do. cap.
Cloth.
Coats } Rofia cloth.
Waiscoats } Rofia cloth.
Gowns } Rofia cloth.
Tippets.
Pouches.
Hats.
Bonnets.
Sandals.
Head-dresses.
Beads of various kinds.
Necklaces and bracelets.

MEDICINAL PURPOSES.

Decoctions of various kinds.
Lozenges.
Emulsion.
Lotion.
Remedy for snake-bites.
Do. for wounds.
Antidote to poison.
Catechu.
Dragon's blood.
Tannin.

DWELLINGS AND DOMESTIC PURPOSES.

Houses.
Thatch.
Flooring.
Rafters.
Pillars and posts.
Window-shutters and blinds.
Lattice screens.
Cradles.
Chairs.
Hammocks.
Carpets and mats.
Mattresses and sofa-stuffing.
Chests of Drawers.
Cooking vessels.
Drinking do.
Plates, dishes, bowels.
Cups, ladles, spoons.
Water-pails.
Cylinders, strainers
Graters, sieves.
Shaving-dishes.
Lamps, lanterns.
Candles, torches.
Soap.
Scrubbing-brushes.
Brooms.
Tinder.
Panniers, baskets, sacks, bags, combs, brushes.
Coffins.

MISCELLANEOUS.

Churches.
Bridges.
Canoes.
Palanquin roofs.
Bee-hives.
Pack-saddles.
Water-troughs and gutterings.
Fences.
Well-sweeps.
Fishing-nets, rods, lines, hooks.
Bows, arrows, and bowstrings.
Harpoons.
Blowpipe and arrows.
Spears.
Bullets, ramrods.
Drums.
Æolian harps.
Trumpets.
Flageolets.
Viols.
Bird-cages.
Insect-boxes.
Chests, bonnet-boxes.
Packall or pegall.
Egyptian games, with sticks.
Marbles.
Books, paper, pens, stylets, ink, letter-cases.
Walking, parasol, umbrella sticks.
Knobs and frames to do.
Umbrellas, fan sunshades.
Bottle-stopper and screws.
Cordage and sail-cloth.

In the highly interesting and admirably arranged museums at Kew, may be seen very many of the curious and varied products of palm trees. In striking proximity are articles of everyday use amongst ourselves, and strange and almost inexplicable things brought from the dwellings of savages.

33. *A list of the multifarious uses of palms, from Sophy Moody,* The Palm Tree *(1864).*

hothouse and then contemplate their uses in the museum.[9] In the museum guide, Hooker drew visitors' attention to notable exhibits. Of the fourteen plants of particular interest, seven were species of palm.[10] 'It would require a volume to notice the several uses that mankind derives from Palms', Hooker observed in his guide. 'They yield timber, fibre of every variety, oil, wax, starch, sugar, daily food, mild and intoxicating drink; it is rather difficult to say what they do not afford, and impossible in a brief catalogue to notice a tythe of the contents of this collection'.[11]

Among the collectors of palm material for the museum was a young naturalist, Alfred Russel Wallace, who would later become famous for proposing the theory of evolution, independently of Darwin. Wallace was entirely self-taught, having left school at the age of thirteen. He became interested in natural history while he was working as a surveyor and teacher. Entranced by the travel narratives of Darwin and Humboldt, Wallace dreamt of visiting the tropics. Like many of his generation, he was hugely excited by the anonymous publication of *Vestiges of Natural History of Creation* (1844), a bravura account of the formation of the universe that proposed an evolutionary narrative for life on earth (and scandalized many who adhered to the biblical version).[12] Wallace would be preoccupied by the 'great problem of the origin of species' for much of his life. 'I fully believed that a full and careful study of the facts of nature would ultimately lead to a solution of the mystery', he wrote in his autobiography.[13]

At the age of twenty-five, Wallace and his even younger friend, the self-taught entomologist Henry Walter Bates, boldly determined on an expedition up the Amazon and Rio Negro. They would finance their travels through the sale of natural-history specimens. Before their departure, Wallace and Bates sought expert advice from curators at the British Museum (which then included a natural-history section) and Sir William Hooker at Kew.[14] Embarking at Liverpool on the charmingly named *Mischief*, the pair reached Pará (today's Belém) in Brazil in May 1848.

On arrival, Wallace was delighted by the sight of the forest, 'overtopped by palms and plantains . . . appearing doubly beautiful from the presence of those luxuriant tropical productions in a state of nature, which we had so often admired in the conservatories of Kew and Chatsworth'.[15] Bates was equally struck by the glasshouse parallel: 'the hot moist mouldy air, which seemed to strike from the ground and walls, reminded me of the atmosphere of tropical stoves at Kew'.[16] The experience of the hothouses of Kew conditioned their response to the tropics and provided a model for imagining the rain-forest environment. Bates suggested that the 'reader who has visited Kew may form some notion by conceiving vegetation like that of the great palm-house spread over a large tract of swampy ground'.[17]

During the initial months of collecting, Wallace packed up a box of dried palm material, which he dispatched to the Kew museum (charging Hooker the sum of ten pounds). He offered to send living plants and specimens of particular interest, such as the stilt-rooted *paxiúba* palm (*Socratea exorrhiza*). The *paxiúba* grew 'on three legs so high that you may stand with 50 feet of stem perpendicular over your head', he wrote to Hooker.[18] But Wallace's main interest lay in studying primates, birds, insects and fish. Given the abundance of wildlife in the region, he did not know how much time he would be able to devote to plants. Still, he promised Hooker to preserve any vegetable curiosities that he came across for the museum.

Sir William, however, was not dependent on Wallace for his supply of Amazonian plants. In 1849, Hooker encouraged the Yorkshire botanist Richard Spruce to undertake a collecting expedition to the Amazon with the aim of reaching the headwaters of the Orinoco and the Andes. On the voyage out, Spruce accompanied Wallace's younger brother, Herbert, who was joining the expedition. Soon after their arrival in Pará, Spruce met the older Wallace and his companion, Bates. Spruce and Alfred Russel Wallace became close friends. Whenever their paths converged, they would discuss their discoveries and Spruce would give Wallace botanical advice. In 1851, Wallace showed Spruce some drawings that he had made of palms. 'I pointed out to him which seemed to be new', Spruce wrote, 'and encouraged him to go on'.[19] Spruce proposed that they might work together on a study of palms: Wallace providing the pictures, and he the botanical descriptions. But Wallace did not wish to collaborate. Anticipating that Wallace might pre-empt him in publishing his findings, Spruce ceded the palms to Wallace.[20] There remained more than enough to occupy Spruce. He would eventually spend fifteen years in South America, learn twenty-one languages, map three previously uncharted rivers and collect an astonishing 7,000 species of flowering plants.

Some months into the expedition, Wallace and Bates parted company. Venturing alone into remote regions, Wallace was thrilled to encounter people whom he regarded as 'absolute uncontaminated savages', who 'walked with the free step of the independent forest-dweller'.[21] He was also beguiled by the life of the villagers in Javíta, on the Rio Negro, with whom he spent one rainy season. With all their needs met by river and forest, the people appeared to Wallace happily untroubled by the pursuit – and inequalities – of wealth. From an early age, Wallace had been influenced by the socialism of Robert Owen, and, during his time in Javíta, he found himself 'in a state of excited indignation against civilised life in general'.[22] To express his sentiments, Wallace turned to Wordsworthian blank verse. His 'Description of Javíta' compared the joys of the carefree existence of the villagers to the miseries of a life devoted to moneymaking:

> I'd be an Indian here, and live content
> To fish, and hunt, and paddle my canoe[23]

The self-sufficiency of the villagers was based on the all-providing palms of the forest:

A palm-tree's spreading leaves supply a thatch
Impervious to the winter's storms and rain.
No nail secures the beams or rafters, all
Is from the forest, whose lithe, pendent cords
Bind them into a firm enduring mass.
From the tough fibre of a fan-palm's leaf
They twist a cord to make their hammock-bed,
Their bow-string, line, and net for catching fish.[24]

Supplying virtually everything needed to sustain life, the palms of the region fascinated Wallace.

Although he held Humboldt in great esteem, Wallace adopted a less exalted view of the tropics, and occasionally debunked the heroic image of the naturalist. He represented himself as floundering barefooted through the swamps: 'some overhanging bough would knock the cap from my head or the gun from my hand; or the hooked spines of the climbing palms would catch in my shirt-sleeves, and oblige me either to halt and deliberately unhook myself, or leave a portion of my unlucky garment behind'.[25] Spiked stems would often 'seize the insect-net of the ardent Entomologist just as he is making a dash at some rare butterfly'.[26] Accompanied by naked guides and porters, Wallace supposed that they 'no doubt looked upon me as a good illustration of the uselessness and bad consequences of wearing clothes upon a forest journey'.[27]

To Wallace's mind, the barbed climbing palm, *jacitára* (*Desmoncus polyacanthos*), provided a form of natural protection for the indigenous people 'against the incursions of the white traders, who often attack them in their most distant retreats, carry fire and sword into their peaceful houses and take captive their wives and children'.[28] Paddling unharmed along *jacitára*-wreathed streams in their canoes, the local people never cleared the thickets, and so effectively remained hidden. 'Thus does the thorny "jacitára"', Wallace concluded, 'help to secure the independence of the wild Indian in the depths of the forests which he loves'.[29]

After four years of collecting, Wallace was in poor physical shape. His health impaired by recurrent bouts of fever, he made his way back to Pará for the return voyage. There, he learnt that his younger brother, Herbert, who had been intending to return home, had died of yellow fever. The grieving Wallace loaded his large collection of animal, bird, fish and insect specimens, including over fifty living creatures, onto the *Helen*, a trading vessel heading to Britain. But, three weeks into the voyage, the *Helen* caught fire. As flames swept through the hold, the order was given to abandon ship. Wallace snatched up a tin box stuffed with a few shirts, his watch, purse and a couple of notebooks of drawings of palms and fish, 'which were luckily at hand'.[30] He and the crew scrambled for lifeboats and stared aghast at the 'magnificent and awful sight' as the ship 'rolled over, looking like a huge cauldron of fire, the whole cargo of rubber, etc. forming a liquid burning mass at the bottom'.[31]

For ten days, the men survived in the lifeboats on meagre rations of biscuit, raw pork and water. Finally, spotting a sail, they rowed desperately towards it, and were taken on board an old-fashioned brig, the *Jordeson*. Thankful as they were to have been rescued, the survivors then had to endure a long voyage on poor provisions. Arriving at last in Deal, in Kent, the men rushed ashore. 'Oh, glorious day!' Wallace exclaimed in a letter to Spruce. 'Such a dinner with our two captains! Oh, beef-steaks and damson tart, a paradise for hungry sinners'.[32]

But Wallace's entire collection had been lost, including four years' worth of drawings, notes and journals. This was to have been the material on which Wallace founded his career as a naturalist. The sale of the live animals and specimens might have raised £500, which would have kept him solvent while he wrote up his findings. The hundreds of new species of insects and birds in his own private collection would have kept him busy for years. 'So you will see', he lamented to Spruce, 'that I have some need of philosophic resignation to bear my fate with patience and equanimity'.[33]

Now, there was nothing for it but to use his own recollections and the saved notebooks. Remarkably, Wallace managed to produce two books which were published the following year: a short study, *Palm Trees of the Amazon and their Uses* (1853), and an account of his journey, *A Narrative of Travels on the Amazon and Rio Negro* (1853). *Palm Trees of the Amazon* was illustrated with lithographs worked up from Wallace's salvaged sketches by Walter Hood Fitch, the botanical artist patronized by Hooker. To augment the portraits of palms, Fitch illustrated their fruits from specimens in the Kew museum. Although Wallace did not attempt conventional botanical descriptions, he claimed to have discovered a number of new species of palm. But the main focus of the book was on the many uses of palms. 'Suppose then', Wallace addressed the reader in the introduction, 'we visit an Indian cottage on the banks of the Rio Negro'.[34] Wallace listed the contents of the palm-built and furnished hut: rafters, thatch, twine, door, harpoon, blowpipe, arrows, musical instruments, cloth, chest, hammock, bowstring, fishing line, combs, fish hooks and strainer – all made of palm, not to mention the fruit of the peach palm to eat and açaí-berry juice to drink. With individual entries detailing artefacts made from each species, *Palm Trees of the Amazon* demonstrated the intimate connection between people and plants. Wallace directed readers to view living specimens in the Palm House and preserved fruits and spathes in the museum at Kew.

With a limited print run of only 250 copies, *Palm Trees of the Amazon* was reviewed by two journals. The book was praised by the *Annals and Magazine of Natural History* as offering the 'most curious account of the almost endless uses to which palms are applied by the

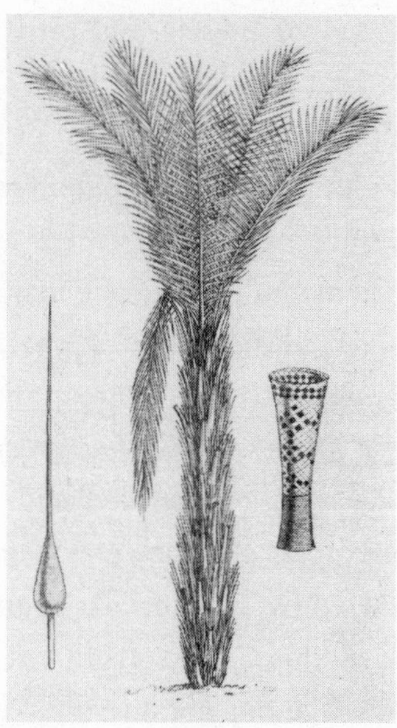

34. Oenocarpus bataua, *with blowpipe arrow and quiver, from Wallace's* Palm Trees of the Amazon *(1853)*.

inhabitants of tropical countries'.[35] Hooker, however, writing in *Hooker's Journal of Botany*, thought that the text added little to existing botanical knowledge of palms. 'He must be a bold man who would undertake a work on Palms after the splendid and scientific volumes of the illustrious Von Martius', his review opened. 'The present however is of a very humble character'.[36] Hooker criticized Wallace's presumption in attempting to identify new species of palm in the absence of illustrations of fruit and flowers, and looked forward to Spruce supplying more accurate information. Hooker displayed remarkably little sympathy for Wallace's loss of his collection through fire (even though, as a young man, he himself had suffered the same fate when returning from Iceland). 'The work', Hooker wrote, 'is certainly more suited to the drawing-room table than to the library of the botanist'.[37]

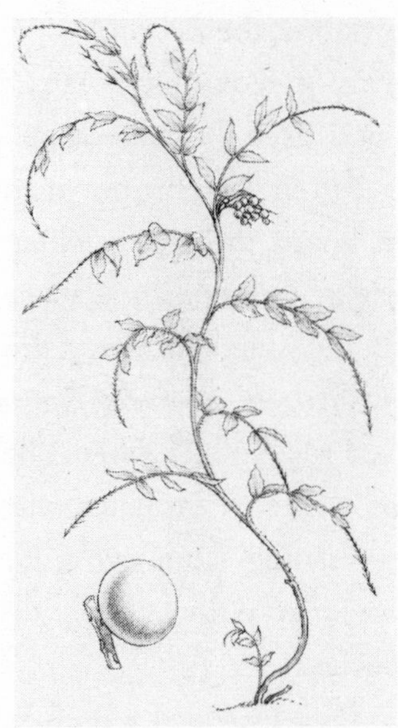

35. Desmoncus polyacanthos, *the barbed climbing palm, from Wallace's* Palm Trees of the Amazon *(1853)*.

Hooker followed up his uncharacteristically sharp review the subsequent year, when he printed an extract of a letter from Spruce in *Hooker's Journal of Botany*. Spruce wrote that he had received a copy of *Palm Trees of the Amazon* from Wallace. The descriptions of palms, Spruce considered 'worse than nothing, – in many cases not a single circumstance that a botanist would care to know'.[38] The illustrations, however, were very pretty and mostly accurate, and the accounts of the uses he judged to be good. Most importantly, Spruce confirmed that two of the palms that Wallace had claimed as previously undescribed were indeed new. Thus Wallace, for whom plants were a mere sideline, managed to achieve botanical success in identifying and naming new species.

One of Wallace's new palms, the *Leopoldinia piassaba*, was particularly significant in terms of economic botany, because it produced *piaçaba* fibre, which was used to make rope and cable in Brazil, and was exported to Britain for broom manufacture (indeed, a quantity had been on board the *Helen* when it had caught fire). One cause of Hooker's irritation with Wallace's book was that he himself had previously identified another palm, *Attalea funifera*, as the source of *piaçaba* fibre, in *Hooker's Journal of Botany* (1849). The mystery was solved for Hooker when Thomas Croxen Archer of Liverpool Customs wrote to explain that two types of fibre – one coarse, one fine – issuing from two different locations, both went by the name of *piaçaba*, so it was likely that they were sourced from two different species.[39]

For Hooker, *piaçaba* fibre provided a useful demonstration of the presence of palm products in the most unexpected areas of British life. As he wrote in *Hooker's Journal of Botany*, 'more use is made of Palms even in England than the public are generally aware'.[40] Who would have thought, for instance, that palm products were essential to civic cleanliness? One of the more unsavoury aspects of nineteenth-century city life was the state of the roads. Horse-drawn traffic meant that thoroughfares were awash with mud composed of horse dung and urine. It was often impossible to find a place to cross the street without dirtying footwear and skirt hems. Crossings were kept clear by road sweepers who were paid pennies to brush the dung into kerbside piles for collection by scavenging carts. In *Bleak House* (1852–3), Dickens chose a homeless sweeper boy, Jo, to represent London's deprived underclass of child labourers. 'No father, no mother, no friends. Never been to school. What's home? Knows a broom's a broom, and knows it's wicked to tell a lie'.[41] Dickens' phrase, 'Knows a broom's a broom', suggests the depths of Jo's ignorance. But, for William Hooker, there was much to know about brooms.

A new fibre had recently been introduced into broom manufacture, Sir William told the readers of *Hooker's Journal of Botany*. It was stiff, yet flexible and water-resistant. It was used both in hand brooms and the brushes of the new cleaning machines that were now seen on the streets of major cities. Most members of the public, Hooker suggested, assumed that the bristles were made from whalebone. 'But no; it is not of animal, but vegetable origin, the coarse fibre of a species of Palm, which grows abundantly in Brazil and is imported to Europe extensively . . . under the native name of "*Piaçaba*"'.[42] The fibre had first come to Britain as packing material in ships' holds, but, the *Mechanics' Magazine* related, a Liverpool brush-maker had picked up a discarded bundle at the docks and found it well suited to the manufacture of brooms.[43] This was an example of exactly the kind of enterprise which Hooker wished to encourage through the Museum of Economic Botany. He placed samples of *piaçaba* fibre, derived from *Attalea funifera*, together with brooms and brushes on display in the palm section of the museum. Next to them were items carved from the mottled brown shell of the same palm's fruit, which was imported under the name of coquilla nut and used to fashion the handles of bell pulls and umbrellas. The items did not have to be spectacular to attract attention. In some ways, the more commonplace the objects, the more remarkable their distant origins.

Berthold Seemann, too, was concerned to illustrate the ubiquity of palm products. He opened his *Popular History of the Palms* with an anecdote. His first acquaintance with palms, Seemann recalled, was neither 'in the great conservatories of Europe, nor in the virgin forests of tropical America or Asia . . . but in a dusty schoolroom of my native town'. It was an acquaintance, wrote Seemann, 'not sought by me; but . . . quite forced upon me'.[44] To keep his class of fifty unruly boys in order, the schoolmaster possessed a number of canes; whenever the opportunity arose, the boys would steal the canes to cut into cigar lengths for smoking practice. The canes were the shoots of an East Indian palm, Seemann told his readers, belonging to the genus *Calamus*, which also supplied the material for chair seats.

Seemann next invited the reader to take a walk with him around the streets of London:

> That ragged boy, sweeping the crossing, and begging you with a faltering voice, real or assumed, to 'remember poor Jack,' holds in his hands a broom, the fibrous substance of which was cut by the wild Indians of Brazil from the stems of a Palm; that gentleman, dressed in the tiptop of fashion, who playfully swings his 'Penang lawyer,' little thinks that, in carrying that walking-cane, he is in fact carrying a young plant of the Licuala acutifida; that fine lady's parasol-knob – what is it but a Coquilla-nut turned into that shape?[45]

Seemann's guided palm tour of London continued at some length. It worked to defamiliarize everyday articles and to suggest the networks of trade and empire that suppled Britain with palm products to manufacture both humble necessities and fashion accessories.

In the Museum of Economic Botany, two display cases were devoted solely to the coconut and its products. Drawing visitors' attention to the display in the introduction of his guide, Hooker described 'the food and raiment, the milk, the oil, the wine (toddy), the cups and bowls, cordage, brushes, mats, in short, the 365 articles ("as many," the Hindoos say, "as there are days in the year") afforded by the

13. Sir William Jackson Hooker, the first director of Kew, by Spiridione Gambardella (1842). Keen to assert the status of the national botanic garden, Hooker determined to build a magnificent new Palm House at Kew.

14. Richard Turner, the iron founder and engineer responsible for the groundbreaking design and construction of the Palm House. The ever-inventive Turner is appropriately pictured here with plans in hand, although his contribution was not always recognized.

15. The architect Decimus Burton in the early 1830s. Well connected and urbane, Burton oversaw the Palm House project, skilfully managing relations between government officials and the unpredictable Richard Turner. For many years, he was credited with the whole design.

16. The first curator of Kew, John Smith. A practical gardener and self-taught botanist, Smith tended the gardens with stern devotion for forty-two years. Always ready to speak his mind, Smith objected to the site chosen for the Palm House – and was to be proved correct.

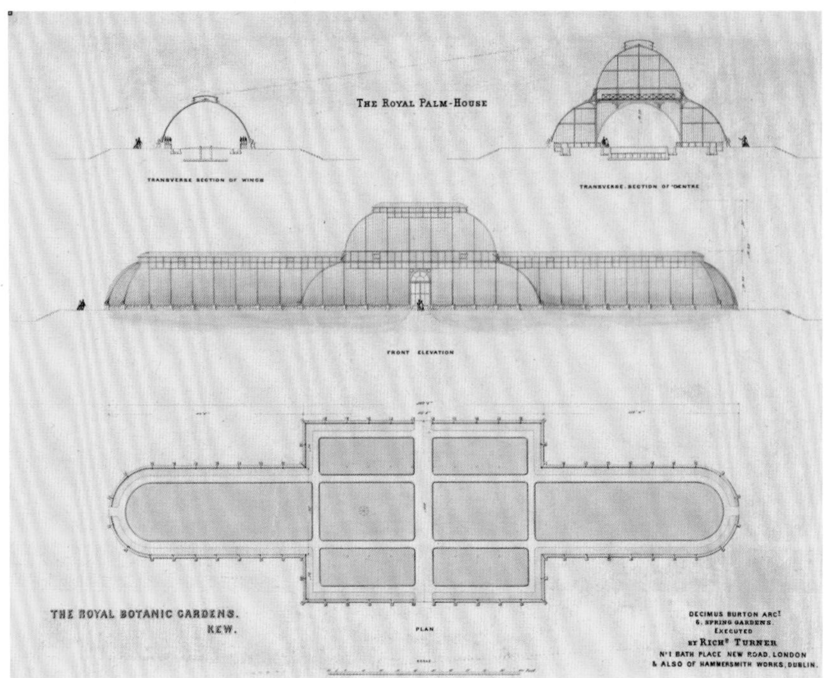


17. A plan of the Palm House produced by Decimus Burton and Richard Turner. Burton was responsible for the pared-down elegance of the design, while Turner devised the innovative wrought-iron frame which used materials borrowed from ship-building and spanned unprecedented widths.

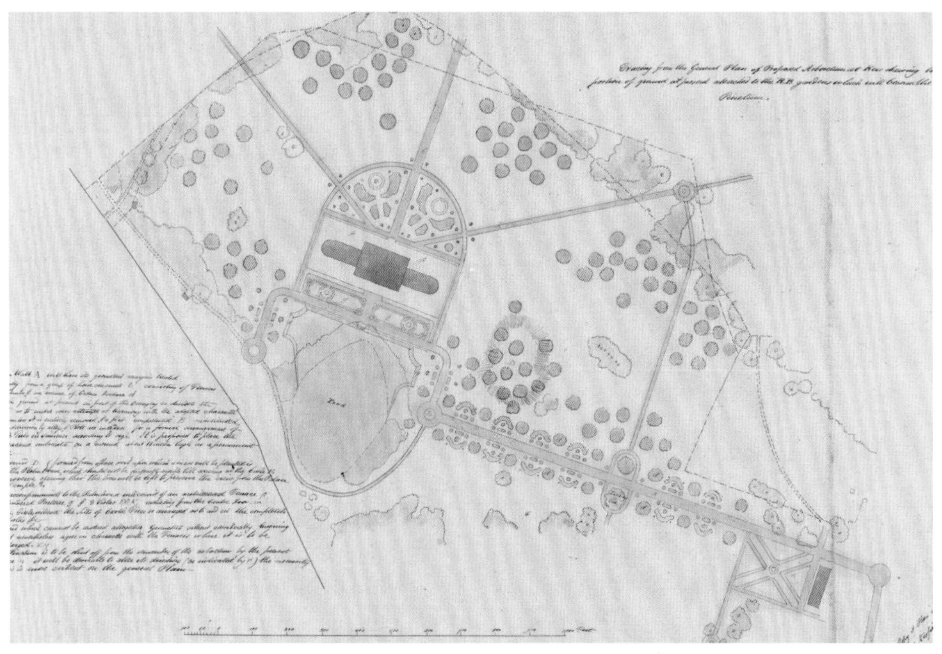

18. A plan of the area around the Palm House by the landscape architect William Nesfield. With a reflecting pond at the front, and three grand vistas radiating at the back, the Palm House would form the spectacular centrepiece of the gardens.

19. Chemist and photographer Robert Hunt, by William Buckler (1842). Pictured here with photographic equipment and a prism, Hunt researched the effect of coloured light on plant growth, and advised on the use of green-tinted glass in the Palm House. At certain times of day, the building had an opalescent gleam.

20. Experimenting with samples of glass and juice extracted from palm leaves, Robert Hunt concluded that the Palm House glass should be tinted a pale green. This diagram records the results of his experiments: nos. 1 and 2 show the spectrum formed by clear and coloured glass; nos. 3 and 4 show the scorching effect.

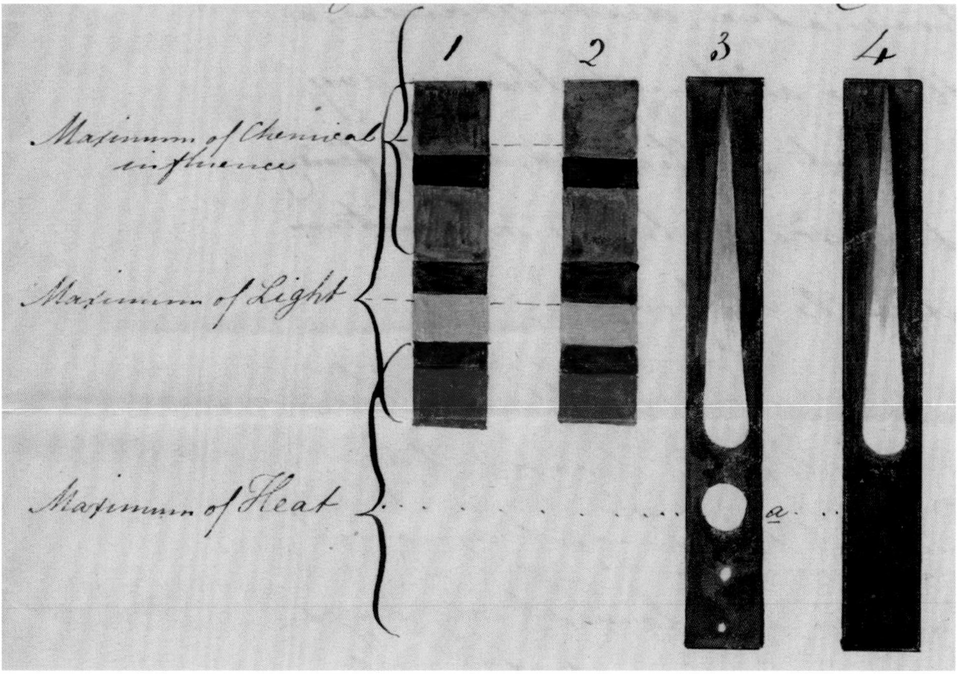

1 2 3 4

Maximum of Chemical influence

Maximum of Light

Maximum of Heat

a

21. A daguerreotype of the Palm House nearing completion by Antoine Claudet (July 1847). Taken a year before the Palm House was opened, the daguerreotype shows the magnificent glazed central section and skeletal wings.

22. Claudet's interior view of the Palm House catches both the grand span of the wrought-iron arches and the delicacy of the spiral staircase and gallery. The identity of the pair in the centre remains a mystery: possibly Richard Turner and Decimus Burton, or Sir William and Joseph Hooker. The figure standing behind in working clothes is perhaps the curator, John Smith.

23. The Palm House proved a popular attraction from the time of its opening. As in most Victorian images of Kew Gardens, the female visitors outnumber the male in this coloured version of a print from the *Illustrated London News* (6 August 1859).

24. Misleadingly squeezing the landmarks of Kew into a single view, this nineteenth-century print presents the gardens as an architectural spectacle. Among the crowd contemplating the scene are a lady artist, two Grenadier guards and a pair of foreign – perhaps Ottoman – visitors in dark robes and fezzes.

25. This 1860s stereoview of the Palm House would have been viewed through a stereoscope for three-dimensional effect. It shows the Victorian display with large palms planted in beds, surrounded by smaller potted plants.

26. Princess Mary (popularly known as 'Fat Mary') lived on Kew Green and took a lively interest in the gardens. In this charming sketch (1858) by Ella Taylor, Princess Mary is pictured in the company of a benign, top-hatted Sir William Hooker, making suggestions to Mr Craig, a Scottish gardener, in broad-brimmed hat and working clothes.

27. Sir William Hooker in his later years. Sir William continued as director of the Botanic Gardens into old age. It was only when he was nearly seventy that Hooker achieved his long-held aim of appointing his son, Joseph, assistant director. Under Sir William's directorship, Kew became a great public institution.

28. Joseph Hooker succeeded his father as director of Kew in 1865. A close friend of Charles Darwin, Joseph Hooker was at the forefront of nineteenth-century science. He made Kew a key part of the scientific establishment.

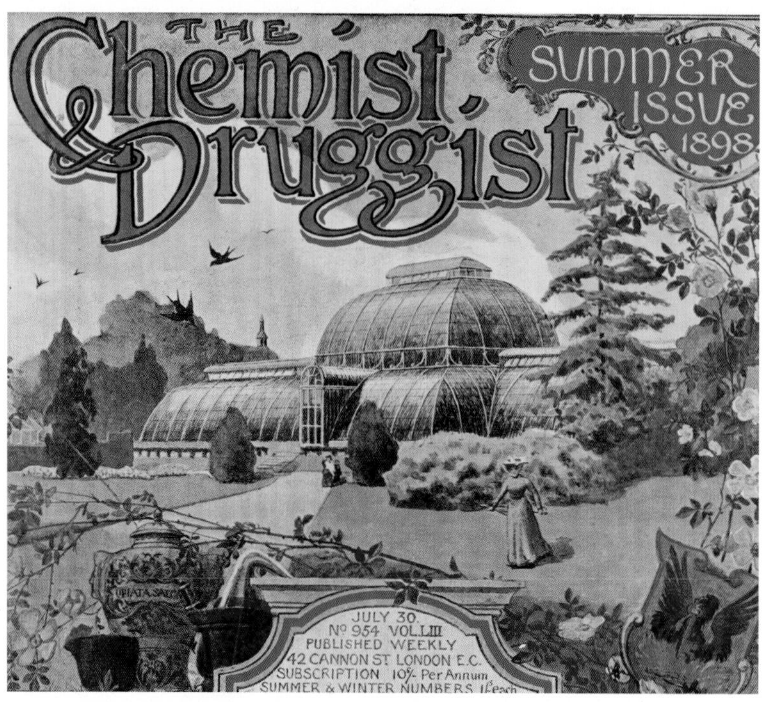


29. The cover of the *Chemist & Druggist* magazine, July 1898. The Palm House, an accompanying article explained, symbolized imperial science: 'the centre of the most important botanical organisation in the world . . . a peculiarly Imperial institution'.

30. Edward Bawden celebrated the distinctive form of the Palm House throughout his career in book illustrations and posters for London Transport. With its bold lines and arresting symmetry, this 1950 linocut demonstrates the influence of the Palm House on modern design and its enduring status as emblem of Kew.

common *Cocoa-nut* alone'.[46] The tendency to itemize the multiple uses of the coconut was parodied by the journalist, John Robertson, in Dickens' *Household Words*, with a comic coco-alphabet:

> Coco bread and coco water, coco almonds, coco butter, coco brushes, coco baskets, coco brooms, coco bowls, coco boxes, coco bonnets, coco cups, coco candles, coco carpets, coco curtains, coco charcoal, coco cream, coco cabbage, coco combs, coco fans, coco forks, coco hats, coco jaggary, coco linen, coco lamps, coco mats, coco masts, coco nets, coco oars, coco oil, coco paper, coco pickles, coco pots, coco pudding, coco ropes, coco spoons, coco sandals, coco sauce, coco ships, coco torches, coco wood, coco vinegar, coco arrack, coco toddy![47]

The coconut's endless capacity for transformation, Robertson suggested, belonged more to the world of fantasy than utility. 'The wonderful bottles of the wizards of the stage', he observed, 'are poor plagiarisms of this single tree'.[48]

Coconuts themselves were of little economic value as a food item in Britain. They were transported as packing material on ships arriving from the West Indies, then sold off cheaply to fruit vendors and bought as a treat for children (or won at fairs on the coconut shy). Coir, the fibre from the coconut husk, was used in mat-making, one of the major prison industries. First the coir had to be picked – unskilled work that, according to the prison governors interviewed by Henry Mayhew, was suitable for 'dull men' and also, because no tools were involved, appropriate for prisoners who had attempted suicide.[49] The coir was next made into cord, and finally was woven on large looms, which, given the stiffness of the material, required considerable physical force to operate. Coir was also used as an alternative to straw to stuff workhouse mattresses. It was cleaner, more durable and did not harbour vermin.

But by far the most valuable product of the coconut was the oil. In 1840, in Ceylon (present-day Sri Lanka), the colonial authorities enacted legislation which converted 90 per cent of land into Crown property. The Crown Lands (Encroachment) Ordinance encouraged the development of British-owned plantations for a number of tropical crops, including coconut. To encourage investors, Peter Lund Simmonds wrote excitedly of the potential profits of coconut plantations, in *The Commercial Products of the Vegetable Kingdom* (1854). 'Take the case of a plantation of 100 acres in extent', he began.[50] The annual gross return in oil alone, he calculated at £1,087: 'a handsome return from 100 acres of any land, *requiring no cultivation or care whatever, after the fourth year, and yielding* the same amount for upwards of half a century! But that is not all'.[51] Adding the returns for the coir and *poonac* (oil cake for animal feed), he calculated that the total return would be at least £1,630. Concluding his triumphant calculations, he exclaimed: 'we have a grand total of £960 sterling expended; for what purpose? To secure a net income of *at least* £1,200 sterling per annum for at least 50 years!'[52]

Coconut oil became such a valuable commodity because of the demand from the soap and candle manufacturers. By the 1840s, vegetable oils were increasingly replacing ill-smelling animal tallow in both industries. At the start of the decade, the entrepreneurial candle manufacturers, Price's, based on the river at Vauxhall, in London, developed a new candle, made of a mixture of coconut oil and tallow, which produced a bright light and did not require snuffing.[53] In a canny marketing move, Price's 'composite' candle was launched just in time for Queen Victoria's wedding, when custom dictated that every household leave a candle burning overnight in the front-room window.

Price's continued to experiment with new ingredients and

processes. To ensure its supply of coconut oil, Price's acquired 1,000 acres of coconut plantation in Ceylon. The company's growth was facilitated by Robert Peel's abolition, in 1845, of the duties on vegetable oils (the same budget that repealed the glass tax). In a period of just fifteen years, Price's workforce rose from seventy-four men and ten boys, in 1840, to 1,098 men and 1,191 boys and girls, in 1855; Price's Patent Candle Company had expanded twenty-seven-fold. By the mid-1850s, it was, indisputably, Britain's leading candle manufacturer.

Price's owed its dazzling expansion to another vegetable oil: palm oil. Extracted from the ripe fruit of the oil palm (*Elaeis guineensis*), palm oil was 'an orange-coloured unctuous mass, with the fragrant smell of violets', according to Sophy Moody.[54] Oil palms grew wild

36. *The oil palm (*Elaeis guineensis*).*

in West and Central Africa, and, in villages in the Niger Delta, whole families were involved in cutting, collecting, treading and boiling the fruit to extract the oil. As modern historians have pointed out, the wealthy used slave labour to produce large quantities of palm oil and transport it to the coast.[55] The main centre for the trade was the island of Bonny (in modern Nigeria). On the British side, the palm-oil trade was largely conducted by merchants from Liverpool who had formerly been involved in the slave trade.

Between 1840 and 1854, the quantity of palm oil exported from West Africa to Britain more than doubled. The steep increase was caused by a rise in demand from soap and candle manufacturers, who found, through various technological innovations, that palm oil enhanced the quality of their products. In addition, palm oil's unctuous qualities made it ideal as a mechanical lubricant, particularly on the railways. With increasing mechanization and the expansion of the rail system, the demand for palm oil rose sharply. 'Any one who has travelled on a railway may have observed, when a train stops at a station, that a man passes along the line of carriages, carrying a box of bright yellow oily substance, and puts a lump of it into the box of each wheel', wrote Elizabeth Twining.[56] The lubricating qualities of palm oil were, she noted, 'a most well-timed discovery . . . in these days of constant rapid travelling on railways'.[57]

Despite the involvement of slave labour in its large-scale production, palm oil was perceived in 1840s Britain as an anti-slavery product. The palm-oil trade, it was hoped, would displace the slave trade that persisted between West Africa, Cuba and Brazil. Economic inducements might prove more effective in suppressing human trafficking than the Navy's West Africa Squadron that patrolled the offshore waters. 'The inhabitants of a vast extent of coast have been led to give up the slave-trade', asserted the naval commander Frederick Forbes in 1854, 'and why? Because they have been taught the immense increase of the value of the palm-oil trade over that in slaves'.[58] Moody termed the oil palm 'the Negro's Friend', and Seemann thought that the oil palm and 'the selfish love of gain' would raise the 'Negro races of Africa' from their 'state of debasement'.[59] Indeed, Seemann proposed that the oil palm might offer a subject for the as yet unwritten history of botany: 'showing the direct and indirect influence the occurrence of a plant exercises on the moral and physical condition of a country'.[60] At once eradicating an inhumane practice, oiling the wheels of the ever-expanding railway system and spreading light and hygiene to the working classes, palm oil seemed to overflow with moral, social and commercial benefits.

Price's Patent Candle Company made full use of palm oil's anti-slavery associations in its promotional material. 'Our readers hardly need to be reminded that the trade in palm-oil on the African coast is the chief economical antidote to the slave trade at the present day', the *North British Review* noted in an account of Price's candle factory in 1853, 'and a showy placard, to be seen at many railway stations, pictorially sets forth the fact'.[61] It is possible that the 'showy placard' displayed an image similar to that in a surviving advertisement for Price's Distilled Palm Candles (see illustration 37, below). In the advertisement, a slave trader (in broad-brimmed hat) pulls a resistant slave by a rope, while another crouches, disconsolate, on the shore. But a candle-maker, surrounded by candle moulds, intervenes. Holding a candle to burn through the slave trader's rope, he hands the slave a liberty cap – the sign of freedom. In the background, figures approach, balancing gourds of palm oil on their shoulders.

The humanitarian reputation of Price's Patent Candle Company was only enhanced by reports of its practices at its Vauxhall factory. The works were managed by James Wilson, the son of one of the company's founders (and brother of George, who was responsible for the technical innovations). James Wilson instituted a chapel and paid for a clergyman to tend to the spiritual needs of the factory workers. He set up girls' and boys' schools – both day and night, for the child shift workers. He encouraged the boys to play cricket and to garden after hours, laid on tea parties, and took the children on annual day trips to the country or seaside. James Wilson described his unusual management methods in a report to the proprietors, which attracted considerable interest.

The novelist Elizabeth Gaskell, who was greatly concerned with factory conditions, was much taken with the report, and proposed to Dickens that she write an article on Price's for *Household Words*. Dickens encouraged her, but Wilson (whom Gaskell knew) did not want the factory to become a show place, so Gaskell dropped the idea.[62] The following year, however, Gaskell visited the works in the company of the American abolitionist and author Harriet Beecher Stowe (who had recently published *Uncle Tom's Cabin*). The example of Wilson's regime at Price's, the critic Stephen Gill has argued, influenced Gaskell in the composition of her great novel of industrial life, *North and South* (1854–5).[63]

Other writers were less concerned to respect Wilson's wishes. The

37. *An anti-slavery advertisement for Price's Distilled Palm Candles.*

cleric John Armstrong praised Wilson's methods in a long article for the *Quarterly Review*. If more widely adopted, such an approach, Armstrong thought, 'would turn the tide of Radicalism and infidelity and the worse forms of dissent which leaven the lower districts of our large towns'.[64] The *North British Review* noted the financial rewards of what we might today term ethical trade: 'the disinterested deeds of Price's Candle Company have come back to them in hard cash . . . Many have bought Price's candles because they felt they *ought* to buy them; because in buying them they not only obtained a good article, but one of which the making carried with it a blessing, and not a curse, to nearly a thousand English homes'.[65]

It is impossible today to read of the nineteenth-century enthusiasm for palm oil without a sense of tragic foreboding. In the industrial innovations of the 1840s, we see the origins of our current dependence on palm oil. The same properties that made palm oil the ideal constituent of candles, soap and axle grease have led, in our time, to its omnipresence in an immense range of goods, from shampoo to biscuits, from biodiesel to ice cream. At around the same time that Kew's Palm House opened, the Dutch transferred four oil palms from West Africa to the botanical gardens in Buitenzorg (now Bogor), in Java. Not only did these four palms flourish, but they furnished the seed for all the oil palms grown in the region until the mid-twentieth century. At that point, fresh germ plasm was imported from Africa and new strains of oil palm were bred. Today, Indonesia and Malaysia are responsible for 85 per cent of global palm-oil production, and palm oil is the most widely consumed of all vegetable oils. Oil-palm monoculture is a major cause of deforestation that not only threatens the habitat of endangered species, such as orangutans, but involves child and forced labour. Today, we would probably have to invert the *North British Review*'s verdict to conclude that palm-oil products carry a curse, not a blessing, into our homes.

But, as far as William Hooker and his contemporaries were concerned, palm oil was a commodity that liberated slaves and improved the lot of child workers. It also had unexpected applications. In 1854, George Wilson patented a process for purifying glycerine (a by-product of palm-oil candle production which had previously been discarded) that was found useful in the treatment of skin conditions. Price's Patent Candle Company was among the donors to the Museum of Economic Botany, and Hooker evidently cherished the connection. In the introduction to his guide to the museum, Hooker drew visitors' attention to 'the fruits and nuts of *Elais Guineensis*, which yield the Palm oil of western tropical Africa, now largely imported and consumed by Messrs, Price and Co.; and not those only, but the oil itself and the several preparations it undergoes in its progress towards the perfect candle, in a series of samples presented by that truly philanthropic company'.[66] For Hooker, the company's extraordinary rise and series of innovations demonstrated the boundless potential of vegetable products. Price's provided the best possible proof of Hooker's claim that the Museum of Economic Botany was 'essential to a great commercial country'.[67]

Among the items of economic interest, the museum also exhibited the curiosities of the plant kingdom. The star of the palm display in the museum was the gigantic double coconut (*Lodoicea maldivica*). Extremely rare, highly valued and virtually impossible to cultivate, the double coconut bore the heaviest fruit and largest seed in the world, and enjoyed near mythical status in Europe. Until the eighteenth century, it was believed to grow under the sea – hence the popular French name, *coco de mer*. The rounded, divided form of the nut – which resembles, on one side, a female pelvis, and, on the other, a pair of buttocks – gave the plant its early botanic name, *Lodoicea callipyge*: 'beautiful rump'. The black or dark brown nuts, highly polished, set in silver and inlaid with gems, found their way into aristocratic cabinets of curiosity. The French discovery in 1769 of double-coconut groves, with palms up to a hundred feet high, on a handful of islands in the Seychelles led to their commercial exploitation and near extinction. By the 1840s, the palm only survived in two locations: the islands of Praslin and Curieuse (where it remained largely undisturbed because the island was the site of a leper colony). 'It is even probable that, in the course of time, the Seychelles Palm may entirely disappear from the face of the earth', the *London Saturday Journal* warned in 1839. 'Let us hope that . . . the "Coco de Mer" may not share the fate of the almost apocryphal bird, the Dodo'.[68]

While still Professor of Botany at Glasgow, Hooker chose to feature the double coconut in the first volume of *Curtis's Botanical Magazine* that he edited (see Plates 4 and 5). Following the usual botanical descriptions and illustrations, Hooker included an account of the many tales told of the double coconut. It was the splendidly named seventeenth-century German botanist Georg Rumphius, who described its submarine habitat and repeated stories that it grew 'near the island of Java, with its leaves and branches rising above the water, in which a monstrous bird or griffin, had its habitation, whence it used to sally forth at night, and tear to pieces Elephants, Tigers and Rhinoceroses with its beak'.[69] In China and south-east Asia, the double coconut was highly prized as an aphrodisiac, an antidote for poisons, and universal cure-all. The nuts commanded astronomic prices: 'some kings have been so greedy of obtaining these fruits', related Hooker, 'as to have given a loaded ship for a single one'.[70] Hooker was clearly aiming to attract a popular readership with his article, which was much repeated in subsequent journalistic accounts. The *Eclectic Review* commented that the tales of the double coconut 'might figure advantageously among the fantasticalities of the Arabian Nights'.[71]

In the museum were specimens of the fabled nuts and preserved male and female inflorescences, fleshy spikes covered with scales and flowers, up to four feet long. But the greater attraction, the almost unrealizable horticultural dream, would be to cultivate a double coconut in the Palm House. According to the *London Saturday Journal*, neither Loddiges' Nursery in Hackney nor the Chelsea Physic Garden had managed to coax double-coconut seeds into germination. 'We have frequently seen the one sent to the Apothecaries' Garden in Chelsea, reposing on its bed of state', reported the paper in 1839, 'to all appearance exactly the same when first placed there'.[72] A double coconut had never been successfully cultivated in Europe. With his spectacular new Palm House, Hooker desperately wanted to claim the prize for Kew.

In July 1849, Hooker wrote to Wenceslaus Bojer, a Bohemian botanist stationed in Mauritius, to ask if he could supply a living double coconut. Two and a half years later, in January 1852, Bojer wrote excitedly to Hooker to say that, after twenty years of failed attempts, he could finally convey 'the good news' of his 'being in possession of a beautiful germinated plant of the celebrated "Double Cocoa Nut" from the Seychelles'. What was more, Bojer wrote, 'this novelty is destined for your Royal Garden at Kew'.[73] But how could the plant be safely transported to Britain? The nut was planted in a large cask; the whole, Bojer estimated, weighed some two tons. Heavy items were usually not allowed on a ship's deck, he explained to Hooker, but the plant would suffer if placed in the hold. The captain, Bojer wrote, in his hyperbolic, if slightly stilted style,

> should be informed before hand of the care he must bestow in carrying home the Prince of Princes of the whole vegetable kingdom, whom he must treat with all due honor and attention on board his vessell, and if he is successful in bring this noble Palm home alive, & deliver it to you in good condition, he should be rewarded by Her Majesty the Queen with the cross of St. Patrick, or of any other Saint that HM might be pleased to select.
>
> This is merely a joke – write immediately by overland and tell me what you have decided, during the time I shall nourse my precious plant well.[74]

To ensure the safe passage of nut and barrel, Bojer had already made enquiries of the captain of one of the vessels of the Screw Propelling Steam Company which stopped at Mauritius en route between Calcutta and Plymouth. He advised Hooker to approach the company's directors in London.

By October that year, all the arrangements had been made. The double coconut now had two leaves, one five feet long. Bojer had planned to enclose the whole in glass, like a massive Wardian case, but the second leaf had emerged at a right angle, making this impossible. On 13 October 1852, a day of torrential rain, Bojer anxiously accompanied the double coconut down to the docks to supervise its loading onto the *Queen of the South*, a large and well-appointed steamer. He worried that the young plant would suffer from prolonged exposure to sea air.

Four days into the voyage, the *Queen of the South* developed faults: one of the fans of the screw propeller broke off; then a blade of the screw was lost and another damaged. The vessel only managed to make it to the Cape under sail and half steam, and then was delayed at the dock for over a week for repairs. When Bojer learnt of the problems, he became anxious that the plant would be harmed by arriving in Britain in the midst of winter weather. Two months after it had set out from Mauritius, the steamship finally docked at Plymouth in mid-December.

A week later, Sir William wrote joyfully to inform Bojer that the double coconut had safely reached Kew. Hooker lost no time in

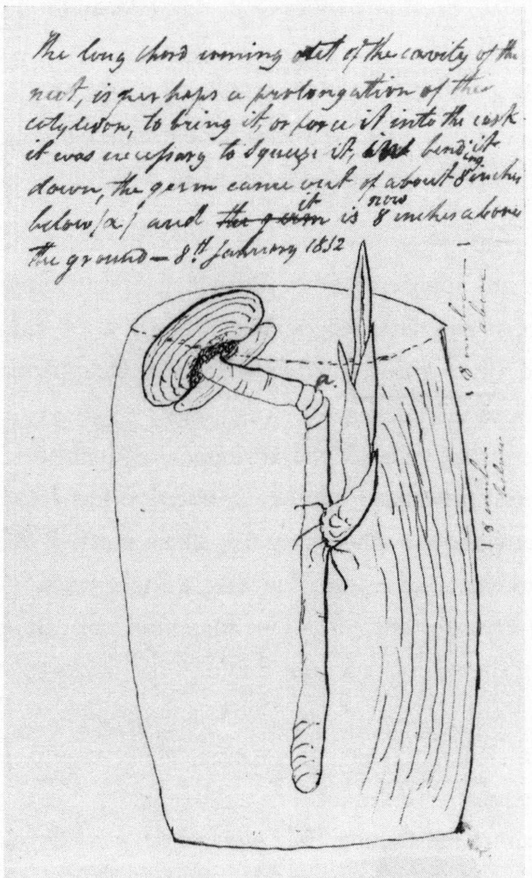


38. *A sketch of germinating double coconut in cask, in letter from Wenceslaus Bojer.*

trumpeting the horticultural coup. 'All lovers of Palms', he informed readers of the *Journal of Botany*, 'will be interested to learn that the Royal Gardens of Kew have just received a valuable addition to their collection, in the safe arrival of a healthy young plant of the famous *Coco de Mer*, or *Double Seychelles Cocoa-nut*, the first ever imported alive to Europe'.[75] He gave full acknowledgement to the part played by Bojer and the shipping company: 'For this we are indebted to Professor Bojer of the Mauritius; and for its safe and speedy conveyance to this country, to Messrs. Blyth and Greene and the Directors of the new screw-propelled steamers, who, in the most generous manner, on hearing what was expected to come from Mauritius to the Royal Gardens of Kew, volunteered to give the cask with the plant . . . a free passage in the "Queen of the South," and every care to be taken of it'.[76]

Bojer warned Hooker that the double coconut was of extremely slow growth, so that Hooker should not be concerned if it remained the same size for years. But despite even John Smith's close attention, the double coconut failed to thrive. After two years, it sadly died. Smith made many subsequent attempts to cultivate the double coconut. In his *Records of the Royal Botanic Gardens* (1880), he noted that eight nuts had, at different times, germinated at Kew, but that no plant had ever survived. The double coconut remained more legendary than real; the ultimate palm, forever just out of reach.

Hooker's appeals for exhibits for the Museum of Economic Botany had proved more than successful. There was no more room in either the cabinets or the corridors for the exhibits. The endlessly growing collection was catalogued by Alexander Smith in 1855. The younger Smith carried out his duties with such careful deliberation that, the following year, at the age of twenty-three, he was appointed curator of the museum, on an annual salary of £104. His father was no doubt delighted to see him so well settled at such a young age. According to Berthold Seemann, 'there was no one who had a better or sounder knowledge of the subject, or took a keener delight in collecting and verifying every scrap of information'.[77] Raised at Kew, and occupied with economic botany since his early teens, Alexander Smith – much like Joseph Hooker – was born to the job.

With the museum swamped with material, Hooker managed to persuade the Commissioners that more accommodation was required. They approached Decimus Burton to design a purpose-built museum. He came up with a plan for a plain but serviceable brick building, three storeys high. As ever at Kew, there was considerable debate about where the building should be situated. The First Commissioner of Works, Sir Benjamin Hall, overruled Hooker, and selected a prime site, across the ornamental pond from the Palm House. In his original landscape design, William Nesfield had left this area with trees and sloping grass banks as a naturalistic contrast to the formal Palm House terrace and parterre. A correspondent to Lindley's *Gardeners' Chronicle* lamented in 1856, the year before the new building opened, that 'so much of the beautiful piece of water, so many noble trees, and so picturesque a part of the garden have been needlessly sacrificed, it is difficult to conceive what head could have planned such a monstrosity'.[78]

While the rhetoric may have been overblown, Burton's design was certainly undistinguished. Without Richard Turner's brilliance, Burton easily slipped into the conventional. But at least the museum had eleven large windows on every floor. If visitors tired of inspecting dried roots and fruits, they could turn to gaze across the water at the streams of visitors heading towards the spectacular Palm House.

# 13

# The Public

Situated at the axis of radiating vistas, the Palm House formed the translucent centrepiece of the Gardens. The green frame etched the outline against the sky. Seemingly weightless, vast and yet light, it floated free from architectural convention. It was at once monumental and ethereal; an enclosed space rather than a solid building. Its elongated, curved form was reflected in the waters of the ornamental pool. From a distance, the crowns of the palms within were silhouetted in the central dome; close to, banana leaves thrust themselves against the glass. At certain times of day, especially towards sunset, the green tint of the glass was distinctly visible. When the sun struck the glass at a particular angle, it presented 'a most curious and beautiful appearance, the whole surface . . . glowing like a mass of gigantic fiery opals'.[1]

As they wandered the Gardens and arboretum, visitors repeatedly caught sight of the Palm House, framed at the end of William Nesfield's long avenues: a glittering, enticing goal. From inside the Palm House, at gallery level, visitors could turn from the tropical scene to look out across the whole grounds. Levels of humidity in the Palm House today are such that condensation obscures the view, but this was not the case in the nineteenth century. Running around the entire nave, the gallery offered a 360-degree viewing platform: a glorious panorama of flower beds, pond, lawns, shrubberies and plantations, stretching all the way to the Chinese Pagoda. With its commanding position, the Palm House dominated the landscape.

The Palm House became the emblem of Kew, even before it was constructed. Three years in advance of its completion, Sir William, with his unerring instinct for marketing, commissioned a vignette of the design to adorn the title page of *Curtis's Botanical Magazine*, one of the many botanical journals that he edited (but the only one to persist to the present day). The frontispiece of *Curtis's Botanical Magazine* located this vision of the future in an improbably rustic scene, with a fisherman in a boat in the foreground. Beneath the engraving, a tailor-made epigraph declared:

> Nature and Art t'adorn the page combine
> And flowers exotic grace our northern clime

The couplet and illustration celebrated the transportation of the tropics to the temperate zone – the happy union of science, art and nature at Kew.

The Palm House more than fulfilled Hooker's hopes that it would form the grand attraction at Kew. The building was greeted with near universal acclaim. 'The erection of the Palm-stove at Kew may be expected to mark an era in the history of horticultural architecture', declared Charles Knight.[2] It was judged 'so remarkable a work' that the *Builder* detailed its design, technical innovations and dimensions in an article that was reproduced in a range of publications, including those aimed at a female market, such as the *Lady's Newspaper*.[3] The Palm House was hailed by the *Florist and Garden*

CURTIS'S

# BOTANICAL MAGAZINE,

COMPRISING THE

**Plants of the Royal Gardens of Kew,**

AND

OF OTHER BOTANICAL ESTABLISHMENTS IN GREAT BRITAIN;

WITH SUITABLE DESCRIPTIONS;

AND

A SUPPLEMENT OF BOTANICAL AND HORTICULTURAL INFORMATION;

BY

SIR WILLIAM JACKSON HOOKER, K.H., D.C.L., OXON.

L.L.D, F.R.S., and L.S., Vice-President of the Linnæan Society, and Director of the Royal Gardens of Kew.

VOL. I.

OF THE THIRD SERIES;

(*Or Vol.* LXXI. *of the whole Work.*)

" Nature and Art t'adorn the page combine
And flowers exotic grace our northern clime."

LONDON:

REEVE, BROTHERS, KING WILLIAM STREET, STRAND;

1845.

39. *Frontispiece of* Curtis's Botanical Magazine *(1845)*.

*Miscellany* as a national status symbol: 'an erection matchless in the world, and worthy of Old England and her true greatness'.[4]

There were a few dissenting voices. One came, surprisingly, from Hooker's old friend and ally, John Lindley. In an article for the *Gardeners' Chronicle* that otherwise applauded Hooker's innovations at Kew, Lindley criticized both the site and design of the Palm House: 'It is decidedly placed too low; and its natural heaviness of style is thus unnecessarily increased'.[5] Lindley took particular exception to the upper row of clerestory windows: the 'queer, long, narrow shallow birdcages (for so they seem) that ride along the tops of the arches'.[6] In a later comment, he somewhat modified his criticism by commending the practical interior arrangements of 'the magnificent conservatory'. But, for Lindley, aesthetics and utility remained incompatible: 'external architectural beauty is unattainable in plant-houses fit for the use of gardeners'.[7] Another critic was the landscape gardener Edward Kemp, who had worked with Joseph Paxton on the creation of Birkenhead Park, the first public park, across the Mersey from Liverpool. Without trees in its vicinity, the Palm House appeared to Kemp to break all picturesque rules, standing harshly exposed in the landscape. 'This extreme nakedness and rawness – which the transparency of the material of which it is composed renders all the more glaring – are among its most defective characteristics, pictorially viewed'.[8] For both Lindley and Kemp, Turner's innovative design was too bold, the shock of the new too great.

There were also those who criticized the Palm House on political grounds. Over the course of its four-year construction, with Hooker's repeated requests to Parliament for extra funding, the Palm House became notorious for its expense. It was cited in the press as an example of government mismanagement of public funds. In August 1847, for instance, the *Evening Mail* called the Palm House 'an indulgence to vegetable aristocracy' (a sly dig at Linnaeus's description of palms as the princes of the vegetable kingdom).[9] In January 1849, the *Stirling Observer* reported a speech at a public meeting of the radical Edinburgh Financial Reform Association which asked why the people of Great Britain should expend £36,000 on palms when 'it would be better to give it to grow potatoes'.[10] With Ireland still in the grip of the terrible famine, this was not a joke.

In April and May 1848, a Select Committee of the House of Commons investigated the costs involved in building the Palm House. In June that year, the social reformer Douglas Jerrold noted the 'great outcry . . . raised amongst those who peruse a certain class of weekly newspapers about the amount of public money granted to erect a Palm House at Kew'.[11] He deplored the campaign of disinformation – the rumour that the Palm House had been erected exclusively for the Queen – with which the working classes had been 'led astray and deceived'.[12] But Jerrold was less interested in the 'policy of sinking so much as £30,000 and upwards in a scheme not reproductive in itself, at a time when a financial crisis threatens to ruin the country', than in his view that the public derived no more benefit from Kew than from any London park.[13] In Jerrold's opinion, those who profited from Kew were nurserymen who procured plants free of charge and members of the gentry and nobility who might '*cum privilegio*, carry away the choicest and rarest gems'.[14] For Jerrold, Kew was failing in its role as a public institution – in particular, in its mission to educate the middle and working classes.

In the uncertain political climate of 1848, both Kew and the Palm House appeared particularly vulnerable to attack, not only in the press, but also on the ground. The year of European revolutions, 1848 was marked in Britain by a rise in Chartist activity. The campaign for democratic reform and universal manhood suffrage attracted wide support. Chartist protests were associated with violence against property, in particular smashing windows. The vast expanse of glass in the Palm House – 16,000 individual panes – seemed eminently breakable. In February 1848, Lindley warned in an editorial for the *Gardeners' Chronicle* that activists might have infiltrated the Botanic Gardens; workers were advised to 'prove by their acts that they are worthy of the favour of her MAJESTY'S Government', and to separate themselves 'from any evil spirits that may have found their way among them'; the authorities at Kew 'should instantly discharge all disturbers of the peace'.[15] In April 1848, Chartist leaders organized a mass demonstration in London; troops were mobilized, the police readied and the city placed in a state of high alert. On the eve of the demonstration, Hooker had sixty of the workforce sworn in as special constables to defend the Gardens. In the event, the London demonstration was smaller than anticipated and the protestors dispersed peacefully; the threat to Kew had proved more imagined than real. But the need to prove the Gardens' public utility and value for money remained.

In Ireland, the European revolutions of 1848 had rekindled hopes of repeal and the nationalist aspirations of the Young Ireland movement. Following a mass demonstration in County Tipperary in July 1848, the British government suspended the Habeas Corpus Act – so that suspects could be detained without trial – and ordered the arrest of nationalist leaders. In response, there was an uprising in Tipperary, which was easily put down. For Richard Turner, in Dublin, the political unrest was of less immediate concern than his own distressing personal circumstances. In December 1848, he wrote of his difficulties to Henry Booth, secretary of the London and North-Western Railway: 'I've had much domestic trouble lately in my Family in the dying state of my son-in-law and the loss of my eldest son's reason'.[16]

Not only was Turner's daughter soon to be widowed, but the mental deterioration of his son, Richard, a Church of Ireland cleric, was the prelude to his death, two months later, aged only thirty-two.[17]

Adding to Turner's family woes were his financial worries. He had seriously underestimated the cost of the construction of the Palm House. Drawing up his final accounts, Turner was alarmed to discover the full extent of his losses: a staggering £7,000. How could his estimates have been so wrong? Of course, there had been his initial eagerness to win the contract. And his decision to substitute deck beam for cast iron had entailed the construction of expensive new machinery. He had not anticipated the price of freight from Dublin to London. Then the workers at Kew had gone on strike, and he had been forced to raise their wages. But, above all, it was Turner's perfectionism that was his undoing. He had always prioritized the excellence of the design over the cost. Now, he had to face the financial consequences.

The only recourse that he could imagine was to write to the Commissioners of Woods and Forests. In a long and at times impassioned letter, Turner set out a narrative of the construction process: his inexperience and miscalculations, his innovations and setbacks, his desire to create a masterpiece. He reminded the Board that the Palm House had won the approval of the architect, the director and the curator, and Her Majesty the Queen herself. The loss of £7,000, claimed Turner, 'would involve myself and Family in utter ruin'. He begged the Commissioners to give 'such a liberal consideration' of his position 'as will avert the calamity, which will otherwise be inevitable'. It was in the Board's power to 'avert the ruin to which in my anxiety to render the Palm House, as a National Structure, worthy of the Age . . . I have unhappily exposed myself'.[18]

The Commissioners were, as ever, less than sympathetic. With the current close scrutiny of public spending, Turner's request seemed inadmissible. They acknowledged that Turner had made improvements to the Palm House at his own cost, but, if they were to reimburse him, they would risk undermining the whole tendering system. The Commissioners recommended a payment of £528 *2s. 2d.* to cover some additional works which Burton had precisely itemized, but refused to reimburse the 'alleged loss upon his whole contract'.[19] Informing the Treasury, the Commissioners stated that Turner had guaranteed to substitute deck beam for cast iron at no extra expense. They pointed out that Turner had incurred his losses through his keenness to gain the contract, insufficient knowledge of timescales and prices, and 'a considerable want of Method and regularity in conducting his works'.[20] The sum of £528 *2s. 2d.* would only be paid on condition that Turner renounced all other claims by sending a receipt in full. Ever persistent – or perhaps desperate – Turner answered by expressing the hope that payment might be forthcoming, 'if not now, at some future time, when the circumstances of the country can better afford it'.[21] Clearly exasperated, the Commissioners responded curtly: 'the Board have no intention to deviate from their decision in this subject already communicated to you'.[22]

But even financial crisis and family distress could not slow Turner down. In February 1849, he was in Liverpool, consulting on his plan to build a vast single-span roof at Lime Street Station. He had finally won the London and North-Western Railway Board's agreement for his hugely ambitious scheme. But Turner's rackety finances and tendency to overstate his case meant that even his own older brother, Timothy, whom Richard had approached to act as his security for the Lime Street contract, was mistrustful of his claims. Before he would agree to stand as security, Timothy demanded to see a copy of the railway company minutes, for proof of his brother's financial arrangements.[23]

Whatever the actual state of his bank balance, Turner's public persona was always that of the successful entrepreneur. In August

1849, in an attempt to show concern for Ireland, still suffering from the effects of famine and civil unrest, the royal family embarked on a tour of the cities of Cork, Dublin and Belfast. On royal visits, it was common civic practice to welcome the monarch by erecting triumphal arches along the carriage route. These were sponsored either by committees or private individuals. Given that wrought-iron arches were Turner's stock in trade, this was too good an opportunity to miss. First in the line of the royal procession was a massive decorated archway erected outside the Hammersmith Works in Ballsbridge. It was topped by an enormous crown and the greeting, 'HAIL VICTORIA AND ALBERT'; beneath the crown, in even larger letters, was the single word: 'KEW'. With its central arch buttressed by two side half-arches, the design artfully recreated a cross section of the Palm House. Festooned with flowers and flags, the archway at once demonstrated Turner's loyalty and claimed ownership of the Palm House project. Even better, an engraving of the royal procession featuring the archway and the grand gateway of the Hammersmith Works, emblazoned with Turner's name, was printed in the *Illustrated London News*, spreading his fame and achievement nationwide.

40. *The triumphal arch outside Hammersmith Works,* Illustrated London News, *11 August 1849.*

The accompanying text, most likely supplied by Turner himself, stated that Turner 'designed the great Palm House at Kew Gardens and is now erecting the monster roof, on his patent principle, over the Liverpool station of the London and North-Western Railway Company'.[24] The report offered one of the few public acknowledgements of Turner's role as Palm House designer.

At Kew, Hooker was keen to demonstrate the popularity of the Gardens as a means to justify the public expenditure. The turnstile at the gate allowed him to keep accurate tallies of visitor figures, which always featured in his annual reports to Parliament. After the opening of the Palm House, visitor numbers more than doubled, rising from some 64,000 in 1847 to nearly 138,000 in 1849. Located outside London, an omnibus, train or steamer ride away from the city, the Gardens were a popular destination for a half-day excursion, as the many guide books, magazine and newspaper articles printed about Kew testified.[25] 'Every Londoner and every London visitor should be familiar with Kew', the penny pamphlet *Summer Days Recreations* declared.[26] The London and South-Western Railway opened a station at Kew Bridge in 1849, which 'rendered Kew at once accessible to the mass of the working classes of the Metropolis', noted John Smith, 'and with the erection of the Palm house Kew Gardens became a point of attraction'.[27] Trains left Waterloo for Kew every hour, and a second-class return ticket cost 1*s.* 1*d.* For 'the mechanic and his family, the Loop-line, now open to Kew Bridge, affords a speedy and cheap conveyance', observed the *Florist and Garden Miscellany*.[28] The journey by rail was delightful, according to *Summer Days Recreations*: 'You are in the country – to all appearance – when you get beyond Vauxhall, and fields and meadows are stretched out on every side, with prettily situated cottages, and grey old hostels, and quiet cattle grazing in the pastures'.[29] For the return fare of a shilling, visitors could board steamers that left Chelsea pier every quarter of an hour for Kew, 'taking you away into quiet country parts . . . If below bridge all is bustle, and a forest of masts bespeaks the commercial greatness of England, up the Thames all is calm repose'.[30] Should the train or boat be beyond visitors' means, Kew was an easy six-mile walk from Piccadilly.

Contemporary journalism depicted a visit to Kew as a holiday away from 'London's dirty, crowded, pestiferous courts and alleys'.[31] Slum-dwellers were supposed to derive moral benefit from the clean air, space and beauty of the Gardens. According to Hooker, 'the minds of the middling and lower ranks are enlarged and enlightened by a display of all that is most beautiful and lovely in the vegetable creation'. From this, Hooker argued, 'a gradual improvement must ensue in the habits and morals of the people'.[32] A visit to Kew was considered rational recreation: an improving activity for the working classes, which would 'tempt them away from the gin-palace, the public house and the beer-shop', to quote the *Florist and Garden Miscellany*.[33] The Palm House provided a vision of the exotic for the working classes. 'Now that Kew has become the favourite resort of Londoners', the *Gardeners' Chronicle* observed, 'even the shop boy who never heard of St. Pierre or the great Prussian physicist [Humboldt] carries with him the vivid impression of their [palms'] graceful forms, after wandering through the delicious Palm grove there'.[34]

Following the example of institutions such as the British Museum and the National Gallery, entry to the Gardens was free of charge. They were open to all, or at least all those who could afford to be 'respectably attired'.[35] To allow for work in the Gardens, members of the public were only admitted from one o'clock. Some journalists saw morning closure as an unnecessary constraint on public access (Kew's opening hours would later become a highly contentious issue, leading to debates in the House of Commons).[36] In his annual reports, Hooker repeatedly asserted the success of free admission. Far from being the dangerous experiment feared by some, the policy had been more than vindicated. The way to encourage respectable conduct from the lower classes was not to police them too closely, but to demonstrate confidence in their sense of responsibility. Hooker was pleased to report that there had been little damage to plants and few instances of visitor misconduct.[37]

But, however great Hooker's liberal faith in the public, he also issued a list of strict regulations to control behaviour. 'Smoking, or eating and drinking, or the carrying provisions of any kinds into the Garden' were absolutely forbidden.[38] 'I would seriously recommend a hearty breakfast, or early lunch', the *Leisure Hour* advised.[39] There was no 'amusement of the cockney kind': no picnics, no drinking

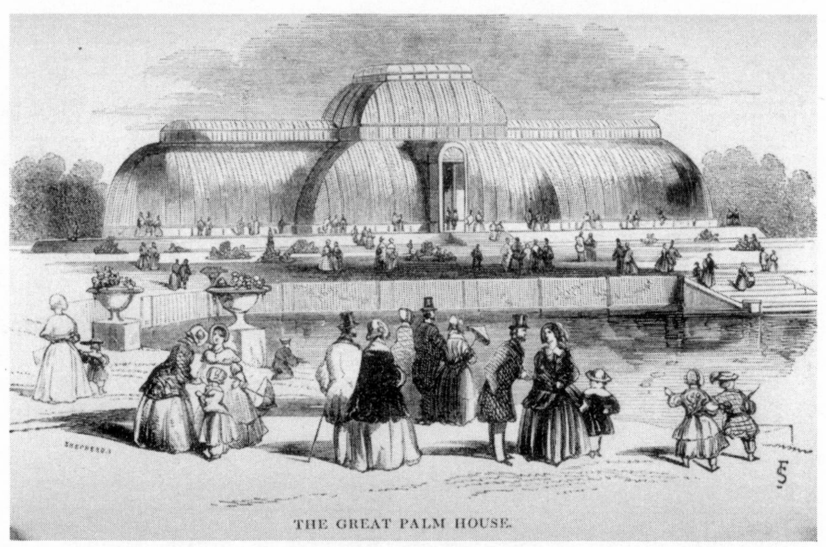


41. *Visitors at Kew (1851).*

booths, no gingerbread stalls, no sporting activities of any kind.[40] Packages or parcels were prohibited (in case they were used for purposes of concealment), and visitors were not allowed to touch the plants. The conduct of visitors was carefully noted, but 'the lower classes' were 'not the people who pick and pilfer', observed the *Quarterly Review*; these offences were more likely to be committed by members of the middle classes: amateur gardeners and collectors who secreted cuttings and pocketed ferns.[41]

The Gardens were supposed to provide the opportunity for the acquisition of knowledge. To this end, all plants were clearly labelled. The Chartist writer and advocate of popular education, Eliza Cook, praised the clarity of these labels: 'the visitor has no difficulty in ascertaining the name, the botanic order, and the country to which the specimens belong'.[42] Hooker received instructions from the Board to compile a cheap guide. Available for sixpence at the gate, *Kew*

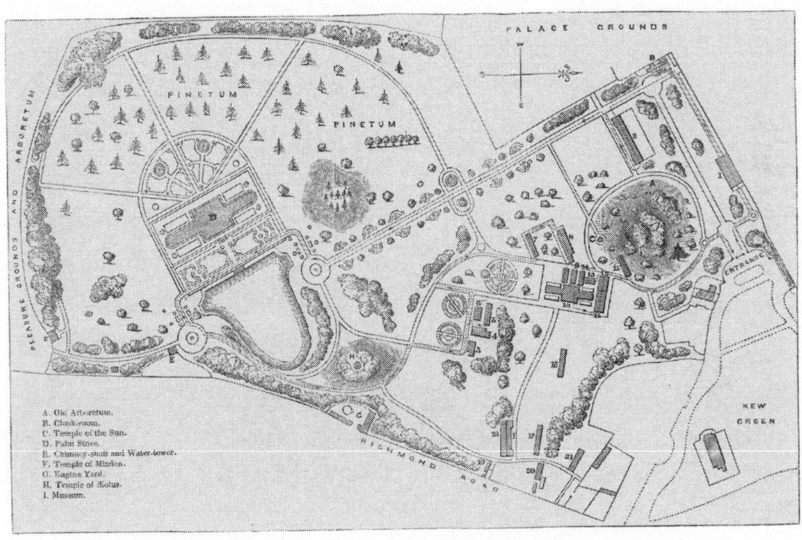


42. *Visitors' map from William Hooker's* Kew Gardens, or, a Popular Guide *(1847).*

*Gardens, or, A Popular Guide to the Royal Botanic Gardens of Kew* (1847) lived up to its name, going through thirteen editions and selling over 32,000 copies in eight years. Praising the guide as 'the most perfect little thing of the kind', the public educator and writer Charles Knight recommended that every visitor purchase a copy.[43] Illustrated with eighty woodcuts, the *Popular Guide* aimed to bring botany to a wider audience: 'the very peasant who never read a book on the subject', claimed Hooker, 'may here see attached to the plant itself the name, vernacular and scientific, of the more useful kinds; while the child from school may acquire an impression of the form and general aspect of many Plants whose names he has learnt in books'.[44]

Hooker suggested a route around the Gardens, provided titbits of information about the plants, their structure, qualities and uses, and illustrated their particular beauties with lines of poetry. He devoted considerable space to the design, dimensions, materials, heating and plumbing arrangements of the Palm House, 'the glory of the Gardens'.[45] The 'noble stove' was 'especially intended for the cultivation of the "Princes" of the vegetable kingdom, but by no means wholly confined to them', observed Hooker. 'The Palms constitute, however, a splendid and striking feature of its vast area, and are seen to most advantage from the gallery above'.[46] With guide in hand, visitors followed a route around the Palm House, with their attention directed to particular specimens and viewing spots. A trip to the Gardens was itself an object lesson in botany, according to the pamphlet *Summer Days Recreations*: 'Kew Gardens is the best botany book every published'.[47] For Eliza Cook, visiting the Gardens was an overwhelmingly textual experience: 'Kew Gardens, so to speak, have been admirably *edited*; and while walking over them you may read them like a book, of which the actual living trees form the graphic illustrations'.[48]

43. *The Palm House interior, with folding artist's stool to the left.*

Botany was the one science that girls were actively encouraged to pursue, honing their skills of observation, identification and illustration. From the start of the century, women had been publishing books on botany, aimed at an audience of mothers, teachers and children. Often these pedagogic texts took epistolary form or were set out as dialogues between mother and child.[49] In an attempt to demystify the language and science of botany, Jane Loudon published *Botany for Ladies* (1842). Loudon wrote in the introduction that she had first learnt the rudiments of botany in order to be an informed companion to her husband, the horticultural writer John Claudius Loudon. (In fact, Jane Loudon played a central role in all aspects of Loudon's numerous publishing activities, and had herself, at the age of twenty, anonymously published a novel, *Mummy!* (1827), which not only inaugurated the genre of Egyptian mummy fiction, but also imagined a futuristic twenty-second-century world powered by steam, where an ancient mummy could be resurrected by means of galvanic batteries.)[50]

While many of the female-authored texts concentrated on domestic botany, those published in the mid-century increasingly included reference to exotic plants. From 1849 to 1855, the botanic artist and philanthropist Elizabeth Twining produced a lavish two-volume collection of engravings and botanical descriptions, *Illustrations of the Natural Orders of Plants* (see Plate 8). Twining was a member of the wealthy tea-merchant dynasty of the same name, with a family home in Twickenham, not far from Kew. Her cousin, Thomas Twining, corresponded with Hooker, and Elizabeth visited Kew to draw plants from life. In addition to such expensive publications, Twining wrote popular guides to botany, based on lectures that she had delivered to young women who attended classes at the Working Men's College in Ormond Street, London. Founded by Christian socialists in 1854, the Working Men's College was intended to increase working-class access to education, and formed part of the Christian socialist response to the 1848 Chartist demonstration. Twining's *Short Lectures on Plants for Schools and Adult Classes* (1858) first outlined the various parts of plants – seeds, root, stem, leaf, flower and fruit – and then moved directly on to the palm family. 'We cannot learn about any country in the hot regions of the world', Twining observed, 'without perceiving that Palms are most important trees, surpassing all others in the variety of materials they yield'.[51] Twining's lectures were reprinted in *The Plant World* (1866). Embellished with gold embossed palms, the book's very cover announced the primacy of palms in the plant world.

Palms also made their way into female-authored works of a genre that might be termed theological botany. *Juvenile Conversations on the Botany of the Bible* (1850) was written by Catherine Mary McNab, the daughter of William McNab, curator of the Edinburgh Botanic Garden (who had initially worked at Kew, and had trained John Smith at Edinburgh). Combining plants with piety, McNab's book staged didactic exchanges between a mother or teacher figure and dutifully enthusiastic pupils. 'Will you be so kind as to tell us about the palm?' prompts a young character named Georgina. 'I should like to know why it has been chosen as the emblem of victory by God, and also by heathen nations who did not know God.'[52] Georgina's question provided the premise of a later text, Sophy Moody's *The Palm Tree* (1864), which united biblical commentary with a comprehensive synthesis of popular writing on palms. Drawing heavily on the works of Humboldt and Seemann, Moody described over twenty species of palm, and informed readers that they could view living specimens in the Palm House at Kew.

In her introduction, Moody made grand claims for the unique status of palms. The palm was the only tree to delight humans on earth that was 'mentioned by name in the word of God, as hereafter to be given in heaven'; the branches of the palm were the only offering that the people of Judea made to the Messiah. Every part of the palm was devoted to mankind's service. It was the only tree to encircle the globe and to be 'found in every varied locality – on desert sands – in luxuriant forests – on mountains, fourteen thousand feet high – and on wave-washed coral reefs in the middle of the ocean'.[53] The text was illustrated with generic images of palms in these various locations (see Plates 9, 10 and 11).

The supreme utility of palms made them objects of fascination to proponents of natural theology – that is, to those who believed the natural world provided evidence of divine purpose. The multiple uses of palms testified of the existence of a benign Creator, ever solicitous to provide for mankind. In 1852, the Religious Tract Society published *The Palm Tribes and their Varieties*. This was the only volume of their Monthly Series – a set of one hundred cheap educational texts encompassing history, biography, geography, science and economics – to be devoted to a single family of plants. Most of the text was purely instructive, but, by way of conclusion, readers were exhorted to consider 'the wonderful wisdom and goodness of God, as manifested in the adaptation of the palm tribe and its products to supply the wants and minister to the comforts of man'.[54] The same year, the Society featured Kew in each of the twelve monthly instalments of *The Child's Companion and Juvenile Instructor*, which bore a print of the Palm House as its frontispiece. Again, the articles were largely informative, but topped and tailed with piety and social concern. The Gardens were 'filled with the wonderful works of God' and were open to all: 'the poor are welcome to enjoy its sights as freely as if they were amongst the princes of the land'.[55] Four of the articles were devoted to the Palm House, with the issues for May and June focusing on palms. 'Those that should first have our notice are the tribe of trees which give their name to the place', the child readers were informed. 'The palms have been called "the princes among trees", to which honour their stately growth, beautiful foliage, and useful productions may entitle them'.[56]

The most engaging of the accounts informed by natural theology was *Wanderings through the Conservatories at Kew*, written anonymously in 1857 by the Nonconformist preacher and naturalist Philip Henry Gosse.[57] The same year, Gosse, who was famous for introducing Victorian Britain to the delights of seashore rock pools and indoor aquariums (a word of his own coining), would ruin his scientific reputation with the publication of *Omphalos*, an eccentric attempt to reconcile geology with the biblical account of creation.[58] For Gosse, the Palm House offered a tropical spectacle that would help the work of evangelism. 'There are probably few persons', he declared, 'however ignorant of botanical science, whose attention could not be roused, if informed that, within the distance of an hour's walk from London, could be seen, without expense or trouble, the vegetable glories of the tropics'. It was Gosse's hope that, 'while beholding some of the fairest works of the vegetable creation', visitors might 'have their thoughts elevated to Him who had formed them and all things for his own glory'.[59] Gosse wrapped his devotion in gloriously florid prose. He promised readers 'the odours and fantastic beauties of the tropics, the fairy-like vegetation of a clime more favoured in this respect than our own, and such a bewitching sight of exotic loveliness as may nowhere else be obtained'.[60]

Never one to stint his superlatives, Gosse described the Palm House as 'a magnificent work, worthy of this great nation, and of the delightful science the interests of which it is so eminently calculated to advance'.[61] To introduce readers to 'the royal tribe of palms', Gosse expanded Linnaeus's figure of the princely palm to populate a whole 'vegetable court':

> Here stands a court-beauty, whose tall and polished stem exults in up-bearing a coronet of plumes thirty or forty feet high; there another, which casts around its long and pointed leaves over a vast area; there a third whose broad and shadowy leaves invite the wanderer to shelter and repose; and arrayed around the peers and commoners of the court, stand grisly old trees with looks so fierce and arms so horrid with spines, that we are by fancy led to believe them to be none other than the warriors and great fighting ones of the army of Queen Flora.[62]

With this extravagant conceit, Gosse offered an extreme version of the anthropomorphic vision of palms, first proposed by Linnaeus. Gosse's extended courtly metaphor highlights the irony implicit in so many accounts of the Palm House: that the emblem of public Kew was actually more regal than anything that had existed in the former Royal Gardens.

The various informative texts, articles and guide books that were published on the Palm House helped Hooker in his aim of promoting Kew as an institution devoted to public education. The accompanying illustrations suggested that Kew was a place of general resort. Contemporary engravings of the Palm House always featured visitors, both to provide a sense of scale and to suggest that it was a popular attraction. In the illustrations, female visitors typically outnumber male ones (see, for instance, Plate 23). Kew features as a respectable destination for women to visit, either alone, in pairs, or attended by men in family groups. Strikingly, the visitors do not seem so much to be inspecting the plants as strolling and conversing. In these images, the Palm House becomes a space for leisure and sociability.

Much as Hooker insisted that Kew provided useful instruction, the suspicion remained that excursionists did not actually attend

44. *Promenading around the Palm House gallery.*

to the information provided. John Smith was characteristically sceptical of the educational benefits to visitors: 'it must be admitted that of this class of visitors few desire any more advantage, than if they were walking through a narrow path. Not one in a thousand could tell what they had seen'.[63] Shortly after the Palm House opened, *Punch* satirized the educational aims of Kew with a wonderfully garrulous contribution from one of its 'correspondents', the 'Old Lady':

> to think of there being a vegetable world, and I, fifty-five my last birth-day, and never saw it, and accustomed to greengrocers all my life . . . so I determined to pay a visit to this vegetable world . . . hearing it was to be seen in Q. Gardens . . . it's well I expected to see vegetables, for

> there isn't no flowers to signify; but hot-houses upon hot-houses. How the coals are paid for isn't my business. And such a Conservatory; all made of glass, and covering I don't know how much ground; all under the care of SIR WILLIAM HOKEY . . . This was the vegetable world I wanted to see, where you've trees that grow umbrellas and chair-bottoms, and trees that grow bread equal to hot-rolls, and custards, and cocoa-nuts, and chocolate, and tea and coffee and other groceries . . . dear knows I saw plenty, and almost fainted among the Palms.[64]

With her domestic preoccupations and garbled information, the Old Lady remained resolutely unenlightened (and unmoved to Humboldtian rapture) by the Palm House display. Her monologue ridiculed both Sir William Hokey's claims to enlarge 'the minds of the middling and lower ranks', and the notion that women might understand botany.

In the autumn of 1849, just over a year after the Palm House opened, Richard Turner learnt about Prince Albert's idea for a Great Exhibition of the Works of Industry of all Nations. Immediately, he and his architect son, Thomas, started to draw up plans. A Great Exhibition building appealed to Turner as the ultimate showpiece for his ambitions. Before the Royal Commission for the Exhibition had even convened, let alone invited tenders, Turner arranged for a model to be dispatched for display at the new Houses of Parliament.[65] In advance of their first meeting in January 1850, Prince Albert and the Commissioners had the opportunity to view Turner's futuristic scheme: a great iron and glass dome, 200 feet high, linked by covered walkways to four satellite domes. Steam engines would pump fresh air into the structure, and a train would transport visitors around the site. Turner proposed Green Park as a suitable location for the complex, which could, after the Exhibition, be used as a winter garden or a venue for 'monster concerts'.[66] Estimated at £300,000, the building completely overshot the Commission's envisaged budget. The Commission wanted a quickly erected, cheap, temporary structure, financed through a subscription scheme. And, in any case, there would have to be an open competition.

Turner and his son returned to the drawing board. Their second plan was for a light wrought-iron and glass hall, a vast, uninterrupted space, with central arched transept, nearly 2,000 feet long and over 400 feet wide. Of the 245 plans submitted, their design was one of two schemes selected as outstanding. But, to Turner's great frustration, the Building Committee decided not to award the contract. What good was an honourable mention? Turner's sense of exasperation grew when the Commission invited tenders for a plan of their own devising, which was heavily criticized in the press. Obdurate as ever, Turner refused to tender for a structure which he considered inferior to his own. Disregarding the fact that the Building Committee had not chosen his design (most likely because they doubted his

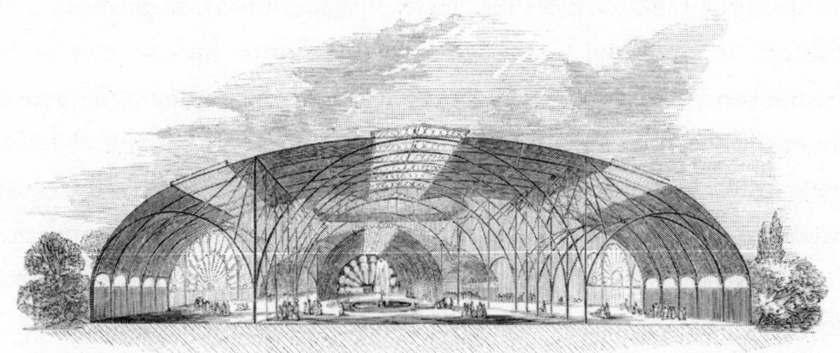

45. *Richard and Thomas Turner's design for the Great Exhibition.*

ability to produce the vast quantity of wrought iron required in time), he tendered for his own plan, which he costed as the very reasonable – although not entirely credible – price of £69,800.

It was at this late stage in the proceedings that Joseph Paxton entered the arena. He submitted a hastily drawn-up plan for a huge modular building made of cast iron, glass and wood. All the components could be prefabricated in bulk, which would allow the building to be erected at speed to meet the very tight time frame set by the Commission. Paxton's impromptu and somewhat irregular intervention was exactly the kind of behaviour to which Turner himself was prone, which made it all the more infuriating to him. He could not bear to see someone else circumventing the rules. The estimate for Paxton's plan came in at £79,000 – a significant £10,000 higher than that for Turner's scheme. And yet, the Commission awarded the contract to Paxton.

Turner chose a very public occasion to express his disappointment and fury. In the winter of 1850, he was elected to the Institution of Civil Engineers. Membership of such a prestigious body was a sign of Turner's social and professional ascent from iron founder to engineer. But Turner did not always respect codes of gentlemanly conduct. Just a month after his election, Turner chose to address the Institution's January meeting on the subject of the competition. The Exhibition Building Committee, he declared, had awarded the contract to Paxton, 'with how much, or rather with how little justice, he would not permit himself to say; but he must submit, that the second design proposed by him, and for which he tendered, would have been a more imposing and a more stable structure, and one more in accordance with the instructions of the Committee than that now in course of construction'.[67]

Having read the account of Paxton's plan published in the *Illustrated London News*, Turner proceeded to criticize almost every element of the building. The exterior canvas shades – which would have been unnecessary had the building been glazed with tinted glass as Turner had proposed – were a 'slovenly, and, positively, dangerous contrivance, which, he thought, would be found to seriously militate against the presumed beauty of the Crystal Palace'.[68] The columns did not have sufficiently strong foundations and might heel over in a gale; the galleries might collapse under the vibrations caused by the crowds; the glass was insufficiently thick and might smash in a hailstorm. Although Turner was clearly motivated by personal animus, his concerns about the stability of the structure were shared by as eminent a figure as the Astronomer Royal, Professor George Bidell Airy.[69] For Turner, the main danger was posed by fire. Unlike his own design, made entirely from fireproof materials, there 'existed great liability of accident from fire in this building which really seemed to be constructed for the express purpose of perishing in a conflagration'.[70] (Turner's warnings proved strangely prophetic. After the Great Exhibition, the Crystal Palace was relocated to Sydenham, where it was re-erected on an expanded scale. In 1866, the northern wing burnt down. Then, one night in 1936, fire took hold; in a matter of hours, the entire building lay in smoking ruins.)

Despite his very public expression of outrage, Turner participated in the Great Exhibition. As an entrepreneur, he could not afford the luxury of hurt pride. In the 'Civil Engineering, Architecture, and Building Contrivances' section, located in the north gallery of the Crystal Palace, he displayed models of his own designs, including the Winter Garden in Regent's Park, the roof over Lime Street Station and, of course, the Palm House. It must have been galling indeed to set up his display within his rival's mammoth structure. After the Exhibition had closed, Turner wrote to the Royal Commission to seek compensation for all the costs involved in his unsuccessful bid: 'several expensive models which we could not afford', lithographed plans, travel and carriage expenses, 'besides all the Time & deep thought & consideration'.[71] He made the case that his design had been one of two to gain an honourable mention in the competition (the other, submitted by the French architect Hector Horeau, he dismissed as 'so inferior to ours'). What was more, of the 245 entries in the competition, his had been the only one to propose a transept. With this unusual insistence on the transept, Turner alluded to his suspicion that Paxton had borrowed the idea of the Crystal Palace transept from him. Turner concluded by reminding the Commissioners 'how much we were disappointed at not being given the contract for erecting the Structure, which the Estimate were so apparently deserving'.[72] Requesting reimbursement and hinting at the impropriety of both the Commissioners' and Paxton's conduct, Turner was behaving in a distinctly unprofessional manner. But then he never played by the rules.

Much as Turner deplored the Crystal Palace, its existence benefited the Palm House. In 1851, when London, as well as the Great Exhibition, was on display, the Palm House became one of the capital's major attractions. Like Paxton's building, the Palm House was now also described as a palace. The Palm House was 'a beautiful glass palace', announced the *Leisure Hour*, 'which even in these glass-palatial days can well afford to hold its own and maintain a rank above them'.[73] A coloured print of the Palm House was chosen as the frontispiece to *London Exhibited in 1851*, a visitors' guide to the diversions provided by the capital.[74] That year, visitor numbers to Kew more than doubled again, leaping to nearly 328,000 – an increase of some 190,000 on the figure for 1849. So numerous were the visitors ascending to the Palm House gallery that Hooker had to order the erection of a second spiral staircase. The two glass structures were often compared, either explicitly or implicitly, and the Palm House was always judged the more beautiful. According to the *Quarterly Review*, the Palm House was 'certainly the most elegant if not the most bulky glass structure in the world'.[75] The *Illustrated London Almanack* declared the Palm House 'without question, the most elegant building of its kind extant'.[76]

But, rather than exhibiting masterpieces of manufacturing, the Palm House displayed the marvels of nature. 'It is a crystal palace', pronounced *Summer Days Recreations*, 'a great glass house filled with nature's wonders, collected from various parts of the world'.[77] Just as the Great Exhibition was claimed as a defining moment of the era, so too was the Palm House display. There could be no greater testimony to Britain's technological prowess than the palace of palms. 'We live in a wonderful age', proclaimed the *Illustrated London Almanack* for 1853, 'when these gigantic children of the sun can be induced to live and flourish amongst us'.[78]

# 14

# Closing *the* Door

In 1855, after more than a decade of plotting and petitioning, Sir William Hooker finally succeeded in creating a post for his son at Kew. As assistant director, the thirty-eight-year-old Joseph – who now had a wife and three children to support – was guaranteed a salary of £400 a year and a large house on Kew Green. Although he had turned seventy, Sir William showed no inclination to retire. But he was now confident that his son was in prime position to inherit the directorship.

Much as he owed to his father's influence and network of contacts, Joseph Hooker was also gifted with scientific talent and a capacity for hard work. By 1855, he enjoyed a growing reputation and had achieved an impressive record of publication. He had completed substantial works on the floras of New Zealand and India, and a two-volume account of his Indian travels. Through his friendship with Darwin, he was in the vanguard of scientific thought of the day. In recognition of his achievements, the Royal Society had awarded him the Royal Medal in 1854.

John Smith never reconciled himself to Joseph Hooker's

appointment at Kew. With the creation of the post of assistant director, Smith had effectively been demoted. He found it particularly galling to be overruled by Joseph, a theoretical horticulturalist, lacking in any practical expertise. Joseph won Smith's undying contempt by instituting a policy of pruning in the Palm House. Concerned about the free circulation of air, Joseph ordered the removal of the creepers from the spiral staircase and gallery rails. 'Sir W. Hooker thought his son very clever in doing so', Smith commented sourly; 'I only looked upon such as freaks of the Dr's pretended knowledge of horticulture'.[1]

Worse still, Sir William and Dr Hooker decided to thin out the Palm House collection, destroying plants that Smith had nurtured for decades. This appeared to Smith as wanton mischief. 'Sir William would fix his eyes on a plant, ask its history, then say "Away with it" and in a moment the foreman's big knife made the bark hang in ribbons'.[2] Marking these occasions as black days in his diary, Smith recorded the death toll and memorialized the fallen plants: '*Cocos Plumosa*, Height of stem 10 ft., Length of leaves 2 ft. A splendid plant, but ordered to be destroyed with as little concern as if had been a geranium'.[3]

Smith's increasing gloom may have been affected by the infirmities of age. His vision was deteriorating and, by 1864, he could no longer see sufficiently to work. In his annual report for that year, Sir William paid handsome tribute to Smith: 'The most important [change] that has occurred since 1841, when I was appointed Director, has been the retirement (owing to an affection of the eyes) of our able and highly valued curator, Mr. John Smith, who, for upwards of 30 years has superintended all departments of the Royal Gardens, and whose services and fidelity have been recognized by the Treasury in granting him the highest scale of pension'.[4] But Sir William was far from young himself, and this would be his final report. The following August, aged eighty, he contracted a septic disease of the throat, and, within the week, was dead.

In accordance with his father's instructions, Joseph wrote to inform the First Commissioner that Sir William wished that his most prized possession, the herbarium, should find a permanent home at Kew. The herbarium consisted, according to an inventory of Sir William's collections, of 'not fewer than a million of named specimens of plants from every known part of the Globe'. The specimens were 'for the most part named, and all ticketed with the names of their Country and Donors or Collectors'. They were 'in perfect order, systematically arranged, and accessible without trouble'. Botanists from across Europe and North America had resorted to the herbarium for the past half century, and its contents were referred to 'in almost every Botanical work published during that period'.[5] A month after Sir William's death, Joseph Hooker was offered the directorship of Kew. The following year, the government agreed to buy the herbarium for the very moderate sum of £5,000. From beyond the grave, Sir William had managed to pull off his most audacious scheme of all.

Thanks to Sir William's masterly manipulation, the Hooker family remained in control of Kew until 1905 (the dynasty continued with William Thiselton-Dyer, Joseph's son-in-law). Less adept at handling those in power than his father, Joseph prioritized his research. His activities laid the groundwork of modern botany and built the reputation of Kew as a centre of imperial science. For twenty years, Joseph's major intellectual passion was the *Genera Plantarum* (1862–83), co-authored with George Bentham. This monumental work of global plant classification identified over 7,500 genera and nearly 100,000 species: a true botanical landmark.

In his last years at Kew, Joseph Hooker devoted many months to the classification of the palm family. In June 1881, he told Charles Darwin that he had been 'doing the Palms for 16 months at least;

46. *Joseph Hooker, flanked by palms, during his presidency of the Royal Society (1873–8).*

the most difficult task I ever undertook. They are evidently a very ancient group and much dislocated, structurally and geographically'.[6] Having laboured long and hard over the palms, Hooker turned his attention to those cultivated at Kew. In 1882, he reported that he had identified 420 species, making Kew's palm collection second only in Europe to that of Herrenhausen, the gardens of the Hanoverian court. For Hooker, the 'unexpected richness' of Kew's collection was testimony to the priority accorded to palms from the inception of the national botanic gardens: 'no pains have been spared to obtain seeds of these attractive plants for the cultivation of which Kew possesses peculiar facilities, from our numerous correspondents in all parts of the world'.[7]

Unlike the Hooker family, the contribution of Richard Turner, the man who designed the palms' magnificent home and helped to build Kew's reputation, was rarely acknowledged during his lifetime. Through a combination of colonial and class assumptions, the Palm House was routinely attributed to the architect Decimus Burton. Richard Turner was simply regarded as the ironwork contractor. In March 1880, however, the year before the death of both Turner and Burton, the Dublin architect Thomas Drew wrote to the *Building News* to set the record straight: Turner, not Burton, should be credited with the design of the great Palm House at Kew. The editor of the *Building News* responded with scepticism to the claim, but John Smith, then in his eighties, blind and long retired, dictated a letter to the *Building News* to confirm that Turner had been the sole designer. Even after the passage of more than thirty years, Smith still had a vivid recollection of Turner's impromptu working methods: 'He took the paper, folding it, to make a crease in the middle, then, with a pen, quickly traced a vertical profile of one half of the intended house, on one side of the crease, then, folding the other half of the paper on the inked part, and, on opening it, there was a section of the whole length of the palm-house, as it was afterwards erected'.[8]

Turner was excluded from the project to build Kew's second great glasshouse. In 1859, Burton was instructed to draw up plans for a Temperate House. Conceived on an even larger scale than the Palm House, the Temperate House was to be constructed from iron, brick, masonry and wood, with separate areas for plants requiring different climatic conditions. Hearing of the scheme, Turner approached Burton to tender for the contract, but was rejected. Justifying his decision to the Commissioner of Works, Burton claimed that Turner was less competent than other contractors to undertake the project, given the variety of materials involved. But the architect might also have lost patience with Turner's unorthodox business methods, his cavalier disregard for directions and deadlines.[9] In the event, government finances extended only as far as the central portion and two side octagons of the Temperate House. The wings had to wait for Thisleton-Dyer's tenure as director. The full structure was finally completed in 1897, sixteen years after Burton's death. Even when finished, the Temperate House, for all its scale, lacked the audacious grandeur of the Palm House.

Having failed to be considered for the Temperate House, Turner sought ever larger contracts. In 1861, he entered a competition to construct the Embankment along the Thames from Westminster to Blackfriars Bridge. His plan comprised wharves, a railway, sewer, thoroughfare, promenade and, characteristically, a winter garden. Turner lost out to the more experienced Joseph Bazalgette, chief engineer of the Metropolitan Board of Works. Around the same time, Turner published an even more daring design: a submarine railway between England and France, one of several Victorian schemes for a Channel tunnel. Predictably, Turner's plan for an iron tube running twenty-one miles under the Dover Strait found few backers. Ultimately, Turner's career foundered on his overconfidence and irrepressible inventiveness.

Smith's intervention to rehabilitate Turner's reputation suggests the strength of the two men's relationship. Despite their temperamental differences, the two men appear to have been friends. They were a similar age, and, in terms of their origins and class, were both outside the English establishment. In a letter to Hooker, Turner referred to Smith as 'my friend, your Curator'. Unlike the ever-optimistic and charming Turner, Smith was typically gloomy and forthright. He wrote a history of Kew, 'so candid', the *Oxford Dictionary of National Biography* observes, that it 'has never been published'.[10] But even Smith was capable of humour. In his retirement, he composed a heavy-handed parody, *Adam Spade; the*

*Gardener* (1879), which consisted of a sequence of laboured botanic puns. Adam Spade had studied botany, and was one of the few gardeners considered 'Solomons in their profession'.[11] Through his comic alter ego, Smith presented his situation, poised midway between gardener and botanist, at once humble and learned. Working without a microscope and using only his powers of observation, Smith devised a new scheme of fern classification which was posthumously recognized as groundbreaking. His herbarium of some 2,000 species of ferns was purchased by the British Museum in 1866, and is now listed as one of the important collections of the Natural History Museum.

With their associations of triumph, abundance and nobility, palms were readily adopted as regal trappings. Queen Victoria's state visits were festooned with palm fronds. For the wedding of her daughter, Princess Victoria, to Prince Frederick of Prussia, in 1858, the Chapel Royal at St James's Palace was decorated with garlands of holly, ivy and palm leaves. In addition, the widespread distribution of palms across Asia, Africa and the Caribbean made them fitting emblems of empire.

To mark Queen Victoria's Diamond Jubilee of 1897, Rudyard Kipling composed 'Recessional', a poem that would later be set to music and sung as a hymn by churchgoers, school children and soldiers across the world. The first verse opens:

> GOD of our fathers, known of old,
> Lord of our far-flung battle-line,
> Beneath whose awful Hand we hold
> Dominion over palm and pine[12]

With poetic economy, Kipling suggests the vast extent of the empire. Southern and northern hemispheres are represented as palm and pine respectively. Opposed as types of tropical and temperate vegetation, palm and pine are nevertheless united through alliteration and divinely ordained British rule. By the end of the century, palms were firmly established in the symbolic repertoire of monarchy and empire.

A touch of this regal and imperial glamour was brought into the domestic realm in the closing decades of the century. The hardy Kentia palm (*Howea forsteriana*), native to Lord Howe Island in the Pacific, was found capable of tolerating the curtain-swathed gloom of the Victorian home. A particular favourite with Queen Victoria, the Kentia palm was introduced into many of her residences. With such royal endorsement, the fashion for palms spread to hotels and tea rooms, to middle-class conservatories and drawing rooms across the land. From the glittering glass palace to the corner plant stand, the palm became an integral part of British culture over the course of Victoria's reign.

In advance of her death in 1901, Queen Victoria gave detailed instructions for the preparation of her body, the items to be placed inside her coffin and the conduct of the funeral. It is likely that she also stage-managed the arrangements for her lying-in-state. At both Osborne House, where she died, and the Albert Memorial Chapel at Windsor, where her coffin lay for two days, the scene was the same. The casket was draped with a royal standard and topped with a crown. At its corners were tall candles, and floral tributes were placed all around. Four Grenadier Guards, their heads bowed in postures of respect, stood constant vigil. Overarching it all were Kentia palms, their graceful drooping fronds a symbol of the nation's – and empire's – grief. Palms, of course, were also associated with virtue, triumph and resurrection. Attended by the princes of the vegetable kingdom, the monarch played out her final act.

47. *Queen Victoria's coffin lying in state in the Albert Memorial Chapel, Windsor Castle, 1901.*

As a living display, the Palm House collection was in a continual state of flux and renewal. Plants that grew vigorously inevitably had to be felled and replaced. Fifteen years after the Palm House opened, the great licuri palm (*Syagrus coronata*) – which had travelled to Kew from Sir George Staunton's Hampshire estate by train – reached the roof, and had to be cut down. Fortunately, the palm had flowered and produced viable seeds, so many of its offspring were raised in the nursery stoves.

For some time, the plants were subject to the vagaries of boilers and inadequate flues. Over the summer of 1867, the heating system began to fail. Leaves yellowed and drooped, and plants started to die. So denuded was the Palm House that it was possible to look through an entire wing – sixteen parallel rows of plants – to the opposite side. By the winter, the surviving plants had to be removed and the Palm House closed to the public. But, with an alteration to the design of the flues, the heat in the Palm House rose by ten degrees, back to the ideal temperature for the palms. A new spray system was installed in the roof to disperse a fine mist from above. The palms started to grow, and the fruit on the bananas and plantains ripened once more.

In 1873, when the crowns of the palms once again threatened the Palm House roof, the *Edinburgh Review* posed the playful question: 'Why may not the glass roof be made to lift so as to accommodate these tropic growths?' The writer indulged in some fanciful speculation about 'telescopic columns that could be lifted by machinery', but concluded that even the inventions of the future would probably not solve the 'incessant struggle between Art and Nature in the stove-houses'.[13]

Fanciful as it was, the *Edinburgh Review*'s vision of extendable pillars expressed a truly Victorian faith in the possibilities of engineering. Of course, the Palm House itself occupied a key position in the evolution of iron and glass technology. The structure broke new ground both in terms of its construction and design. As one of the earliest examples of prefabrication, the Palm House pioneered the building process that would come to dominate construction in the modern age. With its innovative combination of slender wrought iron and curved glass, the Palm House defied architectural convention and gave visitors an entirely new experience of space and light. Throughout the nineteenth century, the Palm House functioned as the model for glasshouses across the globe: in Copenhagen (1872), Adelaide (1875), Brussels (1876), San Francisco (1878),

Vienna (1882) and New York (1902). For the architectural historian Nikolaus Pevsner, it is 'one of the boldest pieces of nineteenth-century functionalism in existence – much bolder indeed, and hence aesthetically much more satisfying than the Crystal Palace ever was'.[14]

From a contemporary viewpoint, the Palm House is often seen as a forerunner of twentieth-century modernism. With its confident union of form and function, clean lines and organic shape, the Palm House still looks improbably contemporary. It continues to be featured in textbooks for students of engineering, architecture and design. In recent years, the Palm House has provided the inspiration for one of London's current icons: the London Eye. For the designers, Julia Barfield and David Marks, the Palm House offered 'the perfect symbiosis of architecture and engineering'.[15]

The Palm House is the finest surviving Victorian glass and iron building in the world. Whereas Paxton's glasshouses no longer exist (the Chatsworth Conservatory was demolished in 1920 and Crystal Palace was destroyed by fire in 1936), the Palm House has proved remarkably resilient. It weathered a devastating hailstorm in August 1879, when hailstones five inches across smashed over 40,000 panes of glass across the Gardens. By the final decades of the nineteenth century, replacement panes of green glass were not free of manganese oxide, as had originally been specified by Robert Hunt. This resulted – as Hunt had predicted – in the green glass fading and acquiring a pinkish hue. The growing pollution of London and regular winter fogs cut down on the available sunlight and coated the Palm House glass with filth. By 1895 it was decided to abandon the use of green glass altogether.[16] Painted battleship grey, the Palm House came through the bombing of the Second World War. By the 1950s, however, the building had deteriorated to such an extent that it was threatened with demolition. Various schemes were drawn up, including one that planned to replace the entire structure with a new

48. *A design to rebuild the Palm House using arches from Elizabeth II's Coronation.*

glass house that reused the ceremonial arches erected for the coronation of Elizabeth II. Happily, the Ministry of Works intervened and, over the period from 1955 to 1957, the building was renovated and re-glazed instead.

From 1985 to 1988, a more thoroughgoing restoration was painstakingly executed. The whole building was dismantled, with individual components numbered and laid out, like an immense Meccano kit, to be inspected and either replaced or repaired. It was at this point, during an analysis of the ironwork, that the conservation team discovered the Palm House had initially been painted a deep blue-green. Rather than pursue authenticity, they decided to keep the frame the familiar white. Meticulously reconstructed, and re-glazed with toughened glass, the palace of palms rose again, strengthened and gleaming, ready to receive its princely inhabitants once more.

More than thirty years after its restoration, the Palm House is again starting to show signs of wear and tear. Few buildings have had to endure such constant interior assault as the Palm House. With the high levels of humidity, the surfaces and structural elements are continually wet. In the 1980s, Turner's wrought-iron glazing bars were replaced by stainless-steel versions, but many of the original iron components of the Palm House were retained. Inevitably, these are beginning to corrode. The white paint is starting to peel, revealing the red primer beneath. Small patches of rust are appearing along the edges of staircase railings. A light patina of algae blooms in corners of the stonework. There is a singular beauty to these traces of decay, but soon it will be time for another renovation.

A visit to the Palm House remains an educational experience. Just as William Hooker directed visitors' attention to plants of particular commercial and cultural interest in his *Popular Guide*, so information panels in the Palm House point out plants like the oil palm and rarities such as the coco de mer. But, these days, the emphasis falls on biodiversity and conservation. Visitors are informed of the environmental impact of massive oil-palm plantations and the endangered status of the coco de mer. In ways that William Hooker could not have anticipated, the Palm House has assumed renewed significance. Never before has it been so urgent to communicate the importance of the rainforest. A tour of the Palm House serves as a reminder of the wonders of a fast-vanishing world.

At Kew, current research on palms focuses on the conservation, diversity and evolution of palms across the globe. Palms are especially vulnerable to extinction because many species are endemic – that is, they only grow in specific geographic locations. Kew scientists are engaged on a project to sequence hundreds of genes from representatives of every palm species. Here, again, the Palm House comes into its own. The cultivated specimens furnish material for the scientific team to use for genome sequencing, dissection and anatomical study. Science, spectacle and public education have long been united at Kew.

Visiting the Palm House today, you may come across gardeners at work in the undergrowth. Many are horticultural students from around the world, training at Kew. Others are volunteers who give a day each week to tidying the jungle. Assigned a section of the Palm House to monitor, volunteers log the dates when particular plants are in flower or fruit. They say that they feel privileged to work in so famous a building. Besides the heat in summer, the only hindrance is backing unawares into a spiny cycad. For the volunteer gardeners, the task of maintaining the artful disarray is evidently a labour of love.

A walk through the Palm House is as immersive and absorbing as a great theatrical performance. The Palm House has always been a site of the imagination. Part artificial, part natural, the building and plants combine to form a space of spectacular beauty. Time slows as you stare at the patterns of fronds, leaves, arches and ribs. But it is also too humid, too hot, too overwhelming. You head for the door. At last, you can breathe again. It is cool and there is space all around. You close the Palm House door with a mixture of relief and regret. Behind you lies a tropical dreamscape, more vivid, more intense, more alive than the everyday world. Even as you leave, you know that you will have to return.

# *Notes*

## Chapter 1: Opening the Door

1 Virginia Woolf, *The Complete Shorter Fiction of Virginia Woolf* (London: Hogarth Press, 1985), p. 89.

## Chapter 2: The Inspectors

1 Joseph Paxton to Sarah Paxton, 14 February 1838, P/44, Paxton Papers (PP), Chatsworth.
2 Royal Gardens, Committee of Inquiry, Work 6/297: no. 8, NA.
3 Robson's *Directory of Middlesex* (1837), cited in Janet McNamara, 'Brentford High Street Project' http://www.bhsproject.co.uk/history.shtml
4 *Spectator*, 18 April 1840, p. 379.
5 John Lindley, 'Observations upon the Effects produced on Plants by the Frost which occurred in England in the Winter of 1837–8', *Transactions of the Horticultural Society of London*, Second Series, vol. 2 (1842), p. 225.
6 John Smith, *Records of the Royal Botanic Gardens, Kew* (1880), pp. 261–2, Archives RBGK.
7 Richard Hankins, Secretary Office of Woods, to John Lindley, 3 February 1838, T90/189: f. 69, NA.
8 *Gardener's Magazine* 2 (1827), p. 315.
9 *Gardeners' Gazette*, 7 October 1837, reprinted in *Annals of Horticulture* (1849), p. 100; *Gardeners' Gazette*, 11 November 1837, p. 714; *Gardeners' Gazette*, 21 October 1837, p. 664.
10 *Gardeners' Gazette*, 7 October 1837, reprinted in *Annals of Horticulture* (1849), p. 100.
11 *Colonial Magazine and Commercial Maritime Journal*, vol. 2 (May–August 1840), p. 213.

12 For Lindley's career, see William T. Stearn (ed.), *John Lindley 1799–1865* (1998), pp. 15–72.
13 Richard Hankins, Secretary Office of Woods, to John Lindley, 3 February 1838, T90/189: f. 69, NA.
14 Royal Gardens, Committee of Inquiry, Work 6/297: nos. 91, 92, 94, NA.
15 John Lindley, *Report upon the present Condition of the Botanical Garden at Kew*, Parliamentary Paper 292 (House of Commons, 1840), p. 2.
16 Royal Gardens, Committee of Inquiry, Work 6/297: Appendix A; nos. 105, 110, 112, NA.
17 Lindley, *Report*, p. 3.
18 *Ibid.*
19 Lindley, *Report*, p. 2.
20 Lindley, *Report*, p. 3.
21 *Ibid.*
22 Lindley, *Report*, p. 4.
23 *Ibid.*
24 *Ibid.*
25 *Ibid.*
26 Lindley, *Report*, p. 5.
27 *Ibid.*
28 *Ibid.*
29 Royal Gardens, Committee of Inquiry, Work 6/297: f. 12, NA.
30 Queen Victoria's Journals, 30 April 1838, Lord Esher's typescript, vol. 5, p. 137, http://www.queenvictoriasjournals.org
31 Queen Victoria's Journals, 24 January 1839, Lord Esher's typescript, vol. 9, p. 259, http://www.queenvictoriasjournals.org
32 Queen Victoria's Journals, 24 January 1839, Lord Esher's typescript, vol. 9, p. 259; 28 February 1839, vol. 9, p. 84. The pair revert to the topic of Kew on 12 April 1839: 'Lord M. was for giving it quite up, which I am for, but the Duke of Bedford and others say, that wouldn't do. Talked of the new proposition for the gardens, – which Lord M. has sent to the Duke of Argyll, who is ill again, but Surrey will look over it', and 24 November 1839: 'Talked of that Botanic Garden being such a dreadful pressure as Erroll said, upon the Lord Steward's department, in which Lord M. quite agreed, and said, he would see what could be done about it.' http://www.queenvictoriasjournals.org

## Chapter 3: The Contenders

1 Frederick Scheer, *Kew and its Gardens* (London: B. Steill, 1840) p. v.

2 J. Paxton to S. Paxton, 14 February 1838, P/44, Paxton Papers (PP), Chatsworth.

3 J. Paxton to S. Paxton, 20 February 1838, P/45, PP, Chatsworth.

4 *Ibid.*

5 J. Lindley to W. Hooker, London, 12 February 1838, Director's Correspondence (DC) 11 (1838), f. 60, Archives RBGK.

6 W. Hooker to J. Lindley, Glasgow, 20 February 1838, Dr Lindley's Official Correspondence, f. 469, Archives RBGK.

7 *Ibid.*

8 J. Lindley to W. Hooker, London, 24 February 1838, DC 11 (1838), f. 61, Archives RBGK.

9 W. Hooker to D. Turner, Glasgow, 13 March 1838, 'Extracts from Letters relating to the Royal Botanic Gardens, Kew, written by Sir W. J. Hooker to Dawson Turner, 1834–50', f. 4, Archives RBGK.

10 Richard Drayton, *Nature's Government: Science, Imperial Britain, and the 'Improvement' of the World* (New Haven: Yale University Press, 2000), p. 158.

11 W. Hooker to W. H. Fox Talbot, Glasgow, 10 April 1838, Fox Talbot Collection, British Library, see http://foxtalbot.dmu.ac.uk/letters/letters.html

12 W. H. Fox Talbot to W. Hooker, 1 May 1838, Archives RBGK, EL 11.146, see http://foxtalbot.dmu.ac.uk/letters/letters.html

13 Charles Lyell, *Life, Letters, and Journals of Sir Charles Lyell*, K. M. Lyell (ed.), 2 vols. (1881), vol. 1, p. 41.

14 J. D. Hooker, 'A Sketch of the Life and Labours of Sir William Jackson Hooker', *Annals of Botany*, vol. os-16:4 (December 1902), p. xii.

15 For Dawson Turner's family life, see Nigel Goodman (ed.), *Dawson Turner: A Norfolk Antiquary and his Remarkable Family* (Chester: Phillimore, 2007).

16 W. Hooker to D. Turner, Glasgow, 13 March 1838, 'Extracts from Letters', f. 4, Archives RBGK.

17 W. Hooker to D. Turner, Glasgow, 18 January 1839, 'Extracts from Letters', f. 8, Archives RBGK.

18 W. Hooker to D. Turner, Inveresk Cottage, 27 July 1839, 'Extracts from Letters', f. 11, Archives RBGK.

19 *Gardener's Magazine* n. s. 4 (1838), p. 194.

20 *Gardeners' Chronicle*, 18 March 1876, p. 363.

21 *Gardener's Magazine* 1 (1826), p. 25.

22 See, for instance, J. Wighton, 'On the Preference for Scotch Gardeners', *Gardener's Magazine* n. s. 6 (1840), pp. 244–6; *Gardeners' Chronicle*, 6 April 1872, pp. 461–2.

23 John Smith, 'History of the Royal Gardens, Kew', 1: f. 98, Archives RBGK.

24 For a discussion of Scottish gardeners, see Rod McEwen, 'The Northern Lads: The Migration of Scottish Gardeners with especial reference to the Royal Botanic Gardens Kew', *Sibbaldia: The Journal of Botanic Garden Horticulture* 11 (2013), pp. 109–23.

25 *Gardeners' Chronicle*, 18 March 1876, p. 363.

26 J. W. Thomson, 'Reminiscences of an Old Kewite', *Journal of the Kew Guild* 1.3 (1894), p. 35.

27 J. W. Thomson, 'Reminiscences of an Old Kewite', *Journal of the Kew Guild*, p. 34.

28 Trial of Robert Sweet, 18 February 1824, *The Proceedings of the Old Bailey*, Ref. t18240218-88, https://www.oldbaileyonline.org

29 *Morning Chronicle*, 25 February 1824, p. 4.

30 Trial of Robert Sweet, 18 February 1824, *The Proceedings of the Old Bailey*, Ref. t18240218-88, https://www.oldbaileyonline.org

31 *Morning Chronicle*, 25 February 1824, p. 4.

32 Smith, 'History of the Royal Gardens', 3: f. 502.

33 Ray Desmond, 'John Smith, Kew's First Curator', *Journal of the Kew Guild* (1965), p. 580.

34 *Gardeners' Gazette*, 28 April 1838, p. 264.

35 *Gardeners' Gazette*, 28 April 1838, p. 264, p. 265.

36 *Gardeners' Gazette*, 8 September 1838, p. 568.

37 W. Hooker to J. Hooker, Glasgow, 2 February 1840, JDH/2/10 f. 97, Archives RBGK.

38 Harold Lambert, 'The other Dr Hooker: William Dawson Hooker', *Journal of Medical Biography* (2011) 19.4, pp. 141–4.

39 W. Hooker to J. Hooker, Glasgow, 13 April 1840, JDH/2/10 f. 100, Archives RBGK.

40 Donald Beaton, *Cottage Gardener*, 15 October 1855, p. 35, cited in Brent Elliott, *The Royal Horticultural Society: A History 1804–2004* (Chichester: Phillimore, 2004), p. 343.

41 J. Lindley to W. Hooker, 11 August 1840, DC 15, f. 37, Archives RBGK.
42 *The Royal Botanic Society of London. 1841* (London: Richard and John E. Taylor, 1841), n.p.
43 *The Pictorial Handbook of London* (London: Henry G. Bohn, 1854), p. 488.
44 W. Hooker to Dawson Turner, Glasgow, 4 August 1838, 'Extracts from Letters', f. 5, Archives RBGK.
45 Guy Meynell, 'The Royal Botanic Society's Garden, Regent's Park', *London Journal*, vol. 6:2 (1980), p. 145.
46 W. Hooker to Dawson Turner, Glasgow, 4 August 1838, 'Extracts from Letters', f. 5, Archives RBGK.
47 Drayton, *Nature's Government*, p. 160.
48 A. Lambert to J. Smith, 13 February 1840, Aylmer Bourke Lambert Letters, Archives RBGK.
49 John Smith, 'A Record of a Few Special Events and Matters Relative to the Royal Botanic Garden at Kew' (Brentford: W. H. Jackson, n.d.), p. 14, Archives RBGK.
50 Heward is identified as the anonymous author of the letter to *The Times* in a footnote to an article on Smith in the *Gardeners' Chronicle*, Jan–June 1876, p. 363, in Heward's obituary notice in the *Gardeners' Chronicle*, July–Dec 1877, p. 571, and in a footnote to Berthold Seemann's obituary of Frederick Scheer, in the *Journal of Botany, British and Foreign*, vol. 7 (Jan 1869), p. 270.
51 *The Times*, 21 February 1840, p. 3.
52 A. Lambert to J. Smith, 27 February 1840, Aylmer Bourke Lambert Letters, Archives RBGK.
53 *Ibid.*
54 *Morning Chronicle*, 4 March 1840, p. 1.
55 A. Lambert to J. Smith, 27 February 1840, Aylmer Bourke Lambert Letters, Archives RBGK.
56 A. Lambert to J. Smith, 9 March 1840, Aylmer Bourke Lambert Letters, Archives RBGK.
57 The report was widely circulated, having been reprinted in the *Gardener's Magazine*, n.s. 6 (1840), pp. 365–71.
58 W. Hooker to D. Turner, 3 March 1840, 'Extracts from Letters', f. 14, Archives RBGK.
59 William Hooker, *Copy of a letter addressed to Dawson Turner Esq. FRA & LS . . . on the occasion of the death of the late Duke of Bedford* (Glasgow: George Richardson, 1840), p. 20.

60 W. Hooker to D. Turner, 4 April 1840, 'Extracts from Letters', f. 16, Archives RBGK.
61 Smith, 'History of the Royal Gardens', 3: f. 502.
62 W. Hooker to D. Turner, 29 April 1840, 'Extracts from Letters', f. 20, Archives RBGK.
63 W. Hooker to D. Turner, 20 April 1840, 'Extracts from Letters', f. 17; W. Hooker to D. Turner, 23 June 1840, 'Extracts from Letters', f. 23, Archives RBGK.
64 W. Hooker to J. Hooker, London, 21 June 1840, JDH/2/10, f. 101, Archives RBGK.
65 W. Hooker to D. Turner, 26 April 1841, 'Extracts from Letters', f. 46, Archives RBGK.

## Chapter 4: The Horticultural Tour

1 W. Hooker to J. Hooker, Glasgow, 9 May 1841, JDH/2/10, f. 114, Archives RBGK.
2 J. Hooker to W. Hooker, HMS 'Erebus', Falkland Islands, 5 April 1842, JDH/1/f/85, Archives RBGK.
3 Joseph Hooker, 'A Sketch of the Life and Labours of Sir William Jackson Hooker', *Annals of Botany*, vol. 16:4 (December 1902), p. lv.
4 'A type of true English gentleman', from Alphonse de Candolle, 'La vie et les écrits de Sir W. Hooker', *Archives des Sciences de la Bibliothèque universelle de Genève* (Jan 1866); Joseph Hooker, 'A Sketch of the Life and Labours of Sir William Jackson Hooker', *Annals of Botany*, vol. 16:4 (December 1902), p. lxxxviii.
5 J. Smith to W. Hooker, Royal Botanic Gardens, 4 August 1841, DC 16, f. 332, Archives RBGK.
6 James Forbes, *Journal of a Horticultural Tour through Germany, Belgium and Part of France* (London: James Ridgway, 1837), p. 16.
7 James Forbes, *Hortus Woburnensis* (London: James Ridgway, 1833), p. iii.
8 D. Cameron to W. Hooker, Birmingham, 29 October 1841, DC 16, f. 71, Archives RBGK.
9 Charles McIntosh, *The Book of the Garden* (Edinburgh: William Blackwood & Sons, 1853), vol. 1, p. 374.
10 *Ibid.*
11 *Paxton's Magazine of Botany* 8 (1841), p. 256.

12 *Imperial Magazine* 11 (1829), p. 1124.
13 *Derby Mercury*, 5 May 1841, p. 3.
14 'The ultimate conservatory', *Magazine of Horticulture, Botany and all useful Discoveries in Rural Affairs* 7 (1841), p. 425.
15 *The Times*, 21 September 1840. The massive palm was part of a larger collection of palms which were offered to the Duke of Devonshire on the death of Lady Tankerville. The actual cost for the transfer of the entire collection was £726.18*s*. See Kate Colquhoun, *The Busiest Man in England* (Boston: David Godine, 2006), p. 267.
16 Charles Knight, *The Land We Live In* (London: Charles Knight, 1847–50), vol. 3, p. 79.
17 *Chambers's Edinburgh Journal* 7 (22 May 1847), p. 336.
18 G. Lawson, 'Palm Trees', *Hogg's Instructor* 5 (July–December 1855), p. 199.
19 'Palm Trees and their Products', *Illustrated Magazine of Art*, vol. 3:16 (1854), p. 227.
20 *Chambers's Journal of Popular Literature, Science and Arts* 8 (15 August 1857), p. 108.
21 *Chambers's Edinburgh Journal* 7 (22 May 1847), p. 333.
22 See, for instance, Archibald Bennie, *Discourses* (Edinburgh: William Blackwood, 1847), pp. 380–99.
23 See, for instance, Sophy Moody, *The Palm Tree* (London: T. Nelson and Sons, 1864), pp. 38–9, pp. 83–5, pp. 365–6, p. 370, p. 397.
24 Charles Knight, *Library of Entertaining Knowledge*: *A Description and History of Vegetable Substances* (London: Charles Knight, 1830), vol. 42, p. 351.
25 *Chambers's Journal* 8 (15 August 1857), p. 108.
26 Charles Knight, *Library of Entertaining Knowledge*, vol. 42, p. 351.
27 *Chambers's Journal* 19 (21 February 1863), p. 113.
28 *Ibid.*
29 See, for instance, the *Penny Magazine of the Society for the Diffusion of Knowledge* (5 December 1835), pp. 475–6; *The Church Scholar's Reading Book* (London: John Parker, 1840), vol. 1, p. 65; *Chambers's Journal* (15 August 1857), p. 108.
30 Sir John Malcolm, *Sketches of Persia* (London: John Murray, 1861), p. 40.
31 Malcolm, *Sketches of Persia*, p. 41.
32 R. M. Ballantyne, *The Coral Island* (London: W. Chambers, 1870), p. 228.

33 John Robertson, 'Coco-Eaters', *Household Words* (31 January 1857), p. 101.
34 *Ibid.*
35 *Ibid.*
36 Herman Melville, *Omoo* (London: John Murray, 1847), p. 265.
37 *Ibid.*
38 *Ibid.*
39 Hugh Murray et al., *Historical and Descriptive Account of British India* (Edinburgh: Oliver & Boyd, 1843), vol. 3, p. 168.
40 Anon, *The Palm Tribes and their Varieties* (London: Religious Tract Society, 1852), p. 73.
41 Melville, *Omoo*, p. 267.
42 See, for instance, Henry Marshall, 'Contribution to a Natural and Economical History of the Coco-Nut Tree', *Memoirs of the Werniarian Natural History Society*, vol. 5:1 (1824), p. 114; Murray et al., *Historical and Descriptive Account of British India*, vol. 3, p. 168.
43 Jacques-Henri Bernardin de S. Pierre, *Harmonies of Nature*, vol. 1 (London: Baldwin, Craddock & Joy, 1815), pp. 68–9; John Robertson, *Household Words* (15 January 1857), p. 67.
44 *Chambers's Edinburgh Journal* 7 (22 May 1847), p. 333.
45 Marshall, 'Contribution to a Natural and Economical History of the Coco-Nut Tree', *Memoirs of the Werniarian Natural History Society*, vol. 5:1 (1824), p. 118.
46 Marshall, 'Contribution to a Natural and Economical History of the Coco-Nut Tree', *Memoirs of the Werniarian Natural History Society*, vol. 5:1 (1824), p. 119.
47 John Fisher Murray, 'The World of London', *Blackwood's Edinburgh Magazine* 51 (1842), p. 380.
48 John Claudius Loudon, 'Hints for Breathing Places for the Metropolis', *Gardener's Magazine* 5 (1829), p. 687.
49 Murray, 'The World of London', *Blackwood's Edinburgh Magazine* 51 (1842), p. 381.
50 *Report from the Select Committee on Public Walks* (House of Commons, 1833), p. 9.
51 'Minutes of Evidence Taken before the Select Committee on National Monuments', *Parliamentary Papers: Reports from Committees* 6 (1841), p. 71.
52 W. Hooker to D. Turner, Kew, 13 July 1843, 'Extracts from Letters', f. 50, Archives RBGK.

53 Joseph Hooker, 'A Sketch of the Life and Labours of Sir William Jackson Hooker', *Annals of Botany*, vol. 16:4 (December 1902), p. lxii.
54 W. Hooker to D. Turner, Kew, 4 October 1842, 'Extracts from Letters' f. 48, Archives RBGK.
55 W. Hooker to J. Hooker, Kew, 1 May 1842, JDH/2/10, f. 121, Archives RBGK.
56 M. Hooker to J. Hooker, Kew, 30 July 1842, JDH/2/10, f. 140, Archives RBGK.
57 W. Hooker to D. Turner, Kew, 22 May 1843, 'Extracts from Letters', f. 50, Archives RBGK.
58 *Report from Sir William Hooker on the Royal Botanic Gardens and the Proposed new Palm House at Kew* (House of Commons, Accounts and Papers, vol. 45, 1845), p. 12.
59 John Smith, 'History of the Royal Gardens, Kew', 3: f. 504, Archives RBGK.
60 *Gardeners' Chronicle*, 14 August 1841, p. 535.
61 *Gardeners' Chronicle*, 19 February 1842, p. 123.
62 *Gardeners' Chronicle*, 14 August 1841, p. 535.

## Chapter 5: Father and Son

1 Leonard Huxley, *Life and Letters of Sir Joseph Dalton Hooker* (London: John Murray, 1918), vol. 1, p. 16.
2 Huxley, *Life and Letters of Sir Joseph Dalton Hooker*, vol. 1, p. 37.
3 Huxley, *Life and Letters of Sir Joseph Dalton Hooker*, vol 1, p. 27.
4 Huxley, *Life and Letters of Sir Joseph Dalton Hooker*, vol. 1, p. 28.
5 William Jackson Hooker, *Journal of A Tour in Iceland in the summer of 1809*, 2 vols. (privately published 1811; 2nd ed., London: Longman, Hurst, Rees, Orme, Brown and John Murray, 1813).
6 W. Vernon Harcourt, 'President's Address', British Association of the Advancement of Science, *Report of the Ninth Meeting* (1840), p. 4.
7 W. Hooker to J. Hooker, Glasgow, 14 September 1839, JDH/2/10, f. 93, Archives RBGK.
8 *Literary Gazette*, 28 September 1839, p. 621.
9 J. Hooker to W. Hooker, St Helena Roads, 3 February 1840, JHC281, f. 2, Joseph Dalton Hooker Correspondence Project (JDHCP), http://jdhooker.kew.org/p/jdh
10 J. Hooker to M. McGilvray, HMS *Erebus*, Hobarton, 18 August 1840, JHC286, f. 1, JDHCP, http://jdhooker.kew.org/p/jdh

11 W. Hooker to J. Hooker, Glasgow, 13 February 1840, JDH/2/10, f. 98, Archives RBGK.
12 J. Hooker to W. Hooker, Hobart Town, 7 September 1840, JHC288, f. 1, JDHCP, http://jdhooker.kew.org/p/jdh
13 W. Hooker to J. Hooker, Glasgow, 13 February 1840, JDH/2/10, f. 98, Archives RBGK.
14 *Ibid.*
15 J. Hooker to W. Hooker, Hobarton, 16 August 1840, JHC285, f. 2, JDHCP, http://jdhooker.kew.org/p/jdh
16 J. Hooker to W. Hooker, Hobarton, 3 November 1840, JHC290, f. 1, JDHCP, http://jdhooker.kew.org/p/jdh
17 Joseph Dalton Hooker, *The Botany of the Antarctic Voyage* (London: Reeve, 1844), vol. 1, p. vii.
18 J. Hooker, Antarctic Journal Typescript, JDH/1/1, f. 146, Archives RBGK.
19 *Literary Gazette*, 28 September 1839, p. 621.
20 J. Hooker to W. Hooker, Hobarton, 5 April 1841, JHC292, f. 3, JDHCP, http://jdhooker.kew.org/p/jdh
21 *Athenæum*, 4 March 1843, p. 212.
22 J. Hooker to W. Hooker, 'Erebus', Lat. S71.0 Long. W16, 7 March 1843, JHC327, f. 11, JDHCP, http://jdhooker.kew.org/p/jdh
23 *Ibid.*
24 W. Hooker to J. Hooker, Kew, 5 January 1843, JDH/2/10, f. 121, Archives RBGK.
25 *Ibid.*
26 Huxley, *Life and Letters of Sir Joseph Dalton Hooker*, vol. 1, p. 77.
27 See Jim Endersby, *Imperial Nature: Joseph Hooker and the Practices of Victorian Science* (Chicago: University of Chicago Press, 2008), pp. 45–7; R. J. Berry, 'Hooker and Islands', *Biological Journal of the Linnean Society*, vol. 96:2 (2009), pp. 462–81.
28 J. Hooker to Lady Hooker, Falkland Islands, 6 December 1842, JHC324, f. 9, JDHCP, http://jdhooker.kew.org/p/jdh
29 Elizabeth Hooker to J. Hooker, West Park, December 1841, JDH/2/10, f. 173, Archives RBGK.
30 J. Hooker, Antarctic Journal Typescript, JDH/1/1, f. 149, Archives RBGK.
31 Huxley, *Life and Letters of Sir Joseph Dalton Hooker*, vol. 1, p. 62.
32 Elizabeth Hooker to J. Hooker, West Park, December 1841, JDH/2/10, f. 173, Archives RBGK.

33 J. Hooker to W. Hooker, Falkland Islands, 5 December 1842, JHC323, f. 7, JDHCP, http://jdhooker.kew.org/p/jdh

34 Lady Hooker to J. Hooker, West Park, 20 March 1842, JDH/2/10, f. 145, Archives RBGK.

35 W. Hooker to J. Hooker, Athenaeum, 29 March 1842, JDH/2/10, f. 120, Archives RBGK.

36 W. Hooker to J. Hooker, Kew, 9 July 1842, JDH/2/10, f. 107, Archives RBGK.

37 J. Hooker to W. Hooker, Cape of Good Hope, 20 April 1843, JHC334, f. 14, JDHCP, http://jdhooker.kew.org/p/jdh

38 J. Hooker to W. Hooker, HMS *Erebus*, 7 March 1843, JHC327, f. 22, JDHCP, http://jdhooker.kew.org/p/jdh

39 W. Hooker to J. Hooker, Kew, 9 July 1842, JDH/2/10, f. 107, Archives RBGK.

40 W. J. Hooker, *Notes on the Botany of the Antarctic Voyage* (London: H. Baillière,1843), dedication.

41 Hooker, *Notes on the Botany of the Antarctic Voyage*, p. 1.

42 Hooker, *Notes on the Botany of the Antarctic Voyage*, p. 11.

43 Hooker, *Notes on the Botany of the Antarctic Voyage*, p. 25. Compare to the passage in the original letter, where Joseph makes no reference either to commander or Creator, but rather turns the discussion to himself: 'The idea that we have penetrated far farther than was once thought practicable, & there is every thing beyond what we see is enveloped in a mystery reserved for future voyagers to fathom. But you are all this time wondering what are the fruits of this expedition to me especially.' J. Hooker to W. Hooker, Hobarton, Van Diemen's Land, 5 April 1841, JHC292, f. 3, JDHCP, http://jdhooker.kew.org/p/jdh

44 'Correspondence respecting the Colonization of the Falkland Islands', *Parliamentary Papers* 33 (1843), pp. 38–9.

45 Originally published in the *Star*, Guernsey, 15 September 1842, reprinted in the *Morning Post*, 23 September 1842, *Caledonian Mercury*, 24 September 1842 and *Dublin Evening Packet and Correspondent*, 24 September 1842.

46 W. J. Hooker, 'Tussac Grass', *Journal of the Royal Geographical Society* 12 (1842), pp. 265–6.

47 W. Hooker to J. Hooker, Kew, 5 January 1843, JDH/2/10, f. 121, Archives RBGK.

48 W. Hooker to J. Hooker, Kew, 1 May 1842, JDH/2/10, f. 121, Archives RBGK.
49 *Ibid.*
50 C. Darwin to W. Hooker, Down, 12 March 1843, DCP-LETT-664, Darwin Correspondence Project (DCP), https://www.darwinproject.ac.uk/
51 C. Darwin to W. Hooker, Down, 11 January 1844, DCP-LETT-729, DCP, https://www.darwinproject.ac.uk/
52 W. Hooker to J. Hooker, Kew, 30 June 1843, JDH/2/10, f. 125, Archives RBGK.
53 *Ibid.*
54 *Ibid.*
55 *Ibid.*
56 J. Hooker to W. Hooker, Rio de Janeiro, 21 June 1843, JHC 347, f. 4, JDHCP, http://jdhooker.kew.org/p/jdh

## Chapter 6: The Engineer and the Architect

1 John Lindley, Entry on 'Garden' in Charles Knight (ed.), *Penny Cyclopaedia* (1838), vol. 11, p. 73.
2 John Claudius Loudon, *Encyclopædia of Gardening* (London: Longman, Rees, Orme, Brown, Green and Longman, 1835), vol. 1, p. 201.
3 Loudon, *Encyclopædia of Gardening*, vol. 1, p. 203.
4 Queen Victoria's Journals, 3 October 1843, Princess Beatrice's copies, vol. 16, p. 138, http://www.queenvictoriasjournals.org
5 W. Hooker to D. Turner, Kew, 4 October 1843, 'Extracts from Letters', f. 52, Archives RBGK.
6 *Lloyd's Weekly London Newspaper*, 8 October 1843; *Gardeners' Chronicle*, 30 September 1843, p. 675.
7 W. Hooker to D. Turner, Kew, 4 October 1843, 'Extracts from Letters', f. 52, Archives RBGK.
8 *Ibid.*
9 Charles McIntosh, *The Greenhouse, Hothouse and Stove* (London: W. S. Orr & Co., 1838), pp. 278–9.
10 *Ibid.*
11 *Galignani's New Paris Guide* (Paris: A. and W. Galignani, 1839), p. 441.
12 Loudon, *Encyclopædia of Gardening*, vol. 1, p. 116.
13 Review of Frederick Scheer, *Kew and its Gardens* in the *Colonial Magazine and Commercial Maritime Journal* 2 (May–August 1840), p. 214.

14 *Ibid.*
15 Frederick Scheer, *Kew and its Gardens* (London: B. Steill, 1840), p. 37.
16 Lord Lincoln's evidence, 'Report from the Select Committee on Miscellaneous Expenditure', 27 July 1848, *Reports of Committees*, nos. 543, 346 (House of Commons Papers, 1847–8).
17 John Smith, 'History of the Royal Gardens, Kew', 1: f. 51, Archives RBGK.
18 *Chambers's Edinburgh Journal* 6 (31 October 1846), p. 283.
19 William Adam, *The Gem of the Peak* (London: Longman, 1845), p. 147.
20 *Ibid.*
21 Lord Lincoln's evidence, 'Report from the Select Committee on Miscellaneous Expenditure', 27 July 1848, no. 346.
22 *Gardeners' Chronicle*, 30 September 1843, p. 675.
23 W. Hooker to D. Turner, Kew, 4 October 1843, 'Extracts from Letters', f. 53, Archives RBGK.
24 *Ibid.*
25 *Chambers's Edinburgh Journal* 6 (31 October 1846), p. 281.
26 Loudon, *Encyclopædia of Gardening*, vol. 1, p. 581.
27 *Ibid.*
28 Thomas Drew, *Building News,* 19 March 1880, p. 355.
29 *Sharpe's London Magazine*, 8 May 1847, p. 29, p. 30.
30 R. J. M. Sutherland, *Structural Iron 1750–1850: Studies in the History of Civil Engineering*, vol. 9 (London: Routledge, 2016), p. 15.
31 Andrew Ure, *A Dictionary of Arts, Manufactures and Mines* (London: Longman, Orme, Brown, Green and Longman, 1840), p. 680.
32 *The Times*, 3 September 1833, p. 3.
33 *Gardener's Magazine* 9 (1833), p. 614.
34 E. J. Diestelkamp, 'The Curvilinear Range at the National Botanic Gardens', *Moorea* 9 (December, 1990), p. 8.
35 RBS/8, Records of the Royal Botanic Society of London, Westminster City Archives.
36 *Ibid.*
37 Thomas Drew, *Building News,* 19 March 1880, p. 355.
38 W. Hooker to Lord Lincoln, Kew, 1 February 1844, Ne C 8, 969, Newcastle (Clumber) Collection, Manuscripts and Special Collections, University of Nottingham.
39 R. Turner to W. Hooker, 2 February 1844, DC 22, f. 255, Archives RBGK. See also R. Turner to the Hon. Board, Office of Woods, Work 16/29/8, f. 14, NA.

40 W. Hooker to D. Turner, Kew, 9 March 1844, 'Extracts from Letters', f. 53, Archives RBGK.
41 A Grade II-listed building in Regent's Park's Inner Circle.
42 John Harris, 'C. R. Cockerell's "Ichnographica Domestica"', *Architectural History* 14 (1971), p. 20.
43 See Christopher Jones, 'Picturesque Urban Planning – Tunbridge Wells and the Suburban Ideal: The Development of the Calverley Estate 1825–1855', DPhil. thesis, University of Oxford, 2017.
44 *The Architectural Review*, vol. 17:98 (1905), p. 109.
45 For a discussion of Burton's conservatories, see chapter 4 of Edward J. Diestelkamp,'The Iron and Glass Architecture of Richard Turner', PhD thesis, University College London, 1982.
46 See C. F. Chadwick, 'Paxton and the Great Stove', *Architectural History* 4 (1961), pp. 77–92.
47 *Ibid.*
48 Edward J. Diestelkamp, 'Richard Turner and the Palm House at Kew Gardens', in Sutherland, *Structural Iron*, pp. 185–6.
49 R. Turner to W. Hooker, 23 February 1844, DC 22, f. 259, Archives, RBGK.
50 D. Burton to the Commissioners of HM Woods, 7 March 1844, Work, 16/29/8, ff. 2–3, NA.
51 *Ibid.*
52 *Ibid.*
53 W. Hooker to Lord Lincoln, 20 February 1844, Ne C 8, 971, Newcastle (Clumber) Collection, Manuscripts and Special Collections, University of Nottingham.
54 R. Turner to W. Hooker, 28 February 1844, DC 22, f. 261, Archives RBGK.
55 R. Turner to W. Hooker, 23 February 1844, DC 22, f. 260, Archives RBGK.
56 R. Turner to W. Hooker, 28 February 1844, DC 22, f. 261, Archives RBGK.
57 *Ibid.*
58 R. Turner to W. Hooker, 23 February 1844, DC 22, f. 260, Archives RBGK.
59 D. Burton to W. Hooker, 2 March 1844, DC 21, f. 162, Archives RBGK.
60 Diestelkamp, 'Richard Turner and the Palm House', in Sutherland, *Structural Iron*, p.196.

61 R. Turner to W. Hooker, 23 February 1844, DC 22, f. 264, Archives RBGK.

62 *Ibid.*

63 Diestelkamp, 'Richard Turner and the Palm House', in Sutherland, *Structural Iron*, p. 198.

64 R. Turner to W. Hooker, 4 April 1844, Learmont, DC 22, ff. 268–9, Archives RBGK.

65 *Ibid.*

66 R. Turner to W. Hooker, 27 April 1844, DC 22, f. 269, Archives RBGK.

67 Thomas Drew, *Building News*, 19 March 1880, p. 355.

68 *Ibid.*

69 R. Turner to the Hon. Board, 9 May 1844, Work 16/29/8, ff. 13–14, NA.

70 R. Turner to W. Hooker, 14 May 1844, DC 22, f. 270, Archives RBGK.

71 R. Turner to W. Hooker, 23 May 1844, DC 22, f. 273, Archives RBGK.

72 *Ibid.*

73 *Ibid.*

74 *Ibid.*

## Chapter 7: The Landscape Designer

1 John Smith, 'History of the Royal Gardens, Kew', 1: f. 64, Archives RGBK.

2 Smith, 'History of the Royal Gardens', 1: f. 55.

3 *Ibid.*

4 John Ruskin, *Modern Painters* (Sunnyside: George Allen, 1888), vol. 1, p. 349, p. 344. For Nesfield's life and design principles, see Shirley Evans, *Masters of their Craft: The Art, Architecture and Garden Design of the Nesfields* (Cambridge: Lutterworth Press, 2014).

5 W. Hooker to D. Turner, Kew, 9 March 1844, 'Extracts from Letters', f. 53, Archives RBGK.

6 For an analysis of Nesfield's gardening principles, see Shirley Evans, 'William Andrews Nesfield (1794–1881) Artist and Landscape Gardener', PhD thesis, University College, Falmouth, 2007.

7 W. Hooker to Lord Lincoln, Kew, 1 February 1844, Ne C 8, 969, Newcastle (Clumber) Collection, Manuscripts and Special Collections, University of Nottingham.

8 John Lindley, *Report upon the present Condition of the Botanical Garden at Kew*, Parliamentary Paper 292 (House of Commons, 1840), p. 1.
9 *Ibid.*
10 John Smith, *Records of the Royal Botanic Gardens, Kew* (1880), p. 287, Archives RBGK.
11 Smith, *Records*, p. 260.
12 Smith, *Records*, p. 261.
13 Paul A. Elliott, Charles Watkins, Stephen Daniels, *The British Arboretum: Trees, Science and Culture in the Nineteenth Century* (Pittsburgh: University of Pittsburgh Press, 2011), pp. 46–9.
14 John Claudius Loudon, *Arboretum et Fruticetum Britannicum*, 8 vols. (London: Longman, Green, Brown, Longman, 1844), vol. 1, p. 1.
15 Loudon, *Arboretum*, vol. 1, pp. 3–4.
16 *Annals of Natural History*, vol. 3 (1839), p. 188.
17 *Annals of Natural History*, vol. 3 (1839), p. 189.
18 Smith, *Records*, p. 269.
19 Uvedale Price, *Essays on the Picturesque* (London: J. Mawman, 1810), vol. 1, p. 259.
20 Price, *Essays on the Picturesque*, vol. 1, p. 262.
21 George Sinclair, *Useful and Ornamental Planting* (London: Baldwin and Craddock, 1832), p. 129.
22 *Ibid.*
23 W. Nesfield to W. Hooker, Eton College, Windsor, 15 February 1844, DC 22, f. 131, Archives RBGK.
24 *Ibid.*
25 W. Nesfield to W. Hooker, Eton College, postmarked 2 March 1844, DC 22, f. 133, Archives RBGK.
26 *Ibid.*
27 W. Hooker to D. Turner, Kew, 9 March 1844, 'Extracts from Letters', f. 53, Archives RBGK.
28 W. Nesfield to W. Hooker, Eton College, Windsor, 18 March 1844, DC 22, f. 134, Archives RBGK.
29 W. Nesfield to W. Hooker, Eton College, Windsor, 25 June 1844, DC 22, f. 140, Archives RBGK.
30 *Gardener's Magazine* n. s. 8 (1842), p. 553.
31 D. Burton to W. Hooker, Spring Gardens, 28 January 1845, DC 23, f. 92, Archives RBGK.

32 D. Burton to W. Hooker, 6 Spring Gardens, 18 February 1845, DC 23, f. 109, Archives RBGK.

33 D. Burton to W. Hooker, 6 Spring Gardens, 19 February 1845, DC 23, f. 110, Archives RBGK.

34 D. Burton to W. Hooker, 6 Spring Gardens, 4 June 1845, DC 23, f. 113, Archives RBGK.

35 W. Hooker to Dawson Turner, Kew, 17 May 1845, 'Extracts from Letters', f. 56, Archives RBGK.

36 Report sent by W. Nesfield to D. Burton, 27 May 1845, Kew Pleasure Grounds, f. 216, Archives RBGK.

37 W. Nesfield, 'Report Number Twenty-Four, Royal Botanic Gardens, Richmond', reproduced in Evans, 'William Andrews Nesfield', vol. 2, p. 153.

38 W. Nesfield, 'Report', in Evans, 'William Andrews Nesfield', vol. 2, p. 154.

39 W. Hooker to Dawson Turner, Kew, 9 July 1845, WJH/2/3, f. 56, Archives RBGK.

## Chapter 8: Deck Iron

1 'Richard Turner, of Hammersmith Works, Pembroke-road, in the city of Dublin, manufacturer of Iron, dealer and chapman, to surrender on Wednesday, March 3, and on Friday, April 2', *Dublin Morning Registry*, 20 February 1841.

2 See *Account of the Public Money Expended on each of the Royal Palaces, Gardens, Parks . . . 1843–51* (House of Commons, 6 June 1851).

3 *Civil Engineer & Architects Journal* 1 (1837–8), p. iii.

4 *Civil Engineer & Architects Journal* 7 (1844), p. 409.

5 *Ibid.*

6 Charles E. Peterson, 'Inventing the I-Beam: Richard Turner, Cooper & Hewitt and Others', *Bulletin of the Association for Preservation Technology*, vol. 12:3 (1980), p. 3.

7 R. Turner to W. Hooker, 23 November 1844, DC 22, f. 288, Archives RBGK.

8 R. Turner to W. Hooker, 10 October 1844, DC 22, f. 287, Archives RBGK.

9 R. Turner to W. Hooker, 23 November 1844, DC 22, f. 288, Archives RBGK.

10 W. Hooker to Lord Derby, 14 July 1844, quoted in Edward J. Diestelkamp, 'The Iron and Glass Architecture of Richard Turner', PhD thesis, University College London, 1982, p. 197.
11 *Ibid.*
12 W. Hooker to Lord Derby, 19 December 1844, 920 DER 13/1/82/23, Liverpool Record Office, Liverpool Libraries.
13 Lord Derby to W. Hooker, 12 February 1845, English Letters 23 (1845), f. 165, Archives RBGK; Lord Derby to W. Hooker, 20 October 1846, English Letters 24 (1846), f. 140, Archives RBGK, quoted in Diestelkamp, 'Iron and Glass Architecture', pp. 200–1.
14 R. Turner to W. Hooker, 23 November 1844, DC 22, f. 288, Archives RBGK.
15 Edward J. Diestelkamp, 'Richard Turner and the Palm House at Kew Gardens', in Sutherland, *Structural Iron*, p. 209.
16 D. Burton to W. Hooker, 14 June 1845, DC 23, f. 114, Archives RBGK.
17 *Building News*, 19 March 1880, p. 355.
18 RBS 8, Westminster City Archives (WCA).
19 R. Turner to D. Burton, 16 April 1845, RBS 3, WCA.
20 Minutes of Committee, 29 November 1845, RBS 3, WCA.
21 R. Turner to the Committee, London, 29 November 1845, RBS 3, WCA.
22 Minutes of Committee, 29 November 1845, RBS 3, WCA.
23 R. Turner to J. Sowerby, 29 November 1845, RBS 3, WCA.
24 Minutes of Committee, 4 February 1846, RBS 3, WCA.
25 D. Burton to R. Turner, 4 February 1846, RBS 3, WCA.
26 Charles Knight, *Cyclopaedia of London* (London: Charles Knight, 1851), p. 31.
27 Knight, *Cyclopaedia of London*, p. 32.
28 1846 Annual Report, RBS 3, WCA.
29 *Leigh Hunt's Journal* (18 January 1851), p. 109.
30 R. Turner, 'Description of the Iron Roof over the Railway Station, Lime Street Liverpool', *Minutes of the Proceedings of the Institution of Civil Engineers* 9 (1849–50), p. 211.
31 J. Locke to H. Booth, secretary of the London and North-Western Railway, 12 July 1847, Rail 1008/96/189, NA, quoted in Diestelkamp, 'Iron and Glass Architecture', p. 261.
32 John Weale, *Atlas on the Engravings to illustrate and practically explain the construction of Roofs of Iron* (London: John Weale, 1859), p. 4.
33 Robert B. Leuchars, *A Practical Treatise on the Construction, Heating and Ventilation of Hot-Houses* (New York: C. M. Saxton, 1857), p. 105.

34 J. Locke to H. Booth, 23 September 1848, Rail 1008/96/189, NA, quoted in Diestelkamp, 'Iron and Glass Architecture', p. 264.

35 The *Freeman's Journal*, 19 November 1846, reported Turner's charge against the workers: 'for that they, being his journeymen smiths in his employment, had unlawfully conspired and combined against him to the loss and injury of his trade'. The charge of 'combination' was designed to limit the power of trade unions; the employer was required to prove that threats or intimidation had been used (but the definition of 'threat' was left deliberately vague).

36 *Ibid.*

37 *Builder*, 15 January 1848, p. 31.

38 W. Hooker to D. Turner, 6 September 1846, 'Extracts from Letters', f. 65, Archives RBGK.

39 W. Hooker to D. Turner, 3 October 1846, 'Extracts from Letters', f. 66, Archives RBGK.

40 *Ibid.*

41 *Report from Sir William Hooker on the Royal Botanic Gardens and the Proposed new Palm House at Kew* (House of Commons, 1845), p. 3.

42 R. Turner to D. Burton, 1 July 1846, Work 16/29/8, f. 68, NA.

43 *Ibid.*

44 D. Burton to the Commissioners of Woods, 2 July 1846, Work 16/29/8, ff. 70–71, NA.

45 R. Turner to D. Burton, 27 August 1846, Work 16/29/8, f. 82, NA.

## Chapter 9: The Great Experiment

1 John Claudius Loudon, *The Green-House Companion* (London: John Harding, Triphook and Lepard, 1824), p. 3.

2 D. Burton to W. Hooker, 27 December 1844, DC 23, f. 104, Archives RBGK.

3 *Ibid.*

4 *Ibid.*

5 Joseph had initially planned to travel to Germany, but time ran out and he curtailed his tour after visiting Leiden.

6 J. Hooker to Lady M. Hooker, Paris, 2 February 1845, JHC564, f. 4, JDHCP, http://jdhooker.kew.org/p/jdh

7 J. Hooker to W. Hooker, Brussels, 27 February 1845, JHC570, f. 3, JDHCP, http://jdhooker.kew.org/p/jdh

8 J. Hooker to W. Hooker, Paris, 5 February 1845, JHC567, f. 1, JDHCP, http://jdhooker.kew.org/p/jdh
9 J. Hooker to W. Hooker, Paris, 5 February 1845, JHC567, ff. 7–8, JDHCP, http://jdhooker.kew.org/p/jdh
10 *Gardeners' Chronicle*, 4 March 1848, p. 155.
11 R. Turner to W. Hooker, 27 February 1844, DC 22, f. 260, Archives RBGK.
12 John Smith, 'History of the Royal Gardens, Kew', 1: f. 61, Archives RBGK.
13 J. C. Loudon, *Sketches of Curvilinear Hothouses* (London, 1818), p. 1.
14 J. C. Loudon, *Remarks on the Construction of Hothouses* (London: J. Taylor, 1817), pp. 49–50.
15 J. C. Loudon, *Encyclopædia of Gardening* (London: Longman, Hurst, Orme, Brown, Green, 1824), p. 816.
16 Smith, 'History of the Royal Gardens', 1: f. 61.
17 *Ibid.*
18 Loudon, *Encyclopædia of Gardening*, p. 320.
19 Charles McIntosh, *The Greenhouse, Hot House and Stove* (London: W. S. Orr & Co., 1838), p. 50.
20 *Ibid.*
21 *Sir Robert Peel's New Tariff* (London: James Gilbert, 1845), p. 18.
22 *Mechanics' Magazine* 42 (January–June 1845), p. 281.
23 *Ibid.*
24 R. Turner to A. Milne, 15 November 1845, Work 16/29/8, f. 56, NA.
25 Letter from W. Hooker, 23 November 1845 (no addressee), quoted in Robert Hunt, *Researches on Light in its Chemical Relations* (London: Longman, Brown, Green and Longmans, 1854), p. 376.
26 For Robert Hunt's career, see James Ryan, 'Placing Early Photography: The Work of Robert Hunt in mid-nineteenth-century Britain', *History of Photography*, vol. 41:4 (2017), pp. 343–61.
27 Robert Hunt, 'Researches on the Influence of Light on the Germination of Seeds and the Growth of Plants', *Report of the Twelfth Meeting of the British Association for the Advancement of Science held at Manchester in 1842* (London: John Murray, 1843), p. 80.
28 For a helpful digest of Hunt's findings, see Henrik Schoenefeldt, 'The use of Scientific Experimentation in developing the Glazing for the Palm House at Kew', *Construction History* 26 (2011), p. 29.
29 Hunt, *Researches on Light*, p. 379.

30 *Ibid.*
31 Robert Hunt, 'The Principles upon which the Tinted Glass used in the Construction of the Royal Palm House at Kew has been selected', *Transactions of the Society of Arts for 1846–7* (1848), p. 257.
32 Schoenefeldt, 'The use of Scientific Experimentation', *Construction History*, p. 30.
33 Joseph Hooker, 'On the Vegetation of the Carboniferous Period, as compared with that of the Present Day', *Memoirs of the Geological Survey of Great Britain*, vol. 2.2 (Longman, Brown, Green and Longman), p. 389.
34 Hunt, *Researches on Light*, p. 380.
35 Hunt, 'Principles', *Transactions of the Society of Arts*, p. 256.
36 Smith, 'History of the Royal Gardens', 1: f. 62.
37 Smith, 'History of the Royal Gardens', 1: ff. 62–3.
38 See *Report of the Seventeenth Meeting of the British Association for the Advancement of Science held at Oxford in June 1847* (London: John Murray, 1848), pp. 51–2; *Transactions of the Society of Arts*, pp. 251–9. Hunt included the text of the official correspondence and memoranda as an appendix – 'On the Glass in the Palm House of the Royal Gardens at Kew' – to the second edition of his *Researches on Light*, pp. 376–84.
39 Hunt, 'Principles', *Transactions of the Society of Arts*, p. 257.
40 D. Burton to the Commissioners of Woods, 27 March 1847, PRO Works 16–19, f. 110, NA.
41 C. Daubeny to W. Hooker, 24 December 1846, DC 25, English Letters, f. 124, Archives RBGK.
42 D. Burton to W. Hooker, 2 January 1847, DC 25, English Letters, f. 101, Archives RBGK.
43 W. Hooker to the Commissioners, 8 January 1847, Work 16/29/8, f. 110, NA.
44 *Report of the Seventeenth Meeting of the British Association for the Advancement of Science*, p. 52.
45 Charles McIntosh, *The Book of the Garden* (Edinburgh: William Blackwood & Sons, 1853), vol. 1, p. 535.
46 Smith, 'History of the Royal Gardens', 1: f. 62.
47 'British Association for the Advancement of Science', *Punch* 7 (1844), p. 155.
48 C. Darwin to J. Hooker, 14 July 1855; R. Hunt to C. Darwin, 19 July 1855; C. Darwin to R. Hunt, 22 July 1855; R. Hunt to C. Darwin, 24 July 1855, https://www.darwinproject.ac.uk/letters

49 Elihu Burritt, *Walks in the Black Country and its Green Border Land* (Birmingham: S. Low, Son and Marston, 1868), pp. 279–80. See Isobel Armstrong, *Victorian Glassworlds: Glass Culture and the Imagination 1830–1880* (Oxford: Oxford University Press, 2008) for a brilliant reading of nineteenth-century journalism on glassworks, including accounts of visits to the Smethwick works.

50 Henry Chance, 'On the Manufacture of Crown and Sheet Glass', *Journal of the Society of Arts*, 15 February 1856, p. 227.

51 Chance, 'On the Manufacture', *Journal of the Society of Arts*, p. 224.

52 'Revolutionary Players Making the Modern World: French and Belgian Workers', History West Midlands, http://www.revolutionaryplayers.org.uk/french-and-belgian-workers/

53 Burritt, *Walks in the Black Country*, p. 281.

54 *Ibid.*

55 *Report from Sir W. J. Hooker, on the Royal Botanic Gardens and New Palm House at Kew* (Parliamentary Papers 325, House of Commons, 1846), p. 2.

56 W. Hooker to D. Burton, 22 December 1846, Work 16/29/8, f. 97, NA.

57 Smith, 'History of the Royal Gardens', 1: f. 60.

58 Smith, 'History of the Royal Gardens', 1: f. 64.

59 J. Smith to W. Hooker, 28 October 1848, PRO Works 16–19, f. 168, NA.

60 Smith, 'History of the Royal Gardens', 1: f. 64.

61 The daguerreotype was the first commercially available photographic process, producing images on silvered copper plates.

## Chapter 10: The Princes of the Vegetable Kingdom

1 John Smith, 'History of the Royal Gardens, Kew', 1: ff. 64–5, Archives RBGK.

2 Alfred Tennyson, 'Locksley Hall', l. 160, l. 163, ll. 165–6, l. 168, l. 174, ll. 181–2, *Alfred Tennyson: A Critical Edition of the Major Works*, Adam Roberts (ed.) (Oxford: Oxford University Press, 2000), pp. 102–9.

3 P. Barry Tomlinson, 'The Uniqueness of Palms', *Botanical Journal of the Linnean Society*, vol. 151.1 (2006), p. 5, p. 9.

4 Carl von Linné, *A System of Vegetables: According to their Classes, Orders, Genera, Species*, Lichfield Botanical Society (trans.) (London: Leigh and Sotherby, 1783), vol. 1, p. 3.

5 *Ibid.*

6 The translation is from Alexander von Humboldt, *Personal Narrative of Travels to the Equinoctial Regions of the New Continent, during the years 1799–1804*, Helen Maria Williams (trans.) (London: Longman, Hurst, Rees, Orme and Brown, 1814–29), vol. 5.1, p. 213. The original Latin is '*Habitat intra* Tropicos, *Palmis Lotophagus. Hospitatur extra* Tropicos, *sub nouercante Cerere, carivorus*', Caroli a Linné, *Systema Naturæ . . . in Epitomen Redactumi*, Johann Beckmann (ed.) (Gottingae: Vandenhoeck, 1772).

7 Thanks to Bill Baker at Kew for suggesting this parallel.

8 Hitchcock, a devout Christian, excised the chart from later editions of his book for fear of its association with Darwinian theories of evolution.

9 W. Watson, 'Some Observations upon the Sex of Flowers by W. Watson, F. R. S. occasioned by a letter upon the same subject by Mr. Mylius of Berlin', *Philosophical Transactions of the Royal Society* 47 (1752), p. 171.

10 Carl von Linnaeus, *A Dissertation on the Sexes of Plants*, James Edward Smith (trans.) (Dublin: L. White, 1786), p. 51.

11 Anon, *The Palm Tribes and their Varieties* (London: Religious Tracts Society, 1852), p. 21.

12 H. Walter Lack, William J. Baker (eds.), *Die Welt der Palmen / The World of Palms* (Berlin: Botanisches Museum Berlin-Dahlem, 2011), p. 31.

13 J. H. Bernardin de Saint-Pierre, *Paul and Virginia* (Chiswick: C. Whittingham, 1821), p. 3.

14 J. H. Bernardin de Saint-Pierre, *Paul and Virginia*, Helen Maria Williams (trans.) (Paris, 1795), p. 101.

15 Felicia Hemans, *Selected Poems, Prose and Letters*, Gary Kelly (ed.) (Peterborough, Ontario: Broadview Press, 2002), p. 404.

16 Charles Darwin to William Darwin Fox, Hobart Town, 15 February 1836, DCP – LETT 299 DCP, https://www.darwinproject.ac.uk/

17 Bernardin, *Paul and Virginia*, Williams (trans.), pp. 92–3.

18 Bernardin, *Paul and Virginia*, Williams (trans.), p. 125.

19 Bernardin, *Paul and Virginia*, Williams (trans.), pp. 125–6.

20 There is one episode where the children encounter an emaciated runaway slave in the forest; they dutifully return her to her cruel master, and Virginie intercedes on the slave's behalf. Persuaded by Virginie's elegant form and 'the profusion of her beautiful light tresses', the master refrains from beating the runaway slave. Bernardin, *Paul and Virginia*, Williams (trans.), p. 45.

21 Alexander von Humboldt, *Cosmos*, E. C. Otté (trans.) (London: Henry G. Bohn, 1849), vol. 2, p. 433.
22 The passage which Humboldt recalls is: 'in some parts the cabbage-trees raise their naked columns, more than an hundred feet high, crowned at their summits with clustering leaves, and towering above the wood like one forest piled upon another'. Bernardin, *Paul and Virginia*, Williams (trans.), p. 198.
23 Humboldt, *Personal Narrative*, Williams (trans.), vol. 5.1, p. 46, p. 47.
24 Humboldt, *Personal Narrative*, Williams (trans.), vol. 5.1, pp. 46–7.
25 Alexander von Humboldt, *Aspects of Nature in Different Lands and Different Climates*, Mrs Sabine (trans.), 2 vols. (London: John Murray, 1849), vol. 2, p. 29.
26 *Ibid.*
27 Humboldt, *Personal Narrative*, Williams (trans.), vol. 5.1, p. 138.
28 *Ibid.*
29 Humboldt, *Personal Narrative*, Williams (trans.), vol. 5.1, p. 139.
30 *Ibid.*
31 See, for instance, *The Ladies Monthly Magazine* 16 (1822), p 12; *Monthly Review,* March 1823, p. 267; *Fourth Book of Lessons for the Use of the Irish National School*s (Dublin: Philip Dixon Hardy, 1835), pp. 140–2.
32 Humboldt, *Personal Narrative*, Williams (trans.), vol. 5.1, p. 214.
33 *Ibid.*
34 Humboldt, *Personal Narrative*, Williams (trans.), vol. 5.2, pp. 727–9.
35 Humboldt, *Aspects of Nature*, Mrs Sabine (trans.), vol. 1, p. 198.
36 Humboldt, *Personal Narrative*, Williams (trans.), vol. 5.2, p. 728.
37 *Ibid.*
38 Humboldt, *Personal Narrative*, Williams (trans.), vol. 5.2, p. 729.
39 Humboldt, *Aspects of Nature*, Mrs Sabine (trans.), vol. 1, p. 16; Humboldt, *Personal Narrative*, Williams (trans.), vol. 5.2, p. 729.
40 Humboldt, *Aspects of Nature*, Mrs Sabine (trans.), vol. 2, p. 130.
41 Humboldt, *Aspects of Nature*, Mrs Sabine (trans.), vol. 2, pp. 130–1.
42 L. H. Bailey, 'Palms and their Characteristics', *Gentes Herbarium* 3.1 (1933); see, for instance, P. B. Tomlinson, *The Structural Biology of Palms* (Oxford: Clarendon Press, 1990), pp. 17–18; William J. Baker, Preface, *Botanical Journal of the Linnean Society*, vol. 151.1 (2006), p. 2
43 Michael Dettelbach, 'The Stimulations of Travel: Humboldt's Physiological Construction of the Tropics', in Felix Driver and Luciana

Martins (eds.), *Tropical Visions in an Age of Empire* (Chicago: University of Chicago Press, 2005), p. 46.

44 Humboldt, *Aspects of Nature*, Mrs Sabine (trans.), vol. 2, p. 20.

45 Humboldt, *Aspects of Nature*, Mrs Sabine (trans.), vol. 2, p. 127.

46 *Ibid;* Dettelbach, 'Stimulations of Travel', Driver and Martins (eds.), *Tropical Visions*, p. 46.

47 Charles Rau, *Memoir of C. F. P. Von Martius* (Washington: Smithsonian Institution, 1871), p. 170.

48 For information on the children, see Klaus Schönitzer, 'From the New to the Old World: Two indigenous children brought back to Germany by Johann Baptist Spix and Carl Friedrich Philipp Martius', *Journal Fünf Kontinente* 1 (2014–15), pp. 78–9.

49 Philip Henry Gosse, 'Wanderings through the Conservatories at Kew', *Fraser's Magazine* 40 (1849), p. 130.

50 Henrik Balslev, review of *The Book of Palms*, *Frontiers of Biogeography*, vol. 3.2 (2011), p. 55.

51 *Ibid.*

52 Johann Wolfgang von Goethe, *Zur Naturwissenschaft überhaupt, besonders zur Morphologie*, H. Walter Lack (trans.), Introduction, *The Book of Palms* (Köln: Taschen, 2015), p. 17. I am indebted to Professor Lack's introduction for much of the information on Martius.

53 John Claudius Loudon, *Hortus Britannicus* (London: Longman, Rees, Orme, Brown and Green, 1830), vol. 1, p. 540.

54 See, for instance, Charles McIntosh, *The Greenhouse, Hothouse and Stove* (London: W. S. Orr & Co., 1838), p. 361; Berthold Seemann, *Popular History of the Palms and their Allies* (London: Lovell Reeve, 1856), p. 7.

55 C. F. P. Martius to W. J. Hooker, 1 July 1837, DC/68/91, Archives RBGK.

56 Inventory of the Botanical Collection of Books of the Late Sir W. J. Hooker, 1866, WJH/1/7, f. 113, f. 5, Archives RBGK.

57 B. Elliott, 'The illustrations for the botanical articles in the *Penny Cyclopaedia*', *Occasional Papers from the RHS Lindley Library* 13 (November 2015), pp. 32–56.

58 'The Great Palm-House and Monster Cactus', *Illustrated London News*, 4 January 1845, p. 12.

59 *Ibid.*

60 *Ibid.*

## Chapter 11: The Palm House Spectacle

1 John Smith, 'History of the Royal Gardens, Kew', 1: f. 65, Archives RBGK.

2 'A Present Kewite on Kew', *Journal of the Kew Guild* 1.5 (1897), p. 31.

3 *Ibid.*

4 W. J. Hooker, *Kew Gardens, or, A Popular Guide to the Royal Botanic Gardens of Kew*, 11th ed. (London: Longman, Brown, Green and Longmans, 1852), p. 31.

5 W. J. Hooker, 'Botany', in John Herschel (ed.), *A Manual of Scientific Enquiry* (London: John Murray, 1849), p. 402.

6 James Hannay, 'The Palace of Flowers', *Household Words* 3 (26 April 1851), p. 120.

7 *Quarterly Review* 90 (1851–2), p. 57.

8 *Hooker's Journal of Botany and Kew Garden Miscellany* 1 (1849), p. 204.

9 *Companion to the Botanical Magazine* 73 (1847), p. 19.

10 *Companion*, p. 3.

11 *Companion*, p. 22.

12 *Companion*, p. 23.

13 *Ibid.*

14 *Companion*, pp. 18–19.

15 W. Purdie to W. J. Hooker, 28 September 1848, DC 70/234, Archives RBGK.

16 *London Journal of Botany* 6 (1847), p. 604.

17 *Literary Gazette* (10 August 1850), p. 540.

18 For a detailed discussion of the relations between Darjeeling and Sikkim, see Alex McKay, '"A difficult country, a hostile Chief, and a still more hostile Minister": The Anglo-Sikkim War of 1861', *Bulletin of Tibetology* vol. 45:2 (2009), pp. 31–48.

19 J. D. Hooker, *Himalayan Journals* (London: John Murray, 1855), vol. 1, p. 180.

20 J. Hooker to W. Hooker, Lachung, 25 October 1849, JHC88, f. 5, JDHCP, http://jdhooker.kew.org/p/jdh

21 J. Hooker to W. Hooker, Tumlong Sikkim, 12 November 1849, JHC89, f. 1, JDHCP, http://jdhooker.kew.org/p/jdh

22 J. Hooker to W. Hooker, Tumlong Sikkim, 12 November 1849, JHC89, ff. 3–4, JDHCP, http://jdhooker.kew.org/p/jdh

23 J. D. Hooker, *The Rhododendrons of Sikkim-Himalaya* (London: Reeve, Benham and Reeve, 1849), p. 5.

24 J. D. Hooker, *Rhododendrons*, p. 6.
25 J. D. Hooker, *Rhododendrons*, p. 14.
26 W. Hooker to D. Turner, Kew, 21 August 1848, 'Extracts from letters relating to the Royal Botanic Gardens, Kew, written by Sir W. J. Hooker to Dawson Turner, 1834–50', f. 72, Archives RBGK.
27 *London Journal* 33 (1861), p. 104.
28 *Ibid.*
29 *Punch* 14 (1848), p. 181.
30 *Ladies' Cabinet*, 1 June 1854, p. 289.
31 *Quarterly Review* 90 (1851), p. 46.
32 *Punch's Holidays* (1850), p. 4.
33 *Quarterly Review* 90 (1851), p. 46.
34 Robert Southey, *Thalaba the Destroyer*, Bk. 3, v. 10–18.
35 Thomas Moore, *Lalla Rookh*, Bk. 2, pp. 165–9. Compare to Southey, *Thalaba*, Bk. 2, v. 30.
36 Charles Darwin to Caroline Darwin, Cambridge, 28 April 1831, DCP-LETT-98, Darwin Correspondence Project, https://www.darwinproject.ac.uk/
37 See Chapter 10: The Princes of the Vegetable Kingdom, pp. 200–201.
38 Alexander von Humboldt, *Cosmos*, E. C. Otté (trans.) (London: Henry G. Bohn, 1849), vol. 2, p. 465.
39 Humboldt, *Cosmos*, E. C. Otté (trans.), vol. 2, pp. 459–60.
40 S. T. Coleridge, *Biographia Literaria* (London: Rest, Fenner, 1817), p. 2.
41 Humboldt, *Cosmos*, E. C. Otté (trans.), vol. 2, p. 460.
42 Hannay, 'The Palace of Flowers', *Household Words* 3 (26 April 1851), p. 119.
43 *Ibid.*
44 Berthold Seemann, *Popular History of the Palms and their Allies* (London: Lovell Reeve, 1856), p. 42.
45 Seemann, *Popular History*, pp. 42–3.
46 *Ibid.*
47 *Ibid.*
48 Seemann, *Popular History*, p. 44.
49 For a discussion of Humboldt's attitude to commerce, see M. von Brescius, 'Connecting the New World: Nets, Mobility and Progress in the Age of Alexander von Humboldt', *HiN*, vol. 13:25 (2012), pp. 11–33.
50 *Gardeners' Chronicle*, 28 April 1855, p. 280.

51 Smith, *History of the Royal Gardens*, 1: ff. 66–7.
52 *Quarterly Review* 90 (1851), p. 41.
53 *Quarterly Review* 90 (1851), p. 39.

## Chapter 12: The Museum

1 Museum Entry Book, 1847–55, f. 1, Economic Botany Collection, RBGK.
2 Thomas Croxen Archer, *Popular Economic Botany* (London: Reeve & Co., 1853), p. 2.
3 In his chapter for the Admiralty's *Manual of Scientific Enquiry* (London: John Murray, 1849), Hooker used both names: 'the museum of vegetable products, or it may be called the "Museum of Economic Botany"' (p. 405).
4 Caroline Cornish traces the first use of the term 'economic botany' to Gilbert Burnett, Professor of Botany at King's College London in the 1830s. See Caroline Cornish, 'Curating Science in an Age of Empire: Kew's Museum of Economic Botany', PhD thesis, Royal Holloway, University of London, 2013, p. 25.
5 W. J. Hooker, 'Sir W. J. Hooker's Report on Kew Gardens, 1855' (Royal Gardens, Kew, 31 December 1855), p. 3.
6 W. J. Hooker, 'Sir W. J. Hooker's Report on Kew Gardens, 1852', *Parliamentary Papers, Accounts and Papers: Estimates 1852–3*, 8, p. 11.
7 Caroline Cornish '"Botany Behind Glass": The Vegetable Kingdom on Display at Kew's Museum of Economic Botany', in Carin Berkowitz and Bernard Lightman (eds.), *Science Museums in Transition: Cultures of Display in Nineteenth-Century Britain and America* (Pittsburgh, PA: University of Pittsburgh Press, 2017), p. 194.
8 Sophy Moody, *The Palm Tree* (London: T. Nelson and Sons, 1864), p. 325.
9 W. J. Hooker, *Museum of Economic Botany: or, a Popular Guide to the Useful and Remarkable Products of the Museum of the Royal Gardens of Kew* (London: Longman, Brown, Green and Longmans, 1855), p. 4.
10 *Ibid.*
11 Hooker, *Museum of Economic Botany*, p. 67.
12 See James A. Secord, *Victorian Sensation* (Chicago: University of Chicago Press, 2003) for a brilliant excavation of the impact of *Vestiges of the Natural History of Creation*.
13 Alfred Russel Wallace, *My Life: A Record of Events and Opinions* (London: Chapman and Hall, 1908), p. 144.

14 Sandra Knapp, Lynn Sanders and William Baker, 'Alfred Russel Wallace and the Palms of the Amazon', *Palms*, vol. 46:3 (2002), p. 110.
15 Alfred Russel Wallace, *A Narrative of Travels on the Amazon and Rio Negro* (London: Ward, Lock & Co., 1889), p. 1.
16 Henry Walter Bates, *The Naturalist on the River Amazons* (London: John Murray, 1863), p. 6.
17 Bates, *The Naturalist*, p. 51.
18 A. R. Wallace to W. J. Hooker, 20 August 1848, DC/70/377, Archives RBGK.
19 *Hooker's Journal of Botany and Kew Garden Miscellany* 7 (1855), p. 213.
20 However, in 1869, Spruce delivered a long and detailed paper on palms to the Linnean Society: 'Palmae Amazonicae', *Journal of the Linnean Society London Botany* 11 (1871), pp. 65–183. In the paper, Spruce explained that, since the main aim of his expedition had been to supply herbarium specimens, he did not prioritize palms because of the difficulty of collecting and preserving their very large leaves and inflorescences.
21 Wallace, *My Life*, pp. 150–1.
22 Wallace, *Narrative*, p. 176.
23 Wallace, *Narrative*, p. 180.
24 Wallace, *Narrative*, p. 178.
25 Wallace, *Narrative*, p. 149.
26 Alfred Russel Wallace, *Palm Trees of the Amazon and their Uses* (London: John Van Voorst, 1853), p. 74.
27 *Ibid.*
28 Wallace, *Palm Trees*, p. 75.
29 *Ibid.*
30 Wallace, *My Life*, p. 153.
31 Wallace, *My Life*, p. 155.
32 Wallace, *My Life*, p. 159.
33 Wallace, *My Life*, p. 156.
34 Wallace, *Palm Trees*, p. 9.
35 *Annals and Magazine of Natural History*, 2nd series, 13 (1854), p. 56.
36 *Hooker's Journal of Botany and Kew Garden Miscellany* 6 (1854), p. 61.
37 *Hooker's Journal of Botany and Kew Garden Miscellany* 6 (1854), p. 62.
38 *Hooker's Journal of Botany and Kew Garden Miscellany* 7 (1855), p. 213.
39 *Ibid.* Thomas Croxen Archer was a regular correspondent of Hooker at the time. He had recently published *Popular Economic Botany* (1853) and

was very interested in Kew's Museum of Economic Botany. He established a collection following its model at the Liverpool Institution.

40 *Hooker's Journal of Botany and Kew Garden Miscellany* 1 (1849), p. 122.

41 Charles Dickens, *Bleak House* (Oxford: Oxford University Press: 1996), p. 162.

42 *Hooker's Journal of Botany and Kew Garden Miscellany* 1 (1849), p. 122.

43 *Mechanics' Magazine and Journal of Engineering*, n. s. 6 (1861), p. 176.

44 Berthold Seemann, *Popular History of the Palms and their Allies* (London: Lovell Reeve, 1856), p. 1.

45 Seemann, *Popular History*, pp. 4–5.

46 Hooker, *Museum of Economic Botany*, p. 4.

47 John Robertson, 'The Coco Palm', *Household Words* 15 (17 January 1857), p. 69.

48 *Ibid.*

49 Henry Mayhew and John Binny, *The Criminal Prisons of London and Scenes of Prison Life* (London: Griffin, Bohn and Co., 1862), p. 253, p. 243.

50 P. L. Simmonds, *The Commercial Products of the Vegetable Kingdom* (London: T. F. A. Day, 1854), p. 551.

51 *Ibid.*

52 Simmonds, *The Commercial Products*, p. 554.

53 The company was initially named Edward Price & Co., but changed its name to Price's Patent Candle Co. in 1847.

54 Moody, *The Palm Tree*, p. 142.

55 See, for instance, Trevor R. Getz, *Slavery and Reform in West Africa: Toward Emancipation in Nineteenth-Century Senegal and the Gold Coast* (Ohio: Ohio University Press, 2004), pp. 38–41.

56 Elizabeth Twining, *Short Lectures on Plants for Schools and Adult Classes* (London: David Nutt, 1858), pp. 220–1.

57 Twining, *Short Lectures*, p. 221.

58 F. E. Forbes, *Dahomey and the Dahomens* (Paris: Galignani, 1854), p. 2.

59 Moody, *The Palm Tree*, p. 143; Seemann, *Popular History*, pp. 191–2.

60 Seemann, *Popular History*, p. 191.

61 'Candlemaking and Christianity', *North British Review* 20 (November 1853), p. 89.

62 *The Letters of Charles Dickens: 1850–52*, vol. 6, G. Storey, K. Tillotson and N. Burgis (eds.) (Oxford: Clarendon Press,1988), p. 681.

63 See Stephen Gill, 'Price's Patent Candles New Light on *North and South*', *Review of English Studies* 27 (1976), pp. 313–21.

64 *Quarterly Review* 92 (December 1852), p. 10. See also *Fraser's Magazine* 46 (July 1852), pp. 106–12.
65 'Candlemaking and Christianity', *North British Review* 20 (November 1853), p. 90.
66 Hooker, *Museum of Economic Botany*, p. 5.
67 Hooker, 'Sir W. J. Hooker's Report on Kew Gardens, 1855', p. 3.
68 *London Saturday Journal* 34 (24 August 1839), p. 126.
69 *Curtis's Botanical Magazine*, 2nd Series, 1 (1827), n. p.
70 *Ibid.*
71 *Eclectic Review*, 3rd Series, 2 (1829), p. 403.
72 *London Saturday Journal*, 34 (24 August 1839), p. 125.
73 W. Bojer to W. J. Hooker, 8 January 1852, DC 55/13, Archives RBGK.
74 *Ibid.*
75 *Hooker's Journal of Botany & Kew Gardens Miscellany*, 5 (1853), p. 29.
76 *Ibid.*
77 *Journal of Botany, British and Foreign* 3 (1865), p. 199.
78 *Gardeners' Chronicle*, 6 December 1856, p. 803.

## Chapter 13: The Public

1 *Gardeners' Chronicle*, 4 March 1848, p. 155.
2 Charles Knight, *The Land We Live In* (London: Charles Knight, 1847–50), vol. 3, p. 79.
3 *Builder*, vol. 6:258 (15 January 1848), p. 29; *Lady's Newspaper* 56 (22 January 1848), p. 58.
4 *Florist and Garden Miscellany* 2 (1849), p. 285.
5 *Gardeners' Chronicle*, 24 July 1847, p. 486.
6 *Ibid.*
7 *Gardeners' Chronicle*, 26 February 1848, p. 133.
8 Edward Kemp, *London Exhibited in 1851* (London: John Weale, 1851), p. 471.
9 *Evening Mail*, 18 August 1848.
10 *Stirling Observer*, 4 January 1849.
11 *Douglas Jerrold's Weekly Newspaper*, 24 June 1848, p. 818.
12 *Ibid.*
13 *Ibid.*
14 *Ibid.*
15 *Gardeners' Chronicle*, 26 February 1848, p. 133.

16 R. Turner to H. Booth, 4 December 1848, Rail 1008/96/204, cited in Edward J. Diestelkamp, 'The Iron and Glass Architecture of Richard Turner', PhD thesis, University College London, 1982, p. 265.
17 *Ibid.*
18 R. Turner to the Commissioners of Woods, Work 16/29/8, f. 178, NA.
19 Office of Woods to Treasury, 7 February 1849, Work 16/29/8, f. 197, NA.
20 Office of Woods to Treasury, 7 February 1849, Work 16/29/8, f. 198, NA.
21 Turner writing to D. Burton, quoted by D. Burton to Commissioners 14 March 1849, Works 16/29/8, f. 206, NA.
22 Office of Woods to Decimus Burton, 17 March 1849, Works 16/29/8, f. 207, NA.
23 Diestelkamp, 'Iron and Glass Architecture', p. 265.
24 *Illustrated London News,* 11 August 1849, p. 83.
25 At the archives of the Royal Botanic Gardens, Kew, there is a collection named 'Kewensia' that gathers many such items of Kew ephemera.
26 *Summer Days Recreations*, p. 1.
27 John Smith, 'History of the Royal Gardens, Kew', 2: f. 340, Archives RBGK.
28 *Florist and Garden Miscellany* 2 (1849), p. 284.
29 *Summer Days Recreations*, p. 8.
30 *Ibid.*
31 *Florist and Garden Miscellany* 2 (1849), p. 284.
32 *Report from Sir W. J. Hooker, on the Royal Botanic Gardens, and the proposed new Palm House at Kew* (House of Commons, 1845), p. 4.
33 *Florist and Garden Miscellany* 2 (1849), p. 284.
34 *Gardeners' Chronicle*, 29 December 1855, p. 855.
35 W. J. Hooker, *Kew Gardens, or, A Popular Guide to the Royal Botanic Gardens of Kew* (London: Longman, Green and Longmans, 1847), p. vi.
36 See, for instance, *Florist and Garden Miscellany* 2 (1849), p. 284; for a discussion of the opening hours campaign, see Jim Endersby, *Imperial Nature: Joseph Hooker and the Practices of Victorian Science* (Chicago: University of Chicago Press, 2008), pp. 277–8, pp. 306–7.
37 See, for instance, Hooker's *Reports* for 1845, 1848 and 1855.
38 Hooker, *Kew Gardens*, p. vi.
39 *Leisure Hour* 11 (1862), p. 440.
40 *Ibid.*

41 *Quarterly Review* 90 (1851), p. 61. See also W. J. Hooker, 'Sir W. J. Hooker's Report on Kew Gardens, 1855' (Royal Gardens, Kew, 31 December 1855), p. 2.

42 *Eliza Cook's Journal* 9 (1853), p. 206.

43 Knight, *The Land We Live In*, vol. 3, p. 79.

44 Hooker, 'Sir W. J. Hooker's Report on Kew Gardens, 1855', p. 2.

45 W. J. Hooker, *Kew Gardens, or, A Popular Guide to the Royal Botanic Gardens of Kew*, 11th ed. (London: Longman, Brown, Green and Longmans, 1852), p. 18.

46 W. J. Hooker, *Kew Gardens* (1852), p. 18, p. 20.

47 *Summer Days Recreations*, p. 1.

48 *Eliza Cook's Journal* 9 (1853), p. 206.

49 These two forms were established by Priscilla Wakefield's *Introduction to Botany, in a series of familiar letters* (1796), and *Conversations on Botany* (1817) by Jane Marcet, Sarah and Elizabeth Fitton.

50 According to Jane Loudon, it was *Mummy!* which led her to meet her future husband. She described their first encounter in a memoir published as a preface to John Claudius Loudon's posthumous *Self-Instruction for Gardeners* (1845):

> Mr. Loudon chanced to see the review of this book in the *Literary Gazette*, and, as among other things, I had mentioned a steam-plough, it attracted his attention, and he procured the work from a circulating library. He read it, and was so much pleased with it, that he published, in *The Gardener's Magazine* for 1828, a notice of it under the head of 'Hints for Improvements;' and he had from that time a great desire to become acquainted with the author, whom he supposed to be a man. In February, 1830, Mr. Loudon chanced to mention this wish to a lady, a friend of his, who happened to be acquainted with me, and who immediately invited him to a party, where she promised him he should have the wished-for introduction. It may be easily supposed that he was surprised to find the author of the book a woman; but I believe that from that evening he formed an attachment to me, and, in fact, we were married on the 14th of the following September.

51 Elizabeth Twining, *Short Lectures on Plants for Schools and Adult Classes* (London: David Nutt, 1858), p. 218.

52 Catherine Mary McNab, *Juvenile Conversations on the Botany of the Bible* (Edinburgh: William P. Kennedy, 1850), p. 56.

53 Sophy Moody, *The Palm Tree* (London: T. Nelson and Sons, 1864), p. 17.

54 Anon, *The Palm Tribes and their Varieties* (London: Religious Tract Society, 1852), p. 189.
55 *The Child's Companion and Juvenile Instructor* (1852), vol. 1, pp. 2–3.
56 *The Child's Companion and Juvenile Instructor* (1852), vol. 5, p. 27.
57 *Wanderings through the Conservatories at Kew* appeared first as a short article for *Fraser's Magazine* (August 1849), was expanded in 1855 for the *Home Friend* (a magazine issued by the Society for Promoting Christian Knowledge) and was finally printed by the SPCK as a book in 1857.
58 Philip Henry Gosse's son, Edmund Gosse, wrote a striking account of his father in his 1907 memoir, *Father and Son*.
59 Philip Henry Gosse, *Wanderings through the Conservatories at Kew* (London: SPCK, 1857), p. 1.
60 Gosse, *Wanderings* (1857), p. 19.
61 Gosse, *Wanderings* (1857), p. 40.
62 Gosse, *Wanderings* (1857), pp. 44–5.
63 Smith, 'History of the Royal Gardens', 2: ff. 340–1.
64 *Punch* 14 (1848), p. 181.
65 Diestelkamp, 'Iron and Glass Architecture', p. 285.
66 *Builder*, vol. 8:364 (26 January 1850), p. 45.
67 'On the Construction of the Building for the Exhibition of the Works of all Nations', *Minutes of the Proceedings of the Institution of Civil Engineers*, vol. 10 (1850–1), p. 168.
68 *Minutes*, p. 170.
69 Tom F. Peters, 'Some Structural Problems encountered in the building of the Crystal Palace of 1851', in Robert Thorne (ed.), *Structural Iron and Steel, 1850–1900* (London: Routledge, 2000), p. 6.
70 *Minutes*, p. 170.
71 Richard and Thomas Turner to the Commissioners, 4 December 1851, RC/A/1851/836, 1851 Exhibition Correspondence, Prince Albert Digitisation Project, Royal Collection Trust: https://albert.rct.uk/collections/royal-commission-for-the-exhibition-of-1851/1851-exhibition
72 *Ibid.* In a letter in the possession of the Turner family, dated 30 March 1980, Edward Diestelkamp discusses a manuscript memoir in the Linen Hall Library, Belfast: *Recollections of a Nonagenarian*, written in 1906 by Robert Young. Young recounts that Richard Turner believed his design had been the source for Paxton's semicircular arched ribs over the transept of Crystal Palace. Unfortunately, at the time of writing, the Linen Hall Library had misplaced the manuscript.

73 *Leisure Hour* (1862), p. 469.
74 *London Exhibited in 1851* (London: John Weale, 1851).
75 *Quarterly Review* 90 (1851), p. 42.
76 *Illustrated London Almanack* (1853), p. 14.
77 *Summer Days Recreations*, p. 3.
78 *Illustrated London Almanack* (1853), p. 14.

## Chapter 14: Closing the Door

1 John Smith, 'History of the Royal Gardens, Kew', 1: f. 75, Archives RBGK.
2 Smith, 'History of the Royal Gardens', 1: f. 76.
3 Smith, 'History of the Royal Gardens', 1: ff. 78–9.
4 W. J. Hooker, *Report on the Progress and Condition of the Royal Gardens at Kew, during the year 1864* (HMSO 1865), p. 1.
5 Inventory of the Botanical Collection of the Late Sir W. J. Hooker, purchased by the Commissioners of her Majesty's Works & Public Buildings, 1866, WJH/1/7, ff. 2–3, Archives RBGK.
6 J. D. Hooker to C. Darwin, 12 June 1881, in Leonard Huxley, *Life and Letters of Joseph Dalton Hooker* (London: John Murray, 1918), vol. 2, p. 245.
7 J. D. Hooker, *Report on the Progress and Condition of the Royal Gardens at Kew, during the year 1882* (HMSO 1883), p. 10.
8 *Building News* (26 March 1880), p. 385.
9 Edward J. Diestelkamp,'The Iron and Glass Architecture of Richard Turner', PhD thesis, University College London, 1982, pp. 72–3.
10 D. E. Allen, 'John Smith (1798–1888)', *Oxford Dictionary of National Biography* https://doi.org/10.1093/ref:odnb/59325
11 Abel Doubleway [John Smith], *Adam Spade; the Gardener* (London: Hardwicke and Bogue, 1879), p. 5.
12 Rudyard Kipling, 'Recessional', ll. 1–4, *Stories and Poems*, ed. Daniel Karlin (Oxford: Oxford University Press, 2015), p. 478.
13 *Edinburgh Review* 138 (October 1873), p. 268.
14 Bridget Cherry and Nikolaus Pevsner, *London 2: South* (London: Yale University Press, 2002), p. 510.
15 Deborah Singmaster, 'A Life in Architecture; David Marks, Julia Barfield', *Architects' Journal*, 9 September 1999.
16 'Green Glass in Plant-houses', *Bulletin of Miscellaneous Information*, vol. 98 (1895), pp. 44–5.

# *Bibliography*

## PRIMARY SOURCES

### Manuscripts


*Chatsworth House*

Paxton Papers [PP], vols. 44, 45.

*Liverpool Record Office, Liverpool Libraries*

Papers of Edward Smith-Stanley, Thirteenth Earl of Derby.

*National Archives (NA)*

Work 6/297; 16/29/8.

Royal Gardens Committee of Inquiry T90/189.

*Royal Botanic Gardens Kew (RBGK)*

Aylmer Bourke Lambert Letters.

Director's Correspondence [DC], vols. 11, 15, 16, 21, 22, 23, 25, 55, 68, 70.

Dr Lindley's Official Correspondence, 1832–54.

'Extracts from Letters relating to the Royal Botanic Gardens, Kew, written by Sir W. J. Hooker to Dawson Turner, Esq 1834–50'.

Nesfield, William, 'Kew Pleasure Grounds'.

Sir Joseph Hooker Papers.

Smith, John, 'History of the Royal Gardens, Kew', 3 vols.

*Record of a Few Special Events and Matters relative to the Royal Botanic Garden at Kew* (Old Brentford: W. H. Jackson, n.d.).

*Records of the Royal Botanic Gardens, Kew* (1880).

W. J. Hooker Correspondence, vols. 1, 2.

*University of Nottingham*

Newcastle Clumber Collection, vol. 8.

*Westminster City Archives (WCA)*

Records of the Royal Botanic Society of London.

## Online sources

Brentford High Street Project: http://www.bhsproject.co.uk/history.shtml

Correspondence of William Henry Fox Talbot: http://foxtalbot.dmu.ac.uk/

Darwin Correspondence Project: https://www.darwinproject.ac.uk/

Joseph Dalton Hooker Correspondence Project: http://jdhooker.kew.org/p/jdh

Prince Albert Digitisation Project, Royal Collection Trust: https://albert.rct.uk/collections/royal-commission-for-the-exhibition-of-1851/1851-exhibition

Proceedings of the Old Bailey: https://www.oldbaileyonline.org

Queen Victoria's Journals: http://www.queenvictoriasjournals.org

Revolutionary Players Making the Modern World, History West Midlands: http://www.revolutionaryplayers.org.uk

## Newspapers and Magazines

*Annals of Natural History*

*Architectural Review*

*Athenæum*

*Blackwood's Edinburgh Magazine*

*Builder*

*Chambers's Edinburgh Journal*
*Chambers's Journal of Popular Literature, Science & the Arts*
*Child's Companion and Juvenile Instructor*
*Civil Engineer & Architects Journal*
*Colonial Magazine and Commercial Maritime Journal*
*Curtis's Botanical Magazine*
*Derby Mercury*
*Douglas Jerrold's Weekly Newspaper*
*Dublin Morning Registry*
*Eclectic Review*
*Edinburgh Review*
*Eliza Cook's Journal*
*Evening Mail*
*Florist and Garden Miscellany*
*Fraser's Magazine*
*Freeman's Journal*
*Gardeners' Chronicle*
*Gardeners' Gazette*
*Gardener's Magazine*
*Household Words*
*Illustrated London Almanack for 1853*
*Illustrated London News*
*Illustrated Magazine of Art*
*Imperial Magazine*
*Journal of Botany and Kew Gardens Miscellany*
*Journal of Botany, British & Foreign*
*Ladies' Cabinet*
*Ladies' Monthly Magazine*
*Lady's Newspaper*
*Leigh Hunt's Journal*
*Leisure Hour*

*Literary Gazette*

*Lloyd's Weekly London Newspaper*

*London Journal*

*London Journal of Botany*

*London Saturday Journal*

*Magazine of Horticulture, Botany and all useful Discoveries in Rural Affairs*

*Mechanics' Magazine and Journal of Engineering*

*Monthly Review*

*Morning Chronicle*

*North British Review*

*Paxton's Magazine of Botany, and Register of Flowering Plants*

*Punch*

*Quarterly Review*

*Sharpe's London Magazine*

*Star*

*Stirling Observer*

*The Times*

## Parliamentary Papers

*Account of the Public Money Expended on each of the Royal Palaces, Gardens, Parks . . . 1843–51* (House of Commons, 6 June 1851).

'Correspondence respecting the Colonization of the Falkland Islands', *Parliamentary Papers* 33 (1843).

'Minutes of Evidence Taken before the Select Committee on National Monuments', *Parliamentary Papers: Reports from Committees* 6 (1841).

*Report from Sir W. J. Hooker, on the Royal Botanic Gardens, and the proposed new Palm House at Kew* (House of Commons, 1845).

*Report from Sir W. J. Hooker, on the Royal Botanic Gardens, and the new Palm House at Kew* (House of Commons, 1846).

*Report from Sir W. J. Hooker, on the Royal Botanic Gardens and New Palm House at Kew* (House of Commons, 1847).

*Report from the Select Committee on Miscellaneous Expenditure*, 27 July 1848 (House of Commons, 1848).

*Report from the Select Committee on Public Walks* (House of Commons, 1833).

*Report on Kew Gardens 1852*, *Parliamentary Papers: Accounts and Papers 1852–3*, vol. 8.

*Report on the Progress and Condition of the Royal Gardens of Kew from 1853–59* (London: HMSO, 1859).

*Report on the Progress and Condition of the Royal Gardens at Kew, during the year 1864* (HMSO 1865).

*Report on the Progress and Condition of the Royal Gardens at Kew, during the year 1882* (HMSO 1883).

*Report upon the present Condition of the Botanical Garden at Kew*, Parliamentary Paper 292 (House of Commons, 1840).

*Sir W. J. Hooker's Report on Kew Gardens 1855* (London: HMSO, 1856).

*Sir W. J. Hooker's Report on Kew Gardens 1856* (London: HMSO, 1857).

## Published

Adam, William, *The Gem of the Peak* (London: Longman, 1845).

Anon, *Fourth Book of Lessons for the Use of the Irish National School*s (Dublin: Philip Dixon Hardy, 1835).

Anon, 'Green Glass in Plant-houses', *Bulletin of Miscellaneous Information*, vol. 98 (1895), pp. 43–5.

Anon ('A present Kewite on Kew'), *Journal of the Kew Guild* 1.5 (1897), pp. 30–32.

Anon, Obituary of John Smith, *Proceedings of the Linnean Society* (1887–8), pp. 96–8.

Anon, *Sir Robert Peel's New Tariff* (London: James Gilbert, 1845).

Anon, *Summer Days Recreations* (London: G. Vickers, n.d.).

Anon, *The Palm Tribes and their Varieties* (London: Religious Tract Society, 1852).

Anon, *The Pictorial Handbook of London* (London: Henry G. Bohn, 1854).

Anon, *The Royal Botanic Society of London, 1841* (London: Richard and John E. Taylor, 1841).

Archer, Thomas Croxen, *Popular Economic Botany* (London: Reeve & Co., 1853).

Ballantyne, R. M., *The Coral Island* (London: W. Chambers, 1870).

Bates, Henry Walter, *The Naturalist on the River Amazons* (London: John Murray, 1863).

Bennie, Archibald, *Discourses* (Edinburgh: William Blackwood, 1847).

Bernardin de Saint-Pierre, Jacques-Henri:

*Harmonies of Nature*, 3. vols. (London: Baldwin, Cradock & Joy, 1815).

*Paul and Virginia*, Helen Maria Williams (trans.) (Paris, 1795).

*Paul and Virginia* (Chiswick: C. Whittingham, 1821).

*Paul and Virginia* (London: W. S. Orr, 1839).

*Studies of Nature*, H. Hunter (trans.), 5 vols. (London: C. Dilly, 1796).

Burritt, Elihu, *Walks in the Black Country and its Green Border Land* (Birmingham: S. Low, Son and Marston, 1868).

Chance, Henry, 'On the Manufacture of Crown and Sheet Glass', *Journal of the Society of Arts* (15 February 1856), pp. 222–31.

Coleridge, Samuel Taylor, *Biographia Literaria* (London: Rest, Fenner, 1817).

Dickens, Charles, *The Letters of Charles Dickens: 1850–52*, vol. 6, G. Storey, K. Tillotson and N. Burgis (eds.) (Oxford: Clarendon Press, 1988).

Drew, Thomas, 'The Designer of the Royal Palm-House, Kew Gardens', *Building News* (19 March 1880), p. 355.

Forbes, F. E., *Dahomey and the Dahomens* (Paris: Galignani, 1854).

Forbes, James:

*Hortus Woburnensis* (London: James Ridgway, 1833).

*Journal of a Horticultural Tour through Germany, Belgium and Part of France* (London: James Ridgway, 1837).

*Galignani's New Paris Guide* (Paris: A. and W. Galignani, 1839).

Glenny, George, *Annals of Horticulture* (London: Charles Cox, 1849).

Gosse, Philip Henry:

'Wanderings through the Conservatories at Kew', *Fraser's Magazine*, vol. 40:236 (August 1849), pp. 127–35.

*Wanderings through the Conservatories at Kew* (London: Society for Promoting Christian Knowledge, 1857).

Harcourt, W. Vernon, 'President's Address', British Association for the Advancement of Science, *Report of the Ninth Meeting* (London: John Murray, 1840).

Hemans, Felicia, *Selected Poems, Prose and Letters*, Gary Kelly (ed.) (Peterborough, Ontario: Broadview Press, 2002).

Hooker, Joseph Dalton:

'A Sketch of the Life and Labours of Sir William Jackson Hooker', *Annals of Botany*, vol. os-16:4 (December 1902).

*Himalayan Journals*, 2 vols. (London: John Murray, 1855).

'On the Vegetation of the Carboniferous Period, as compared with that of the Present Day', *Memoirs of the Geological Survey of Great Britain*, vol. 2:2 (Longman, Brown, Green and Longmans), pp. 387–430.

*The Botany of the Antarctic Voyage* (London: Reeve, 1844).

*The Rhododendrons of Sikkim-Himalaya* (London: Reeve, Benham and Reeve, 1849).

Hooker, William Jackson:

'Botany', in John Herschel (ed.), *A Manual of Scientific Enquiry: prepared for the use of Her Majesty's Navy and adapted for Travellers in General* (London: John Murray, 1849), pp. 400–22.

*Copy of a Letter addressed to Dawson Turner* (Glasgow: George Richardson, 1840).

*Journal of A Tour in Iceland in the summer of 1809*, 2 vols. (London: Longman, Hurst, Rees, Orme, Brown and John Murray, 1813).

*Kew Gardens, or, A Popular Guide to the Royal Botanic Gardens of Kew* (London: Longman, Green and Longmans, 1847; London: Longman, Brown, Green and Longmans, 1852).

*Museum of Economic Botany: or, a Popular Guide to the Useful and Remarkable Products of the Museum of the Royal Gardens of Kew* (London: Longman, Brown, Green and Longmans, 1855).

*Notes on the Botany of the Antarctic Voyage* (London: H. Baillière, 1843).

'Piacaba', 'Some Account of the Vegetable Ivory Palm'; *Hooker's Journal of Botany and Kew Garden Miscellany* 1 (1849), pp. 121–3, pp. 204–12; 7 (1855), pp. 213–4.

Review of Alfred Russel Wallace, *Palm Trees of the Amazon*, in *Hooker's Journal of Botany and Kew Garden Miscellany* 6 (1854), pp. 61–2.

'Tussac Grass', *Journal of the Royal Geographical Society* 12 (1842), pp. 265–8.

Humboldt, Alexander von:

*Aspects of Nature in Different Lands and Different Climates*, Mrs Sabine (trans.), 2 vols. (London: John Murray, 1849).

*Cosmos*, E. C. Otté (trans.), 3 vols. (London: Henry G. Bohn, 1849).

*Personal Narrative of Travels to the Equinoctial Regions of the New Continent*, Helen Maria Williams (trans.), 7 vols. (London: Longman, Hurst, Rees, Orme and Brown, 1814–29).

Hunt, Robert:

'On the Coloured Glass employed in glazing the new Palm House in the Royal Botanic Garden at Kew', *Report of the Seventeenth Meeting of the British Association for the Advancement of Science* (London: John Murray, 1848), pp. 51–2.

*Researches on Light in its Chemical Relations* (London: Longman, Brown, Green and Longmans, 1854).

'Researches on the Influence of Light on the Germination of Seeds and the Growth of Plants', *Report of the Twelfth Meeting of the British Association for the Advancement of Science* (London: John Murray, 1843).

'The Principles upon which the Tinted Glass used in the Construction of the Royal Palm House at Kew has been selected', *Transactions of the Society of Arts for 1846–7* (1848), pp. 251–9.

Huxley, Leonard, *Life and Letters of Sir Joseph Dalton Hooker*, 2 vols. (London: John Murray, 1918).

Kemp, Edward, *London Exhibited in 1851* (London: John Weale, 1851).

Kipling, Rudyard, *Stories and Poems*, ed. Daniel Karlin (Oxford: Oxford University Press, 2015).

Knight, Charles:

*Cyclopaedia of London* (London: Charles Knight, 1851).

*Library of Entertaining Knowledge: A Description and History of Vegetable Substances* (London: Charles Knight, 1830).

*The Land We Live In*, 4 vols. (London: Charles Knight, 1847–50).

Lawson, G., 'Palm Trees', *Hogg's Instructor* 5 (July–December 1855), pp. 198–205.

Leuchars, Robert B., *A Practical Treatise on the Construction, Heating and Ventilation of Hot-Houses* (New York: C. M. Saxton, 1857).

Lindley, John:

'Garden', in Charles Knight, *Penny Cyclopaedia* 11 (1838), pp. 70–8.

'Observations upon the Effects produced on Plants by the Frost which occurred in England in the Winter of 1837–8', *Transactions of the Horticultural Society of London*, Second Series 2 (1842), pp. 225–46.

Linnaeus, Carl von, *A Dissertation on the Sexes of Plants*, James Edward Smith (trans.) (Dublin: L. White, 1786).

Linné, Carl von, *A System of Vegetables: According to their Classes, Orders, Genera, Species*, Lichfield Botanical Society (trans.) (London: Leigh and Sotherby, 1783).

Loudon, John Claudius:

*Arboretum et Fruticetum Britannicum*, 8 vols. (London: Longman, Green, Brown, Longman, 1844).

*Encyclopædia of Gardening* (London: Longman, Hurst, Orme, Brown, Green, 1824).

*Encyclopædia of Gardening* (London: Longman, Rees, Orme, Brown, Green and Longman, 1835).

*Hortus Britannicus* (London: Longman, Rees, Orme, Brown and Green, 1830).

*Remarks on the Construction of Hothouses* (London: J. Taylor, 1817).

*Sketches of Curvilinear Hothouses* (London, 1818).

*The Green House Companion* (London: John Harding, Triphook and Lepard, 1824).

Lyell, Charles, *Life, Letters, and journals of Sir Charles Lyell*, K. M. Lyell (ed.), 2 vols. (1881).

Malcolm, Sir John, *Sketches of Persia* (London: John Murray, 1861).

Marshall, Henry, 'Contribution to a Natural and Economical History of the Coco-Nut Tree', *Memoirs of the Wernerian Natural History Society*, vol. 5:1 (1823–4), pp. 107–143.

Martius, Karl Friedrich Philipp von, *Historia Naturalis Palmarum*, 3 vols. (Leipzig: T. O. Weigel 1823–53).

Mayhew, Henry and Binny, John, *The Criminal Prisons of London and Scenes of Prison Life* (London: Griffin, Bohn and Co., 1862).

McIntosh, Charles:

*The Book of the Garden*, 2 vols. (Edinburgh: William Blackwood & Sons, 1853).

*The Greenhouse, Hothouse and Stove* (London: W. S. Orr & Co., 1838).

McNab, Catherine Mary, *Juvenile Conversations on the Botany of the Bible* (Edinburgh: William P. Kennedy, 1850).

Melville, Herman, *Omoo* (London: John Murray, 1847).

Moody, Sophy, *The Palm Tree* (London: T. Nelson and Sons, 1864).

Moore, Thomas, *Lalla Rookh: An Oriental Romance* (London: Longman, Hurst, Rees, Orme and Brown, 1817).

Murray, Hugh, et al., *Historical and Descriptive Account of British India* (Edinburgh: Oliver & Boyd, 1843).

Price, Uvedale, *Essays on the Picturesque*, 3 vols. (London: J. Mawman, 1810).

Purdie, William, 'Notice of a Botanical Mission to the West Indies and New Grenada', *Companion to the Botanical Magazine*, in *Curtis's Botanical Magazine* 73 (1847), pp. 2–23.

Rau, Charles, *Memoir of C. F. P. Von Martius* (Washington: Smithsonian Institution, 1871).

Ruskin, John, *Modern Painters* (Sunnyside: George Allen, 1888).

Scheer, Frederick, *Kew and its Gardens* (London: B. Steill, 1840).

Seemann, Berthold, *Popular History of the Palms and their Allies* (London: Lovell Reeve, 1856).

Simmonds, P. L., *The Commercial Products of the Vegetable Kingdom* (London: T. F. A. Day, 1854).

Sinclair, George, *Useful and Ornamental Planting* (London: Baldwin and Craddock, 1832).

Smith, John:

'Green Glass', *Gardeners' Chronicle* (6 March 1880), pp. 307–8.

Letter to the Editor, *Building News* (26 March 1880), pp. 385.

'Napoleon's Willow', *Gardeners' Chronicle*, 2 February 1867, p. 105.

Southey, Robert, *Thalaba the Destroyer* (London: Longman, Hurst, Rees, Orme and Brown) 1821.

Spruce, Richard, 'Palmae Amazonicae', *Journal of the Linnean Society: London Botany* 11 (1871), pp. 65–183.

Tennyson, Alfred, *Alfred Tennyson: A Critical Edition of the Major Works*, Adam Roberts (ed.) (Oxford: Oxford University Press, 2000).

Thackeray, William Makepeace, 'A Prospect of Hampton Court', *Punch's Holidays* (1855), pp. 4–5.

Thiselton-Dyer, W. T., 'Historical Account of Kew to 1841', *Bulletin of Miscellaneous Information*, Royal Botanic Gardens, Kew, 60 (1891), pp. 279–327.

Treloar, Thomas, *The Prince of Palms, being a short account of the Cocoa-nut Tree* (London: Thomas Treloar, 1852).

Turner, Richard:

'Description of the Iron Roof over the Railway Station, Lime Street Liverpool', *Minutes of the Proceedings of the Institution of Civil Engineers* 9 (1849–50), pp. 204–214.

'On the Construction of the Building for the Exhibition of the Works of all Nations', *Minutes of the Proceedings of the Institution of Civil Engineers* 10 (1850–1), pp. 166–70.

Twining, Elizabeth, *Short Lectures on Plants for Schools and Adult Classes* (London: David Nutt, 1858).

Ure, Andrew, *A Dictionary of Arts, Manufactures and Mines* (London: Longman, Orme, Brown, Green and Longmans, 1840).

Wallace, Alfred Russel:

*A Narrative of Travels on the Amazon and Rio Negro* (London: Ward, Lock & Co., 1889).

*My Life: A Record of Events and Opinions* (London: Chapman and Hall, 1908).

*Palm Trees of the Amazon and their Uses* (London: John Van Voorst, 1853).

Watson, W., 'Some Observations upon the Sex of Flowers', *Philosophical Transactions of the Royal Society* 47 (1752), pp. 169–83.

Weale, John, *Atlas on the Engravings to illustrate and practically explain the construction of Roofs of Iron* (London: John Weale, 1859).

Wighton, J., 'On the Preference for Scotch Gardeners', *Gardener's Magazine*, n. s. 6 (1840), pp. 244–6.

Virginia Woolf, *The Complete Shorter Fiction of Virginia Woolf* (London: Hogarth Press, 1985).

## SECONDARY SOURCES

### Unpublished

Cornish, Caroline, 'Curating Science in an Age of Empire: Kew's Museum of Economic Botany' (PhD thesis, Royal Holloway, University of London, 2013).

Diestelkamp, Edward, 'The Iron and Glass Architecture of Richard Turner' (PhD thesis, University College London, 1982).

Evans, Shirley, 'William Andrews Nesfield (1794–1881) Artist and Landscape Gardener' (PhD thesis, University College, Falmouth, 2007).

Jones, Christopher, 'Picturesque Urban Planning: Tunbridge Wells and the Suburban Ideal: The Development of the Calverley Estate 1825–1855' (DPhil. thesis, Oxford, 2017).

### Published

Armstrong, Isobel, *Victorian Glassworlds: Glass Culture and the Imagination 1830–1880* (Oxford: Oxford University Press, 2008).

Arnold, David:

*The Problem of Nature: Environment, Culture and European Expansion* (Oxford: Blackwell, 1996).

*The Tropics and the Traveling Gaze: India, Landscape and Science 1800–1856* (Delhi: Permanent Black, 2005).

Bailey, Peter, *Leisure and Class in Victorian England: Rational Recreation and the Contest for Control 1830–1885* (London: Routledge & Kegan Paul, 1978).

Bailey, L. H., 'Palms and their Characteristics', *Gentes Herbarium* 3.1 (1933).

Baker, William J., Preface, *Botanical Journal of the Linnean Society* (2006).

Barrow, Sasha C., 'Palm Resources at the Centre for Economic Botany at the Royal Botanic Gardens, Kew', *Principes*, vol. 42:3 (1998), pp. 140–4.

Balslev, Henrik, review of *The Book of Palms*, in *Frontiers of Biogeography* vol. 3:2 (2011), pp. 54–55.

Berry, R. J., 'Hooker and Islands', *Biological Journal of the Linnean Society* 96 (2009), pp. 462–81.

Brescius, M. von, 'Connecting the New World: Nets, Mobility and Progress in the Age of Alexander von Humboldt', *HiN*, vol. 13:25 (2012), pp. 11–33.

Brockway, Lucile H., *Science and Colonial Expansion: The Role of the British Royal Botanic Garden* (New Haven: Yale University Press, 2002).

Chadwick, C. F., 'Paxton and the Great Stove', *Architectural History* 4 (1961), pp. 77–92.

Cherry, Bridget and Pevsner, Nikolaus, *London 2: South* (London: Yale University Press, 2002).

Colquhoun, Kate, *'The Busiest Man in England': A Life of Joseph Paxton, Gardener, Architect and Victorian Visionary* (Boston: David R. Godine, 2006).

Cooke, Neil, 'The Forgotten Egyptologist: James Burton', in *Travellers in Egypt* Paul and Janet Starkey (eds.) (London: Tauris Parke, 2001), pp. 85–94.

Cornish, Caroline, '"Botany Behind Glass": The Vegetable Kingdom on Display at Kew's Museum of Economic Botany', in Carin Berkowitz, Bernard Lightman (eds.), *Science Museums in Transition: Cultures of Display in Nineteenth-Century Britain and America* (Pittsburgh, PA: University of Pittsburgh Press, 2017).

Damania, A. B., 'The Coco-de-Mer or the Double Coconut (*Lodoicea maldivica*): Myths and Facts', *Asian Agri-History*, vol. 17:4 (2013), pp. 299–309.

Damodaran, Vinita; Winterbottom, Anna; and Lester, Alan, *The East India Company and the Natural World* (Basingstoke: Palgrave Macmillan, 2015).

Dawson-Brown, Penelope, 'Robert Sweet FLAS 1783–1835', *Linnean*, vol. 12:4 (January 1997), pp. 29–34.

Desmond, Ray:

'John Smith, Kew's First Curator', *Journal of the Kew Guild*, vol. 8:5 (1965), pp. 567–87.

*The History of the Royal Botanic Gardens Kew* (London: Harvill Press with Royal Botanic Gardens, Kew, 1995).

Dettelbach, Michael, 'The Stimulations of Travel: Humboldt's Physiological Construction of the Tropics', in Felix Driver and Luciana Martins (eds.), *Tropical Visions in an Age of Empire* (Chicago: University of Chicago Press, 2005), pp. 43–58.

Diestelkamp, Edward J.:

'Richard Turner and the Palm House at Kew Gardens', in R. J. M. Sutherland, *Structural Iron 1750–1850: Studies in the History of Civil Engineering*, vol. 9 (London: Routledge, 2016), pp. 203–21.

'The Curvilinear Range at the National Botanic Gardens', *Moorea* 9 (December 1990), pp. 6–34.

'The Design and Building of the Palm House, Royal Botanic Gardens Kew', *Journal of Garden History*, vol. 2:3 (1982), pp. 233–272.

Drayton, Richard, *Nature's Government: Science, Imperial Britain, and the 'Improvement' of the World* (New Haven: Yale University Press, 2000).

Driver, Felix, and Martins, Luciana (eds.) *Tropical Visions in an Age of Empire* (Chicago: University of Chicago Press, 2005).

Elliott, Brent, 'The illustrations for the botanical articles in the *Penny Cyclopaedia*', *Occasional Papers from the RHS Lindley Library* 13 (November 2015), pp. 32–56.

*The Royal Horticultural Society: A History 1804–2004* (Chichester: Phillimore, 2004).

Elliott, Paul A.; Watkins, Charles; and Daniels, Stephen, *The British Arboretum: Trees, Science and Culture in the Nineteenth Century* (Pittsburgh: University of Pittsburgh Press, 2011).

Endersby, Jim:

*Imperial Nature: Joseph Hooker and the Practices of Victorian Science* (Chicago: University of Chicago Press, 2008).

'Joseph Hooker: The Making of a Botanist', *Endeavour*, vol. 25:1 (2001), pp. 3–7.

Evans, Shirley, *Masters of their Craft: The Art, Architecture and Garden Design of the Nesfields* (Cambridge: Lutterworth Press, 2014).

Fyfe, Aileen, *Science and Salvation: Evangelical Popular Science Publishing in Victorian Britain* (Chicago: University of Chicago Press, 2004).

Gardiner, B. G., 'Berthold Carol Seemann', *Linnean* 16 (2000), pp. 6–12.

Getz, Trevor R., *Slavery and Reform in West Africa: Toward Emancipation in Nineteenth-Century Senegal and the Gold Coast* (Ohio: Ohio University Press, 2004).

Gill, Stephen, 'Price's Patent Candles New Light on *North and South*', *Review of English Studies* 27 (1976), pp. 313–21.

Goodman, Nigel (ed.), *Dawson Turner: A Norfolk Antiquary and his Remarkable Family* (Chester: Phillimore, 2007).

Grey, Fred, *Palm* (London: Reaktion, 2018).

Grove, Richard, *Green Imperialism* (Cambridge: Cambridge University Press, 1995).

Guthrie, J. L.; Allen, A.; and Jones, C. R., 'Royal Botanic Gardens, Kew: Restoration of Palm House', *Proceedings of the Institution of Civil Engineers*, Part 1, 84 (December 1988), pp. 1145–91.

Harries, Hugh, 'Fun made the fair Coconut Shy', *Palms*, vol. 48:2 (2004), pp. 77–82.

Harris, John, 'C. R. Cockerell's "Ichnographica Domestica"', *Architectural History* 14 (1971), pp. 5–29.

Henderson, Janice, and Osborne, Daphne J., 'The Oil Palm in all our lives: How this came about', *Endeavour*, vol. 24:2 (2000), pp. 63–8.

Herbert, Eugenia W., *Flora's Empire: British Gardens in India* (Philadelphia: University of Philadelphia Press, 2011).

Hix, John:

'Richard Turner: Glass Master', *Architectural Review* 159 (November 1972), pp. 287–203.

*The Glass House* (London: Phaidon, 1974).

Holway, Tatiana, *The Flower of Empire: An Amazonian Water Lily, the Quest to Make it Bloom, and the World it Created* (Oxford: Oxford University Press, 2013).

Johnson, Nuala, *Nature Displaced, Nature Displayed: Order and Beauty in Botanical Gardens* (London: I. B. Tauris, 2011).

Kelley, Theresa M., *Clandestine Marriage: Botany and Romantic Culture* (London: Johns Hopkins University Press, 2012).

Knapp, Sandra, and Baker, William, 'Alfred Russel Wallace and the Palms of the Amazon', *Palms*, vol. 46:3 (2002), pp. 109–19.

Kohlmaier, Georg, and von Sartory, Barna, *Houses of Glass: A Nineteenth-Century Building Type*, John C. Harvey (trans.) (Cambridge, Mass: MIT Press, 1986).

Lack, H. Walter (ed.), *The Book of Palms* by Carl Friedrich Philipp von Martius (Köln: Taschen, 2016).

Lack, H. Walter, and Baker, William J. (eds.), *Die Welt der Palmen, The World of Palms* (Berlin: Botanisches Museum Berlin-Dahlem, 2011).

Lightman, Bernard, *Victorian Popularizers of Science: Designing Nature for New Audiences* (Chicago: University of Chicago Press, 2007).

Lynn, Martin, *Commerce and Economic Change in West Africa: The Palm Oil Trade in the Nineteenth Century* (Cambridge: Cambridge University Press, 2002).

Mackenzie, John, *The Victorian Vision: Inventing New Britain* (London: Victoria and Albert Museum Publications, 2001).

McCalman, Iain, *Darwin's Armada* (London: Simon & Schuster, 2009).

McEwen, Ron, 'The Northern Lads: The Migration of Scottish Gardeners with especial reference to the Royal Botanic Gardens, Kew', *Sibbaldia* 11 (2013), pp. 109–23.

McKay, Alex, '"A difficult country, a hostile Chief, and a still more hostile Minister": The Anglo-Sikkim War of 1861', *Bulletin of Tibetology*, vol. 45:2 (2009), pp. 31–48.

Meynell, Guy:

'Kew and the Royal Gardens Committee of 1838', *Archives of Natural History* 10 (1982), pp. 469–77.

'The Royal Botanic Society's Garden, Regent's Park', *London Journal*, vol. 6: 2 (1980), pp. 135–46.

Minter, Sue, *The Greatest Glass House: The Rainforests Recreated* (London: HMSO, Royal Botanic Gardens, Kew, 1990).

Peters, Tom F., 'Some Structural Problems encountered in the building of the Crystal Palace of 1851', in Robert Thorne (ed.), *Structural Iron and Steel, 1850–1900* (London: Routledge, 2000), pp. 1–15.

Peterson, Charles E., 'Inventing the I-Beam: Richard Turner, Cooper & Hewitt and Others', *Bulletin of the Association for Preservation Technology*, vol. 12:4 (1980), pp. 3–28.

Pietz, William, 'The Fetish of Civilization: Sacrificial Blood and Monetary Debt', in Peter Pels and Oscar Salemink (eds.), *Colonial Subjects: Essays on the Practical History of Anthropology* (Ann Arbor: University of Michigan Press), pp. 53–81.

Ryan, James, 'Placing Early Photography: The Work of Robert Hunt in mid-nineteenth-century Britain', *History of Photography*, vol. 41:4 (2017), pp. 343–61.

Saint, Andrew, *Architect and Engineer: A Study in Sibling Rivalry* (New Haven: Yale University Press, 2007).

Schoenefeldt, Henrik:

'The Palm House Kew, 1844–48: a case study on scientific experimentation and cross-disciplinary working methods in nineteenth century architecture', *Diverse Engagement: Drawing in the Margins – Proceedings of Cambridge Interdisciplinary Graduate Conference* (Cambridge: University of Cambridge, 2010), pp. 174–86.

'The use of Scientific Experimentation in developing the Glazing for the Palm House at Kew', *Construction History* 26 (2011), pp. 19–39.

Schönitzer, Klaus, 'From the New to the Old World: Two indigenous children brought back to Germany by Johann Baptist Spix and Carl Friedrich Philipp Martius', *Journal Fünf Kontinente* (2014–15), pp. 79–97.

Secord, Anne, 'Botany on a Plate: Pleasure and the Power of Pictures in Promoting Early Nineteenth-Century Scientific Knowledge', *Isis*, vol. 93:1 (March 2002), pp. 28–57.

Secord, James A., *Victorian Sensation: the Extraordinary Publication, Reception And Secret Authorship of the Natural History of Creation* (Chicago: University of Chicago Press, 2003).

Singmaster, Deborah, 'A Life in Architecture; David Marks, Julia Barfield', *Architects' Journal*, 9 September 1999, https://www.architectsjournal.co.uk/home/a-life-in-architecture-david-marks-julia-barfield/773615.article

Sivasundaram, Sujit, *Islanded: Britain, Sri Lanka, and the Bounds of an Indian Ocean Colony* (Chicago: University of Chicago Press, 2013).

Stearne, William T. (ed.), *John Lindley 1799–1865: Garden-Botanist and Pioneer Orchidologist* (Woodbridge: Antique Collectors' Club, 1999).

Stepan, Nancy Leys, *Picturing Tropical Nature* (London: Reaktion, 2001).

Sutherland, R. J. M., *Structural Iron 1750–1850: Studies in the History of Civil Engineering*, vol. 9 (London: Routledge, 2016).

Taylor, William M., *The Vital Landscape: Nature and Built Environment in Nineteenth-Century Britain* (Aldershot: Ashgate, 2004).

Tomlinson, P. B.:

*The Structural Biology of Palms* (Oxford: Clarendon Press, 1990).

'The Uniqueness of Palms', *Botanical Journal of the Linnean Society*, vol. 151:1 (2006), pp. 5–14.

Valen, Dustin, 'On the Horticultural Origins of Victorian Glasshouse Culture', *Journal of the Society of Architectural Historians*, vol. 74:4 (December 2016), pp. 403–23.

Whitbourn, Philip, *Decimus Burton, Esquire: Architect and Gentleman (1800–1881)* (Tunbridge Wells: The Royal Tunbridge Wells Civic Society, 2003).

Williams, Guy, *Augustus Pugin versus Decimus Burton: A Victorian Architectural Duel* (London: Cassell, 1990).

Wulf, Andrea, *The Invention of Nature: The Adventures of Alexander von Humboldt, the Lost Hero of Science* (London: John Murray, 2015).

# *Acknowledgements*

The research for this book has led me down many unexpected paths, and I am deeply grateful to everyone who has pointed me in the right direction. As a visiting researcher at Kew, I have been made to feel extremely welcome. I am particularly indebted to Mark Nesbitt for his enthusiastic backing, to Bill Baker and John Dransfield for opening up the world of palms, and to Kiri Ross-Jones for her helpful guidance. Through my association with Kew, I have been lucky enough to make contact with a number of other academics: Felix Driver, who encouraged me in many ways; Luciana Martins, who invited me to talk at Birkbeck's Arts Week; and Caroline Cornish, who shared her knowledge of Kew's Museum of Economic Botany. The reading room at Kew has been a delightful place to work, and the library and archives staff – particularly Fiona Ainsworth, Craig Brough, Julia Buckley, Rosie Eddisford, Kat Harrington, Anne Marshall and Lynn Parker – have all gone out of their way to help with my queries.

I could not have written this book without Edward Diestelkamp's pioneering work on Richard Turner. I owe thanks to Ed for his advice on the architectural and engineering aspects of the Palm House. I am very grateful to Robert Turner and his son Christopher for allowing me to look through their family collection, and for their warm hospitality. The spirit of Turner enterprise has clearly descended to Christopher, whose company, the London Window Cleaner, undertook the complex operation of cleaning the glass of the Palm House, designed and constructed by his great-great-great grandfather.

Through the wise guidance of Clare Alexander, this book has found a wonderful home at Picador. The manuscript benefited from expert editing by Georgina Morley and Marissa Constantinou. Philippa McEwan happily climbed the spiral stairs to gain the full Palm House experience. Laura Carr has skilfully overseen every stage of the production. The design team at Picador has made this a truly beautiful book. It has been a pleasure to work with Gina Fullerlove, Pei Chu and Lydia White at Kew Publishing.

I am very grateful to the University of Roehampton for study leave to undertake the research for this book. I have received great support from colleagues, past and present – in particular, Simon Edwards, Jenny Hartley, Ian Haywood, Nicki Humble, Jane Kingsley-Smith, Zach Leader, Louise Lee, Susan Matthews, Clare McManus, Laura Peters, Martin Priestman, Lisa Sainsbury, Mary Shannon, Shelley Trower, Bea Turner, Sarah Turvey, Amy Waite, Alison Waller and Cathy Wells-Cole. Colleagues at other universities and institutions have encouraged me with their comments and invitations to speak: David Arnold, Rita Banerjee, Rosinka Chaudhuri, Mary Ellis Gibson, Uday Kumar, Nigel Leask, Pramod Nayar and Dan White. I have been sustained by the friendship of Tanvir Hasan, Philippa Park, Srilata Raman, Jonah Siegel, Francis Spufford, Jenny Uglow and Nancy Yousef. I am deeply indebted to Laverne Morey, Alison McIntosh and the staff of Lynde House Care Home.

It is to my family that I owe the greatest thanks: to my kind sister, Helen Rigby; to my two fine children, Jacob and Isaac Loose; and to my loving husband, Julian Loose, who has been with me every chapter of the way.

# Index

Page numbers in **bold** refer to illustrations.


Aberdeen, George Hamilton-Gordon, 4th Earl of 28, 44–5, 47
*Adam Spade* (Smith) 301–2
Africa 62, 210, 257–9
Airy, Professor George Bidell 293
Aiton, William (father) 34
Aiton, William Townsend 13–14, **13**, 16–18, 23, 31, 34, 35–8, 48, 51, 69–71, 133–4, 136
Albert, Prince Consort 21, 45, 87, 88, 94–6, 110, 144, 147, 277, 290–1
Anderson, William 36
*Annals and Magazine of Natural History* 249–50
Antarctic expedition; *see also* Ross, Captain James Clark
  Admiralty secrecy rules 85, 87
  expeditions 74–85, **82**
  J. Hooker's collections 83–4
  J. Hooker's post 76
  *Notes on the Botany of the Antarctic Voyage* (W. Hooker) 88–9, 90
  plans for 74–7
  poem to 77
  supplies and instruments 77
  in Van Diemen's Land 78–9
  vessels 75, 82
Anthaeum, Hove 103–4
arboretum 123–35, **129**, **135**, **Plate 18**
*Arboretum et Fruticetum Britannicum* (Loudon) 125–6
Archer, Thomas Croxen 241, 252
Argyll, Archibald Campbell, 3rd Duke of 123
Argyll, George Campbell, 6th Duke of 26–7
Armstrong, John 261
*Aspects of Nature* (Humboldt) 200–1, 203
*Astrocaryum jauari* **Plate 1**
*Athenæum* 82
*Attalea funifera* 252, 253
Auckland, George Eden, 1st Earl of 223
Augusta, Princess of Wales 9, 45, 69, 95

Bailey, L. H. 204
Ballantyne, R. M. 63–4
Balslev, Henrik 209
Banks, Sir Joseph 11, 14, 25, 30, 74
Barfield, Julia 306
Bates, Henry Walter 244–6
Bawden, Edward 3, **Plate 30**
Bazalgette, Joseph 301
Beaufort, Francis 88
Bedchamber Crisis 21
Bedford, Francis Russell, 7th Duke of 46
Bedford, John Russell, 6th Duke of 26, 29, 31, 46, 54
Bentham, George 298

# Index


Berlin Botanic Garden 95, 97, 191–2, 233
Berlin Experiment 191–2, 194, 199
Bermuda fan palm (*Sabal bermudana*) 1, 215–16
Bernardin de Saint-Pierre, Jacques-Henri 192, 197–8; see also *Paul et Virginie* (Bernardin)
Bernardin statue (Holweck) 197–8, **198**
Bible 61, 62, 66, 285–6
Birmingham Botanical Gardens 55–6, 115
*Bleak House* (Dickens) 252
Bligh, Captain William 215
Bojer, Wenceslaus 264–5, 266, **266**, 267
Bonpland, Aimé 199, 200, 204–5, 222, 235, 236
*Botanical Register* 37
*Botany for Ladies* (Jane Loudon) 284
*Botany of the Voyage of H.M.S. Herald, The* (Seemann) 235
Boussingault, Jean-Baptiste 222
Brentford 7–8, 36, 178
Brick Farm (West Park), Mortlake 49–51, **50**
British Association for the Advancement of Science 74–5, 76–7, 167, 171, 174, 183
British Empire 4, 5, 16, 19–20, 34, 74, 90, 97, 126, 218–19, 241, 302–3
*Builder* 154, 270
*Building News* 300
Burbidge and Healy boilers 180, **181**, 182
Burritt, Elihu 175, 177
Burton, Decimus
  background 108–9
  Colosseum, Regent's Park 17–18, 58
  Great Stove at Chatsworth 57–8, 101, 108, 110, 112, 115, 164
  Kew Gardens
    diplomacy 133–4
    expansion 134
    Museum of Economic Botany 240, 268
    Nesfield, appointment of 131–3
    Palm House
      architect 110–16
      chimney ('campanile') 178–9
      choosing site 119–20, 131–2
      design attribution 115, 300
      designs **5**, 112–13, **156**, **Plate 17**
      designs with Turner 113–15
      finance 138, 157
      flooding 183
      glass 164, 172, 173
      Jones and Clark's Palm House designs 116
      Turner's designs 111–12, 157
      Turner's iron ribs 143
    Temperate House 300–1
  Paris glasshouses 160, 161
  portrait **Plate 15**
  reputation 108, 109–10
  Turner, relationship with 113–15, 118, 144–7, 300–1
  Winter Garden, Regent's Park 144–7
Burton, James 108–9

Calcutta Botanic Garden 218–19
Campbell, Dr Alistair 225–7
Candolle, Alphonse, de 52, 125
Canning, Charles, 1st Earl 154
Caroline, Queen 9
Ceylon (Sri Lanka) 66, 256, 257
Chambers, William 9, 130
*Chambers's Edinburgh Journal* 60–1, 61–2, 98, 100
Chance Brothers glass company, Smethwick 170, 174–8, **175**
Chance, Henry 176
Chartists 273–4
Chatsworth, Derbyshire 15, 17, 21, 56–9, **58**, 98–9, 101, 110, 138, 164, 170, 213, 245, 306

# Index


Chelsea Physic Garden (London) 14–15, 34, 264
*Chemist & Druggist* **Plate 29**
*Child's Companion and Juvenile Instructor, The* (Religious Tract Society) 286–7
*Civil Engineer & Architects Journal* 139–40
Claudet, Antoine 183–4, **Plate 21**, **Plate 22**
Cockerell, Charles 109
coconut oil 256–7
coconut palm (*Cocos nucifera*) 60, 63–6, 194–5, 254–7
coir 255–6
*Colonial Magazine* 14, 97
Colosseum, Regent's Park 57–8, 183
*Commercial Products of the Vegetable Kingdom, The* (Simmonds) 256
consumption/tuberculosis 40–1, 52–3, 67
Cook, Eliza 281, 282
*Coral Island, The* (Ballantyne) 63–4
*Cosmos* (Humboldt) 233–4
Cotman, John Sell 30
Cowper, Charles 170, 172, 178
Crystal Palace, Hyde Park/Sydenham 292–5, 306
Cuban royal palm (*Roystonea regia*) 1
Cunningham, Allan 14
*Curtis's Botanical Magazine* 26, 263–4, 270, **271**

daguerreotypes 166, 183–4, **Plate 21**, **Plate 22**
Dalhousie, Christian Ramsay, Countess of 223
Dalhousie, James Brown-Ramsay, 1st Marquess of 223
Darwin, Charles 84–5, 91–2, 174, 191, 194, 225, 233, 244, 296, 298
Darwin, Erasmus 188–9
date palm (*Phoenix dactylifera*) 60–3, 171, 193, 216, 232, **Plate 12**
Daubeny, Charles 172–3
*Day of the Triffids, The* (Sekely) 3
De la Beche, Sir Henry 166, 167, 169, 241, 242
deck beam iron 140–3, 150, 151–2, 275, 276
Defoe, Daniel 63
deforestation 261
Derby, Edward Smith-Stanley, 13th Earl of 141–2
*Derby Mercury* 59
'Description of Javíta' (Wallace) 246–7
Dettelbach, Michael 204–5
Devonshire, William Cavendish, 6th Duke 15, 23–4, 25, 29, 50, 56, 57, 98–9, 101, 110, 164, 213
Dickens, Charles 252, 260
Diestelkamp, Edward 115
*Dissertation on the Sexes of Plants* (Linnaeus) 191–2
double coconut (*Lodoicea maldivica*) 262–7, **266**, **Plate 4**, **Plate 5**
Drew, Thomas 101–2, 107, 144, 300
Duncannon, John Ponsonby, Viscount 45
Dunn, Patrick 153
Dutch House (Kew Palace) 9

*Eclectic Review* 264
*Edinburgh Review* 305
education, public 12, 19, 34, 68, 167, 212–13, 281, 284–5, 286, 288–90, 308
*Elementary Geology* (Hitchcock) 190–1, **190**
Elliott, Brent 212
*Encyclopædia of Gardening* (Loudon) 101, 163
*Erebus*, HMS 75, 76, 77, 80, 82, 83
*Evening Mail* 272–3
evolution by natural selection 92, 244

Falkland Islands 83, 86, 89–90
Fitch, Walter Hood 86, 87, 249

# Index


*Flora Antarctica* (J. Hooker) 91–2, 169, 223
*Flora Indica* (J. Hooker and Thomson) 228
*Flora of New Zealand* (J. Hooker) 91–2, 296
*Florist and Garden Miscellany* 270, 272, 278, 279
Forbes, Frederick 258–9
Forbes, James 54
Fox Talbot, Henry 29, 166, 183
Franklin, Sir John 79, 235
Frederick of Prussia, Prince 302
Frederick, Prince of Wales 9
*Freeman's Journal* 153

*Gardeners' Chronicle* 71, 99, 268, 272, 274, 279
*Gardeners' Gazette* 13, 39–40
*Gardener's Magazine* 12, 31–2, 33, 39, 44, 48, 67, 125, 132
Gaskell, Elizabeth 260
*Genera Plantarum* (J. Hooker and Bentham) 298
Geological Survey of Britain 166, 169–70
George III 9, 11, 119
George IV 11
Gill, Stephen 260
glasshouses
  Anthaeum, Hove 103–4
  Birmingham Botanical Gardens 55–6, 115
  Crystal Palace, Hyde Park 292–5, 306
  environmental control 159–60
  glass 162–5, 167–9, 170–4, **Plate 20**
  Great Stove at Chatsworth 15, 56–9, **58**, 98–9, 101, 110, 164, 170, 245, 306
  Humboldt's views on 200–1, 233–4
  Jardin des Plantes, Paris 96–7, 160, 161
  Kew Gardens 10–11, 35, 95–6, 97–8, 215–16; *see also* Palm House
  Killakee House conservatory 102, **103**
  Loddiges' Nursery, Hackney 98, 213, 233
  nineteenth-century technology 100–1
  ventilation 161–2
  Winter Garden, Regent's Park 106, 144–9, **148**, 165, 181, 293
glass manufacturers 164–5, 170, 174–8, **175**
glass tax, repeal of 164, 175–6
Glendinning, Robert 132
Glenny, George 13, 39–40
glycerine 262
Goethe, Johann Wolfgang von 199, 209–10
Gordon, Robert 42, 44
Gosse, Philip Henry 208, **231**, 287–8, **310**
Goulburn, Henry 138
Great Exhibition, Hyde Park 290–5, **291**
greenhouses *see* glasshouses
Greenough, George 109
Grissell and Peto building company 138–9, 143, 178
Grissell, Thomas 142, 158
Guarani people, South America 202–3
Gunn, Ronald Campbell 79

Hall, Sir Benjamin 268
Hammersmith Works, Dublin 102, 105–6, **106**, 107–8, 143, 146, 150, 153, 277, **277**
Hannay, James 219, 234–5
Hanover, Ernest Augustus, King 8, 69
*Helen*, SV 248
Hemans, Felicia 193
*Herald*, HMS 235
Herbert, Sidney 106
Herschel, Sir John 166–7, 172
Heward, Robert 43–4

Himalayan fan palm (*Trachycarpus martianus*) 216
*Himalayan Journals* (J. Hooker) 225
*Historia Naturalis Palmarum* (Martius) 207–12, **Plate 1**, **Plate 2**, **Plate 3**
Hitchcock, Edward 190–1, **190**
Hogan, Michael 36–7
Holweck, Louis 198, **198**
Hooker, Elizabeth 40–1, 85, 86
Hooker, Joseph Dalton
  Antarctic expedition
    collections 77–8, 83–4
    contacts and networks 79
    dangers of voyage 81–2
    drawings 86–7
    introduction to Ross 75–6
    learning of brother's death 78–9
    Mount Erebus 80–1
    plant geography 84
    post 76
    public attention 85–9
  classification of palm family 298–9
  Dalhousie, relationship with 223
  Darwin, relationship with 91–2
  Darwin's influence 84–5
  education 72, 73
  Geological Survey work 169–70
  Himalayan trip 223–9, **226**
  Humboldt, relationship with 160–1, 224
  Jardin des Plantes, Paris 161
  Kew assistant directorship 296–7
  Kew directorship 298
  medical qualification 76
  portraits **76**, **299**, **Plate 28**
  tussock grass 89–91
  Victoria and Albert, introduction to 96
  written works 91, 169, 225, 228, 298
Hooker, Lady Maria (née Turner) 30, 41, 69–70, 72–3, 87
Hooker, Mary Harriette 40–1
Hooker, Sir William
  *Arboretum et Fruticetum Britannicum* (Loudon), review of 126
  Buckingham Palace, invitation to 87
  death 297–8
  as director of Kew
    aesthetics 69–70
    appointment 47–8
    arboretum 124, 125, 128, 131, 134
    Brick Farm (West Park) home 49–51, **50**, 51
    Chartist threat 273–4
    expansion 68–9, 70, 83, 127, 133–4, 136
    funding issues 51, 138, 222–3
    *Kew Gardens, or, A Popular Guide* 281–2, **281**
    Lindley's vision, realizing 70
    Museum of Economic Botany 240–4, 253, 254–5, 262, 267, 268
    Nesfield, appointment of 122–3, 132–3, 134
    Palm House
      construction 155–6
      designs 112–13, 116
      early schemes considered 98–100
      environmental control 159–60
      funding 155–6, 160, 272–3
      glass 165, 168, 172–3
      heating system 180
      networking 100
      photographs 184
      site 119–20, 131–2
      stocking 218–20, 221–2
      thinning of collection 297
      Turner, meeting with 107
    plant collectors, commissioning 220, 244, 245
    plant donations, inviting 219, 241–2, 267
    plant exchanges 71, 83
    political changes 154–5

Hooker, Sir William (*cont.*)
- public education/benefits 212–13, 242–3, 253, 279, 281–2, 288
- Royal visits 94–6, 99, 230, **Plate 26**
- salary 30–1, 48, 155
- sending Smith on horticultural tour 53–4
- visitor behaviour 280–1
- visitor numbers 278
- double coconut (*Lodoicea maldivica*) 263–4, 266–7
- as editor
  - *Curtis's Botanical Magazine* 26, 263–4, 270, **271**
  - *Hooker's Journal of Botany and Kew Garden Miscellany* 224–5, 250, 251, 252, 253, 267
  - *London Journal of Botany* 53, 88, 223–4
- family illnesses and bereavements 40–1
- in Glasgow 25–6, 30, 41, 47, 49, 52, 73, 75, 110, 126, 211, 263–4
- herbarium 25, 49, 50, 72, 155, 298
- honours and appointments 26, 52
- Iceland botanical survey 74
- Kew directorship, seeking 26–9, 30–1, 46–7
- networking 52, 218, 224
- *Palm Trees of the Amazon and their Uses* (Wallace), review of 250–1
- *piaçaba* fibre 252–3
- portraits **26, Plate 13, Plate 26, Plate 27**
- relationships
  - Dawson Turner, father-in-law 29–30
  - Lindley 25–6, 27–8, 70–1
  - Martius 211
  - Russell 155
  - Seemann 235
  - Smith 38–9, 52, 53–4, 119–20, 297
  - Turner 141–2
- Royal Botanic Society of London 43
- son Joseph
  - Antarctic expedition 75, 76, 77, 78–9, 83–91
  - Geological Survey work 169
  - plant collecting in Himalayan region 223–4, 224–5, 228–9
  - post-Antarctic career 91–2
  - as successor 72, 155, 296, 298
- written works
  - 'Botany' in *Manual of Scientific Enquiry* (Admiralty) 219, 241
  - *Copy of a Letter address to Dawson Turner* 46–7
  - *Journal of a Tour in Iceland in the summer of 1809* 74
  - *Kew Gardens, or, A Popular Guide* 281–2, **281**
  - *Museum of Economic Botany: or a Popular Guide* **240**, 242–4, 254–5, 262
  - *Notes on the Botany of the Antarctic Voyage* 88–9, 90
  - *Rhododendrons of Sikkim Himalaya, The* (Hooker, ed.) 228–9
  - 'Tussac Grass', *Journal of the Royal Geographical Society* 90–1

Hooker, William Dawson (Willy) 41, 73
*Hooker's Journal of Botany and Kew Garden Miscellany* 224–5, 250, 251, 252, 253, 267
Horeau, Hector 294
Horticultural Society 8, 14, 15, 25, 39, 42, 44, 56, 212, 217
*Hortus Kewensis* (Aiton) 14
*Hortus Woburnensis* (Forbes) 54
hothouses *see* glasshouses
*Household Words* 64, 219, 234–5, 255, 260
Humboldt, Alexander von 88–9, 160–1,

169, 187, 199–205, 207, 210, 221, 222, 224, 233–4, 235–6, 237, 244, 247, 279, 285
Hume, Joseph 44, 45, 47
Hunt, Robert 165–9, 170–2, 173–4, 178, 183, 242, 306, **Plate 19**, **Plate 20**
Huxley, Leonard 73
Huxley, Thomas Henry 73

*Illustrated London Almanack* **289**, 295
*Illustrated London News* **179**, 213, 229, **229**, 277–8, **277**, **283**, 292, **Plate 23**
*Illustrated Magazine of Art* 60
*Illustrations of the Natural Orders of Plants* (Twining) 284, **Plate 8**
*Imperial Magazine* 58
India 139, 223–5, 227–9, 296
Indian wine palm (*Caryota urens*) 216
Indonesia 261
Industrial Revolution 103, 139
Institut National de France 204–5
Institution of Civil Engineers 101, 292–3
International Palm Society 189
Ireland 90, 101–2 105–8, **106**, 110, 137, 152–4, 273, 274, 276–7, **277**
Irish famine 152–4, 273, 277
iron
- adaptability 103
- attractiveness 56–7
- cast-iron 103–4
- changes in architectural thinking 56–7, 100–1
- deck beam 140–3, 150, 151–2, 275, 276
- importance for Industrial Revolution 102–3
- patents 139–40, 142, 151, 278
- railways and ships 139–40, 146, 185–6
- Turner's 'ribs' 105, 142–4, 150, 157
- wrought iron 101, 104–5, 107, 140–1, 148, 150, 178, 277, 291–2, 305, 308

ironworks
- Hammersmith Works, Dublin 102, 105–6, **106**, 107–8, 143, 146, 150, 153, 277, **277**
- Malins and Rawlinson 142, 143

ivory-nut palm (*Phytelephas macrocarpa*) 220–2, **Plate 6**, **Plate 7**

*jacitára* (*Desmoncus polyacanthos*) 247–8, **251**
Jardin des Plantes, Paris 96–7, 160, 161, 197–8, **198**
Java 261, 263
Jerrold, Douglas 273
Jones & Co. (later Jones & Clark) Glasshouses, Birmingham 56, 115–16, 117–18, 157
Jones, John 115, 157
*Journal of a Tour in Iceland in the summer of 1809* (Hooker) 74
*Journal of Researches (Voyage of the Beagle)* (Darwin) 84–5, 199, 225
Juri, Brazilian slave 206–7
*Juvenile Conversations on the Botany of the Bible* (C. McNab) 285

Kemp, Edward 272
Kennedy and Vernon shipbuilders 140, 142, 151
Kentia palm (*Howea forsteriana*) 303, **304**
Kerguelen Land's cabbage (*Pringlea antiscorbutica*) 84
Kew Gardens
- 1838 inspection 1, 10–11, 14–22, 45
- arboretum
  - aesthetics–taxonomy balance 128
  - inspection of trees 131
  - as National Arboretum 134–6, **135**
  - Nesfield's plans 128–31, **129**, 134–6, **135**, **Plate 18**
  - original arboretum 23–4

Kew Gardens (*cont.*)
preparations and purchases 127
Chartist threat 273–4
closure plans/reaction 42–5
criticisms 12–13, 39–40
directorship, contenders for
Hooker 26–9, 31, 38–9, 46–8
Lindley 24–5, 28
Smith 31–5, 39–40
Dutch House (Kew Palace) 9
emblem of Empire 4–5, 19–20, 218–19, **Plate 29**
expansion 68–9, 70, 83, 127, 133–4, 136
funding 51, 138, 155–6, 222–3, 272–3
George III's improvements 9
herbarium 298
Hooker's appointment 47–8
international collections 10–11, 218–20
labelling of plants 17, 18, 39–40, 281
Lindley's report 19–20, 24–5, 45, 70, 90, 123
maps **xviii**, 11, **281**
Museum of Economic Botany *see* Museum of Economic Botany
Napoleon's Willow 9–10
neglect 11–12
Nesfield's appointment 121, 122–3
Pagoda 3, 9, 130, 136, 270
Palm House *see* Palm House
palm stove, old 97–8, 215–16
plant collectors
Bojer 264–7
Hooker, J. 83, 222–9, **226**
Purdie 220–2
Spruce 245–6
Wallace 244–5
plant donations 53–4, 71, 219, 241–2, 264, 267
plant exchanges 71
Princess Augusta's improvements 9
public access 278–82, **280**, **283**, 288–90, **289**
education/benefits 212–13, 242–3, 253, 279, 281–2, 288–9
free admission 279, 286
*Kew Gardens, or, A Popular Guide* 281–2, **281**
map **281**
opening times 279–80
railways 278–9
during Royal ownership 9–12, 18
visitor behaviour 280–1
visitor numbers 278
women visitors 288
public ownership, transfer to 47
Rhododendron Dell 228
Royal visits 94–6, 99, 230, **Plate 26**
state of, on Hooker's arrival 51
Temperate House 3, 300–1
Victoria's interest/indifference 21, 45, 69, 94–6, 230
*Kew Gardens, or, A Popular Guide* 281–2, **281**
Kew village 8
Kipling, Rudyard 302–3
Knight, Charles 59, 61, 62, 148, 270, 282

*Ladies' Cabinet* 230
*Lady's Newspaper* 270
*Lalla Rookh* (Moore) 232
Lambert, Aylmer Bourke 43, 44, 45
*Land We Live In, The* (Knight) 59
Lawson, George 60
*Leisure Hour* 280–1, 294
Leopoldine of Austria 205–6
*Leopoldinia piassaba* 252
*Leopoldinia pulchra* **Plate 1**
Leuchars, Robert 152
licuri palm (*Syagrus coronata*) 216, 217, 304
Lime Street Station, Liverpool 152, 276
Lincoln, Henry Pelham-Clinton, Earl of 100, 101–2, 106, 107, 108, 112, 121, 122–3, 127, 134, 143, 154

Lindley, Dr John
background 14–15
candidacy for Kew directorship 24–5, 28, 30–1, 42
Chartists 274
criticisms of Palm House 272
German royal gardens 95
Hooker, friendship with 25–6, 27–8, 70–1
hothouse ventilation 161–2
Kew closure scheme, reaction to 42
Kew inspection 14, 16–18
Kew report 19–20, 24–5, 45, 70, 90, 123
*Penny Cyclopaedia* articles 212
portrait **24**
Linnaean classification 124–5
Linnean Society 29, 30, 38, 52, 54, 78
Linnaeus, Carl von 29, 124, 188–92, 194, 201–2, 205, 272, 287–8
*Literary Gazette* 77, 80, 224
'Locksley Hall' (Tennyson) 186
Loddiges' Nursery, Hackney 98, 213, 217, 233, 264
*London Exhibited in 1851* (Kemp) 294
London Eye 306
*London Journal* 230
*London Journal of Botany* 53, 88, 223–4
*London Saturday Journal* 263, 264
London Underground posters 3
Loudon, Jane 284
Loudon, John Claudius
arboreta 125–6, 132
*Arboretum et Fruticetum Britannicum* 125–6
call for reforms at Kew 12, 13
*Encyclopædia of Gardening* 101, 163
glasshouse designs **55**, 56, 57, 101, 104, 112
glasshouse environments 159
glasshouse glass 162, 163
'Hints for Breathing Places for the Metropolis' 67
Jardin des Plantes, Paris 97
Kew closure scheme, reaction to 44
Smith for directorship, backing 31–2, 48

McIntosh, Charles 57, 96, 163, 164, 174
McNab, Catherine Mary 285
McNab, William 33, 34
*Magazine of Horticulture* 59
Malaysia 261
Malcolm, Sir John 62–3
Malins and Rawlinson ironworks 142, 143
Malins, William 142
*Manual of Scientific Enquiry, A* (Herschel, ed.) 219, 241
Marks, David 306
Marryat, Frederick 63
Marshall, Henry 66
Marshall, William Calder 196, **197**
Martius, Carl Friedrich Philipp von 95, 205–12, 213, 220, 250, **Plate 1**, **Plate 2**, **Plate 3**
Mary Adelaide, Princess 69, 228, **Plate 26**
*Masterman Ready* (Marryat) 63
Mauritia palm (*Mauritia flexuosa*) 202, 203
Maximilian I Joseph, the King of Bavaria 205–6, 213
Mayhew, Henry 255
*Mechanics' Magazine* 164, 253
Mediterranean fan palm (*Chamaerops humilis*) 191, 192, 199
Melbourne, William Lamb, 2nd Viscount 21, 29
Melville, Herman 64–6
Menzies, Archibald 123
Miranha, Brazilian slave 206–7
Mohl, Hugo 208
Moody, Lieutenant Richard Clement 90
Moody, Sophy 242, **243**, 257, 259, 285–6, **Plate 9**, **Plate 10**, **Plate 11**

Moore, Thomas 232
*Morning Chronicle* 36, 37
Morpeth, George Howard, Viscount 154, 155
Morris, Mr 147
Mount Erebus, Ross Island, Antarctica 80–1, **82**, 86, 87, 89
*Mummy!* (Jane Loudon) 284
municipal gardens 67–8
Murphy, Patrick 7
Murray, John Fisher 67
Museum of Economic Botany
  aims 240
  building 240
  Burton's new building 268
  coconut palm (*Cocos nucifera*) 254–5
  double coconut (*Lodoicea maldivica*) 262, 264
  growth of collection 267–8
  interior view (1855) **240**
  items donated 241–2
  link to Palm House 242–3
  oil palm (*Elaeis guineensis*) 262
  opening to public 239–40
  organization and presentation 241–2
  palms, uses of 242–4
  *piaçaba* fibre 253
  renaming 241
  A. Smith appointed curator 267–8
Museum of Economic Geology 166, 167, 241, 242

*Narrative of the Voyage of H.M.S. Herald* (Seemann) 235
*Narrative of Travels on the Amazon and Rio Negro, A* (Wallace) 249
Nash, John 108
natural classification system 125, 128, 242
natural theology 286–8
Nesfield, William Andrews
  appointment 121, 122–3, 132–3, 134
  arboretum plans 127, 128–31, **129**, 134–6, **135**, **Plate 18**
  background 120–2
  exasperation 131–2, 133
  expansion of Kew 134
  inspection of trees 131
  Palm House as focus of Kew 129, **129**, **130**
*New Monthly Magazine* 193
*North and South* (Gaskell) 260
*North British Review* 259, 261
North, Mary 36
Northumberland, Hugh Percy, 3rd Duke of 130, 220, 222
*Notes on the Botany of the Antarctic Voyage* (W. Hooker) 88–9, 90
*Nova genera et species plantarum Brasiliensium* (Martius) 207
Noyes, Charles 36

Oakshot, Thomas 36
O'Connell, Daniel 105
*Oenocarpus bataua* **250**
Office of Woods and Forest
  bureaucratic delays 111, 133
  Burton's dealings with 108, 111–12, 115, 156–7
  First Commissioners 106, 154; *see also* Lincoln, Henry Pelham-Clinton, Earl
  funding for Kew 131, 138, 222–3
  Hooker's dealings with 47, 51, 99, 154, 155, 173, 268
  Kew report 21
  Kew transferred to 47
  Museum of Economic Geology 242
  Palm House glass 170, 171
  Palm house site 99
  Turner's dealings with 107–8, 117–18, 157–8, 165, 275–6
oil palm (*Elaeis guineensis*) 257–9, **257**, 261–2, 308
*Omoo* (Melville) 64–6
*Omphalos* (Gosse) 287

'On Reading Paul and Virginia in Childhood' (Hemans) 193
Owen, Robert 246

Padua Botanical Garden 199
Palm House
acclaim 230–1, 234–5, 270–2, 294–5, **Plate 23**, **Plate 24**
basement and tunnel 138–9, 178–9, 182–3, **182**, 237–8
Bawden's 1950 linocut **Plate 30**
Burton's involvement *see* Burton, Decimus, Kew Gardens, Palm House
central section 114, 116, 117, 139, 150, 155, **156**, 185
Chartist threat 273–4
chimney ('campanile') 178–9, **179**
construction 150–1, **151**, 156–8, **Plate 21**, **Plate 22**
criticisms 272–3, 289–90
Crystal Palace, benefits from 294–5
*Curtis's Botanical Magazine* frontispiece 270, **271**
daguerreotypes by Claudet 183–4, **Plate 21**, **Plate 22**
designs
Burton 112–13
Jones and Clark 115–16
Robinson 99
Turner 111–12, 114–15
Turner-Burton **5**, 115, **156**, **Plate 17**
door **5**, **310**
emblem of Empire 4–5, 218, **Plate 29**
emblem of Kew 3, 270, **271**, 288, **Plate 30**
emblem of technology 4, 184, 186, 305–6
environmental control 159–60, 217–18
exterior view 3, 269
fantasy 231–5
flooding 183, 237
as focus of Kew 3, 5, 129–30, **129**, **130**, 134, 135–6, **135**, 269–70, **Plate 18**, **Plate 30**
funding 131, 138, 155–6, 160, 272–3
gallery 2, 150, 230, 233, 234–7, 269–70, **289**, 294–5
glass 162–5, 168–9, 170–4, 177–8, **Plate 20**
Grissell and Peto appointed contractor 138
heating system 138–9, 178–83, **181**, **182**, 304–5
interior, descriptions of 1–3, 230–7, 309
interior, images of **229**, **231**, **283**, **289**, **Plate 22**, **Plate 25**
Irish workers 152–4
link to Museum 242–3
model for glasshouses 305–6
modern viewpoint 306
moving plants into 213–17
in Nesfield's arboretum plans 128–30, **129**, **135**, **Plate 18**
opening 229–30, **229**
popularity 278–9, 288, **Plate 23**, **Plate 24**
prefabrication 114, 150, 305
public education/benefits 212–13
rebuild, plans to 306–7, **307**
resilience 306
restoration 307
Royal enthusiasm for construction 99–100
sensory and imaginative experience 1–3, 230–5, 236–7, 309
site, choosing 119–20, 131–2
Smith's concerns 185–6
staircases 2, 150–1, 294–5, 308
stereoview **Plate 25**
stocking 218–20, 221–2
tenders 116–18, 157, 276

Palm House (*cont.*)
  thinning of collection 297
  today 308–9
  Turner's involvement *see* Turner, Richard, Palm House
  ventilation 162
  views of Gardens from within 269–70
  visitor numbers 294–5
  *Wanderings through the Conservatories at Kew* (Gosse) **231**, 287–8, **310**
  watering system 178–9, 217–18, 305
  wear and tear 306, 308
  women visitors **283**, 288–90, **289**, **Plate 23**
  working conditions 182–3, 218, 237, 309
palm oil 257–9, 261–2
*Palm Tree, The* (Moody) 242, **243**, 257, 285–6, **Plate 9**, **Plate 10**, **Plate 11**
*Palm Trees of the Amazon and their Uses* (Wallace) 249–51, **250**, **251**
*Palm Tribes and their Varieties, The* (anon) 192, 286
palms
  association with mankind 61–5, 189–91, 201–3, 243, 246–7
  Bermuda fan palm (*Sabal bermudana*) 1, 215–16
  coconut palm (*Cocos nucifera*) 60, 63–6, 194–5, 254–7
  Cuban royal palm (*Roystonea regia*) 1
  date palm (*Phoenix dactylifera*) 60–3, 171, 193, 216, 232, **Plate 12**
  distribution 60, 64, 66, 208, 210, 302, **Plate 2**, **Plate 3**, **Plate 9**, **Plate 10**, **Plate 11**
  emblem of Empire 302–3
  emblem of the exotic 5, 60
  growth pattern 187–8
  Himalayan fan palm (*Trachycarpus martianus*) 216
  *Historia Naturalis Palmarum* (Martius) 207–12, **Plate 1**, **Plate 2**, **Plate 3**
  *Illustrations of the Natural Orders of Plants* (Twining) **Plate 8**
  Indian wine palm (*Caryota urens*) 216
  International Palm Society 189
  ivory-nut palm (*Phytelephas macrocarpa*) 220–2, **Plate 6**, **Plate 7**
  J. Hooker's classification 298–9
  Kentia palm (*Howea forsteriana*) 303, **304**
  leaves 61, 66, 171–2, 187, 215, 230, 232, 302, **Plate 20**
  licuri palm (*Syagrus coronata*) 216, 217, 304
  literary references 63–6, 193–5, 200, 232
  Mauritia palm (*Mauritia flexuosa*) 202–3
  Mediterranean fan palm (*Chamaerops humilis*) 191–2, 199
  oil palm (*Elaeis guineensis*) 257–9, **257**, 261–2, 308
  *Palm Tree, The* (Moody) 242, **243**, 257, 285–6, **Plate 9**, **Plate 10**, **Plate 11**
  *Palm Trees of the Amazon and their Uses* (Wallace) 249–51, **250**, **251**
  *Palm Tribes and their Varieties, The* (anon) 192, 286
  *paxiúba* palm (*Socratea exorrhiza*) 245
  peach palm (*Bactris gasipaes*) 201–2
  *Popular History of the Palms* (Seemann) 235–7, 253–4
  religious references 60–2, 285–7
  research, current 308–9
  stems 187, 202
  Terra and Phoebus mythology 210, 213, **Plate 2**, **Plate 3**
  uses 59–60, 65, 66, 189, 201–2, 220, 222, 236–7, 242–4, **243**, 247, 249–50, 252–9, 261–2, 263, 286, **Plate 7**, **Plate 12**

Victorian fascination and regard 4–5, 59–61, 187
vulnerability 308–9
wax palm (*Ceroxylon alpinum/ quinduense*) 205, 222
Parliamentary Committee on the Royal Gardens 14, 16, 19, 20, 21, 25, 38, 45
*Paul and Virginia* (Marshall) 196, **197**
*Paul et Virginie* (Bernardin)
coconut palms 194–5
English translations 193
Humboldt's regard for 200
illustrations 195, **196**
life at one with nature 192
plot 193
popularity 193–4
race 196–7
sexual awakening 194–5
visual representations 195–7, **196**, **197**, 198, **198**
*paxiúba* palm (*Socratea exorrhiza*) 245
Paxton, Joseph 15, 23–4, 56–9, **58**, 71, 98–9, 101, 110, 272, 292–3, 294, 306
*Paxton's Magazine of Botany* 15, 57
peach palm (*Bactris gasipaes*) 201–2
Pedro I of Brazil 205–6
Peel, Sir Robert 21, 105, 154, 164, 257
*Penny Cyclopaedia* 212
*Personal Narrative of Travels to the Equinoctial Regions of the New Continent* (Humboldt, trans. Williams) 199–200, 201, 233
Pevsner, Nikolaus 306
photochemistry 166–7
photography 166–7, 183–4, **Plate 19**
*piaçaba* fibre 252–3
*Plant Hunters, The* (Reid) 225
*Plant World, The* (Twining) 285
*Plants of Other Lands* **Plate 12**
*Popular History of the Palms* (Seemann) 235–7, 253–4
*Popular Treatise on the Art of Photography, A* (Hunt) 167
Powell, Baden 172–3
Price, Uvedale 122, 127–8
Price's Patent Candle Company, Vauxhall 256–7, 259–61, **260**, 262
*Principes* 189
public walks 67–8
*Punch* 174, 230, 231–2, 289–90
Purdie, William 220–3, **Plate 6**, **Plate 7**

*Quarterly Review* 219, 230–1, 232, 238, 261, 281, 295
*Queen of the South*, SS 265–6, 267

railways 139, 146, 151–2, 186, 258, 276, 278–9, 301
Raleigh, Sir Walter 202
Rau, Charles 206
'Recessional' (Kipling) 302–3
*Records of the Royal Botanic Gardens* (Smith) 123, 267
Reid, Thomas Mayne 225
*Reise in Brasilien* (Martius and Spix) 207
*Relation historique du voyage* (Humboldt) 199–200
Repeal Association 105, 107, 274
Repton, Humphry 54
*Researches on Light* (Hunt) 167, 184
*Rhododendrons of Sikkim Himalaya, The* (Hooker, ed.) 228–9
Richmond Lodge estate 9
Ridgway, John 36, 37
Robertson, John 64, 255
*Robinson Crusoe* (Defoe) 63
Robinson, Mr 99
Rohault de Fleury, Charles 160, 161
Ross, Captain James Clark 75–6, 77–8, 80, 81, 82, 85, 87, 89
Rowan, Colonel Charles 68
Royal Botanic Society of London 42–3, 106, 109, 110, 144–9, **148**
Royal Geographical Society 90
Rumphius, Georg 263
Ruskin, John 121

Russell, John, Lord (later 1st Earl) 29, 46, 47, 155
Ruthven, George 35–6

Scheer, Frederick 23, 97–8
Seemann, Berthold 235–7, 253–4, 259, 268, 285
Seychelles 263
Schoenefeldt, Henrik 169
*Short Lectures on Plants for Schools and Adult Classes* (Twining) 285
Sikkim 225–7
Sikkim, *Chogyal* of 225, 226–7
Simmonds, Peter Lund 256
Sinclair, George 128
*Sketches of Persia* (Malcolm) 62–3
slavery 192–3, 197, 206–7, 211, 258–9, 260, 262
Smith, Alexander 239, 267–8
Smith, John
  *Adam Spade* 301–2
  background 32–3
  bereavements 40, 52–3
  ferns, study of 38, 53, 302
  herbarium 302
  Hooker, relationship with 38–9, 52, 53–4, 119–20
  on Hooker's Bedford book 47
  job for son Alexander 239, 268
  at Kensington Palace gardens 34
  at Kew
    arboretum 123–4
    attempts to save from closure 43–4, 45
    Glenny's press attack 39–40
    Hogan–Sweet affair 35–7
    Hooker made director 48
    Hooker's leadership 70
    horticultural tour 53–5, 56, 67
    Joseph Hooker's appointment 296–7
    junior gardener 34–5
    Napoleon's Willow 9–10
    Palm House
      designs 113
      flooding 183, 237
      floor 182
      glass 162–3, 171, 174
      heating system 180, 182–3, 237
      industrial appearance 185–6
      moving plants 213–14, 216, 217
      plants thinned 297
      principal foreman 17, 35
      site 119–20, 183
      Turner's role as designer 300
    plant identification 38
    recognition and promotion under Hooker 53
    retirement 297
    Turner, relationship with 301
    visitors 278, 289
  Kew directorship candidacy 31–2, 38–9
  Linnean Society associate 38
  portrait **32, Plate 16**
  published articles 53
  Royal Botanic Society of London 43
  studies 34–5
Soane, John 109
Society for the Diffusion of Useful Knowledge 212
South America, exploration of
  Humboldt 199–205
  Martius and Spix 205–7
  Purdie 220–2
  Spruce 245–6
  Wallace 246–51
  Wallace and Bates 244–5, 245–6
Southey, Robert 232
Spix, Johann Baptist von 205–6, 207, 213
Spring-Rice, Thomas 30–1
Spruce, Richard 245–6, 248–9, 250, 251
Staunton, Sir George 216–17, 304
steamships 139, 186

*Stirling Observer* 273
Stowe, Harriet Beecher 260
*Summer Days Recreations* 278–9, 282, 295
Surrey, Henry Howard, Earl of 15–16, 43
Sweet, Robert 36–7
*System of Vegetables, A* (Linnaeus, trans. E. Darwin) 188–9
*Systema Naturæ* (Linnaeus) 188–9, 189–90

Taylor, Ella **Plate 26**
technological press 139–40
*Terror*, HMS 75, 77, 80
Thackeray, William Makepeace 231–2
*Thalaba the Destroyer* (Southey) 232
Thiselton-Dyer, William 298
Thomson, J. W. 35
Thomson, Thomas 227–8, 229
Tibet 225–7
*Times, The* 44, 59, 104
Tomlinson, P. Barry 187–8
trade, international 237, 240–1, 254, 258–9
Treasury, HM 12, 20–1, 42, 43, 47–8, 137–8, 223, 276, 297
Trinidad Botanic Garden 223
tuberculosis/consumption 40–1, 52–3, 67
Turner, Dawson (Hooker's father-in-law) 29–30, 43, 46–7, 69, 70, 73, 95, 100, 108, 122, 131, 133, 134, 136, 154, 155, 230
Turner, Mary 30
Turner, Richard; *see also* Hammersmith Works, Ireland
  background 101–2
  Channel tunnel design 301
  civil engineer's plans 116–17, 180
  craftsmanship 147–9
  Embankment designs 301
  family illnesses and bereavements 274–5
  finances 137–8, 157–8, 275–6
  glasshouse designs 102, **103**, 104–5, 106–7
  Great Exhibition designs 290–2, **291**, 293–4
  Great Exhibition displays 293
  Hooker, initial meeting with 107
  Institution of Civil Engineers address 292–3
  Lime Street Station, Liverpool 152, 276
  Lincoln, meeting with 106, 107
  Palm House
    appointed subcontractor 138
    Burton's designs 112–13
    decorative ironwork 151
    designs **5**, 111–12, 113–15, **156**, 188, **Plate 17**
    financial losses 275–6
    framework, erection of 150–1
    glass 162–3, 163–4, 165, 170
    heating system 179–80, 181–2
    Irish workers 152–4
    Jones and Clark's designs 115–16, 117–18, 157
    ribs 142–4
    role unacknowledged 115, 300
    tender 116–18, 157, 276
    ventilation 162
    wings 156–8
    winning contract 118
  patented technology 151–2, 278
  Paxton's Crystal Palace, criticism of 292–3
  portrait **Plate 14**
  pro-Union sentiments 105–6
  purlin design 111, 150
  relationships
    Burton 144–7, 300–1
    Hooker 113, 141–2
    Smith 301
  Royal visit to Ireland 277, **277**
  self-publicity 106, 277–8, **277**, 290–1